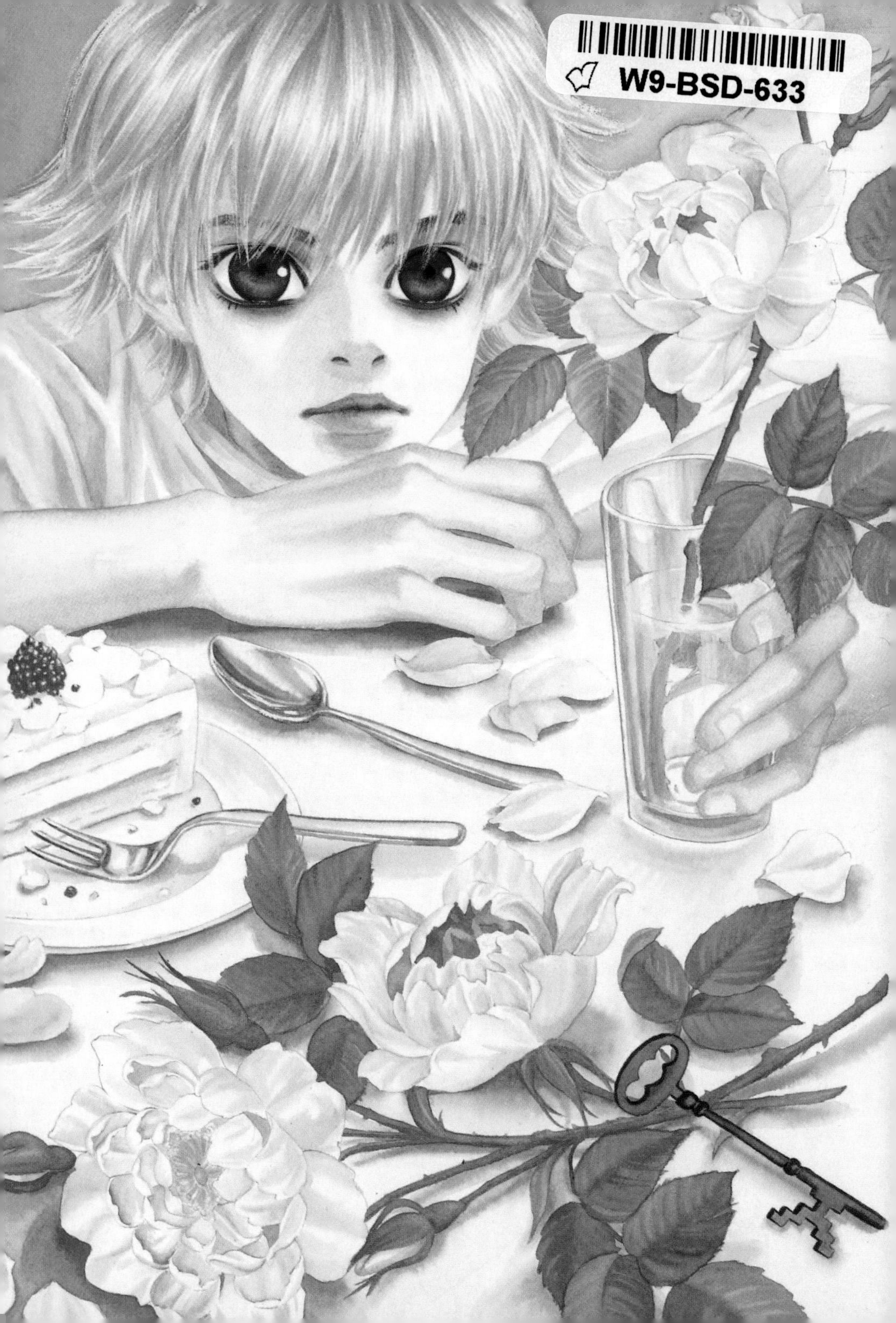

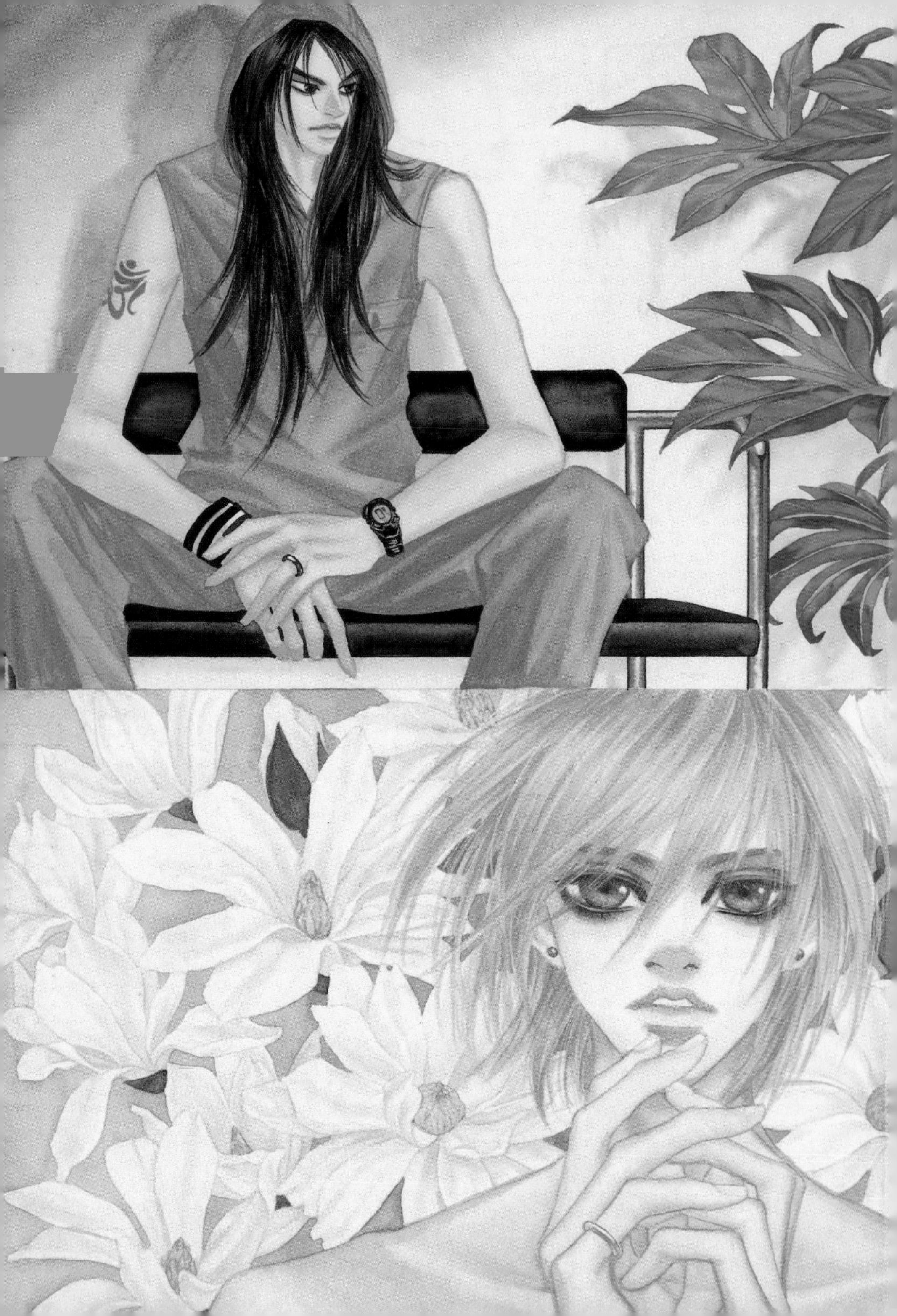

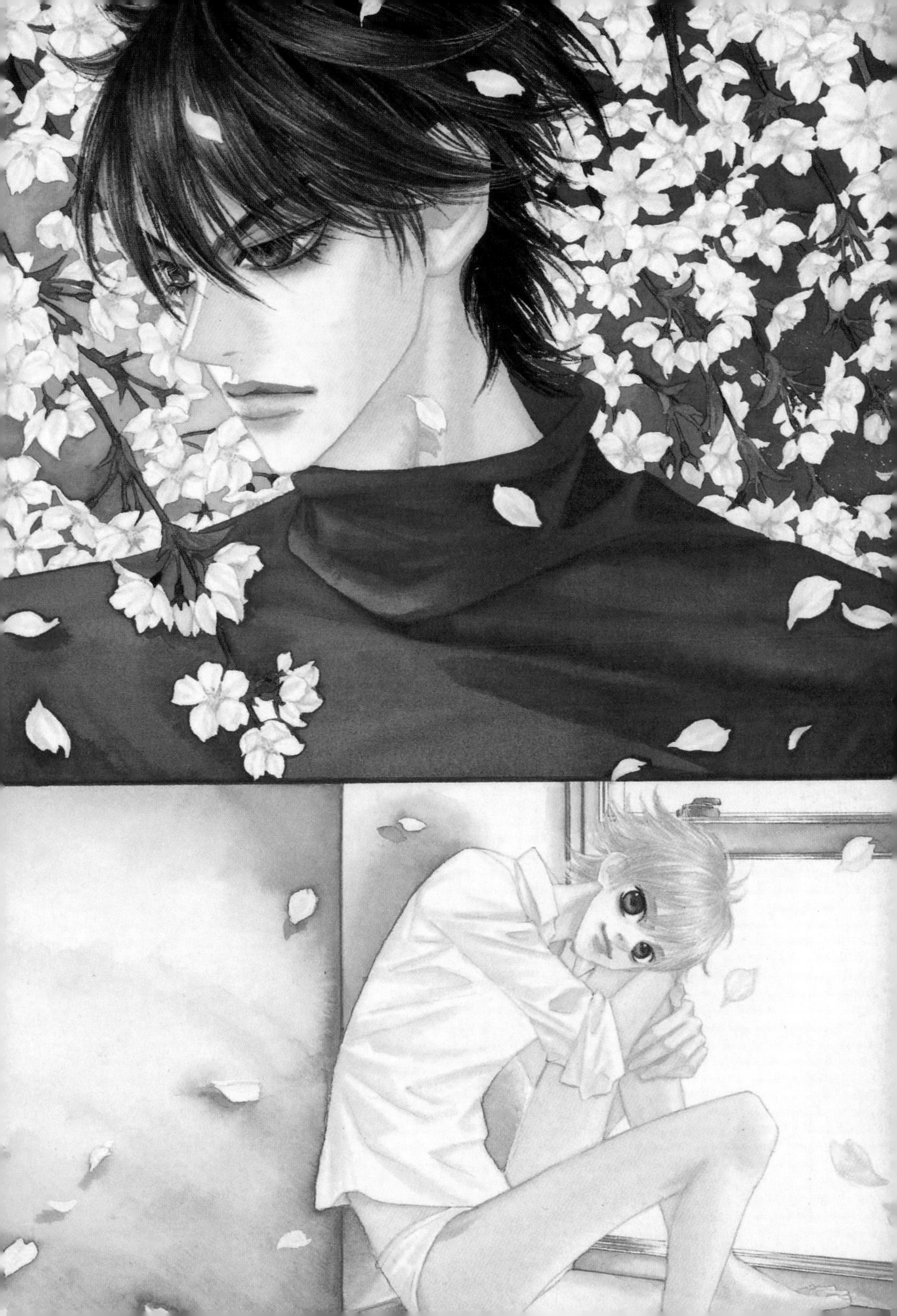

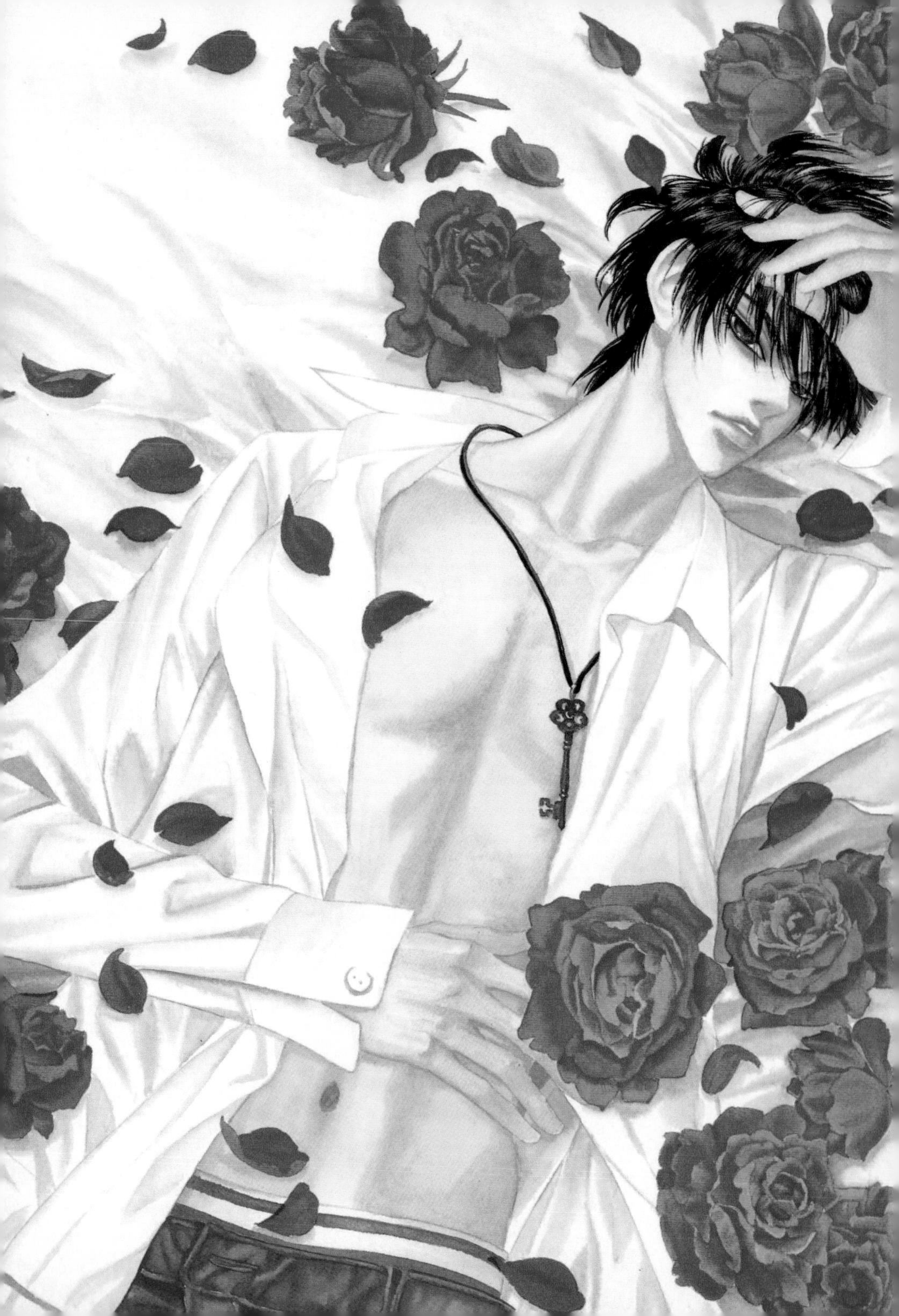

You're So Cool

vol. 3

YoungHee Lee

Yen
Press

THE STORY SO FAR...

SINCERE SCHOOLGIRL NAN-WOO HAD A SIMPLE DREAM. ALL SHE WANTED WAS FOR HER FAMILY TO GET ALONG, GOOD FRIENDS, AND A GENTLE, COOL BOYFRIEND...THAT WAS IT! THEN ONE DAY, HER DREAM CAME TRUE. SHE GOT THE CHANCE TO DATE SEUNG-HA RYU, THE HOTTEST, SMARTEST, AND MOST POPULAR BOY AT HER SCHOOL. BUT THIS HAPPINESS WAS FLEETING... WHEN SEUNG-HA TOOK OFF HIS MASK, NAN-WOO DISCOVERED THAT HE WAS A PERVERTED PSYCHO WITH A SPLIT PERSONALITY! "YEAH, RUNNING AWAY'S THE ONLY SOLUTION!" THOUGHT NAN-WOO, BUT SEUNG-HA CAUGHT HER SOON AFTER. NOW, SHE'S FORCED TO DO HIS CHORES AND PACK LUNCHES FOR HIM, AND SHE CAN NO LONGER HANG OUT WITH HER FRIENDS...SHE WONDERS WHETHER SHE'S DATING A GUY OR BEING TRAINED TO BE THE PERFECT SLAVE. BUT SOMETIMES, WHEN SHE CATCHES SEUNG-HA DEEP IN THOUGHT... AND IN THOSE RARE INSTANCES WHEN HE SPEAKS PROFOUNDLY, NAN-WOO THINKS TWICE. WHY DOES IT BOTHER HER SO MUCH? NAN-WOO, COULD IT BE...?!

...YOU'RE GOING DOWN.

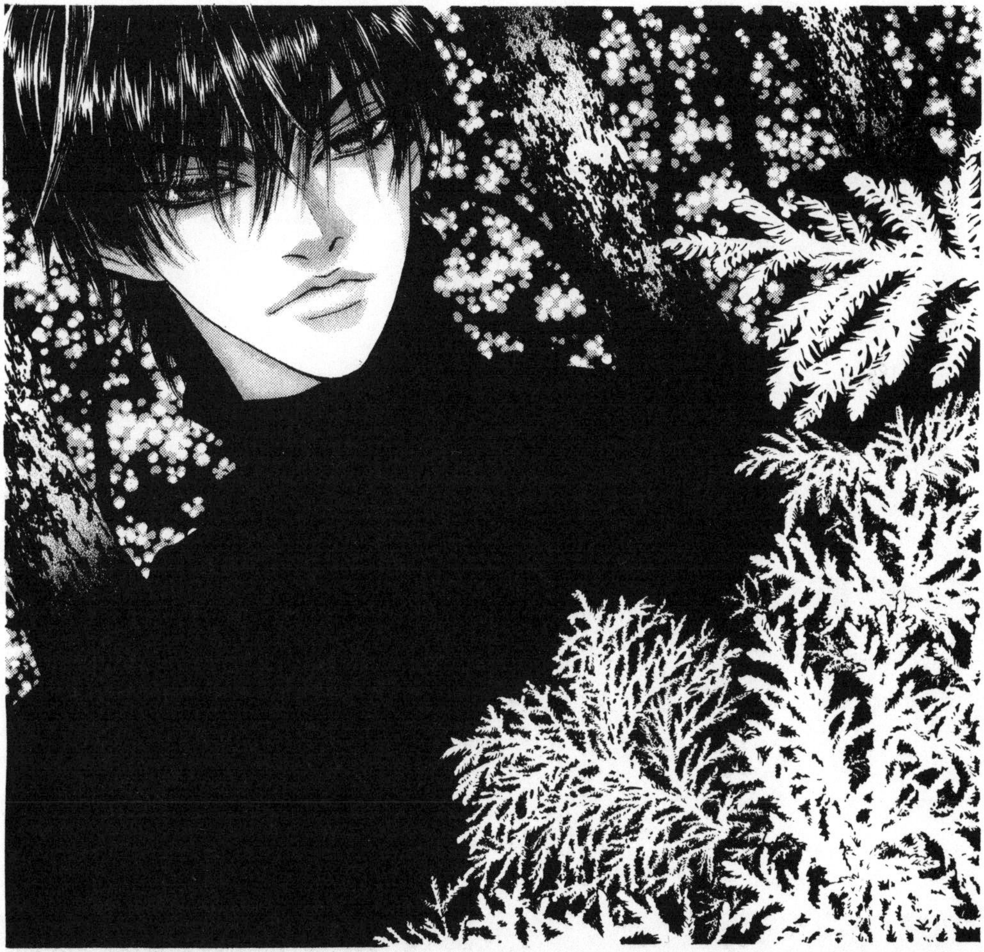

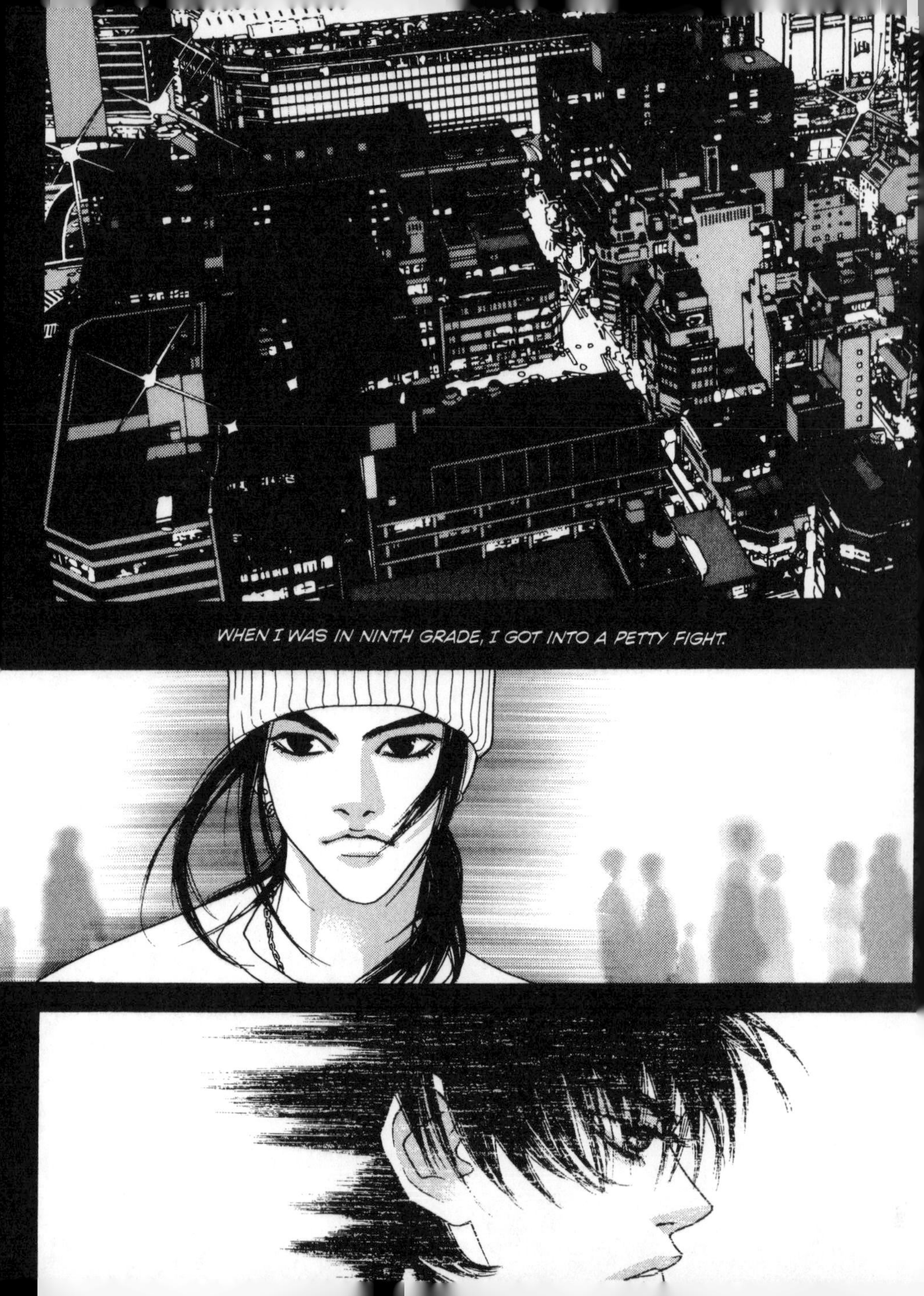
WHEN I WAS IN NINTH GRADE, I GOT INTO A PETTY FIGHT.

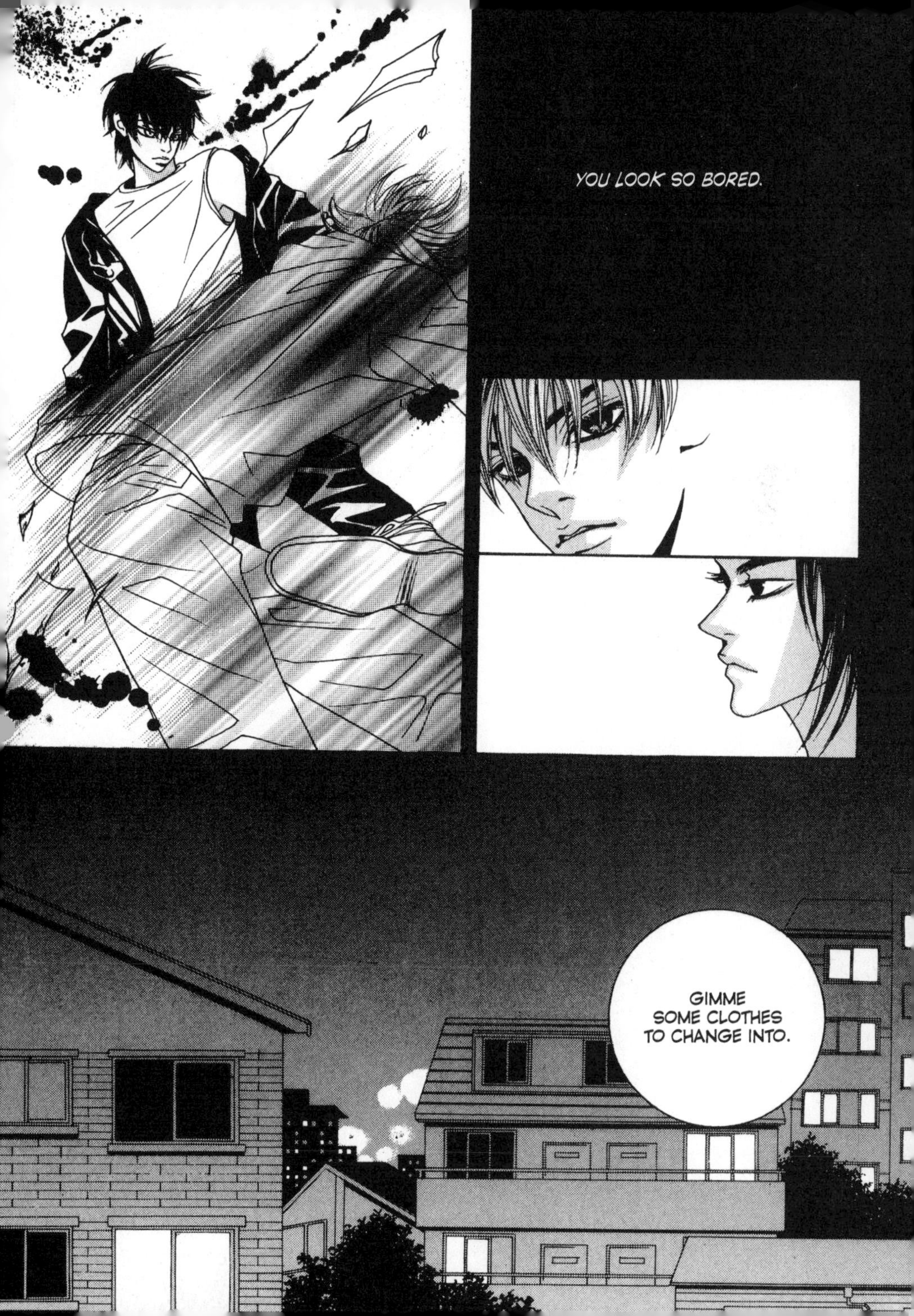
YOU LOOK SO BORED.
GIMME SOME CLOTHES TO CHANGE INTO.

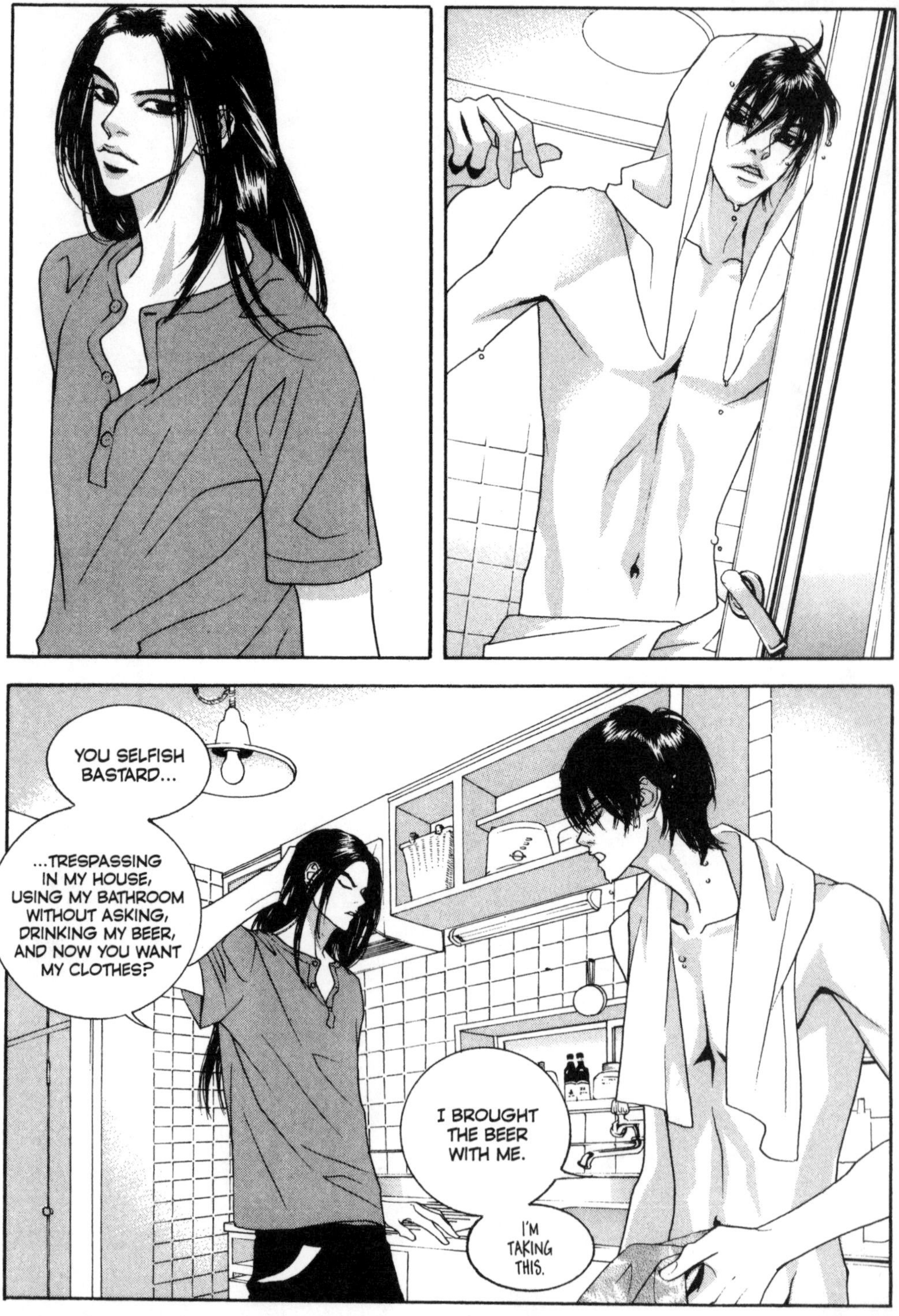
YOU SELFISH BASTARD...
...TRESPASSING IN MY HOUSE, USING MY BATHROOM WITHOUT ASKING, DRINKING MY BEER, AND NOW YOU WANT MY CLOTHES?
I BROUGHT THE BEER WITH ME.
I'M TAKING THIS.

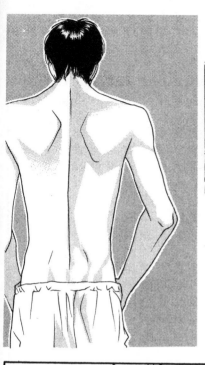

WHY'RE YOU STARING AT ME LIKE THAT?

I DON'T FEEL ANYTHING WHEN THIS JACKASS IS NAKED, BUT...

YOU'RE ACTING WEIRD, BRO.

UGH... STOP STARING AT ME LIKE THAT. I KNOW I'M HOT, BUT I DON'T WANT SOME DUDE CHECKING ME OUT.

YOU WENT SHOPPING?

...SOMEONE MADE IT FOR ME...

...EVEN THOUGH I SAID I DIDN'T WANT IT...

TAKE THIS WITH YOU-- EVEN IF YOU LIVE ALONE, YOU STILL HAVE TO EAT WELL~ IF YOU RUN OUT, JUST COME BACK FOR MORE. ACTUALLY, SHOULD I JUST BRING IT OVER TO YOU INSTEAD?

NO, THAT'S...

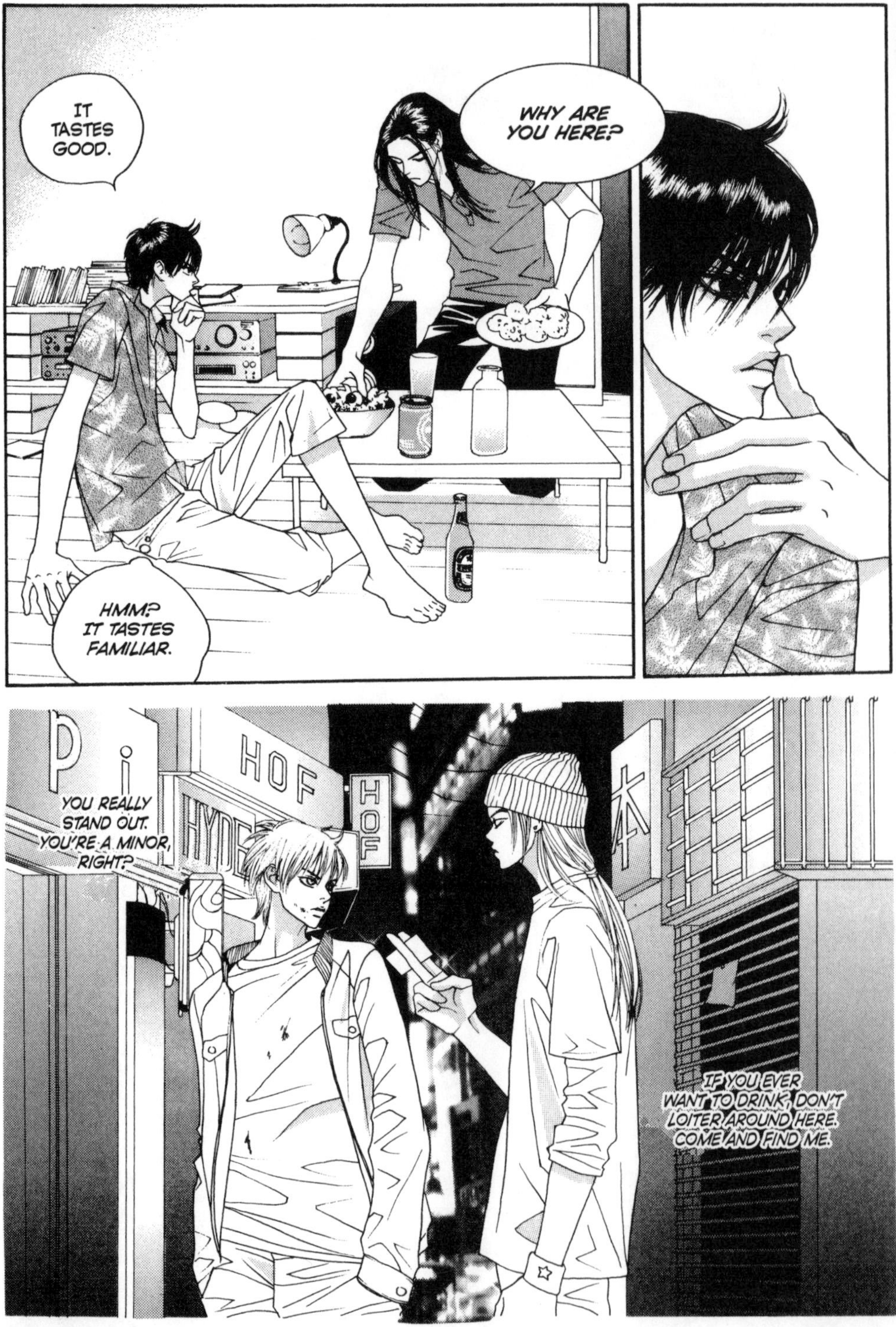
IT TASTES GOOD.
WHY ARE YOU HERE?
HMM? IT TASTES FAMILIAR.
HOF
HYDE
HOF
YOU REALLY STAND OUT. YOU'RE A MINOR, RIGHT?
IF YOU EVER WANT TO DRINK, DON'T LOITER AROUND HERE. COME AND FIND ME.

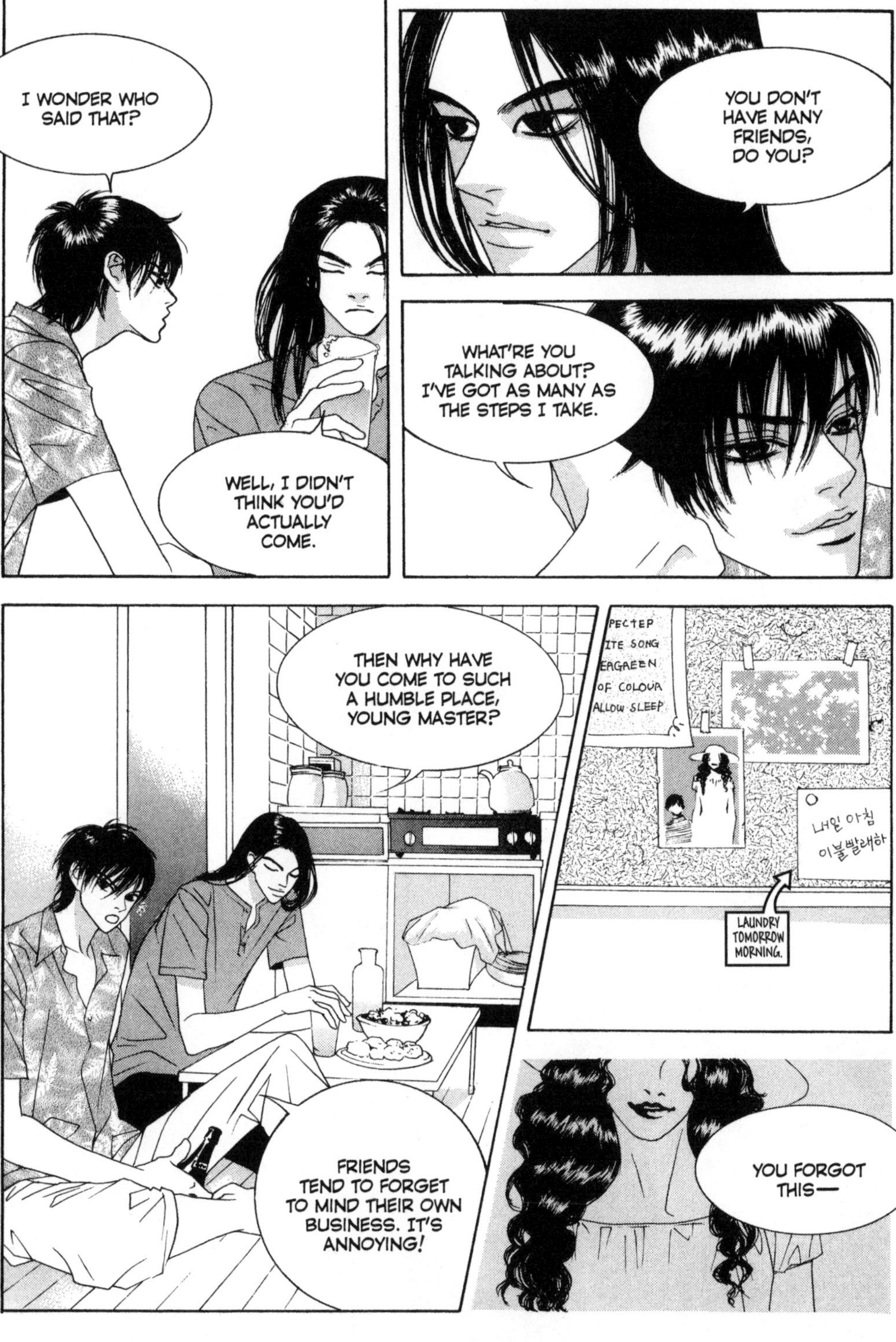
I WONDER WHO SAID THAT?
WELL, I DIDN'T THINK YOU'D ACTUALLY COME.
YOU DON'T HAVE MANY FRIENDS, DO YOU?
WHAT'RE YOU TALKING ABOUT? I'VE GOT AS MANY AS THE STEPS I TAKE.
THEN WHY HAVE YOU COME TO SUCH A HUMBLE PLACE, YOUNG MASTER?
FRIENDS TEND TO FORGET TO MIND THEIR OWN BUSINESS. IT'S ANNOYING!
PECTEP
ITE SONG
EAGAEEN
OF COLOUR
ALLOW SLEEP
내일 아침 이불빨래하
LAUNDRY TOMORROW MORNING.
YOU FORGOT THIS—

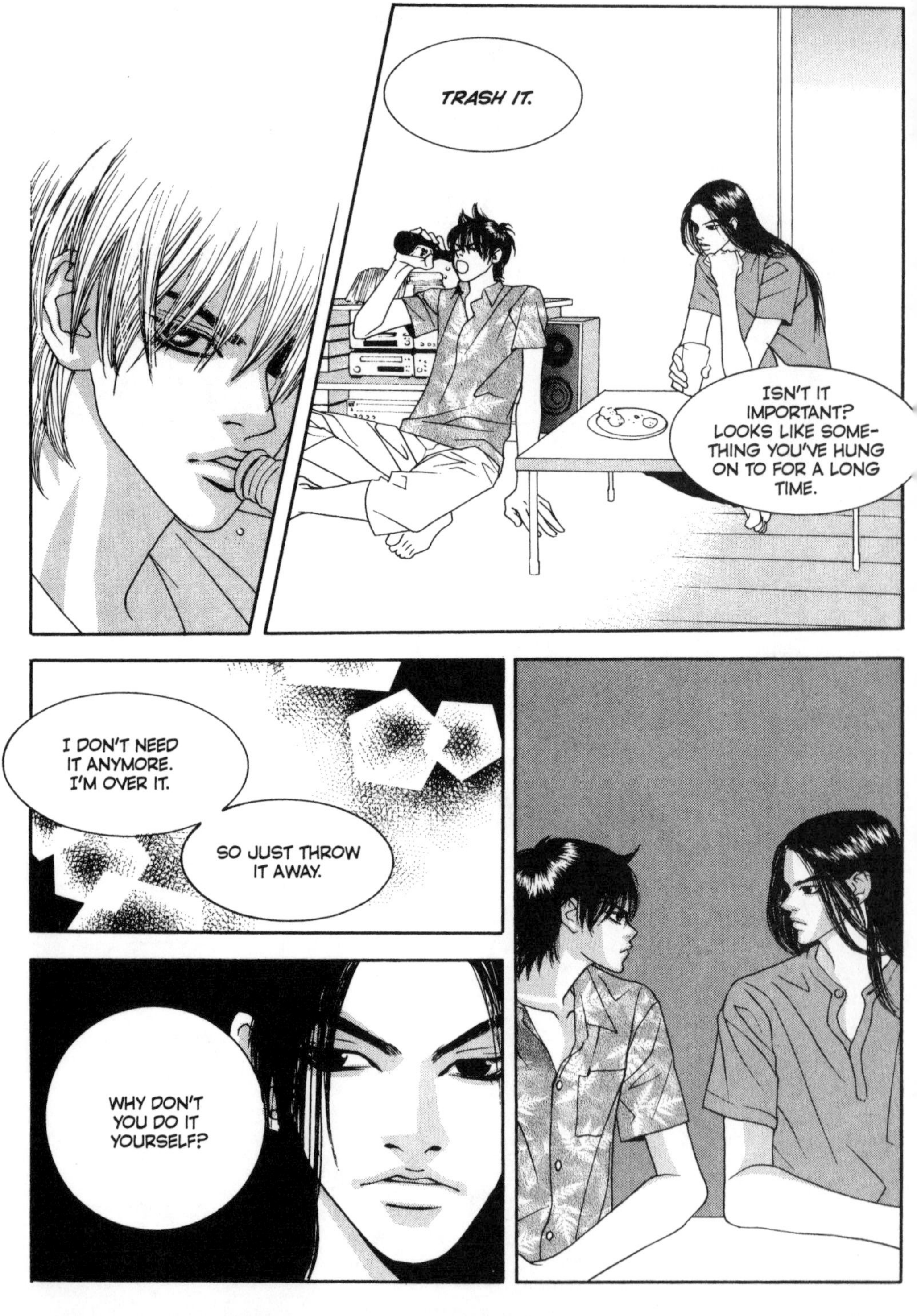
TRASH IT.
ISN'T IT IMPORTANT? LOOKS LIKE SOME-THING YOU'VE HUNG ON TO FOR A LONG TIME.
I DON'T NEED IT ANYMORE. I'M OVER IT.
SO JUST THROW IT AWAY.
WHY DON'T YOU DO IT YOURSELF?

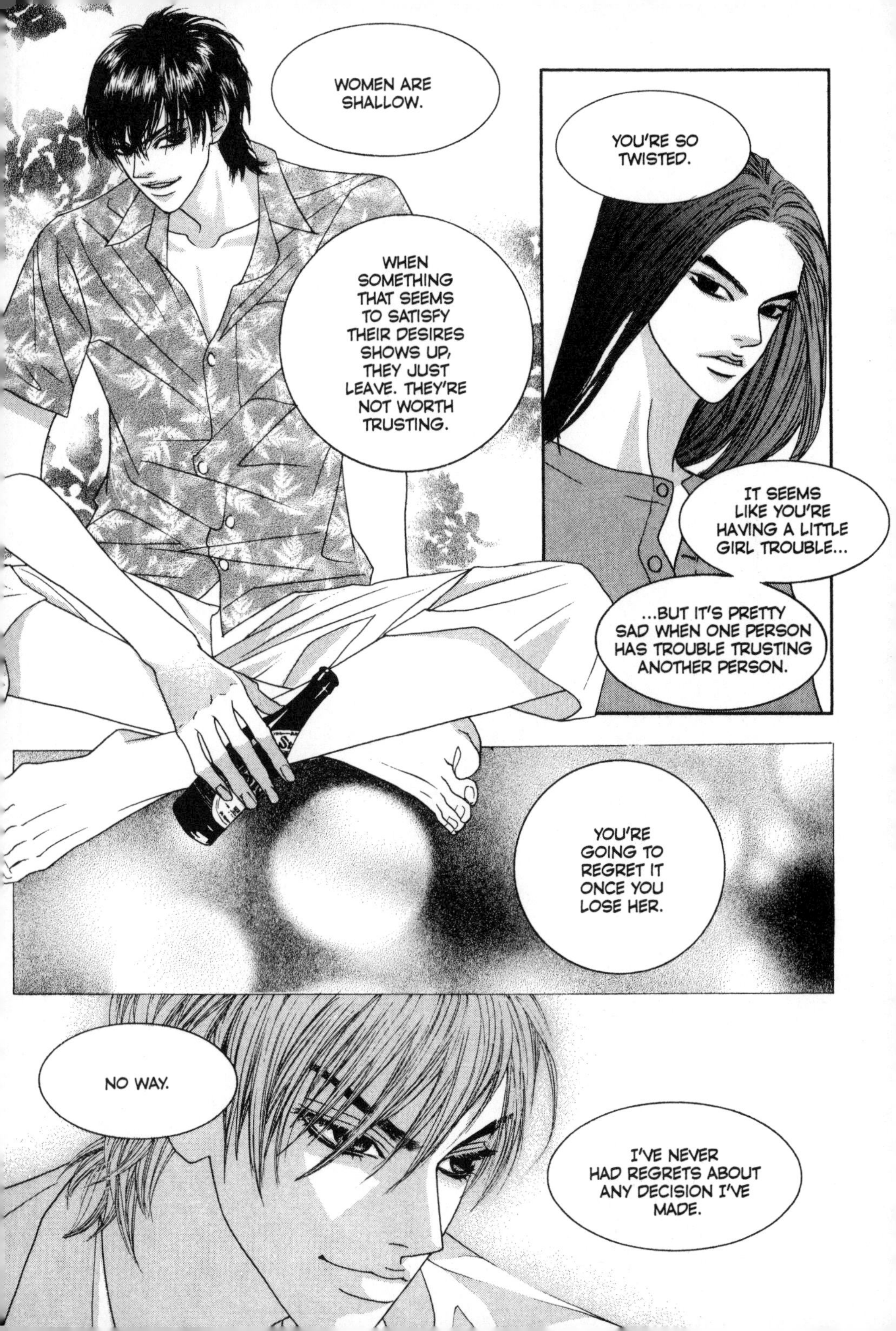
WOMEN ARE SHALLOW.
WHEN SOMETHING THAT SEEMS TO SATISFY THEIR DESIRES SHOWS UP, THEY JUST LEAVE. THEY'RE NOT WORTH TRUSTING.
YOU'RE SO TWISTED.
IT SEEMS LIKE YOU'RE HAVING A LITTLE GIRL TROUBLE...
...BUT IT'S PRETTY SAD WHEN ONE PERSON HAS TROUBLE TRUSTING ANOTHER PERSON.
YOU'RE GOING TO REGRET IT ONCE YOU LOSE HER.
NO WAY.
I'VE NEVER HAD REGRETS ABOUT ANY DECISION I'VE MADE.

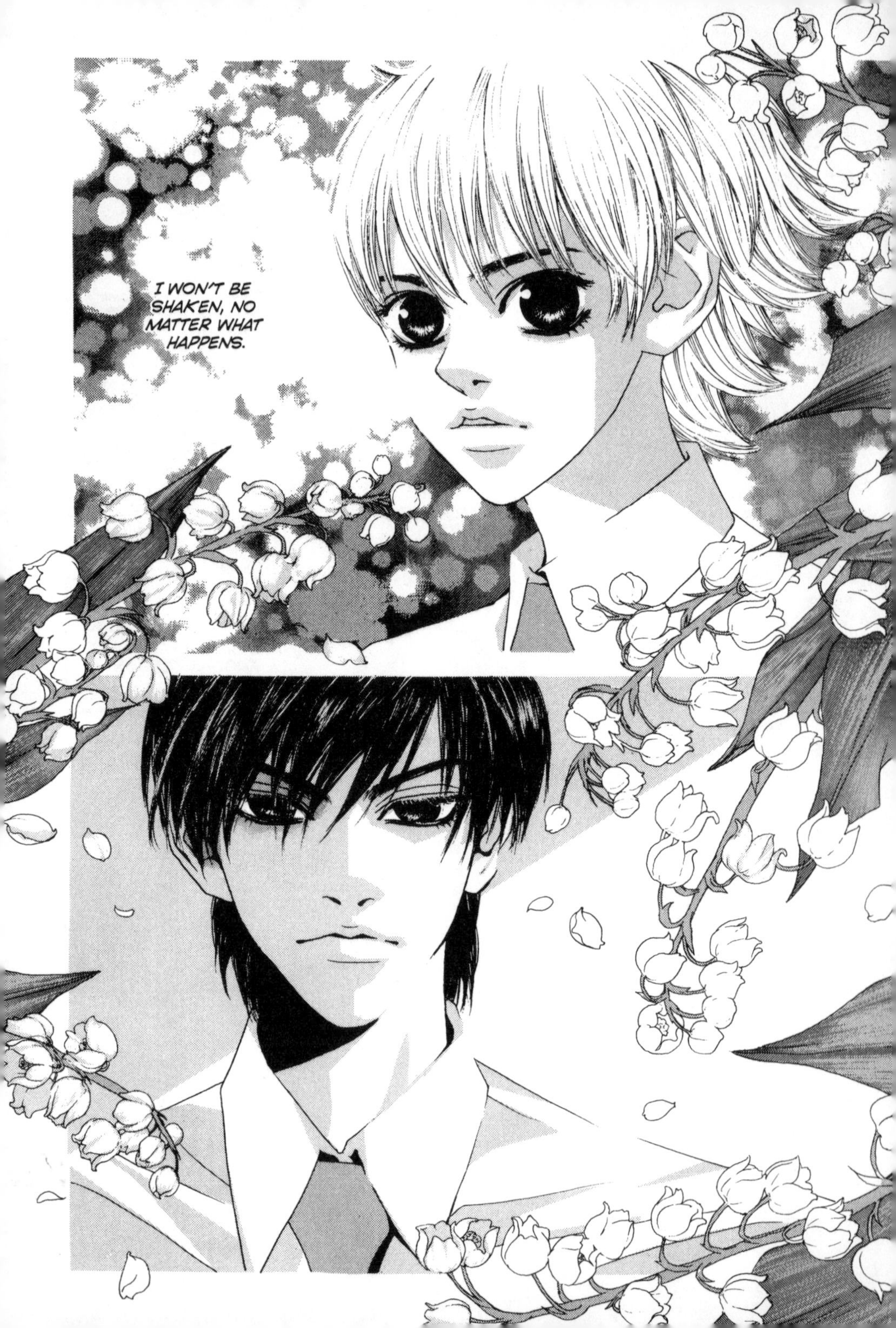
I WON'T BE SHAKEN, NO MATTER WHAT HAPPENS.

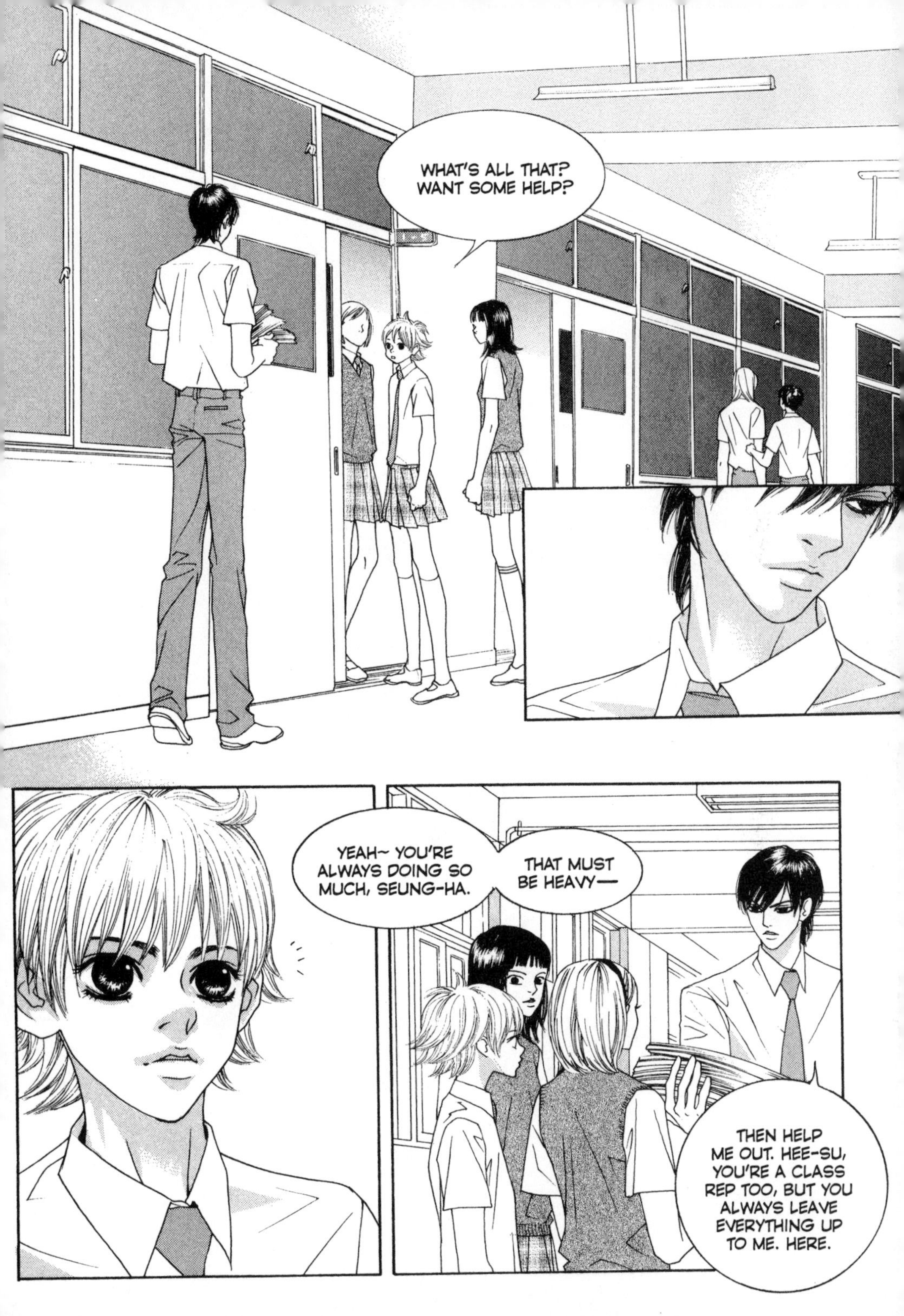
WHAT'S ALL THAT? WANT SOME HELP?
YEAH~ YOU'RE ALWAYS DOING SO MUCH, SEUNG-HA.
THAT MUST BE HEAVY—
THEN HELP ME OUT. HEE-SU, YOU'RE A CLASS REP TOO, BUT YOU ALWAYS LEAVE EVERYTHING UP TO ME. HERE.

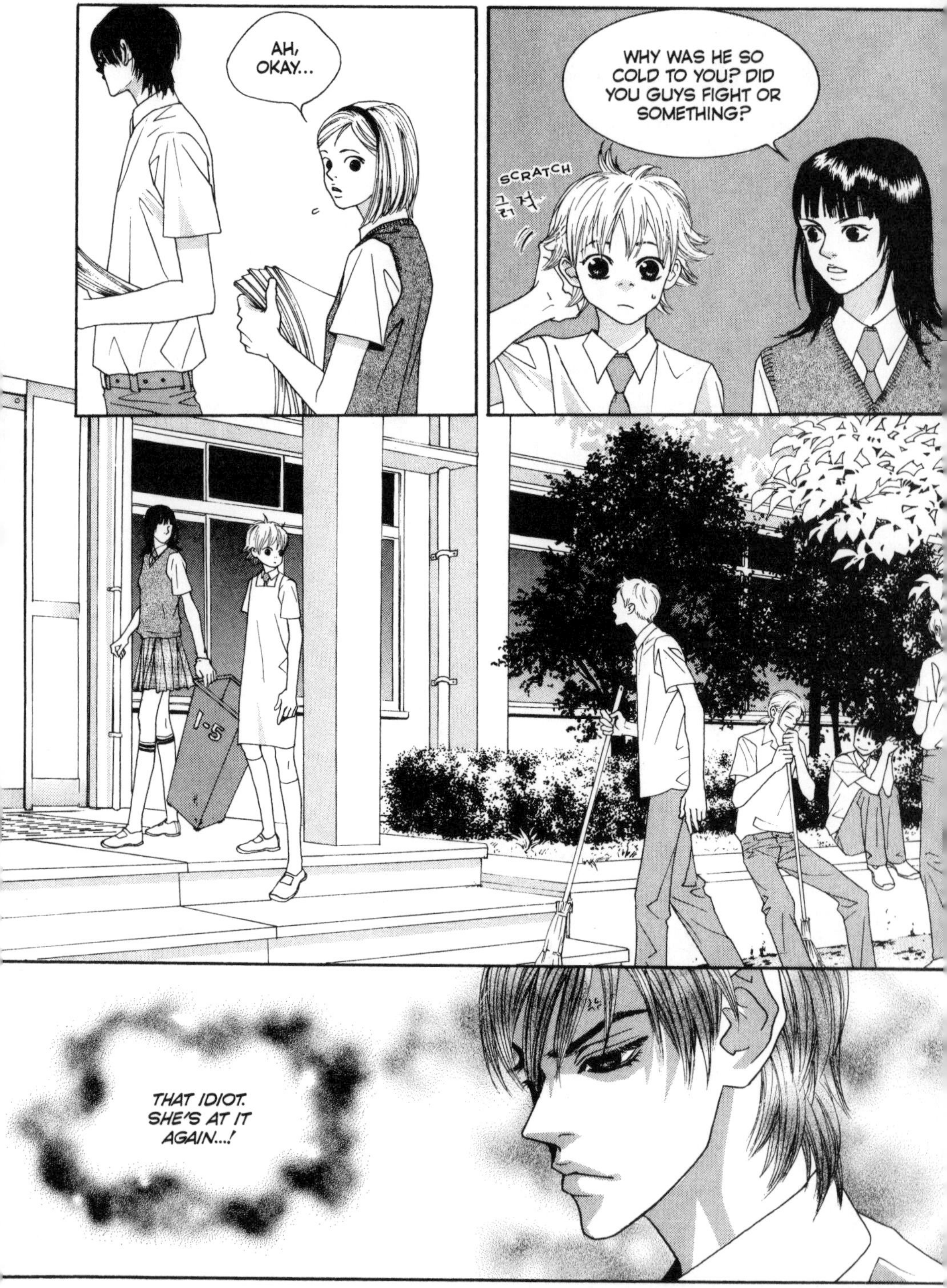
AH, OKAY...
WHY WAS HE SO COLD TO YOU? DID YOU GUYS FIGHT OR SOMETHING?
SCRATCH
긁적
1-5
THAT IDIOT. SHE'S AT IT AGAIN...!

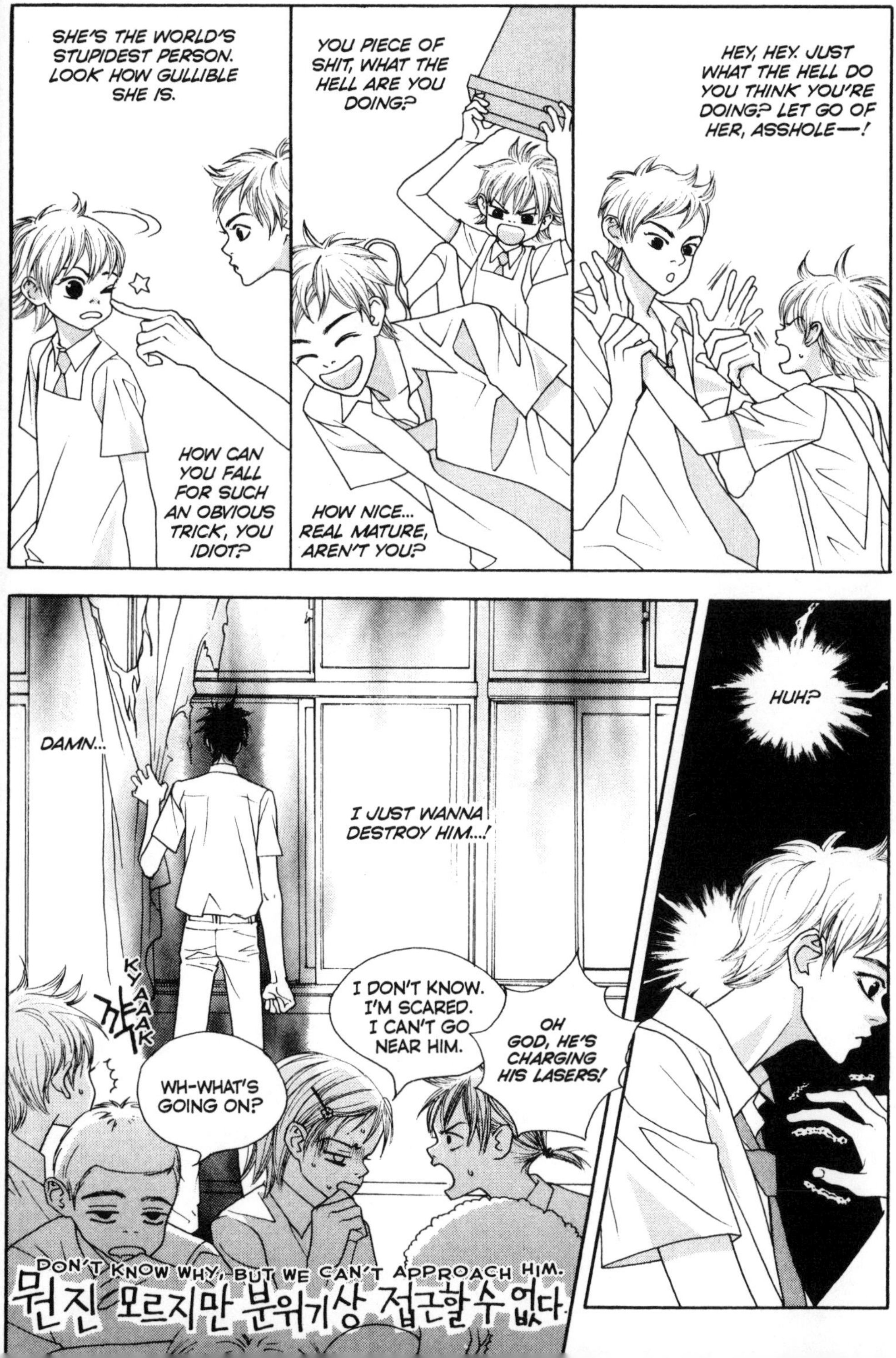
SHE'S THE WORLD'S STUPIDEST PERSON. LOOK HOW GULLIBLE SHE IS.
HOW CAN YOU FALL FOR SUCH AN OBVIOUS TRICK, YOU IDIOT?
YOU PIECE OF SHIT, WHAT THE HELL ARE YOU DOING?
HOW NICE... REAL MATURE, AREN'T YOU?
HEY, HEY. JUST WHAT THE HELL DO YOU THINK YOU'RE DOING? LET GO OF HER, ASSHOLE—!
DAMN...
I JUST WANNA DESTROY HIM...!
KYAAAK
WH-WHAT'S GOING ON?
I DON'T KNOW. I'M SCARED. I CAN'T GO NEAR HIM.
OH GOD, HE'S CHARGING HIS LASERS!
DON'T KNOW WHY, BUT WE CAN'T APPROACH HIM.
뭔진 모르지만 분위기상 접근할수 없다.
HUH?

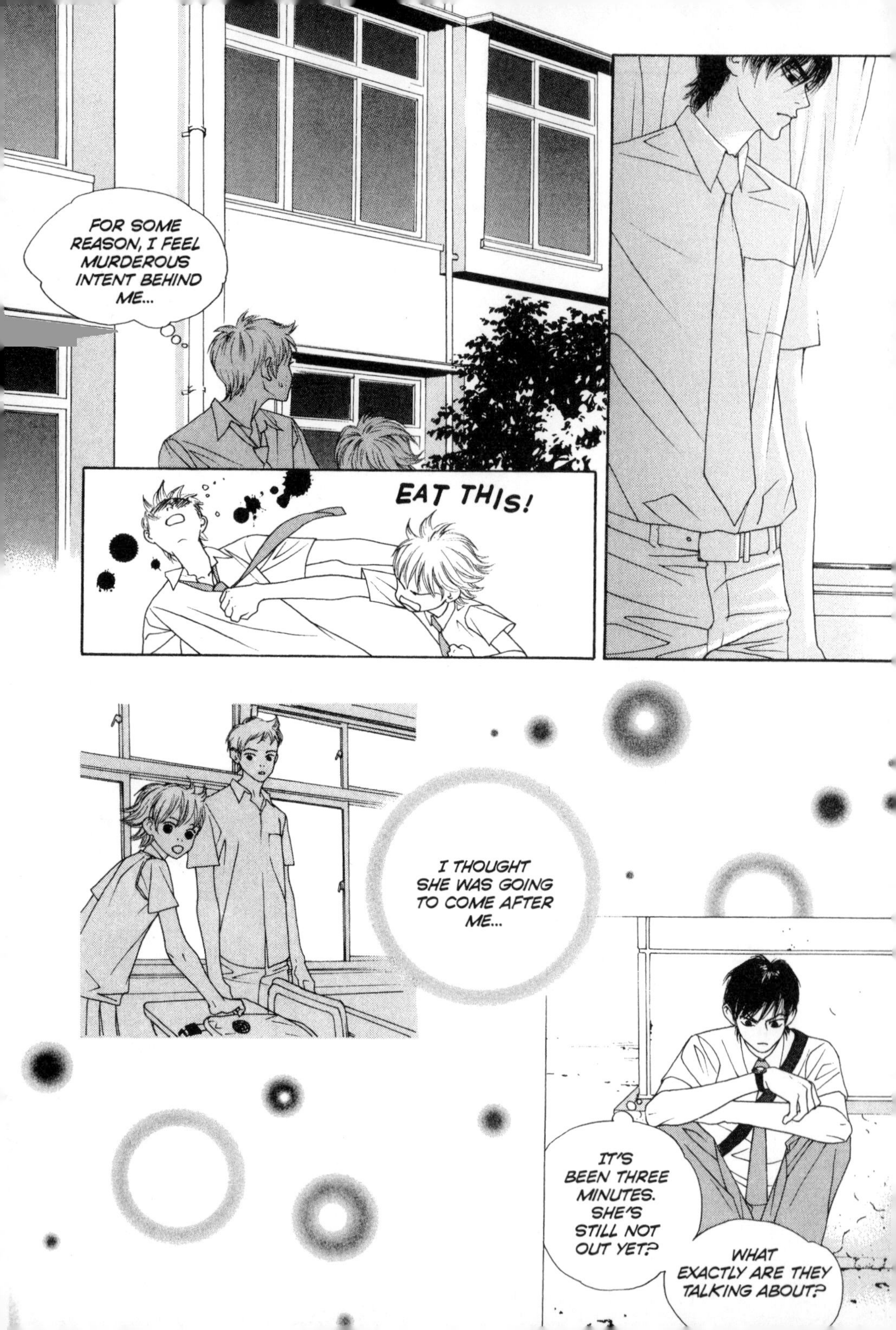
FOR SOME REASON, I FEEL MURDEROUS INTENT BEHIND ME...
EAT THIS!
I THOUGHT SHE WAS GOING TO COME AFTER ME...
IT'S BEEN THREE MINUTES. SHE'S STILL NOT OUT YET?
WHAT EXACTLY ARE THEY TALKING ABOUT?

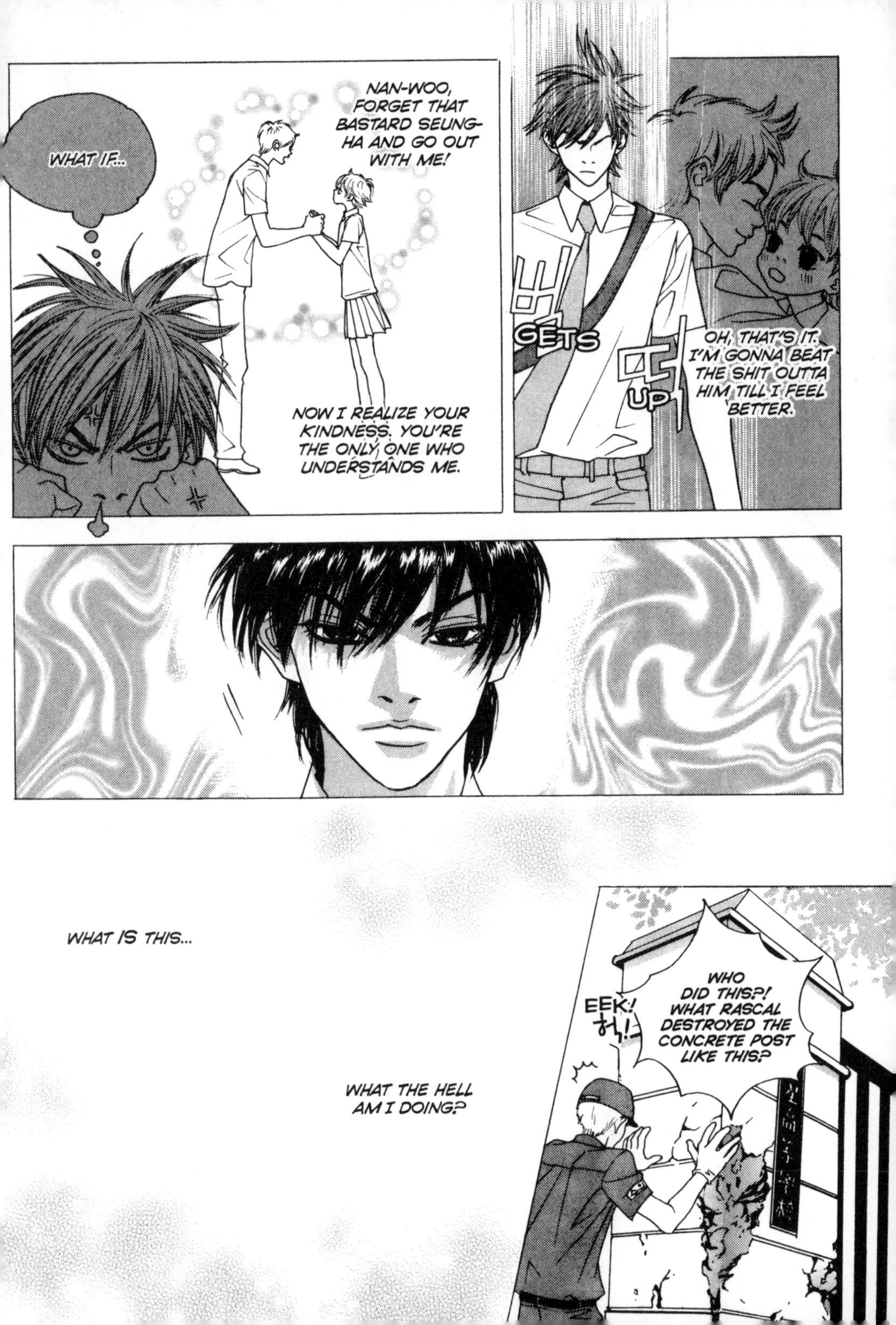
WHAT IF...
NAN-WOO, FORGET THAT BASTARD SEUNG-HA AND GO OUT WITH ME!
NOW I REALIZE YOUR KINDNESS. YOU'RE THE ONLY ONE WHO UNDERSTANDS ME.
GETS UP
OH, THAT'S IT. I'M GONNA BEAT THE SHIT OUTTA HIM TILL I FEEL BETTER.
WHAT IS THIS...
WHAT THE HELL AM I DOING?
EEK!
헉!
WHO DID THIS?! WHAT RASCAL DESTROYED THE CONCRETE POST LIKE THIS?

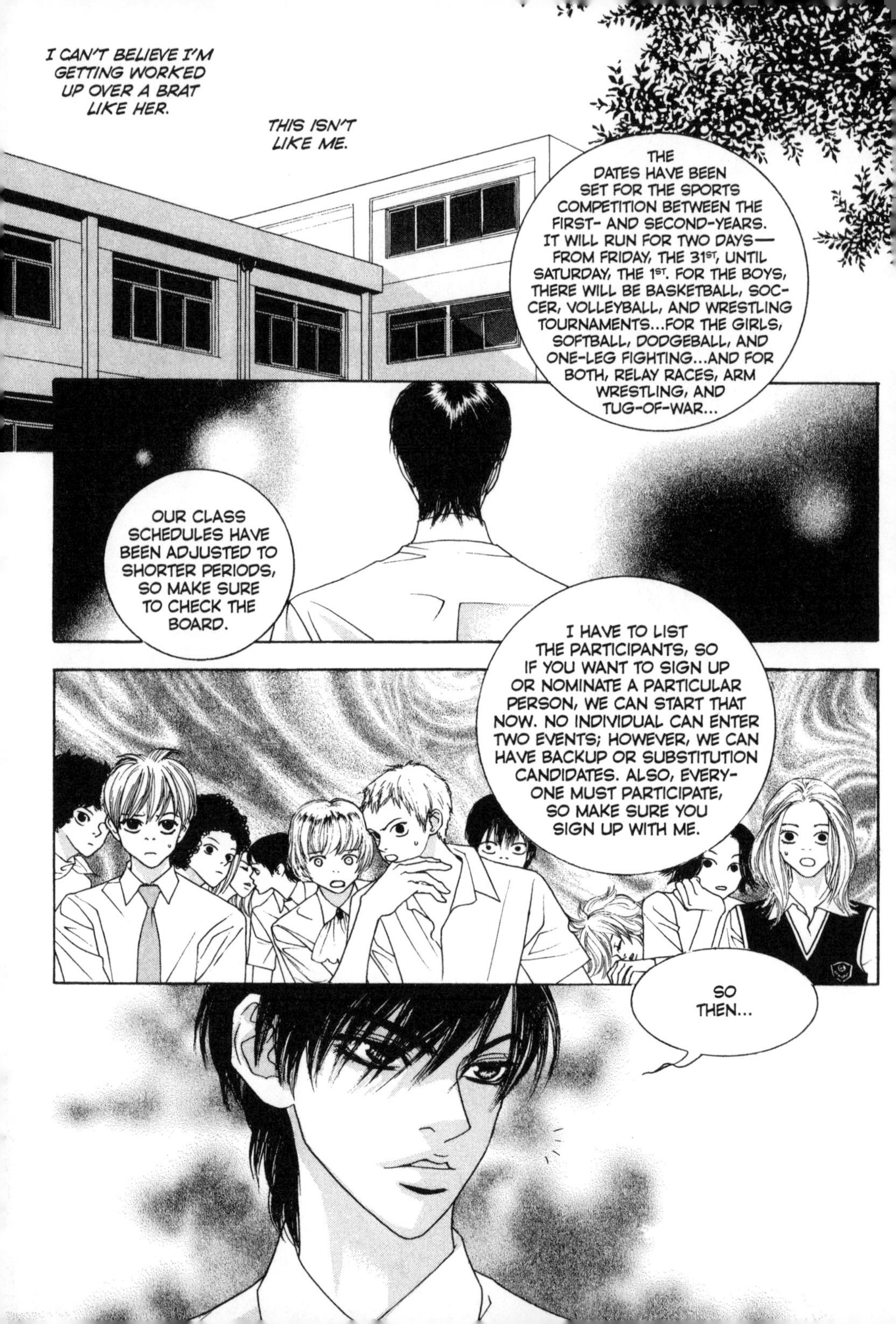
I CAN'T BELIEVE I'M GETTING WORKED UP OVER A BRAT LIKE HER.
THIS ISN'T LIKE ME.
THE DATES HAVE BEEN SET FOR THE SPORTS COMPETITION BETWEEN THE FIRST- AND SECOND-YEARS. IT WILL RUN FOR TWO DAYS— FROM FRIDAY, THE 31ST, UNTIL SATURDAY, THE 1ST. FOR THE BOYS, THERE WILL BE BASKETBALL, SOCCER, VOLLEYBALL, AND WRESTLING TOURNAMENTS...FOR THE GIRLS, SOFTBALL, DODGEBALL, AND ONE-LEG FIGHTING...AND FOR BOTH, RELAY RACES, ARM WRESTLING, AND TUG-OF-WAR...
OUR CLASS SCHEDULES HAVE BEEN ADJUSTED TO SHORTER PERIODS, SO MAKE SURE TO CHECK THE BOARD.
I HAVE TO LIST THE PARTICIPANTS, SO IF YOU WANT TO SIGN UP OR NOMINATE A PARTICULAR PERSON, WE CAN START THAT NOW. NO INDIVIDUAL CAN ENTER TWO EVENTS; HOWEVER, WE CAN HAVE BACKUP OR SUBSTITUTION CANDIDATES. ALSO, EVERYONE MUST PARTICIPATE, SO MAKE SURE YOU SIGN UP WITH ME.
SO THEN...

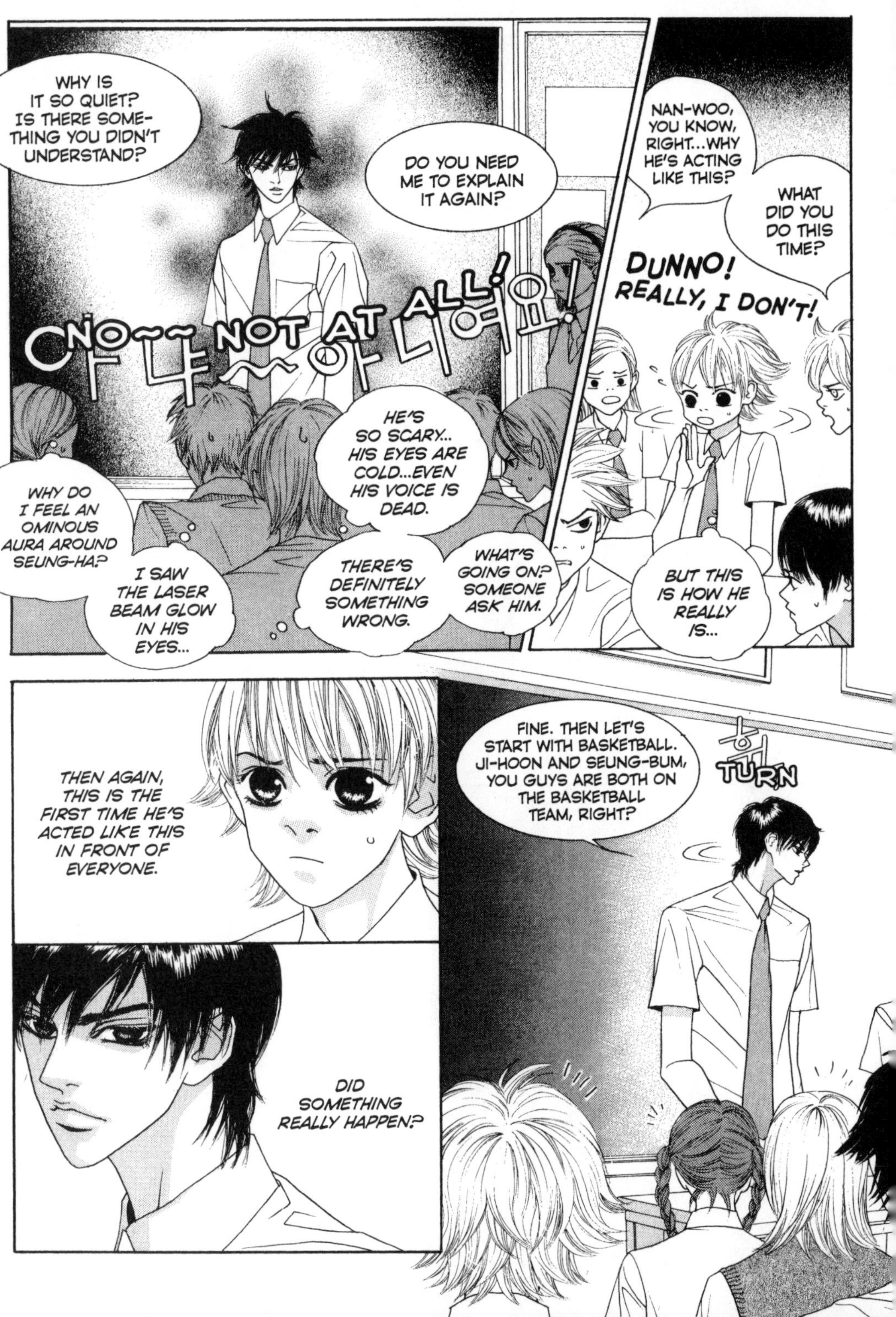
WHY IS IT SO QUIET? IS THERE SOME-THING YOU DIDN'T UNDERSTAND?
DO YOU NEED ME TO EXPLAIN IT AGAIN?
NO~~ NOT AT ALL!
WHY DO I FEEL AN OMINOUS AURA AROUND SEUNG-HA?
HE'S SO SCARY... HIS EYES ARE COLD...EVEN HIS VOICE IS DEAD.
I SAW THE LASER BEAM GLOW IN HIS EYES...
THERE'S DEFINITELY SOMETHING WRONG.
WHAT'S GOING ON? SOMEONE ASK HIM.
NAN-WOO, YOU KNOW, RIGHT...WHY HE'S ACTING LIKE THIS?
WHAT DID YOU DO THIS TIME?
DUNNO! REALLY, I DON'T!
BUT THIS IS HOW HE REALLY IS...
THEN AGAIN, THIS IS THE FIRST TIME HE'S ACTED LIKE THIS IN FRONT OF EVERYONE.
DID SOMETHING REALLY HAPPEN?
FINE. THEN LET'S START WITH BASKETBALL. JI-HOON AND SEUNG-BUM, YOU GUYS ARE BOTH ON THE BASKETBALL TEAM, RIGHT?
TURN

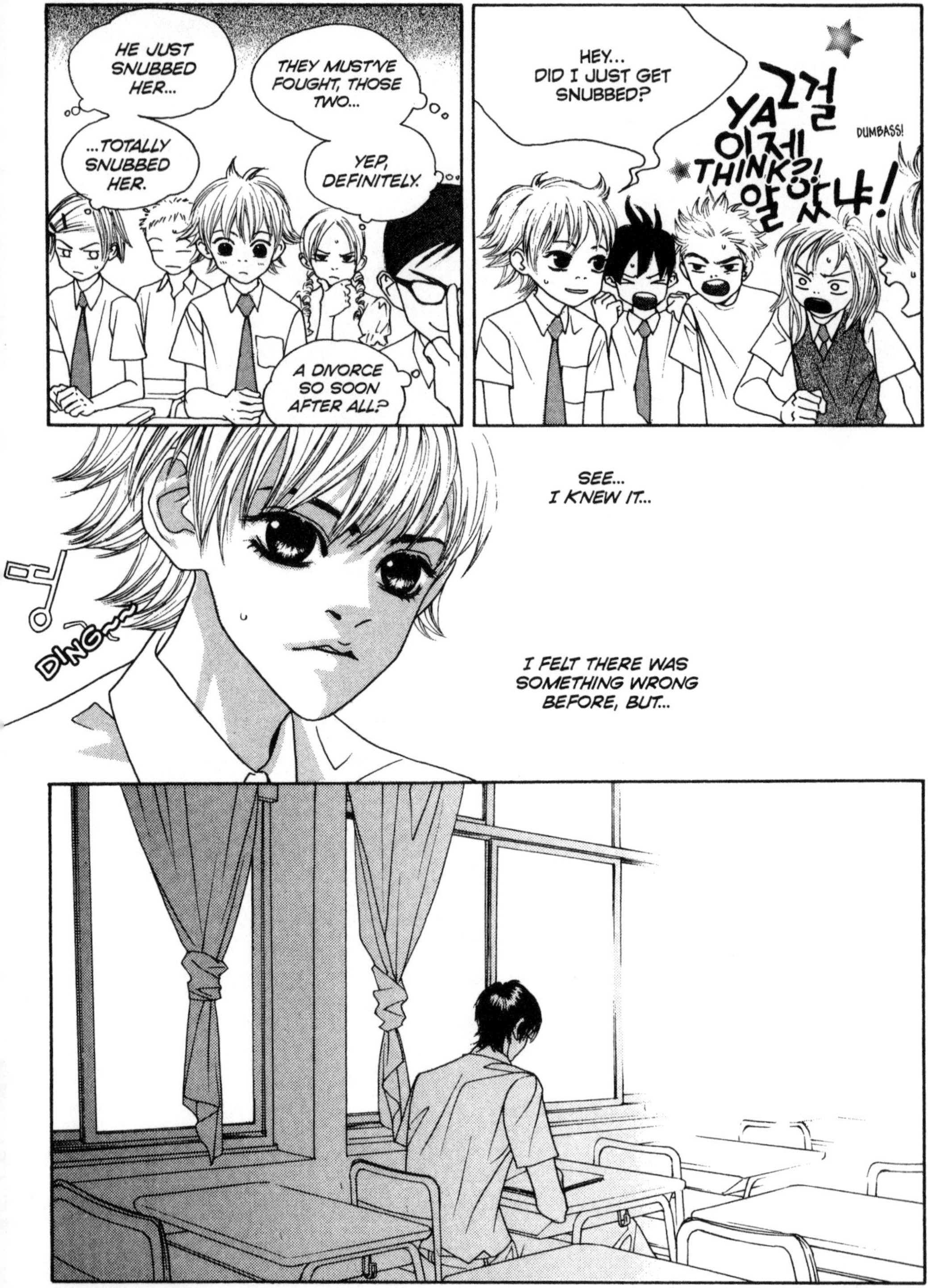
HE JUST SNUBBED HER...
...TOTALLY SNUBBED HER.
THEY MUST'VE FOUGHT, THOSE TWO...
YEP, DEFINITELY.
A DIVORCE SO SOON AFTER ALL?
HEY... DID I JUST GET SNUBBED?
YA THINK?!
고걸 이제 알았냐!
DUMBASS!
띵
DING~~
SEE... I KNEW IT...
I FELT THERE WAS SOMETHING WRONG BEFORE, BUT...

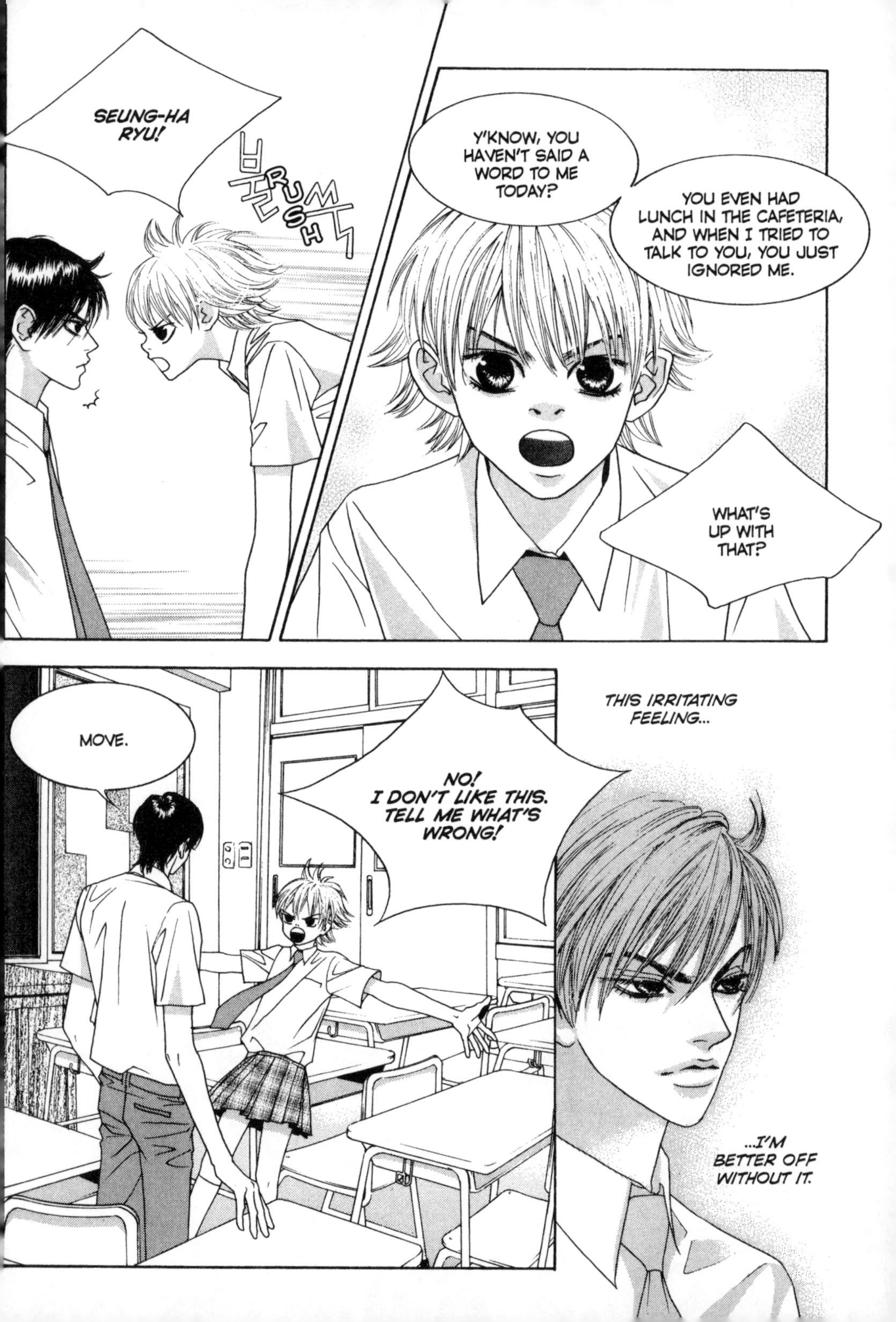
SEUNG-HA RYU!
RUSH
Y'KNOW, YOU HAVEN'T SAID A WORD TO ME TODAY?
YOU EVEN HAD LUNCH IN THE CAFETERIA, AND WHEN I TRIED TO TALK TO YOU, YOU JUST IGNORED ME.
WHAT'S UP WITH THAT?
MOVE.
NO! I DON'T LIKE THIS. TELL ME WHAT'S WRONG!
THIS IRRITATING FEELING...
...I'M BETTER OFF WITHOUT IT.

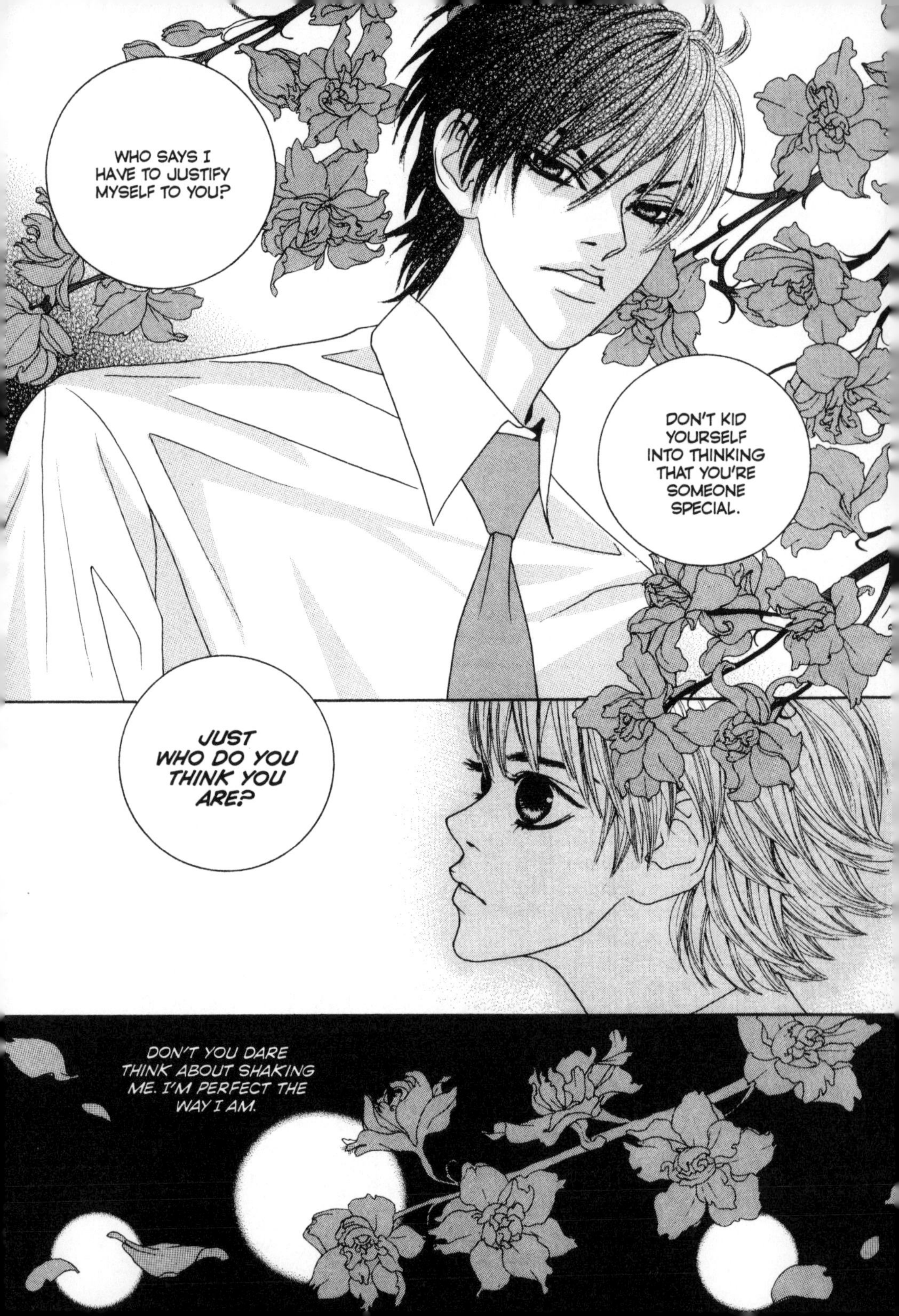
WHO SAYS I HAVE TO JUSTIFY MYSELF TO YOU?
DON'T KID YOURSELF INTO THINKING THAT YOU'RE SOMEONE SPECIAL.
JUST WHO DO YOU THINK YOU ARE?
DON'T YOU DARE THINK ABOUT SHAKING ME. I'M PERFECT THE WAY I AM.

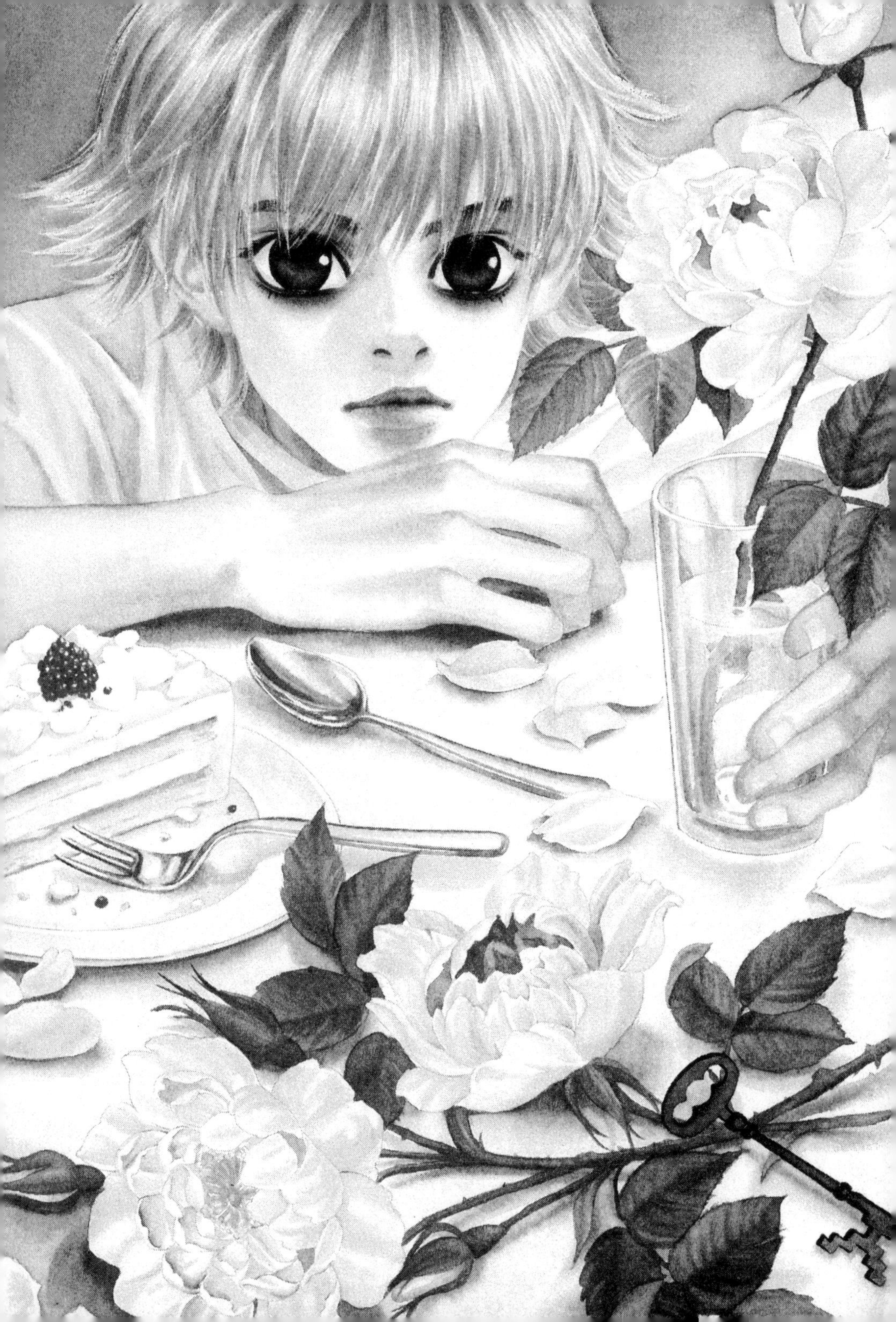

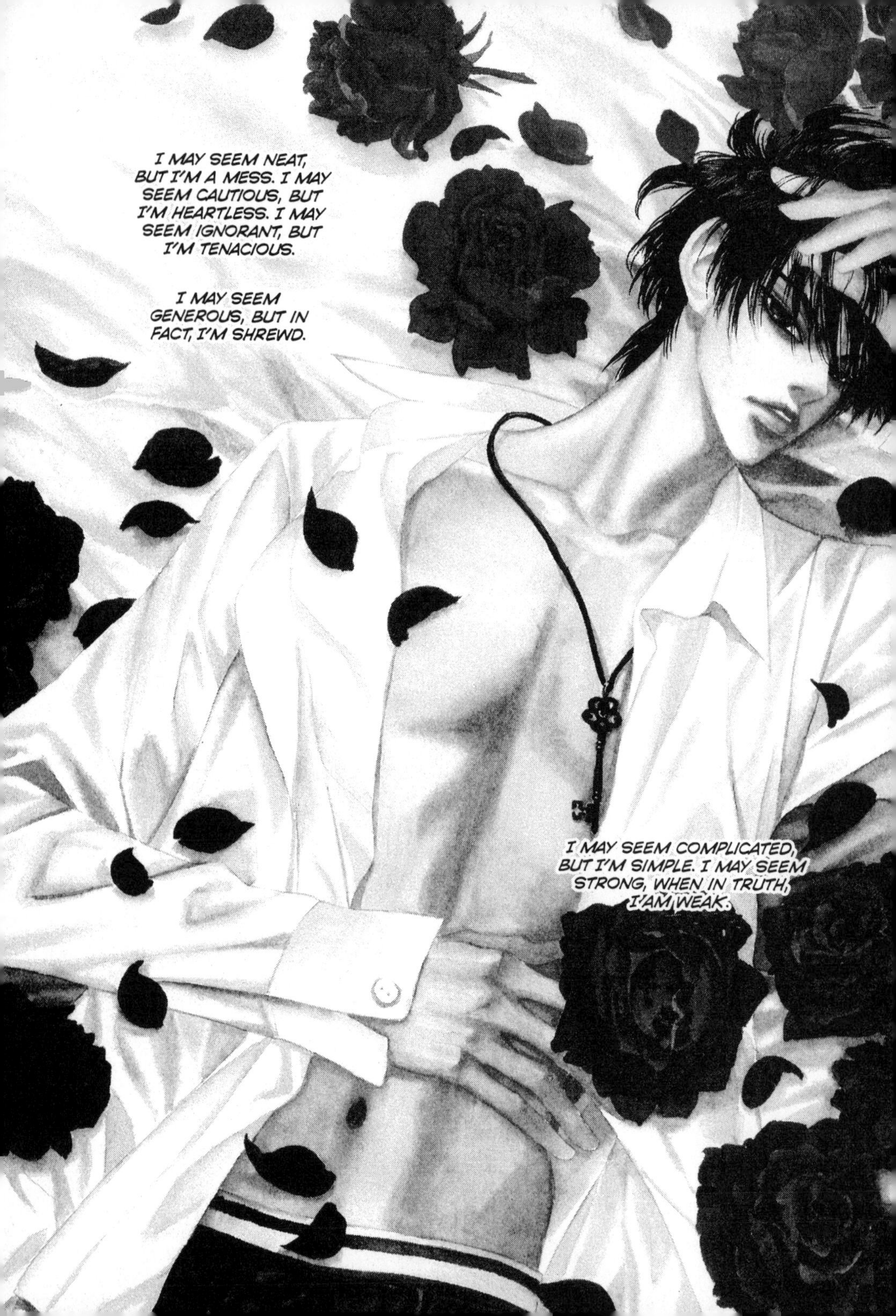
I MAY SEEM NEAT, BUT I'M A MESS. I MAY SEEM CAUTIOUS, BUT I'M HEARTLESS. I MAY SEEM IGNORANT, BUT I'M TENACIOUS.
I MAY SEEM GENEROUS, BUT IN FACT, I'M SHREWD.
I MAY SEEM COMPLICATED, BUT I'M SIMPLE. I MAY SEEM STRONG, WHEN IN TRUTH, I AM WEAK.

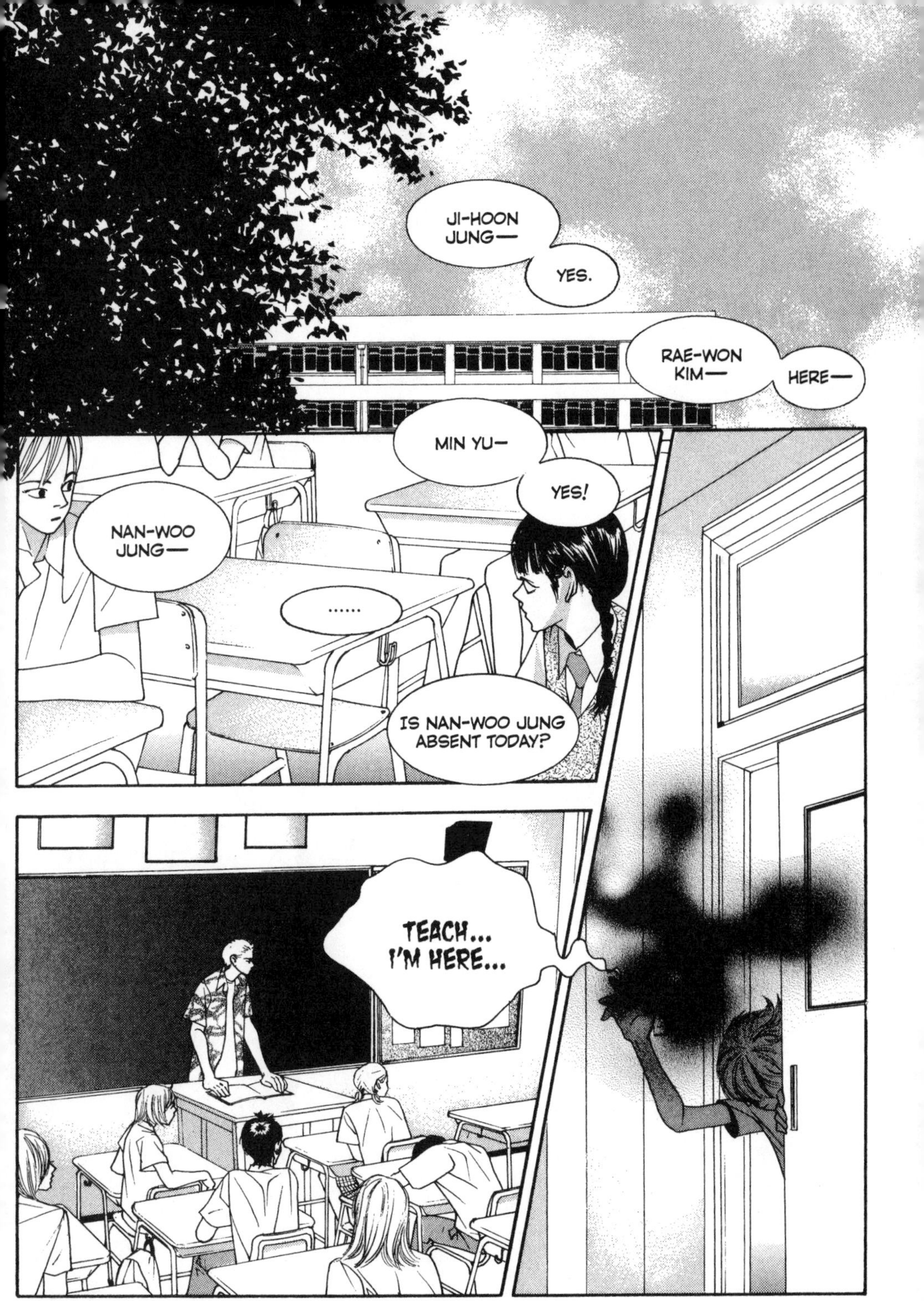
JI-HOON JUNG—
YES.
RAE-WON KIM—
HERE—
MIN YU—
YES!
NAN-WOO JUNG—
......
IS NAN-WOO JUNG ABSENT TODAY?
TEACH... I'M HERE...

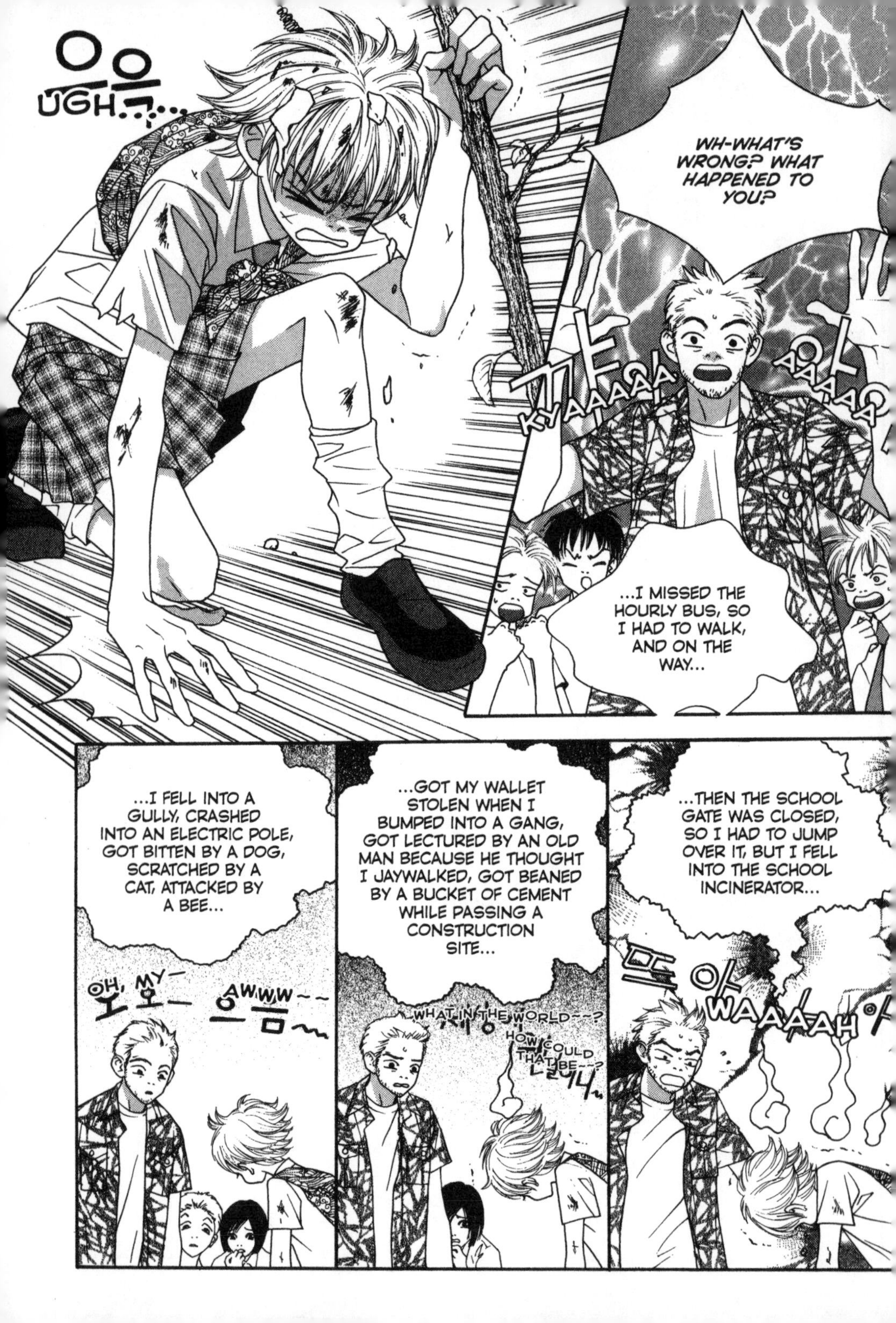
으으
UGH...
WH-WHAT'S WRONG? WHAT HAPPENED TO YOU?
KYAAAAA
AAAAAA
...I MISSED THE HOURLY BUS, SO I HAD TO WALK, AND ON THE WAY...
...I FELL INTO A GULLY, CRASHED INTO AN ELECTRIC POLE, GOT BITTEN BY A DOG, SCRATCHED BY A CAT, ATTACKED BY A BEE...
OH, MY—
AWWW~~
...GOT MY WALLET STOLEN WHEN I BUMPED INTO A GANG, GOT LECTURED BY AN OLD MAN BECAUSE HE THOUGHT I JAYWALKED, GOT BEANED BY A BUCKET OF CEMENT WHILE PASSING A CONSTRUCTION SITE...
WHAT IN THE WORLD~~?
HOW COULD THAT BE~~?
...THEN THE SCHOOL GATE WAS CLOSED, SO I HAD TO JUMP OVER IT, BUT I FELL INTO THE SCHOOL INCINERATOR...
WAAAAAH

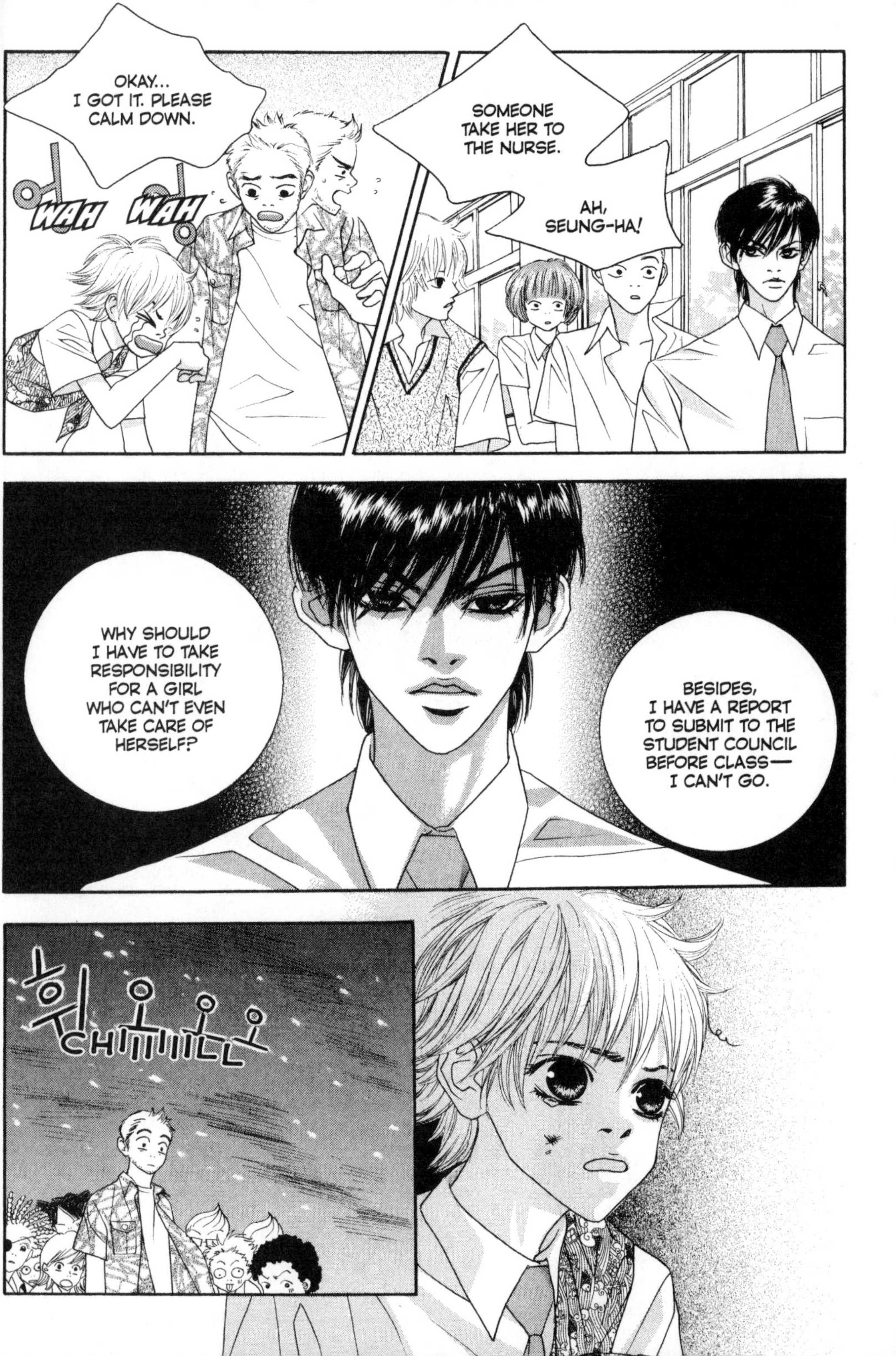
OKAY... I GOT IT. PLEASE CALM DOWN.
WAH WAH
SOMEONE TAKE HER TO THE NURSE.
AH, SEUNG-HA!
WHY SHOULD I HAVE TO TAKE RESPONSIBILITY FOR A GIRL WHO CAN'T EVEN TAKE CARE OF HERSELF?
BESIDES, I HAVE A REPORT TO SUBMIT TO THE STUDENT COUNCIL BEFORE CLASS— I CAN'T GO.
CHIIIIILL

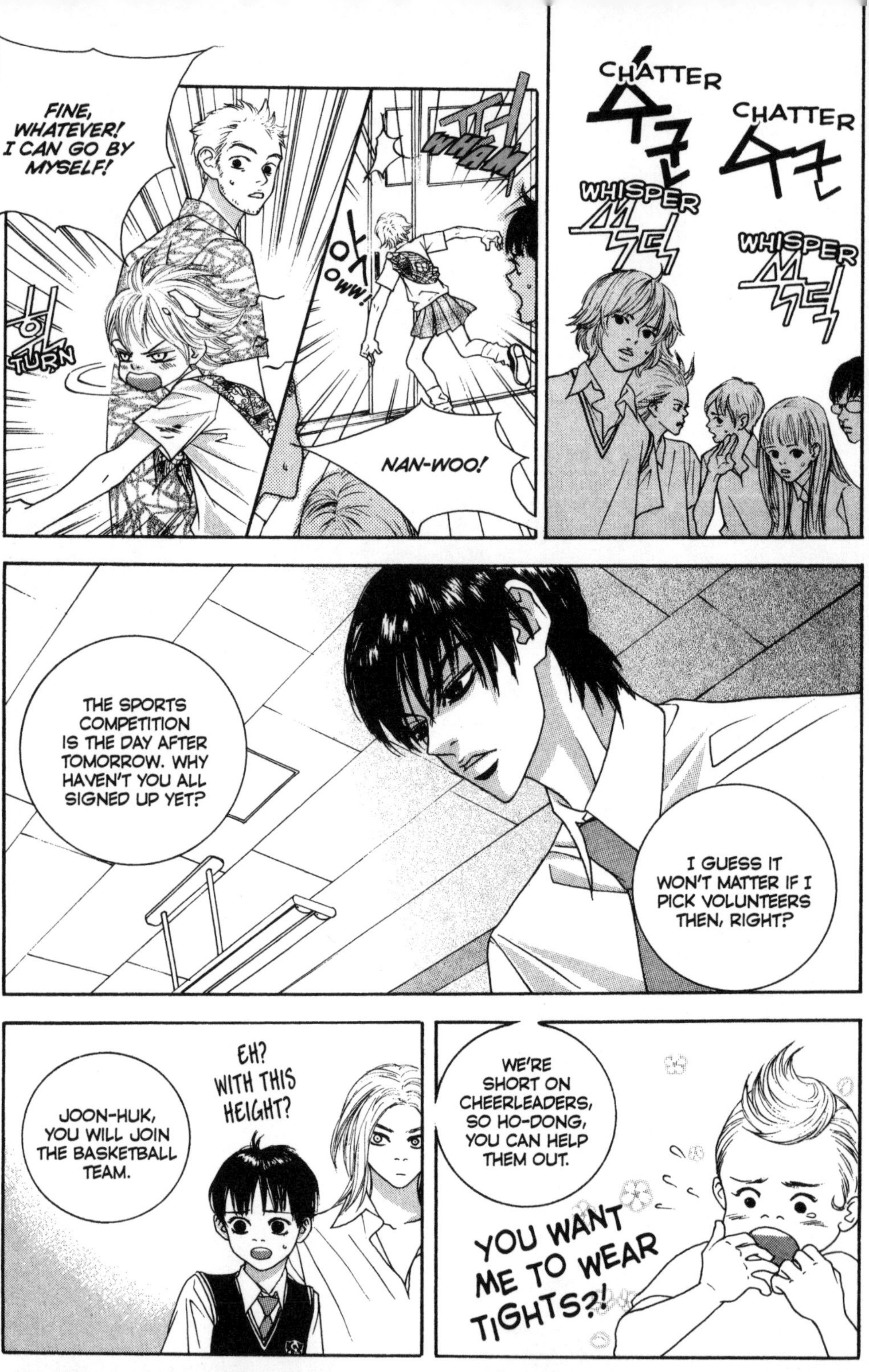
FINE, WHATEVER! I CAN GO BY MYSELF!
TURN
WHAM
OWW!
NAN-WOO!
CHATTER
CHATTER
WHISPER
WHISPER
THE SPORTS COMPETITION IS THE DAY AFTER TOMORROW. WHY HAVEN'T YOU ALL SIGNED UP YET?
I GUESS IT WON'T MATTER IF I PICK VOLUNTEERS THEN, RIGHT?
JOON-HUK, YOU WILL JOIN THE BASKETBALL TEAM.
EH? WITH THIS HEIGHT?
WE'RE SHORT ON CHEERLEADERS, SO HO-DONG, YOU CAN HELP THEM OUT.
YOU WANT ME TO WEAR TIGHTS?!

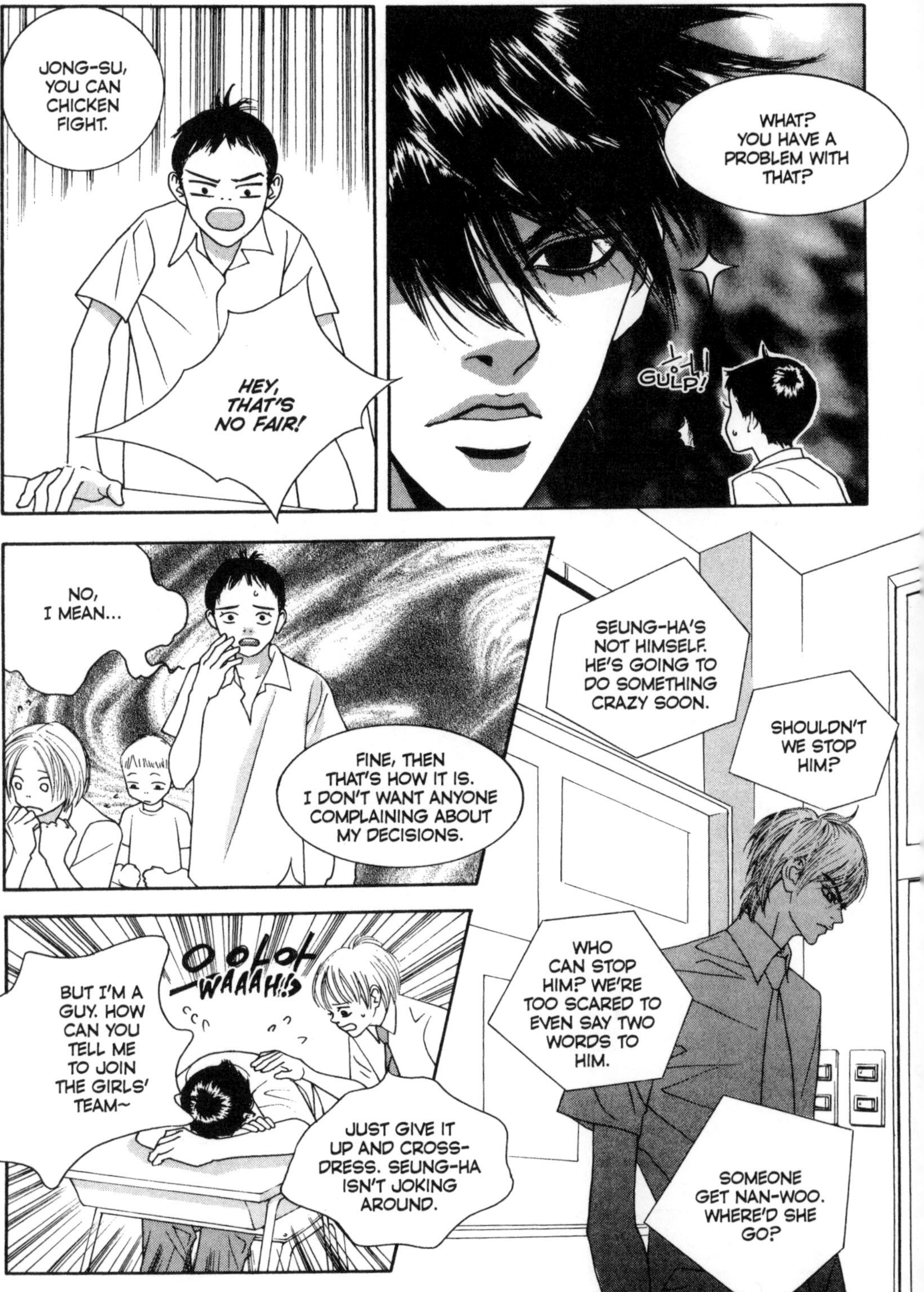
JONG-SU, YOU CAN CHICKEN FIGHT.
HEY, THAT'S NO FAIR!
WHAT? YOU HAVE A PROBLEM WITH THAT?
GULP!
NO, I MEAN...
FINE, THEN THAT'S HOW IT IS. I DON'T WANT ANYONE COMPLAINING ABOUT MY DECISIONS.
BUT I'M A GUY. HOW CAN YOU TELL ME TO JOIN THE GIRLS' TEAM~
WAAAH!!
JUST GIVE IT UP AND CROSS-DRESS. SEUNG-HA ISN'T JOKING AROUND.
SEUNG-HA'S NOT HIMSELF. HE'S GOING TO DO SOMETHING CRAZY SOON.
SHOULDN'T WE STOP HIM?
WHO CAN STOP HIM? WE'RE TOO SCARED TO EVEN SAY TWO WORDS TO HIM.
SOMEONE GET NAN-WOO. WHERE'D SHE GO?

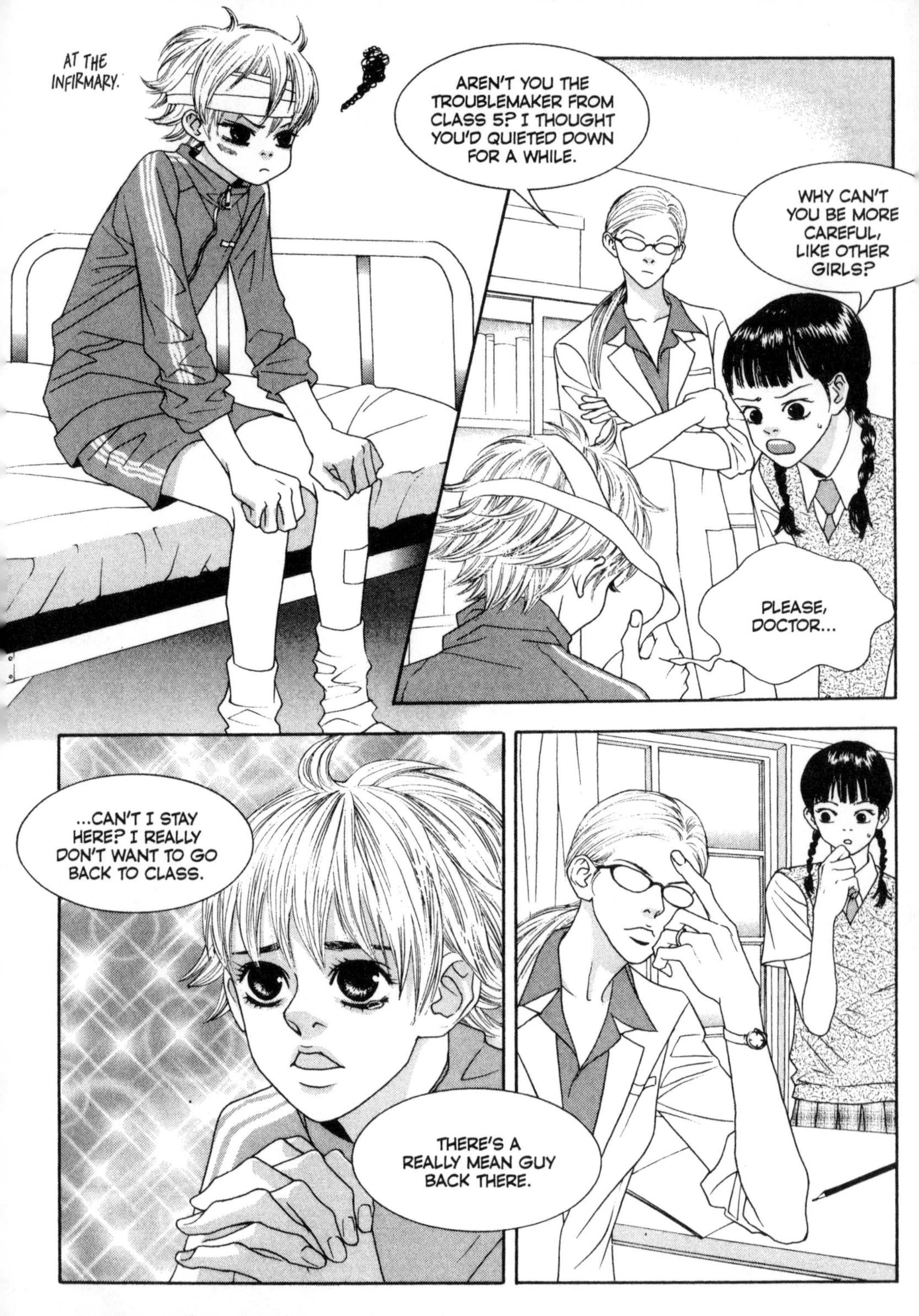
AT THE INFIRMARY.
AREN'T YOU THE TROUBLEMAKER FROM CLASS 5? I THOUGHT YOU'D QUIETED DOWN FOR A WHILE.
WHY CAN'T YOU BE MORE CAREFUL, LIKE OTHER GIRLS?
PLEASE, DOCTOR...
...CAN'T I STAY HERE? I REALLY DON'T WANT TO GO BACK TO CLASS.
THERE'S A REALLY MEAN GUY BACK THERE.

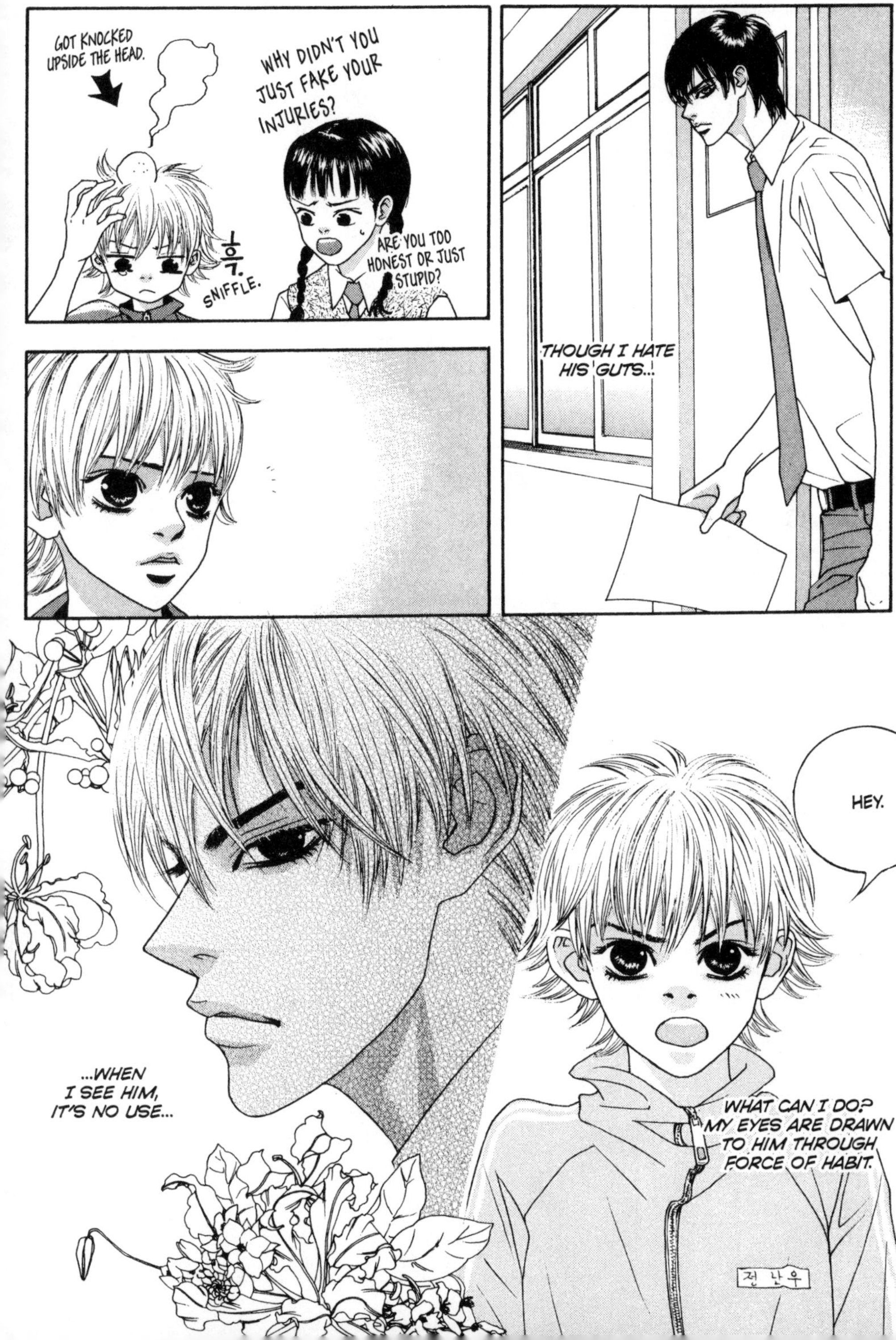
GOT KNOCKED UPSIDE THE HEAD.
WHY DIDN'T YOU JUST FAKE YOUR INJURIES?
흑.
SNIFFLE.
ARE YOU TOO HONEST OR JUST STUPID?
THOUGH I HATE HIS GUTS...
...WHEN I SEE HIM, IT'S NO USE...
HEY.
WHAT CAN I DO? MY EYES ARE DRAWN TO HIM THROUGH FORCE OF HABIT.
전 난우

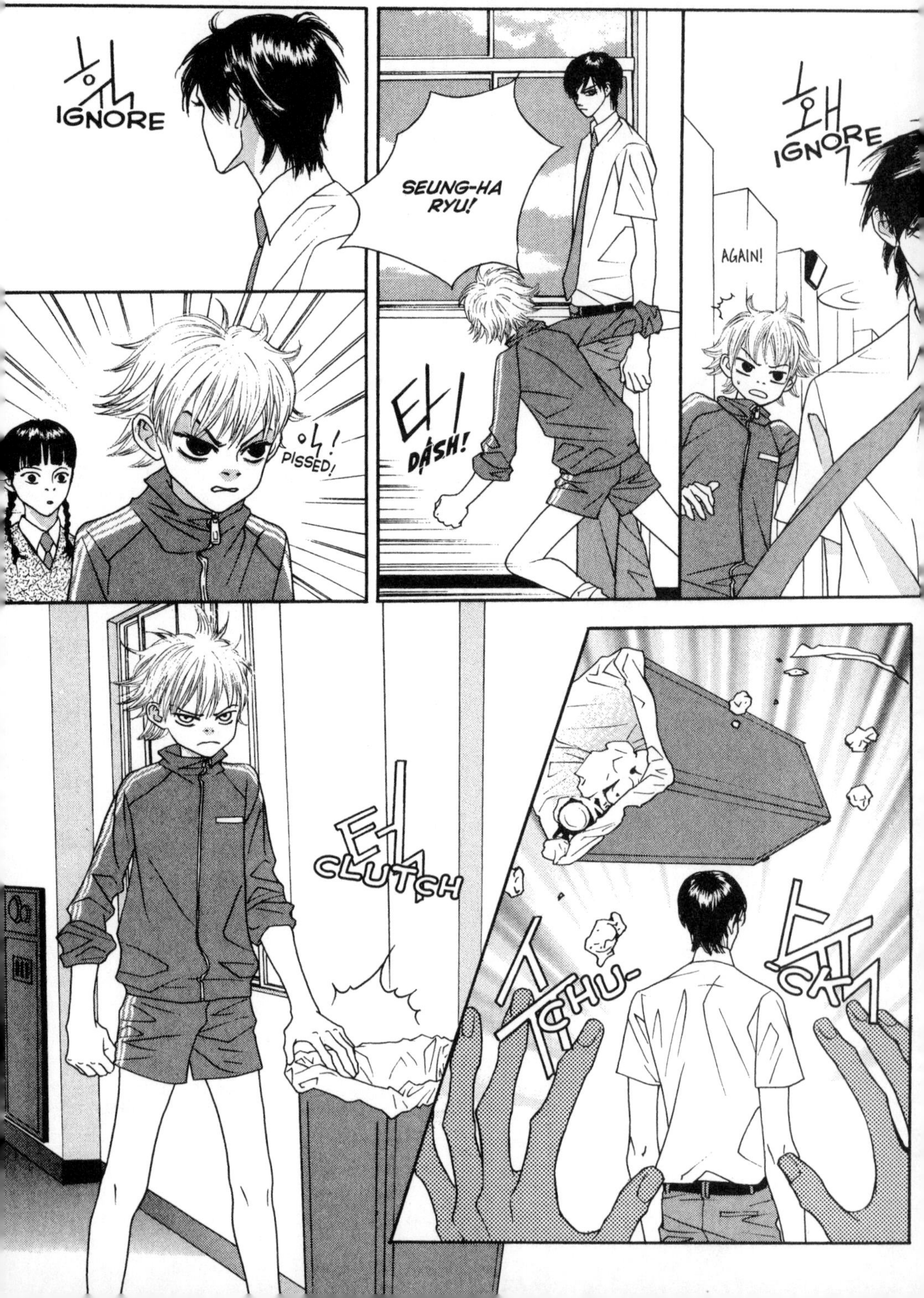
IGNORE
PISSED!
SEUNG-HA RYU!
DASH!
IGNORE
AGAIN!
CLUTCH
TCHU-
CK

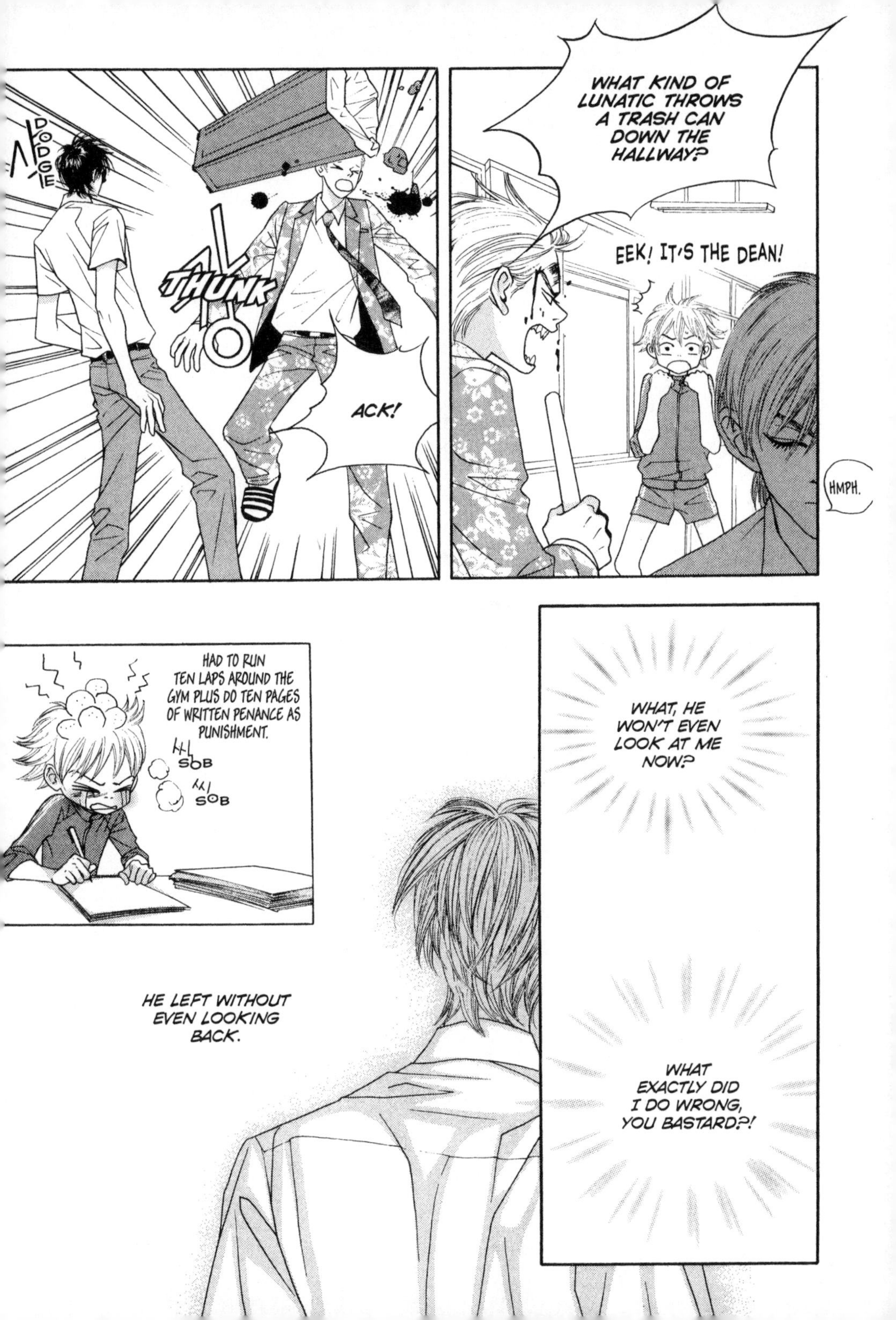
DODGE
THUNK
ACK!
WHAT KIND OF LUNATIC THROWS A TRASH CAN DOWN THE HALLWAY?
EEK! IT'S THE DEAN!
HMPH.
HAD TO RUN TEN LAPS AROUND THE GYM PLUS DO TEN PAGES OF WRITTEN PENANCE AS PUNISHMENT.
SOB
SOB
HE LEFT WITHOUT EVEN LOOKING BACK.
WHAT, HE WON'T EVEN LOOK AT ME NOW?
WHAT EXACTLY DID I DO WRONG, YOU BASTARD?!

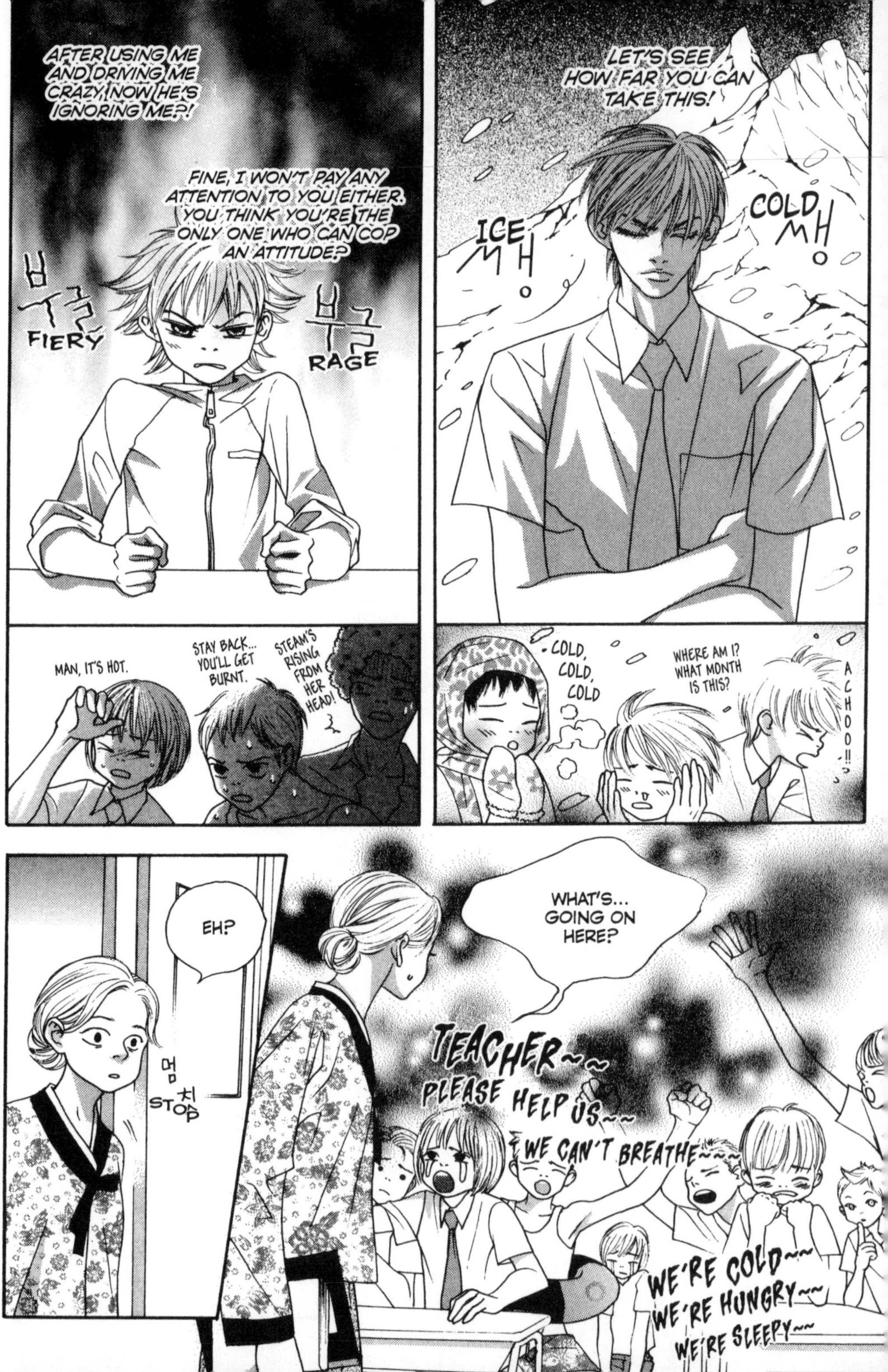
AFTER USING ME AND DRIVING ME CRAZY, NOW HE'S IGNORING ME?!
FINE, I WON'T PAY ANY ATTENTION TO YOU EITHER. YOU THINK YOU'RE THE ONLY ONE WHO CAN COP AN ATTITUDE?
부글 FIERY
부글 RAGE
LET'S SEE HOW FAR YOU CAN TAKE THIS!
ICE
COLD
MAN, IT'S HOT.
STAY BACK... YOU'LL GET BURNT.
STEAM'S RISING FROM HER HEAD!
COLD, COLD, COLD
WHERE AM I? WHAT MONTH IS THIS?
ACHOO!!
EH?
멈칫 STOP
WHAT'S... GOING ON HERE?
TEACHER~~ PLEASE HELP US~~
WE CAN'T BREATHE~~~
WE'RE COLD~~~ WE'RE HUNGRY~~ WE'RE SLEEPY~~

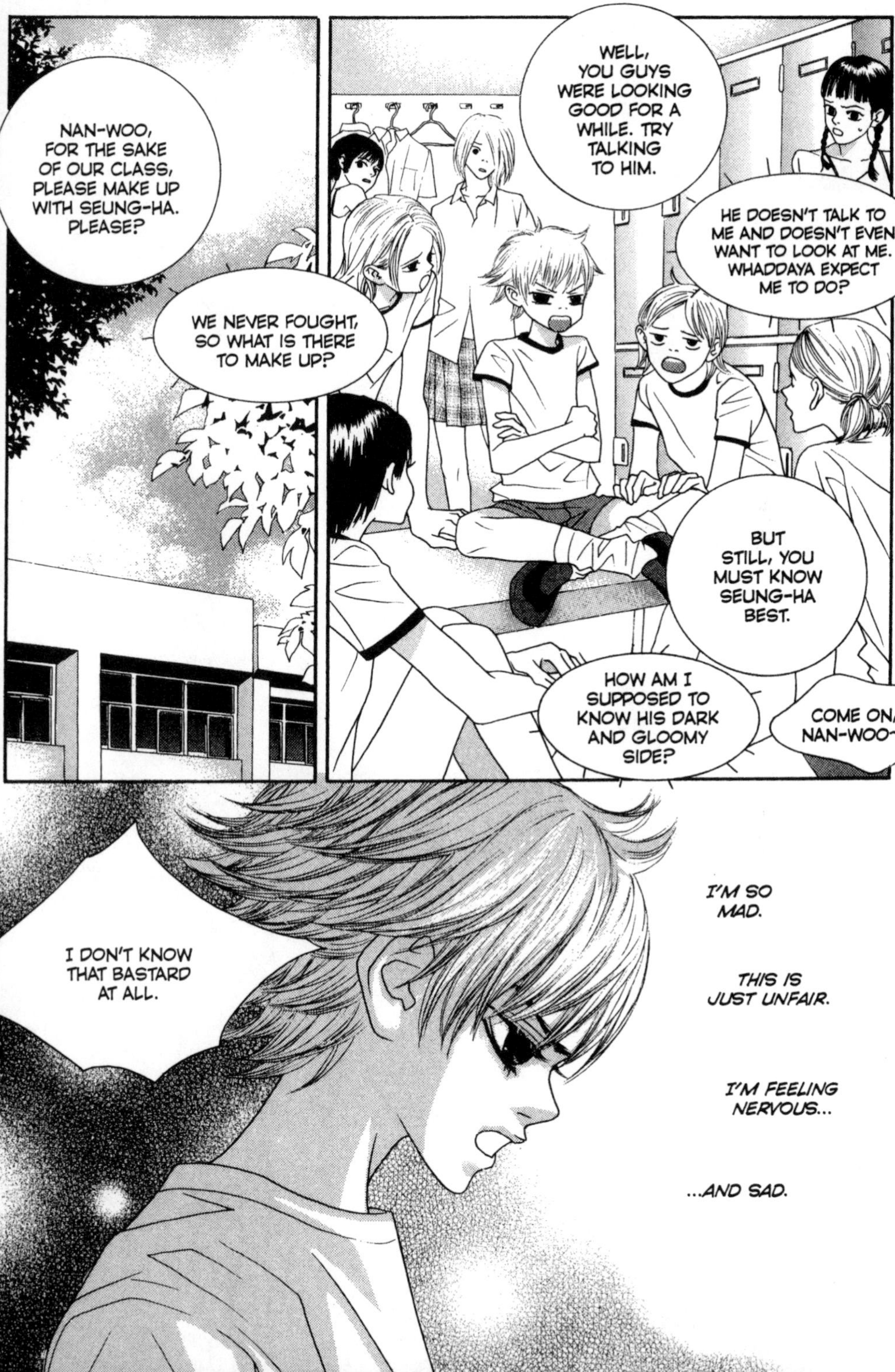
NAN-WOO, FOR THE SAKE OF OUR CLASS, PLEASE MAKE UP WITH SEUNG-HA. PLEASE?
WE NEVER FOUGHT, SO WHAT IS THERE TO MAKE UP?
WELL, YOU GUYS WERE LOOKING GOOD FOR A WHILE. TRY TALKING TO HIM.
HE DOESN'T TALK TO ME AND DOESN'T EVEN WANT TO LOOK AT ME. WHADDAYA EXPECT ME TO DO?
BUT STILL, YOU MUST KNOW SEUNG-HA BEST.
HOW AM I SUPPOSED TO KNOW HIS DARK AND GLOOMY SIDE?
COME ON, NAN-WOO~.
I DON'T KNOW THAT BASTARD AT ALL.
I'M SO MAD.
THIS IS JUST UNFAIR.
I'M FEELING NERVOUS...
...AND SAD.

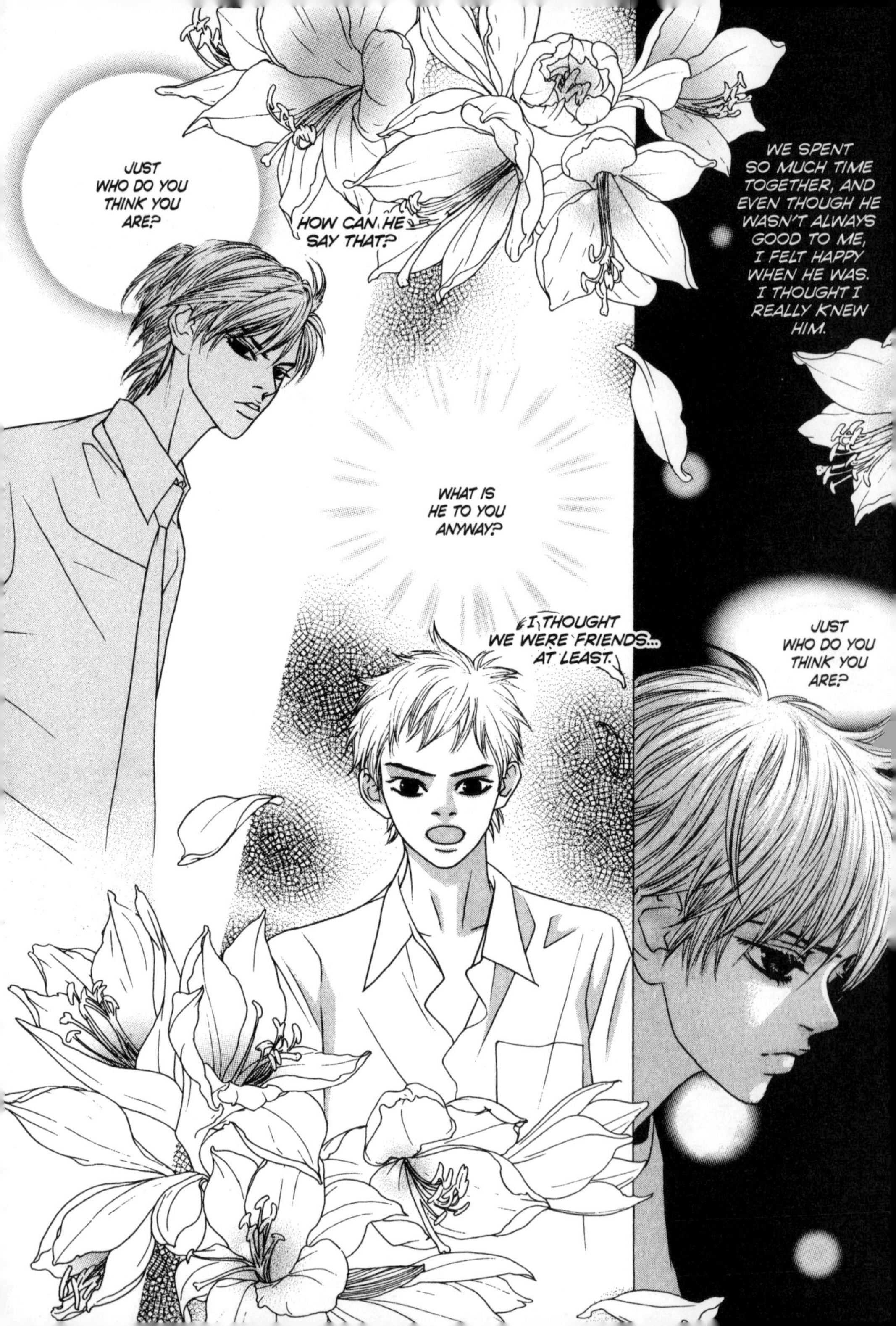
JUST WHO DO YOU THINK YOU ARE?
HOW CAN HE SAY THAT?
WE SPENT SO MUCH TIME TOGETHER, AND EVEN THOUGH HE WASN'T ALWAYS GOOD TO ME, I FELT HAPPY WHEN HE WAS. I THOUGHT I REALLY KNEW HIM.
WHAT IS HE TO YOU ANYWAY?
I THOUGHT WE WERE FRIENDS... AT LEAST.
JUST WHO DO YOU THINK YOU ARE?

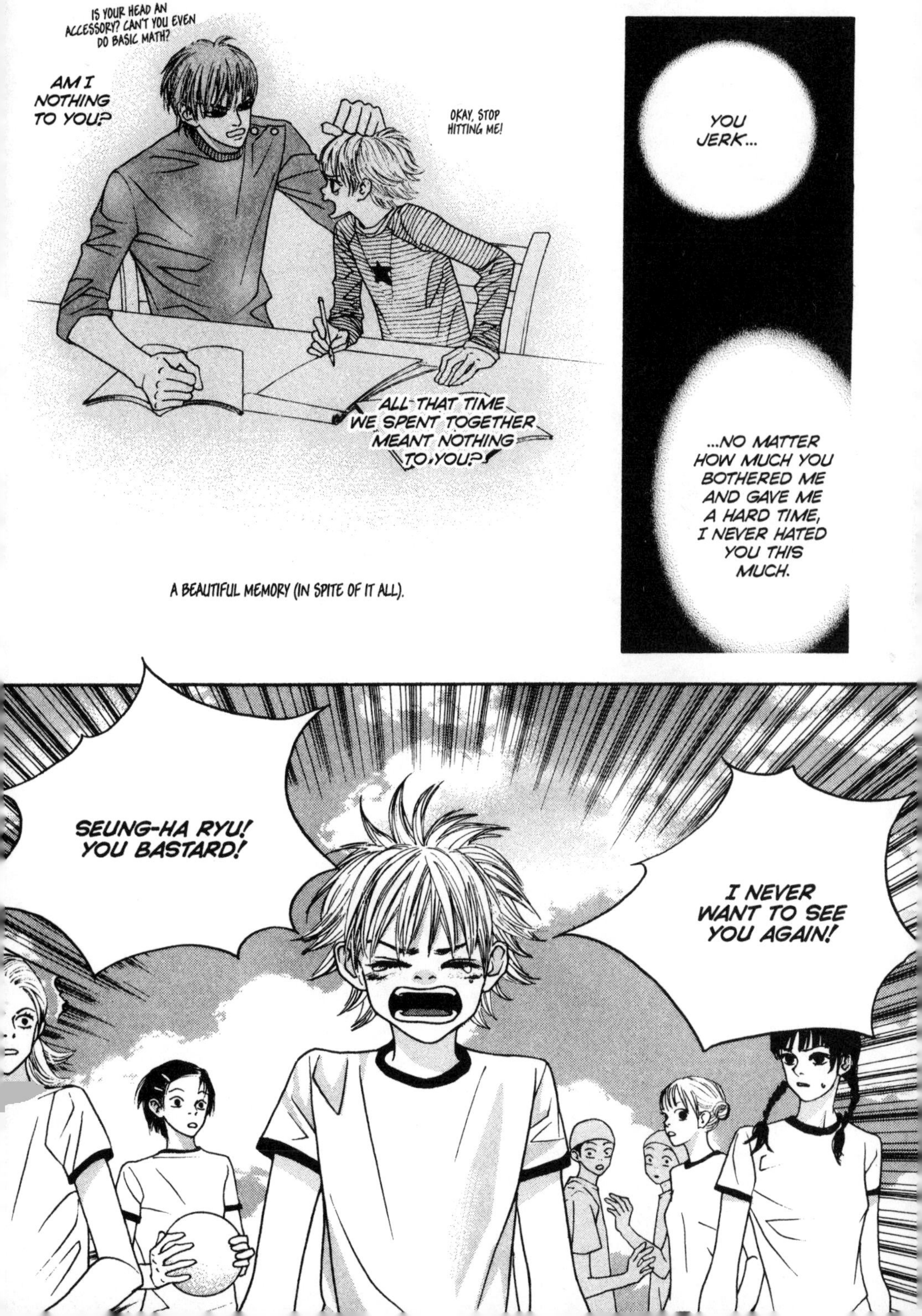

AM I NOTHING TO YOU?
IS YOUR HEAD AN ACCESSORY? CAN'T YOU EVEN DO BASIC MATH?
OKAY, STOP HITTING ME!
ALL THAT TIME WE SPENT TOGETHER MEANT NOTHING TO YOU?!
A BEAUTIFUL MEMORY (IN SPITE OF IT ALL).
YOU JERK...
...NO MATTER HOW MUCH YOU BOTHERED ME AND GAVE ME A HARD TIME, I NEVER HATED YOU THIS MUCH.
SEUNG-HA RYU! YOU BASTARD!
I NEVER WANT TO SEE YOU AGAIN!

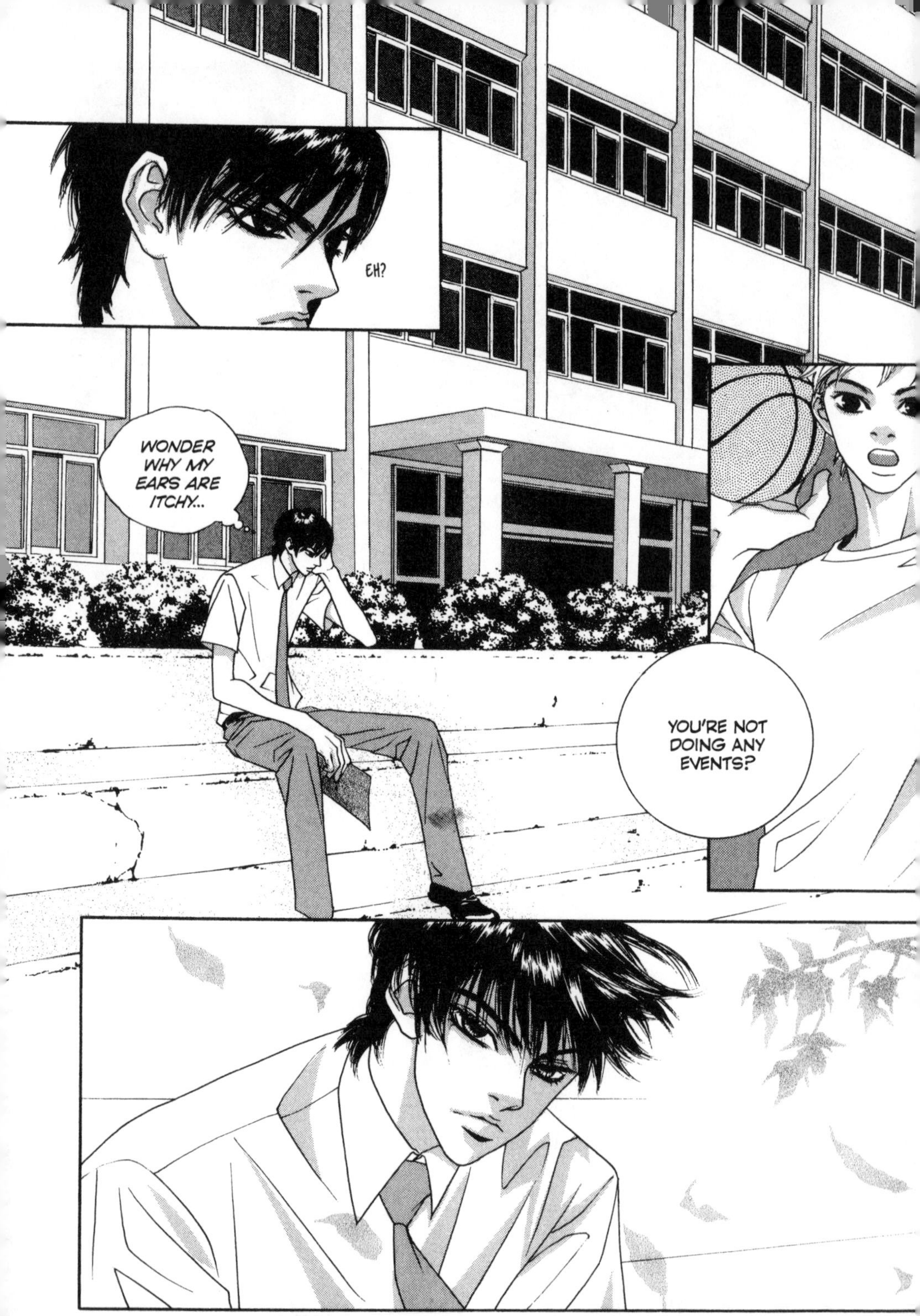
EH?
WONDER WHY MY EARS ARE ITCHY...
YOU'RE NOT DOING ANY EVENTS?

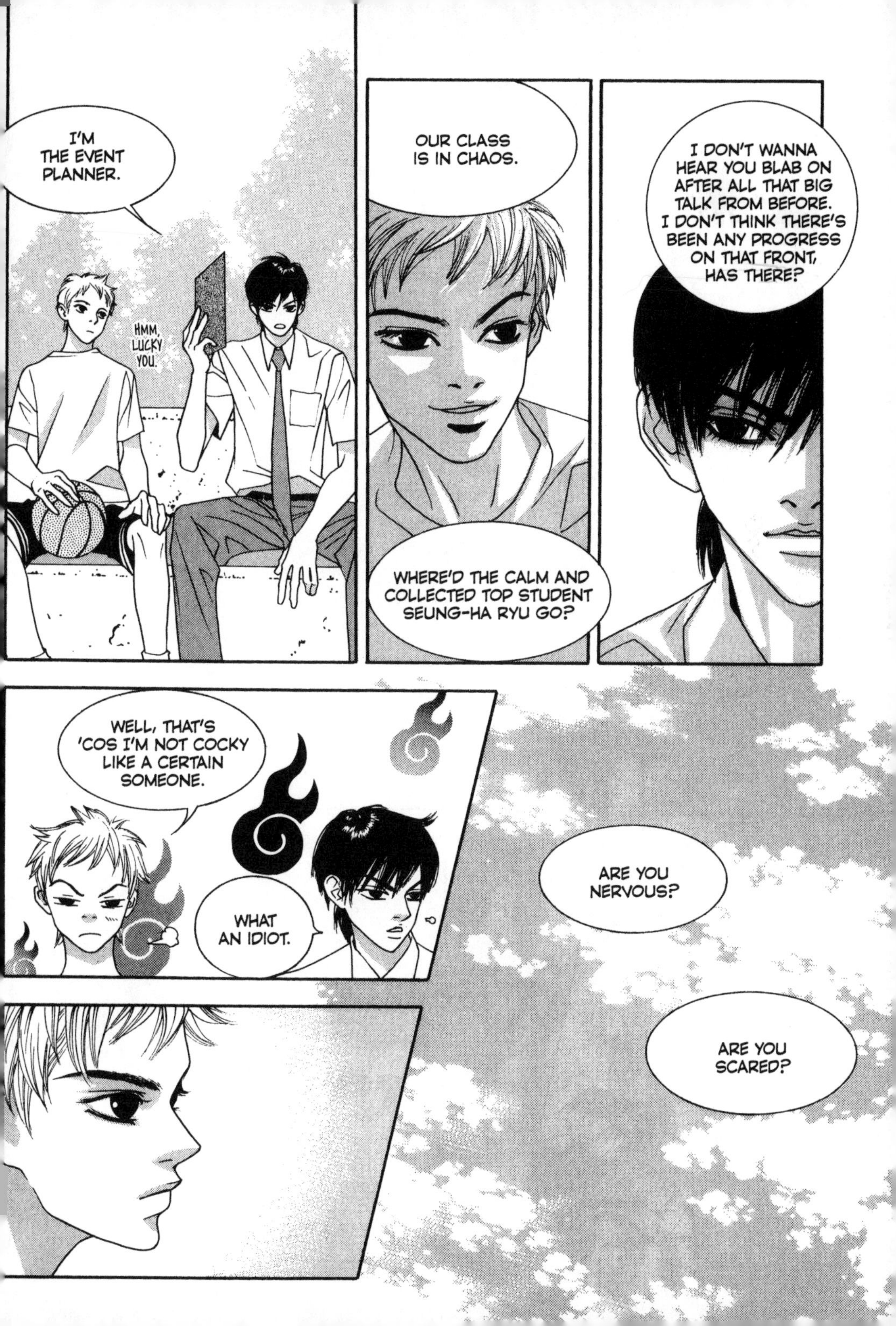
I'M THE EVENT PLANNER.
HMM, LUCKY YOU.
OUR CLASS IS IN CHAOS.
WHERE'D THE CALM AND COLLECTED TOP STUDENT SEUNG-HA RYU GO?
I DON'T WANNA HEAR YOU BLAB ON AFTER ALL THAT BIG TALK FROM BEFORE. I DON'T THINK THERE'S BEEN ANY PROGRESS ON THAT FRONT, HAS THERE?
WELL, THAT'S 'COS I'M NOT COCKY LIKE A CERTAIN SOMEONE.
WHAT AN IDIOT.
ARE YOU NERVOUS?
ARE YOU SCARED?

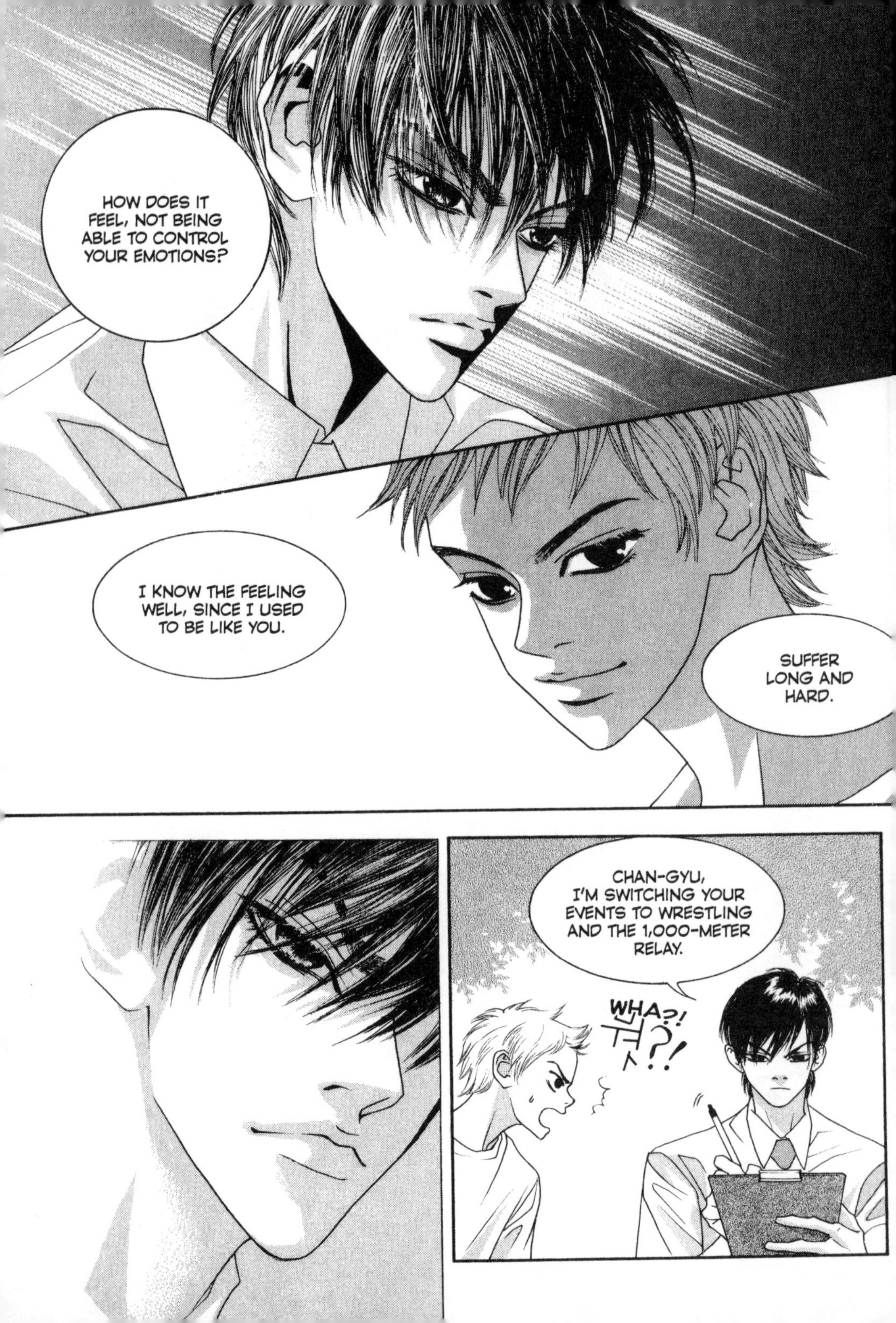
HOW DOES IT FEEL, NOT BEING ABLE TO CONTROL YOUR EMOTIONS?
I KNOW THE FEELING WELL, SINCE I USED TO BE LIKE YOU.
SUFFER LONG AND HARD.
CHAN-GYU, I'M SWITCHING YOUR EVENTS TO WRESTLING AND THE 1,000-METER RELAY.
WHA?!
걱?!

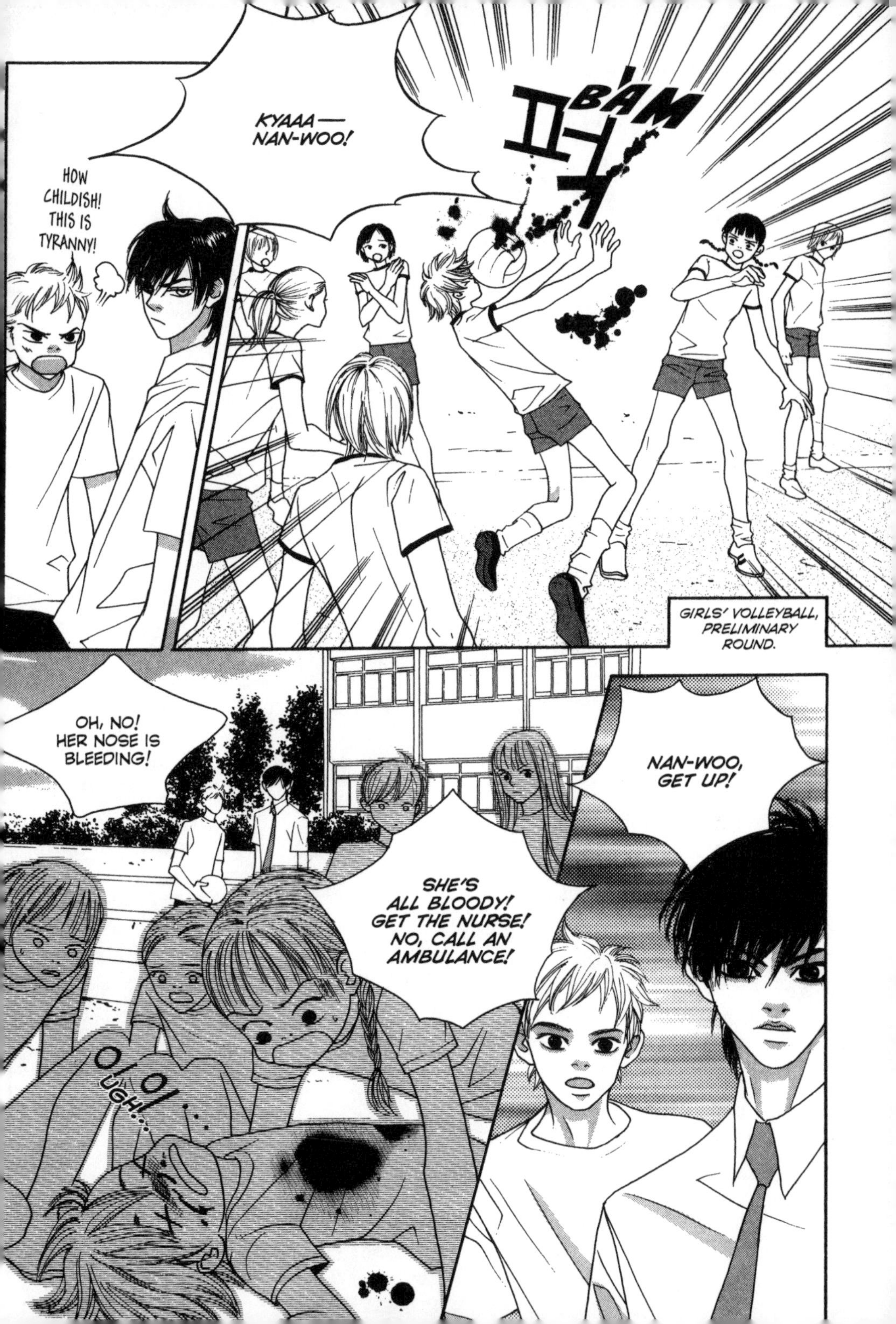
KYAAA— NAN-WOO!
HOW CHILDISH! THIS IS TYRANNY!
B'AM
GIRLS' VOLLEYBALL, PRELIMINARY ROUND.
OH, NO! HER NOSE IS BLEEDING!
SHE'S ALL BLOODY! GET THE NURSE! NO, CALL AN AMBULANCE!
UGH...
NAN-WOO, GET UP!

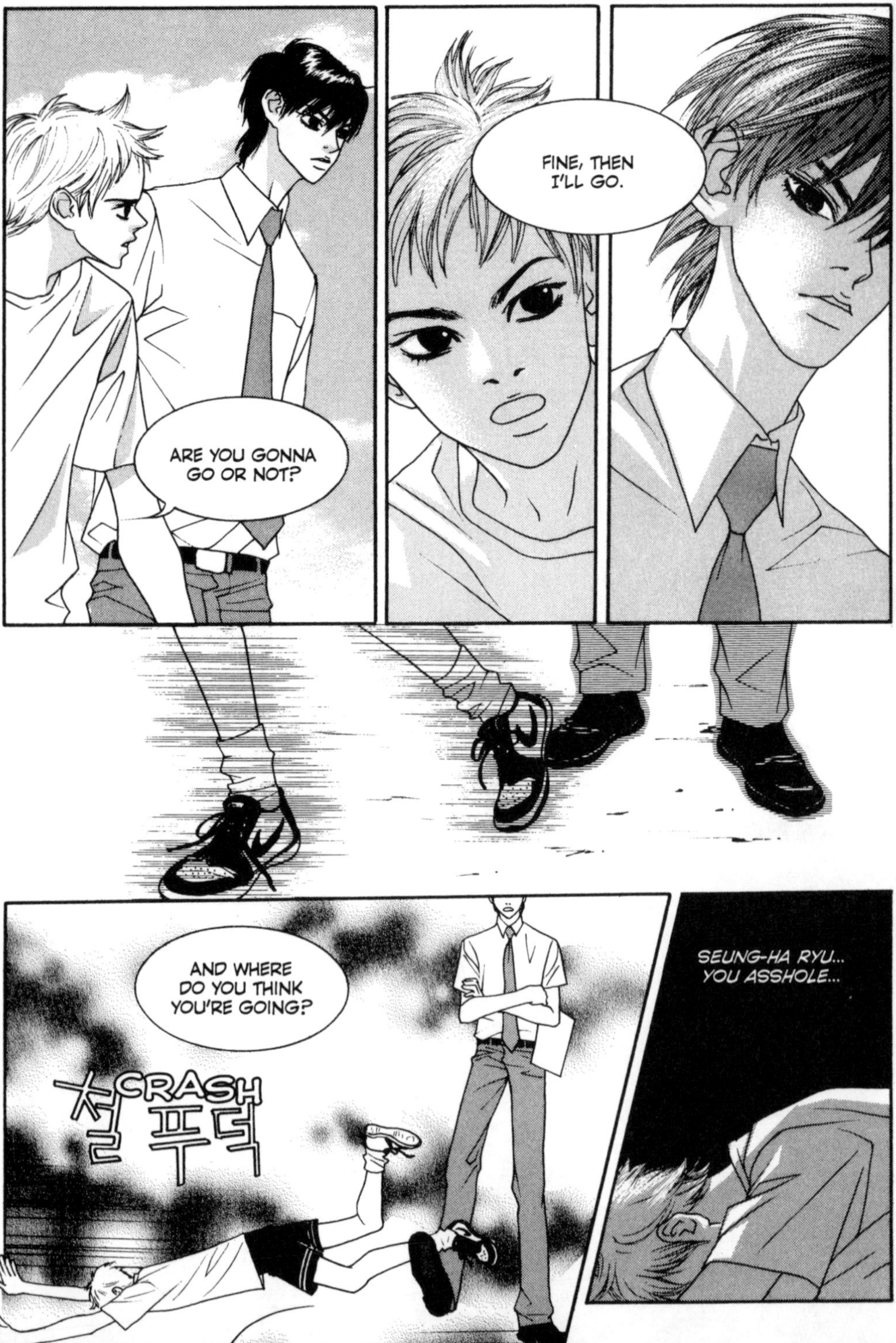
ARE YOU GONNA GO OR NOT?
FINE, THEN I'LL GO.
AND WHERE DO YOU THINK YOU'RE GOING?
CRASH
철푸덕
SEUNG-HA RYU... YOU ASSHOLE...

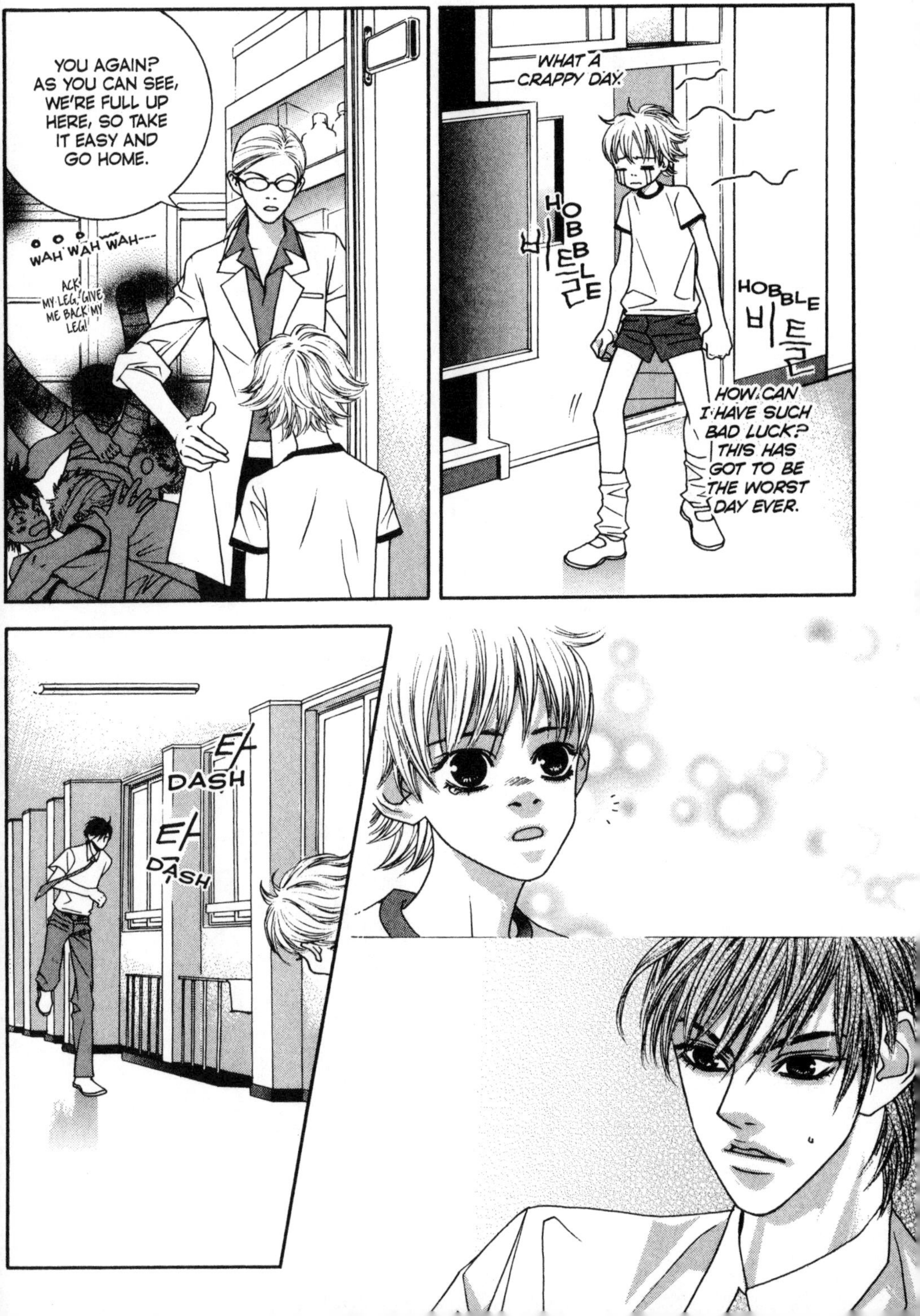

YOU AGAIN? AS YOU CAN SEE, WE'RE FULL UP HERE, SO TAKE IT EASY AND GO HOME.
WAH WAH WAH---
ACK MY LEG! GIVE ME BACK MY LEG!
WHAT A CRAPPY DAY.
HOBBLE 비틀
HOBBLE 비틀
HOW CAN I HAVE SUCH BAD LUCK? THIS HAS GOT TO BE THE WORST DAY EVER.
타 DASH
타 DASH

SHE'S FINE? DAMMIT, I DIDN'T HAVE TO RUN.

YOU'RE IGNORING ME AGAIN?

IS THIS HOW IT'S GOING TO BE FROM NOW ON?

I DON'T WANT TO SEE YOUR BACK ANYMORE.

SEUNG-HA RYU! HOLD IT RIGHT THERE!

...YOU...

DON'T TURN YOUR BACK ON ME.

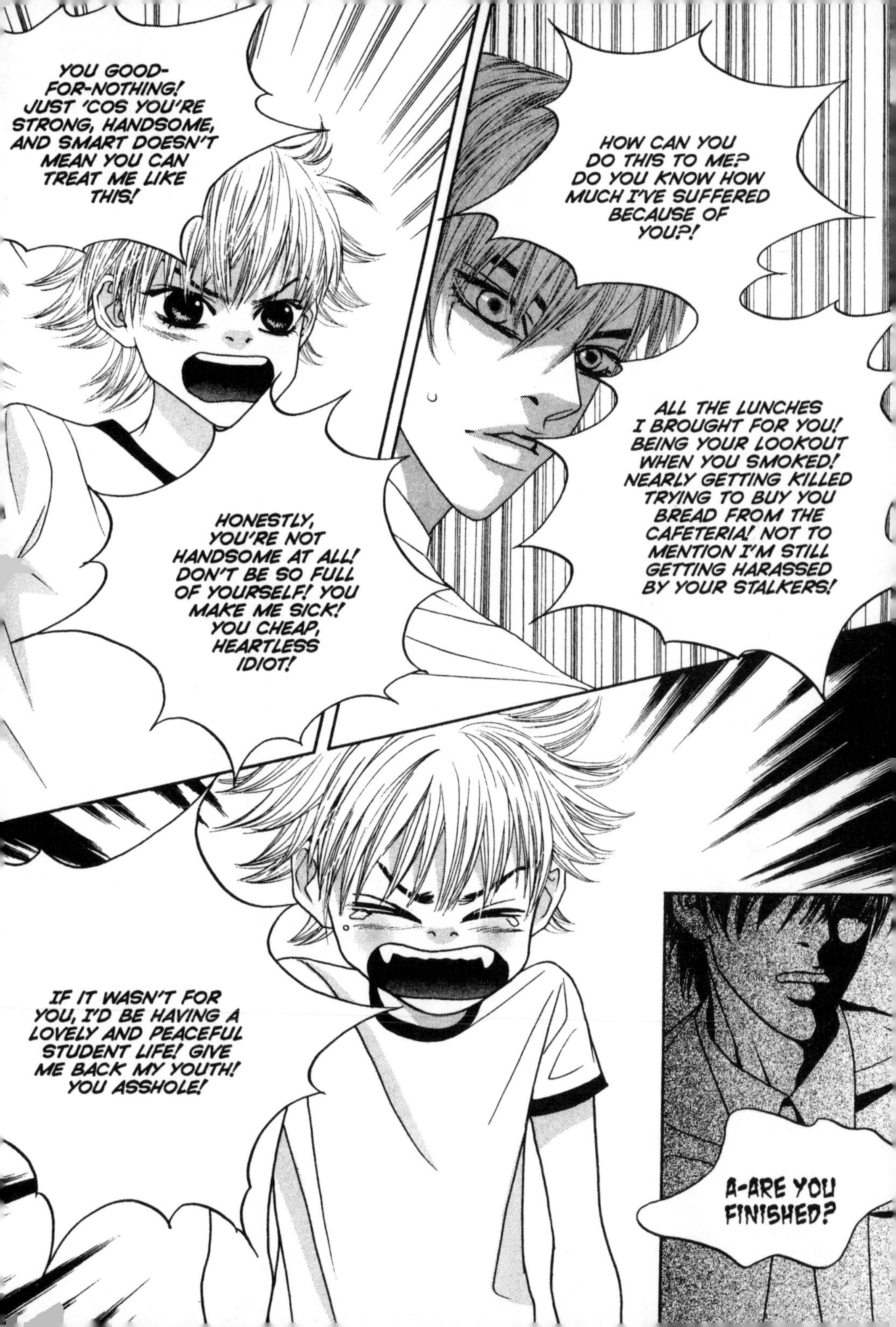
YOU GOOD-FOR-NOTHING! JUST 'COS YOU'RE STRONG, HANDSOME, AND SMART DOESN'T MEAN YOU CAN TREAT ME LIKE THIS!
HONESTLY, YOU'RE NOT HANDSOME AT ALL! DON'T BE SO FULL OF YOURSELF! YOU MAKE ME SICK! YOU CHEAP, HEARTLESS IDIOT!
HOW CAN YOU DO THIS TO ME? DO YOU KNOW HOW MUCH I'VE SUFFERED BECAUSE OF YOU?!
ALL THE LUNCHES I BROUGHT FOR YOU! BEING YOUR LOOKOUT WHEN YOU SMOKED! NEARLY GETTING KILLED TRYING TO BUY YOU BREAD FROM THE CAFETERIA! NOT TO MENTION I'M STILL GETTING HARASSED BY YOUR STALKERS!
IF IT WASN'T FOR YOU, I'D BE HAVING A LOVELY AND PEACEFUL STUDENT LIFE! GIVE ME BACK MY YOUTH! YOU ASSHOLE!
A-ARE YOU FINISHED?

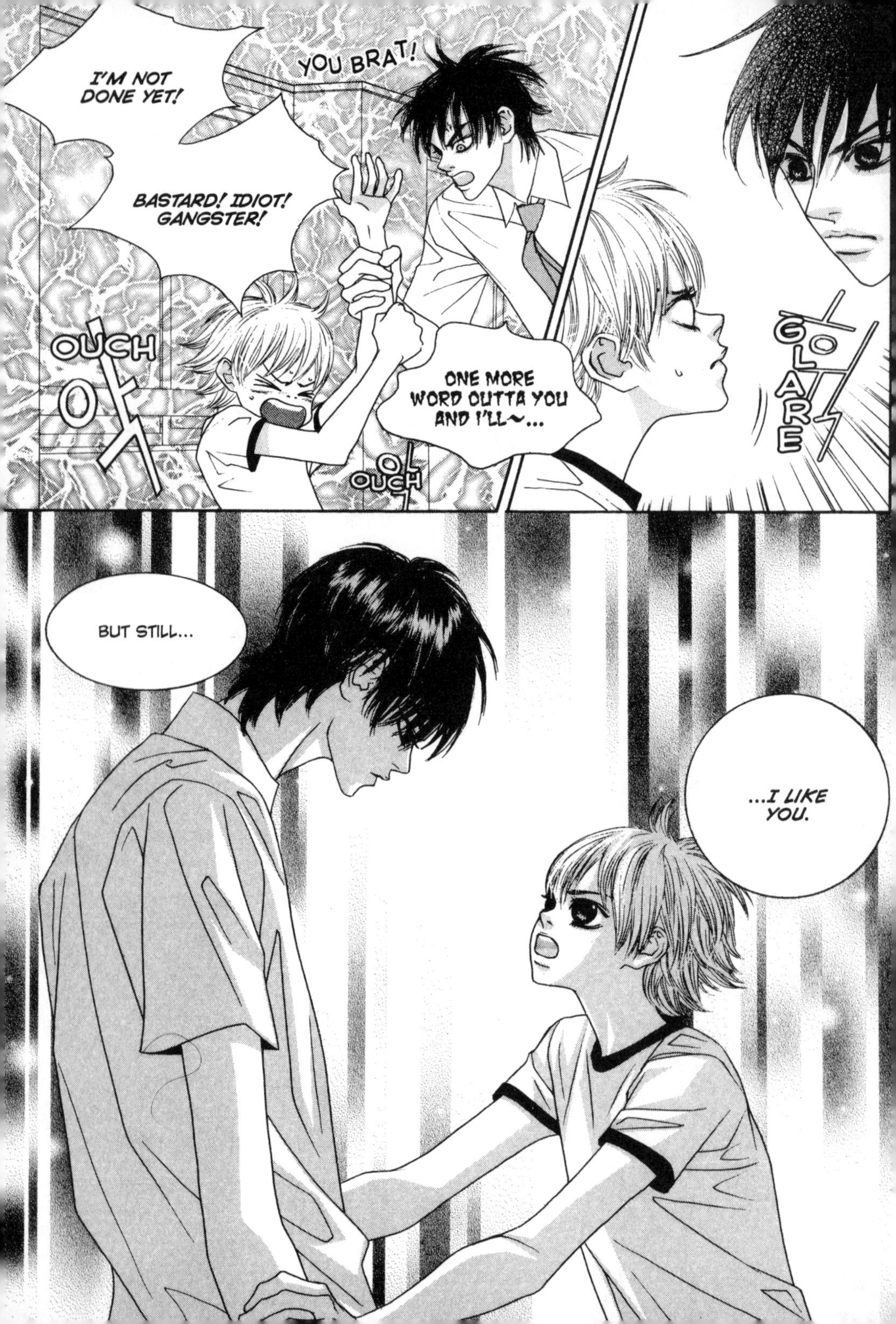
GLARE
YOU BRAT!
I'M NOT DONE YET!
BASTARD! IDIOT! GANGSTER!
ONE MORE WORD OUTTA YOU AND I'LL~...
OUCH
OUCH
...I LIKE YOU.
BUT STILL...

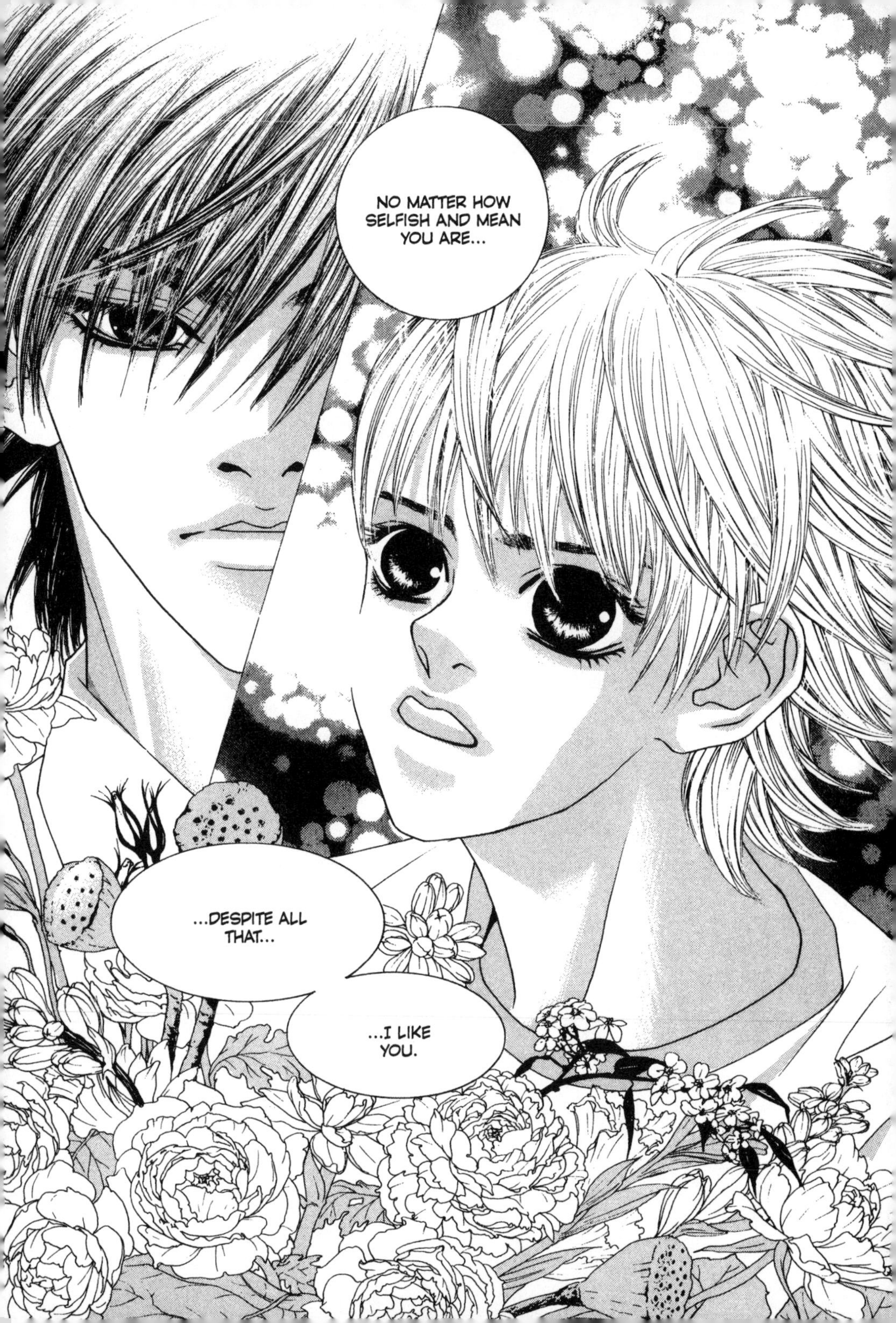
NO MATTER HOW SELFISH AND MEAN YOU ARE...
...DESPITE ALL THAT...
...I LIKE YOU.

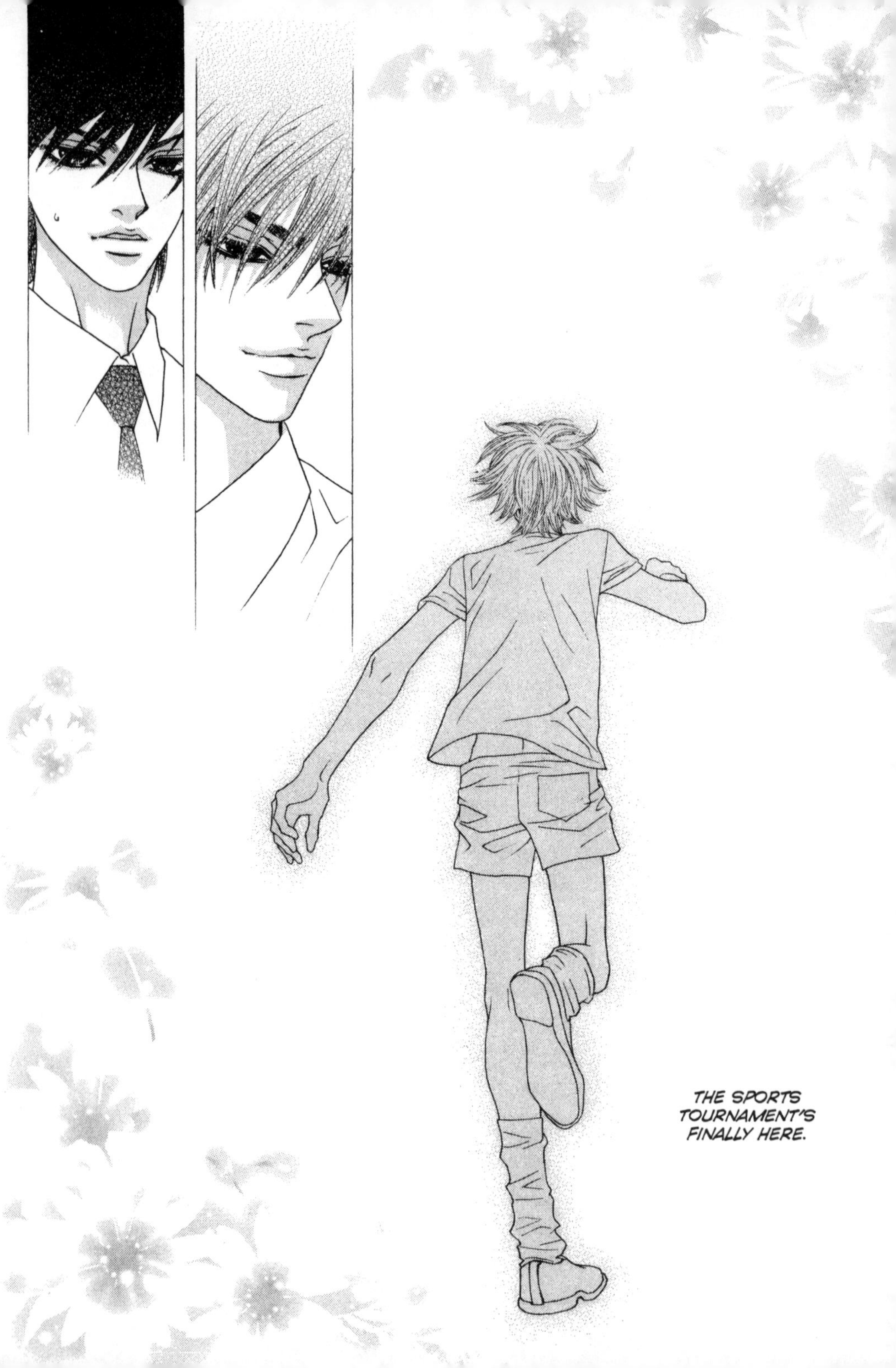
THE SPORTS TOURNAMENT'S FINALLY HERE.

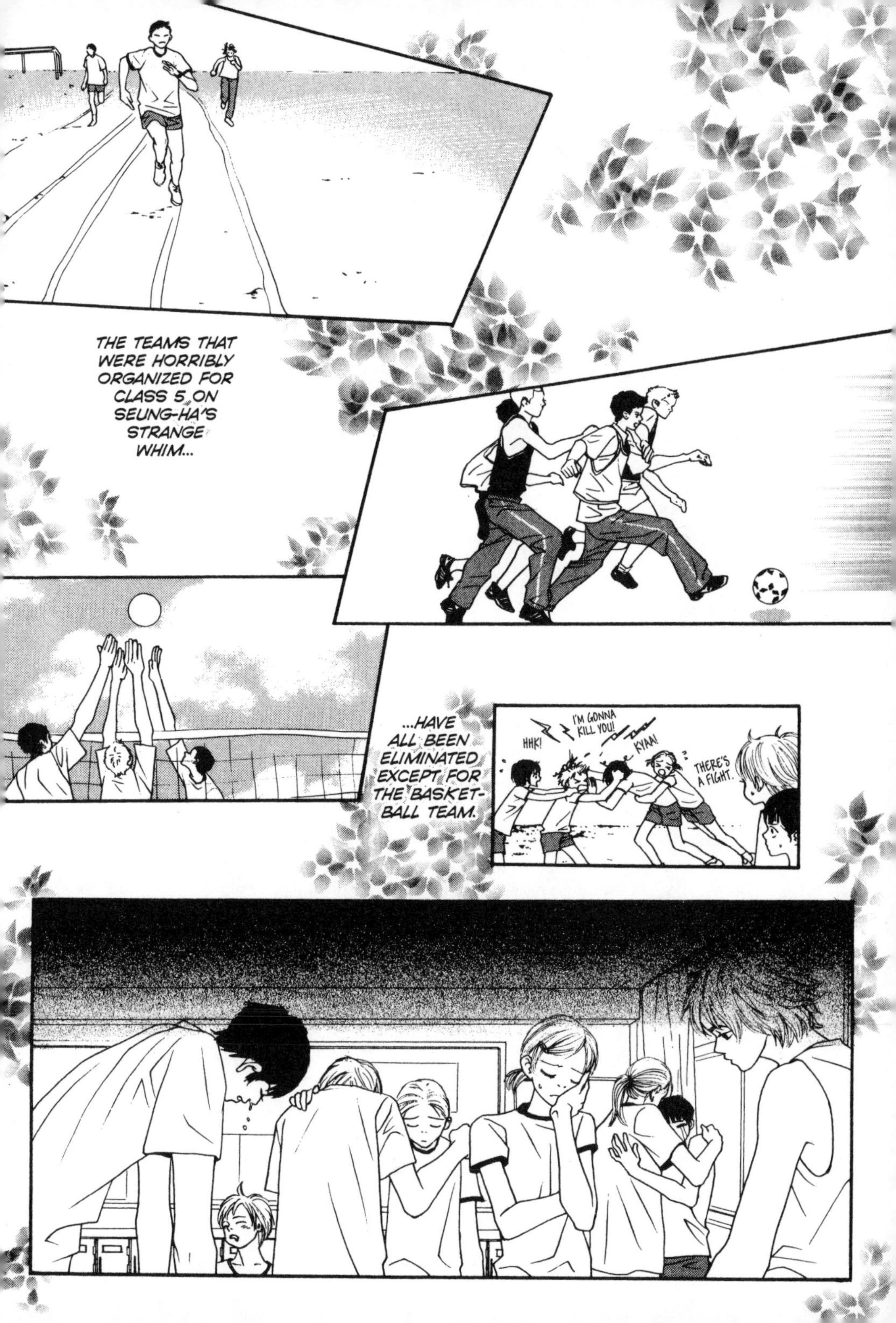
THE TEAMS THAT WERE HORRIBLY ORGANIZED FOR CLASS 5 ON SEUNG-HA'S STRANGE WHIM...
...HAVE ALL BEEN ELIMINATED EXCEPT FOR THE BASKET-BALL TEAM.
HHK!
I'M GONNA KILL YOU!
KYAA!
THERE'S A FIGHT.

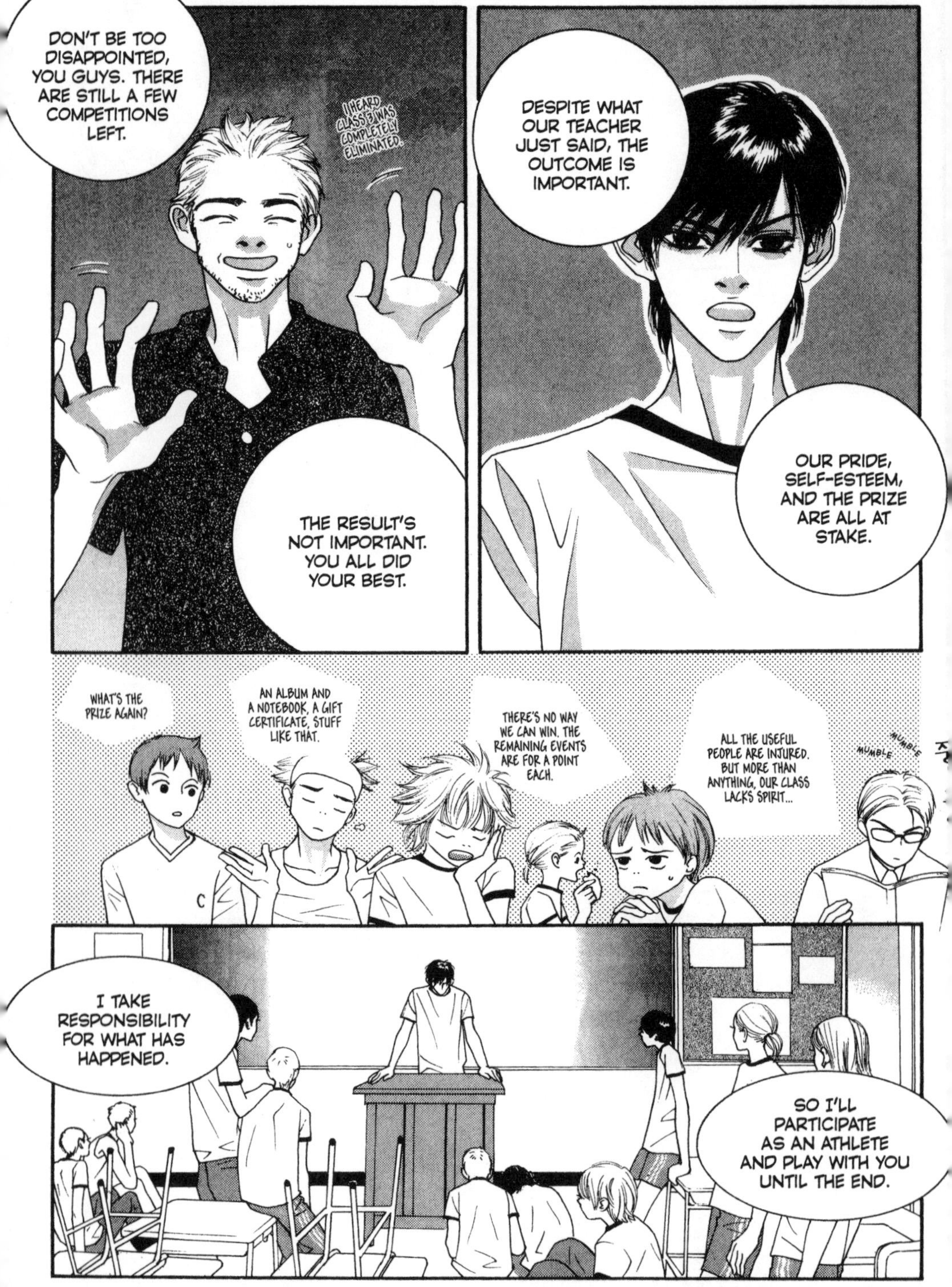
DON'T BE TOO DISAPPOINTED, YOU GUYS. THERE ARE STILL A FEW COMPETITIONS LEFT.
I HEARD CLASS 3 WAS COMPLETELY ELIMINATED.
THE RESULT'S NOT IMPORTANT. YOU ALL DID YOUR BEST.
DESPITE WHAT OUR TEACHER JUST SAID, THE OUTCOME IS IMPORTANT.
OUR PRIDE, SELF-ESTEEM, AND THE PRIZE ARE ALL AT STAKE.
WHAT'S THE PRIZE AGAIN?
AN ALBUM AND A NOTEBOOK, A GIFT CERTIFICATE, STUFF LIKE THAT.
THERE'S NO WAY WE CAN WIN. THE REMAINING EVENTS ARE FOR A POINT EACH.
ALL THE USEFUL PEOPLE ARE INJURED. BUT MORE THAN ANYTHING, OUR CLASS LACKS SPIRIT...
MUMBLE MUMBLE
I TAKE RESPONSIBILITY FOR WHAT HAS HAPPENED.
SO I'LL PARTICIPATE AS AN ATHLETE AND PLAY WITH YOU UNTIL THE END.

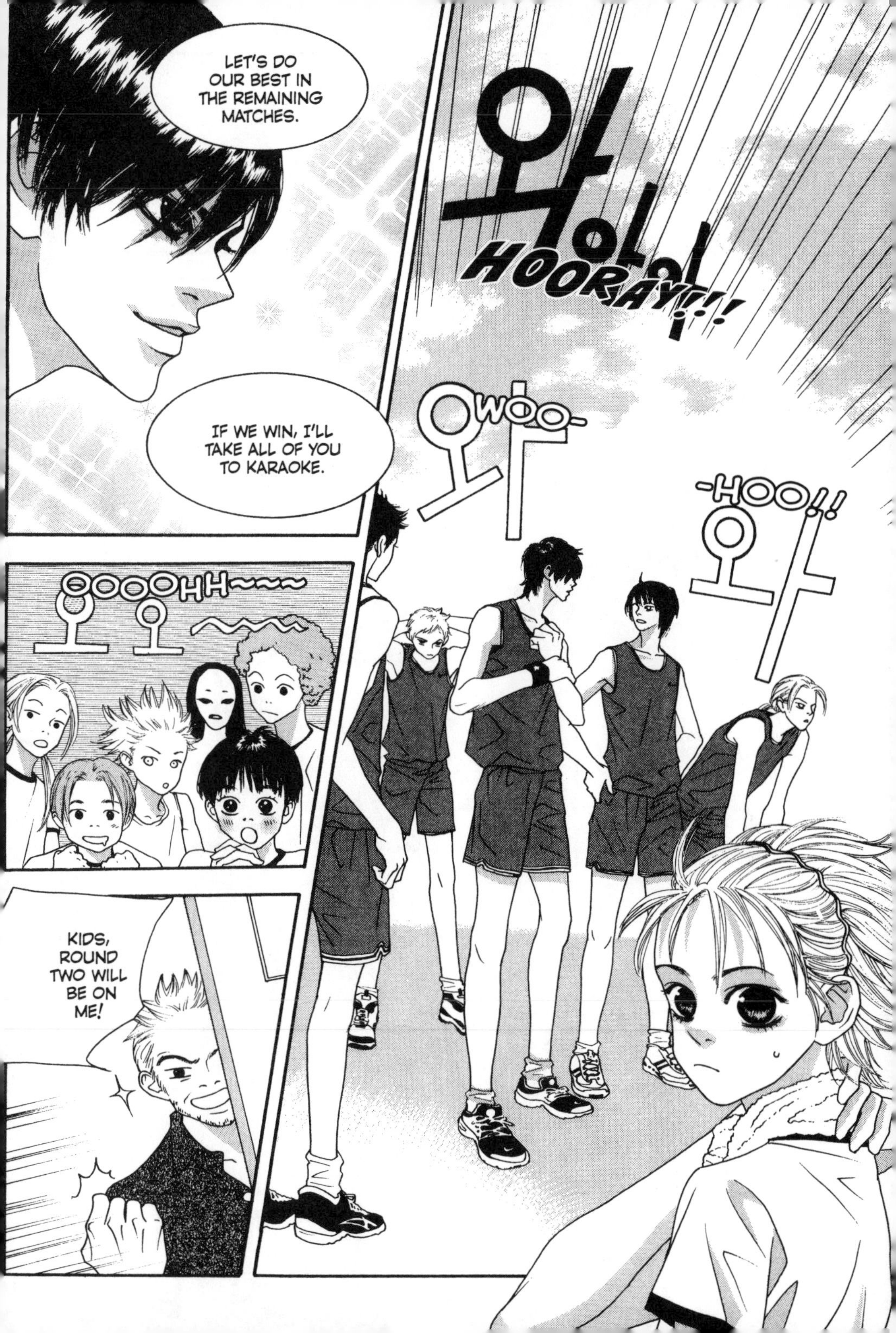
LET'S DO OUR BEST IN THE REMAINING MATCHES.
IF WE WIN, I'LL TAKE ALL OF YOU TO KARAOKE.
OOOOHH~~~
KIDS, ROUND TWO WILL BE ON ME!
HOORAY!!!
WOO-
-HOO!!

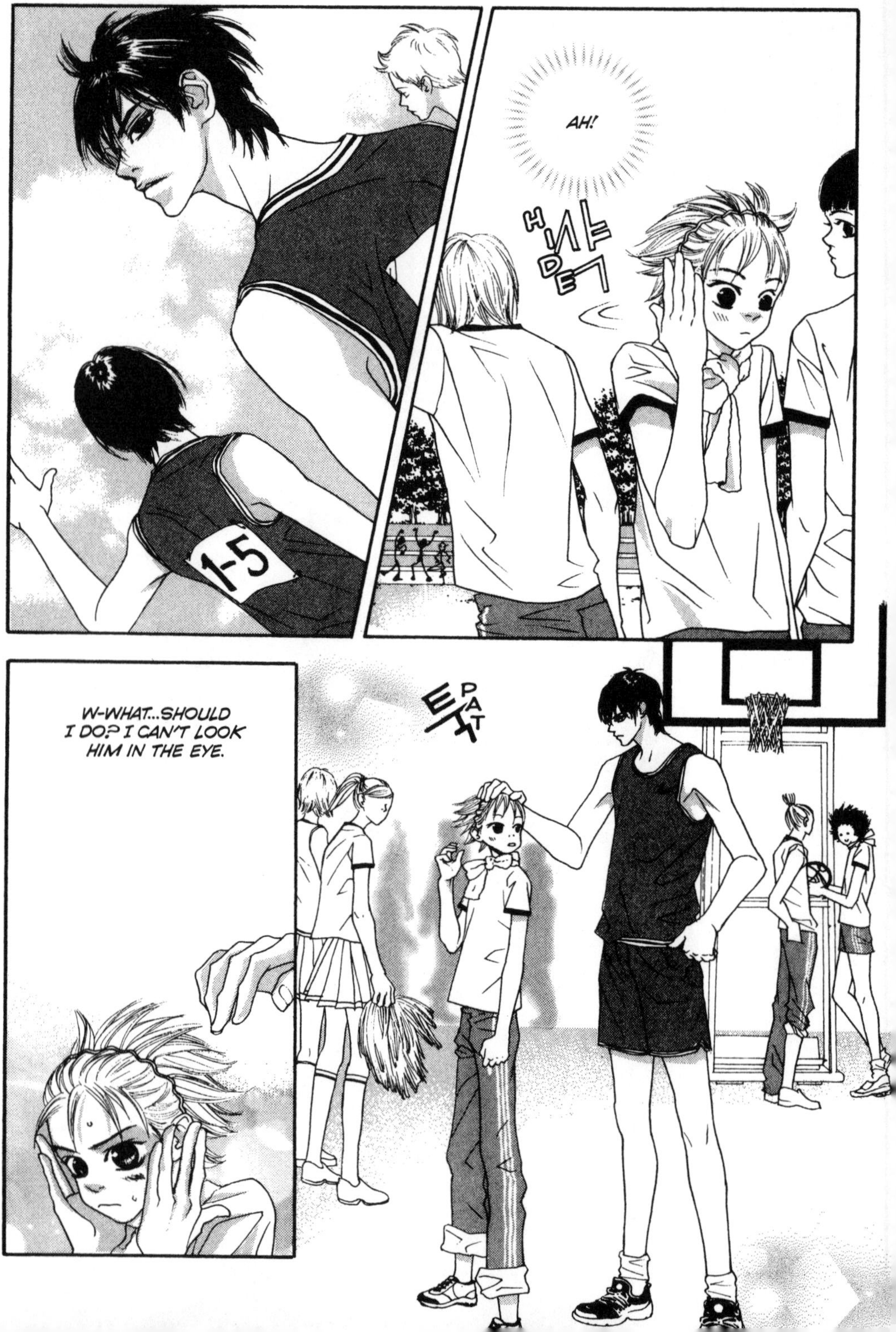

1-5
AH!
HIDE
W-WHAT...SHOULD I DO? I CAN'T LOOK HIM IN THE EYE.
PAT

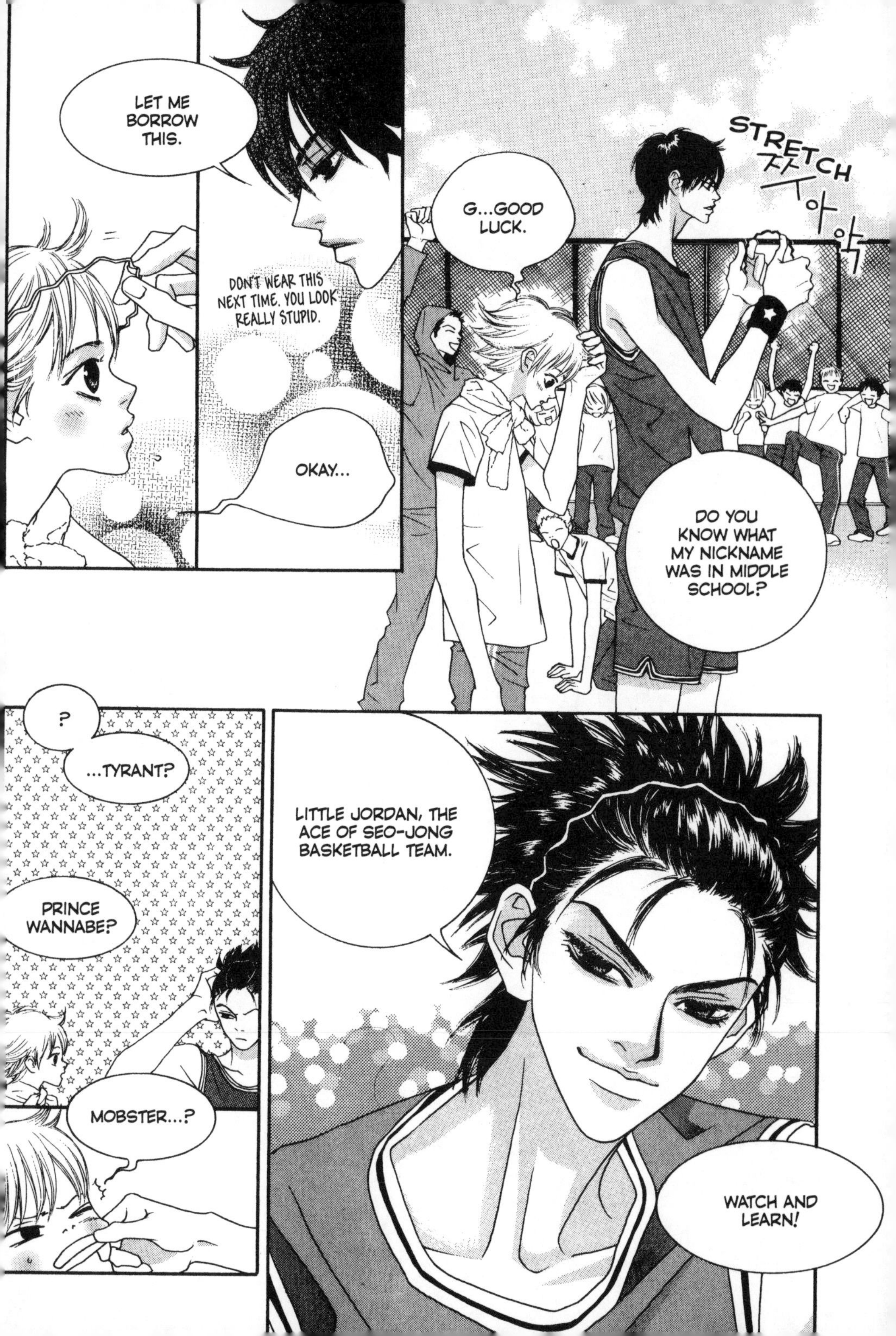
LET ME BORROW THIS.
DON'T WEAR THIS NEXT TIME. YOU LOOK REALLY STUPID.
OKAY...
G...GOOD LUCK.
STRETCH
쭈아악
DO YOU KNOW WHAT MY NICKNAME WAS IN MIDDLE SCHOOL?
?
...TYRANT?
PRINCE WANNABE?
MOBSTER...?
LITTLE JORDAN, THE ACE OF SEO-JONG BASKETBALL TEAM.
WATCH AND LEARN!

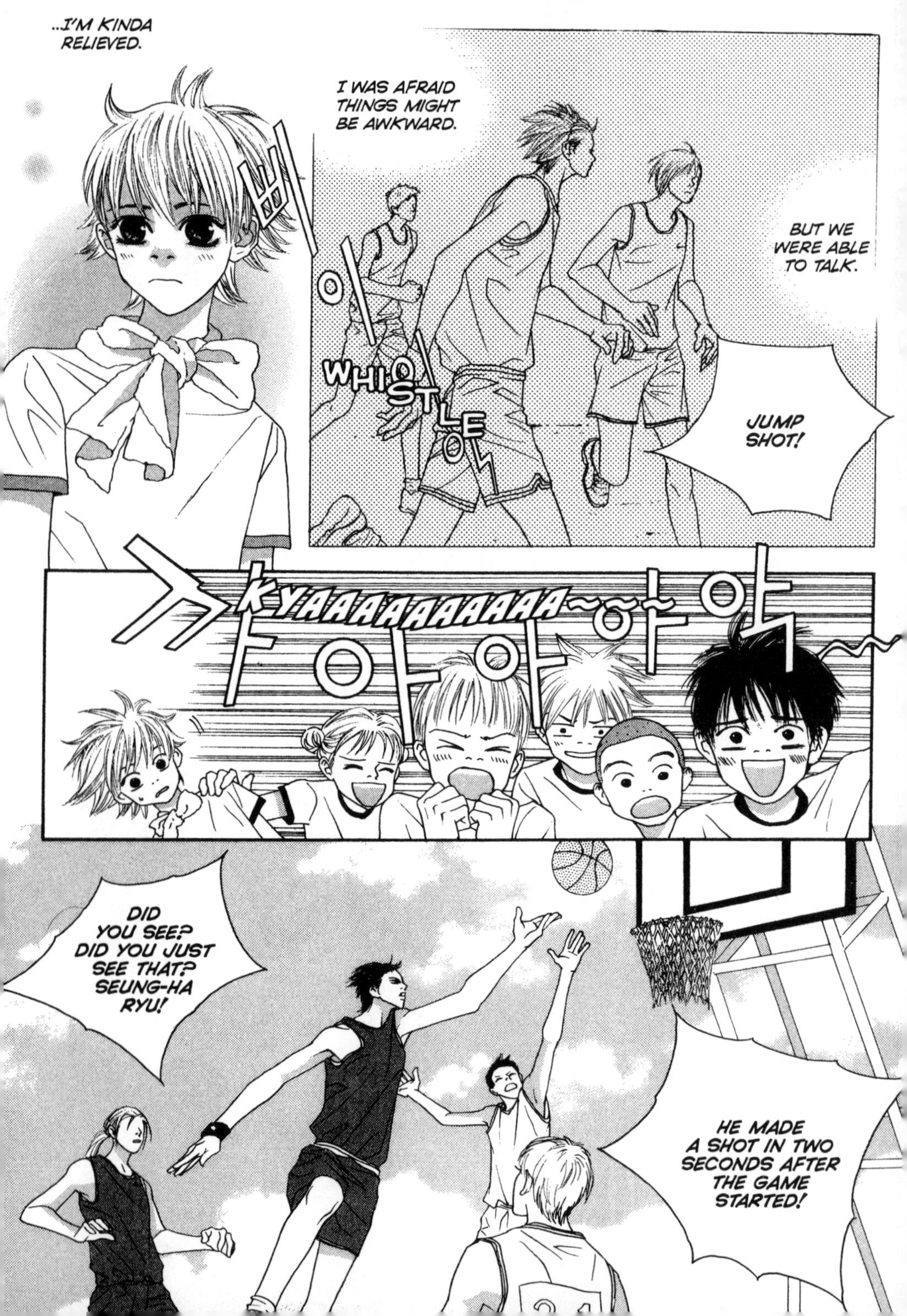
...I'M KINDA RELIEVED.
I WAS AFRAID THINGS MIGHT BE AWKWARD.
BUT WE WERE ABLE TO TALK.
WHISTLE
JUMP SHOT!
KYAAAAAAAAAAA~
DID YOU SEE? DID YOU JUST SEE THAT? SEUNG-HA RYU!
HE MADE A SHOT IN TWO SECONDS AFTER THE GAME STARTED!

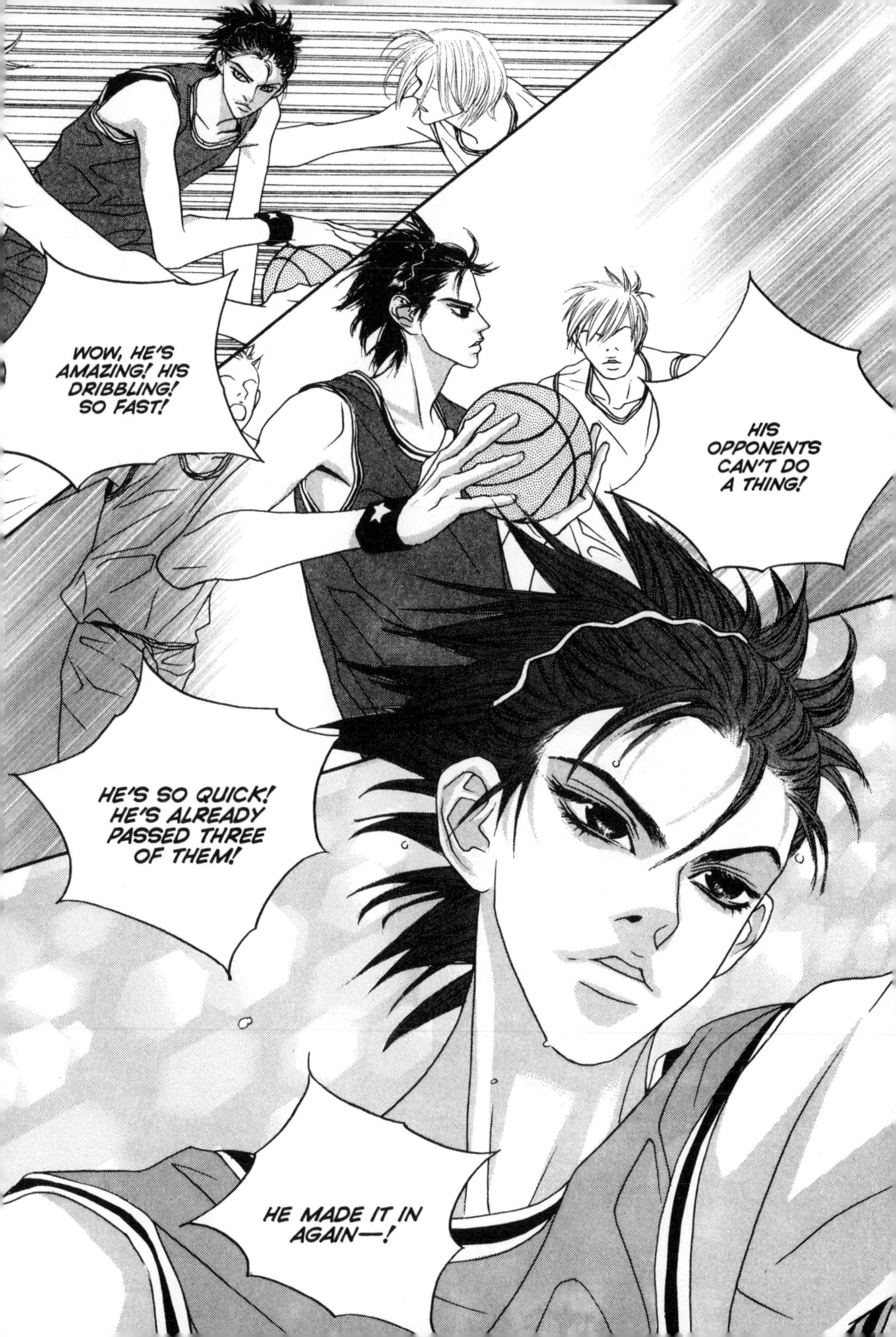
WOW, HE'S AMAZING! HIS DRIBBLING! SO FAST!
HIS OPPONENTS CAN'T DO A THING!
HE'S SO QUICK! HE'S ALREADY PASSED THREE OF THEM!
HE MADE IT IN AGAIN—!

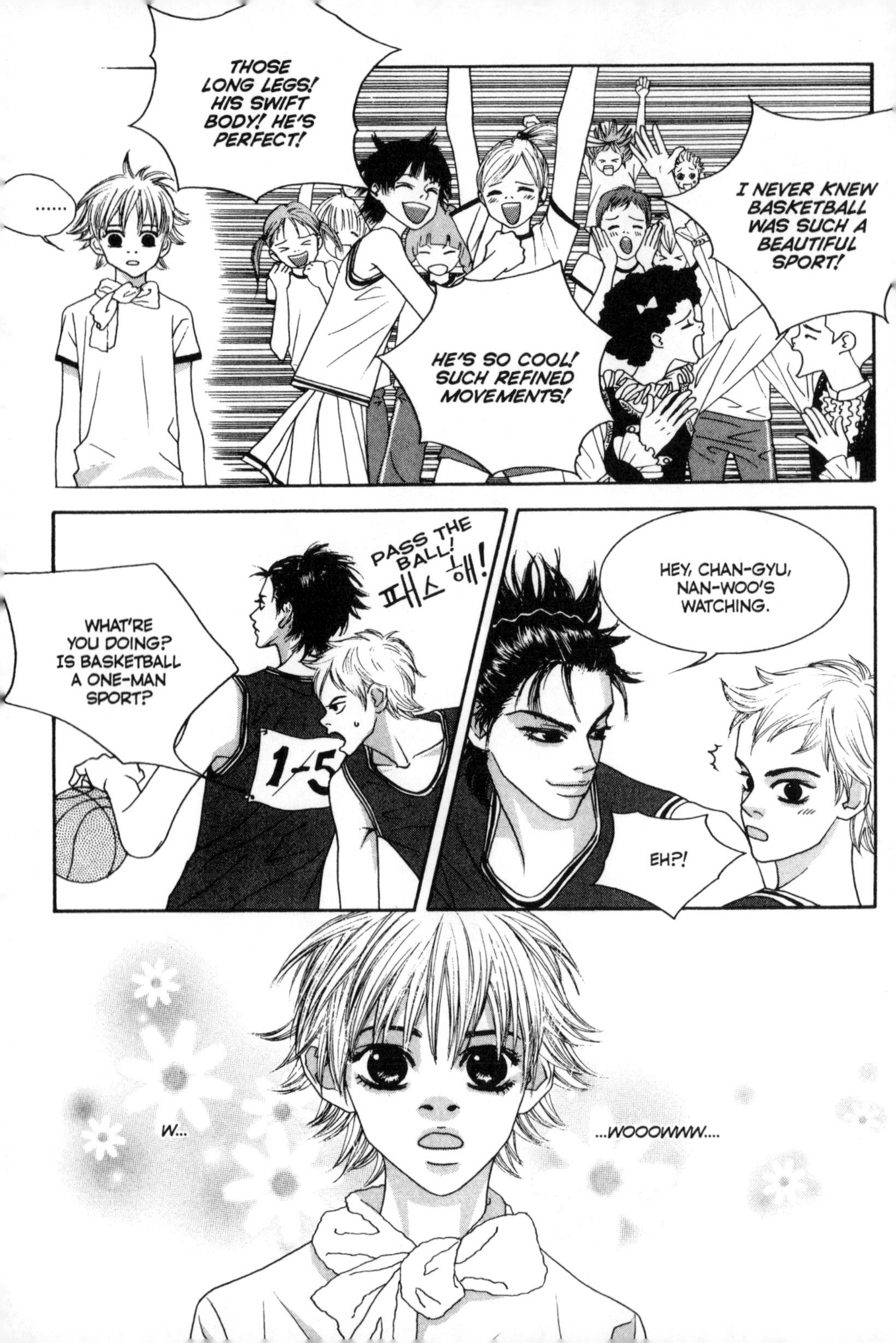
THOSE LONG LEGS! HIS SWIFT BODY! HE'S PERFECT!
......
HE'S SO COOL! SUCH REFINED MOVEMENTS!
I NEVER KNEW BASKETBALL WAS SUCH A BEAUTIFUL SPORT!
WHAT'RE YOU DOING? IS BASKETBALL A ONE-MAN SPORT?
PASS THE BALL!
패스 해!
1-5
HEY, CHAN-GYU, NAN-WOO'S WATCHING.
EH?!
W...
...WOOOWWW....

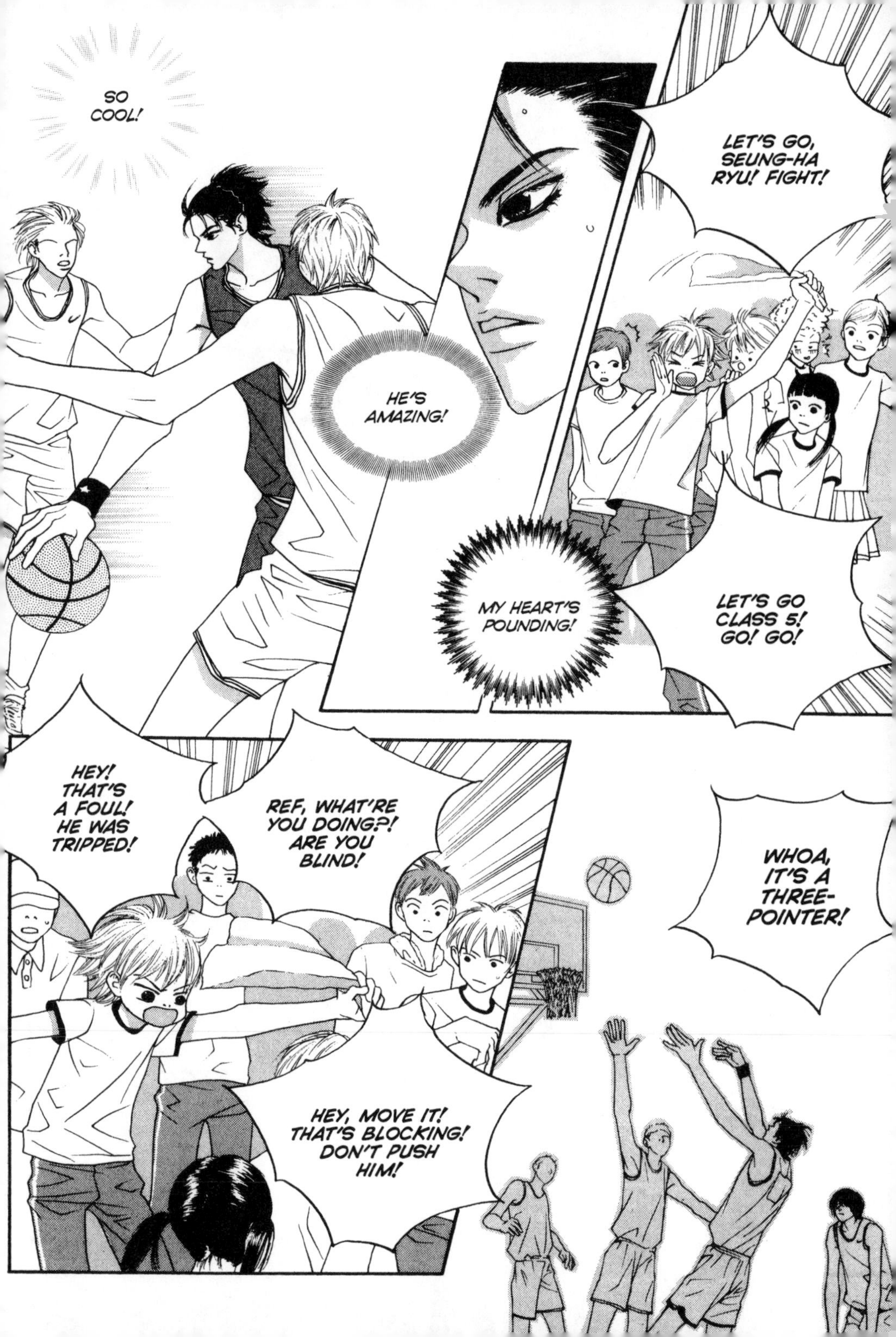
SO COOL!
HE'S AMAZING!
LET'S GO, SEUNG-HA RYU! FIGHT!
MY HEART'S POUNDING!
LET'S GO CLASS 5! GO! GO!
HEY! THAT'S A FOUL! HE WAS TRIPPED!
REF, WHAT'RE YOU DOING?! ARE YOU BLIND!
HEY, MOVE IT! THAT'S BLOCKING! DON'T PUSH HIM!
WHOA, IT'S A THREE-POINTER!

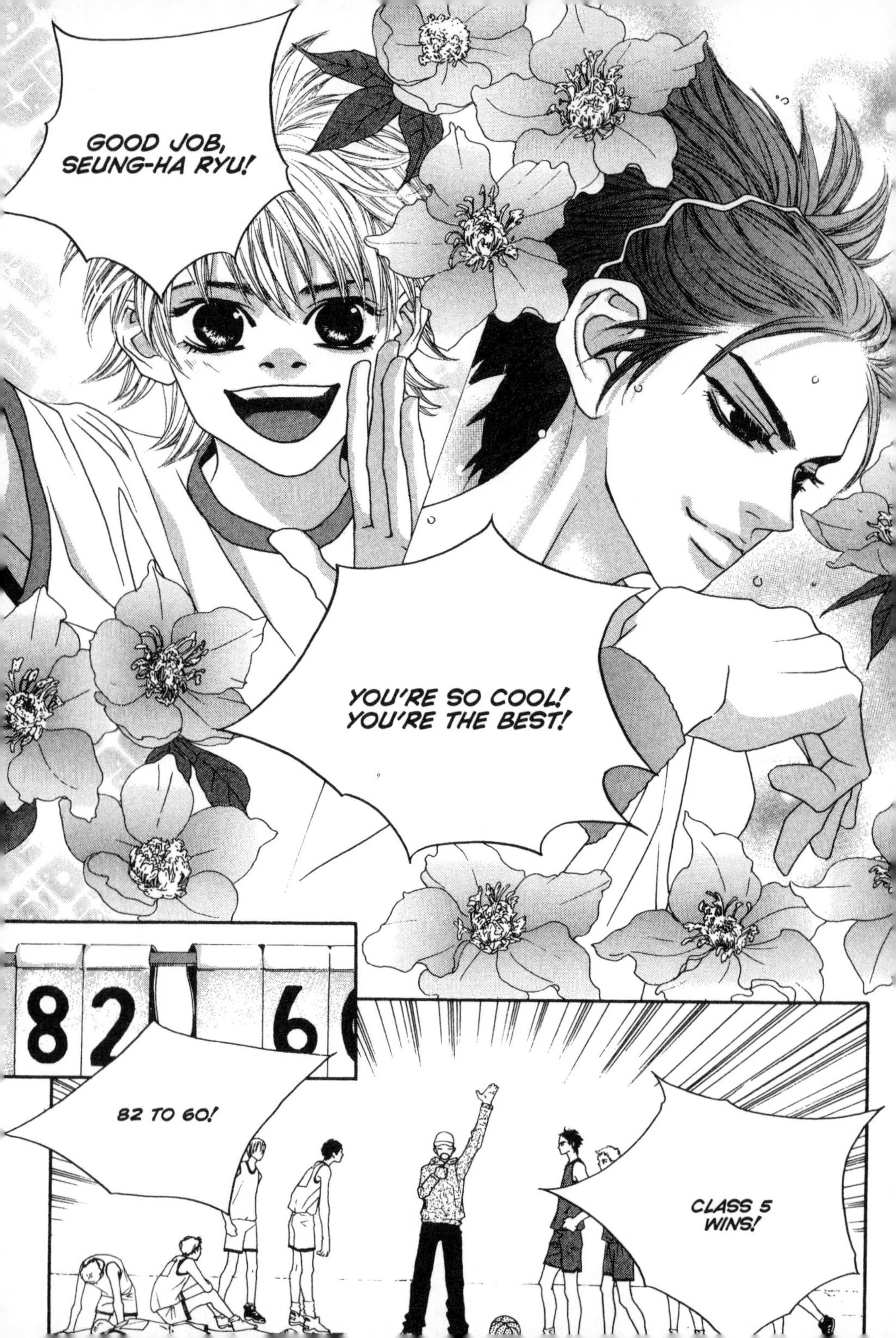
GOOD JOB, SEUNG-HA RYU!
YOU'RE SO COOL! YOU'RE THE BEST!
82
6
82 TO 60!
CLASS 5 WINS!

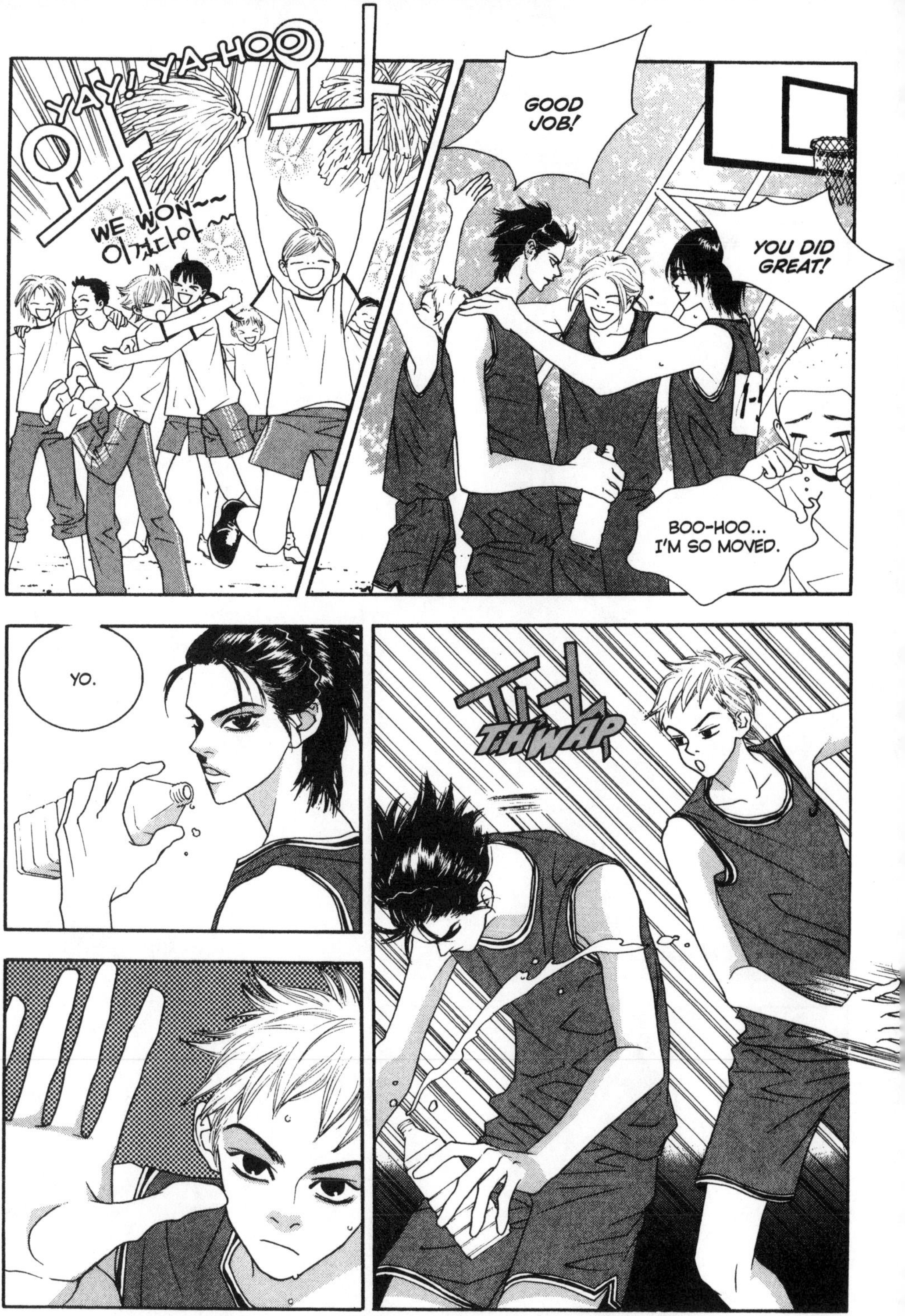
YAY! YA-HOO
와
WE WON~~
이겼다아~~
GOOD JOB!
YOU DID GREAT!
BOO-HOO... I'M SO MOVED.
YO.
THWAP

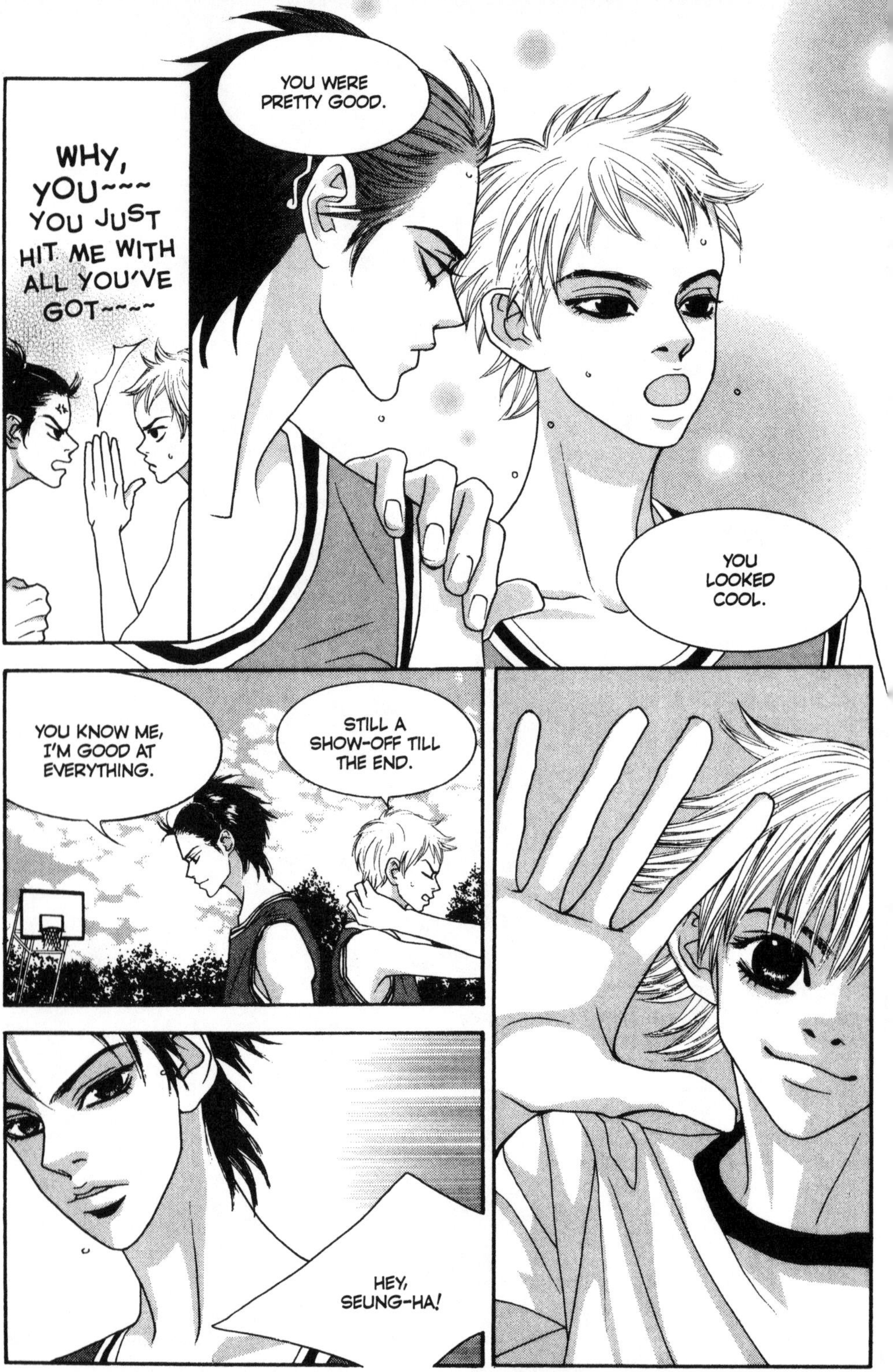
WHY, YOU~~~ YOU JUST HIT ME WITH ALL YOU'VE GOT~~~~
YOU WERE PRETTY GOOD.
YOU LOOKED COOL.
YOU KNOW ME, I'M GOOD AT EVERYTHING.
STILL A SHOW-OFF TILL THE END.
HEY, SEUNG-HA!

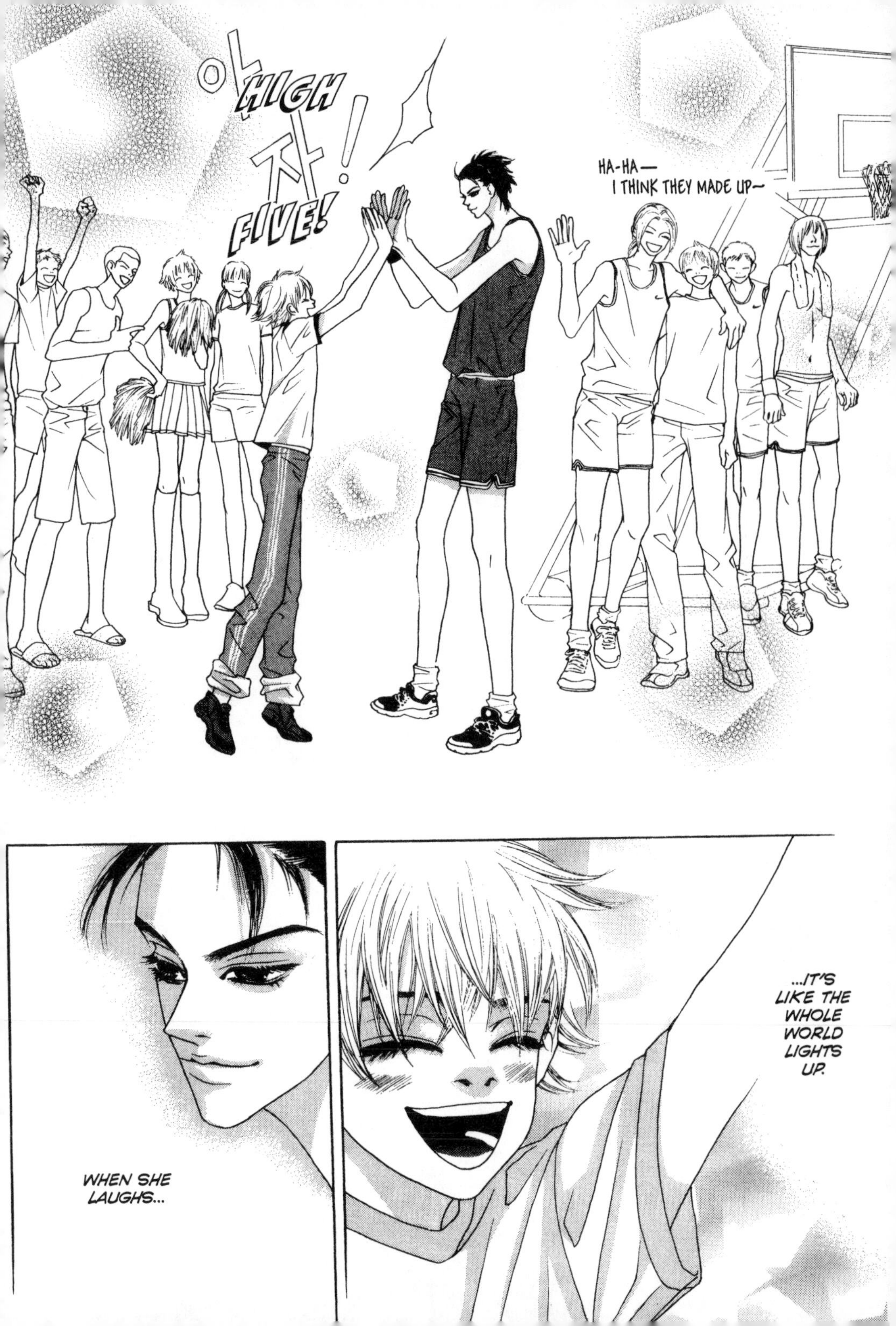
아자!
HIGH FIVE!
HA-HA—
I THINK THEY MADE UP~
WHEN SHE LAUGHS...
...IT'S LIKE THE WHOLE WORLD LIGHTS UP.

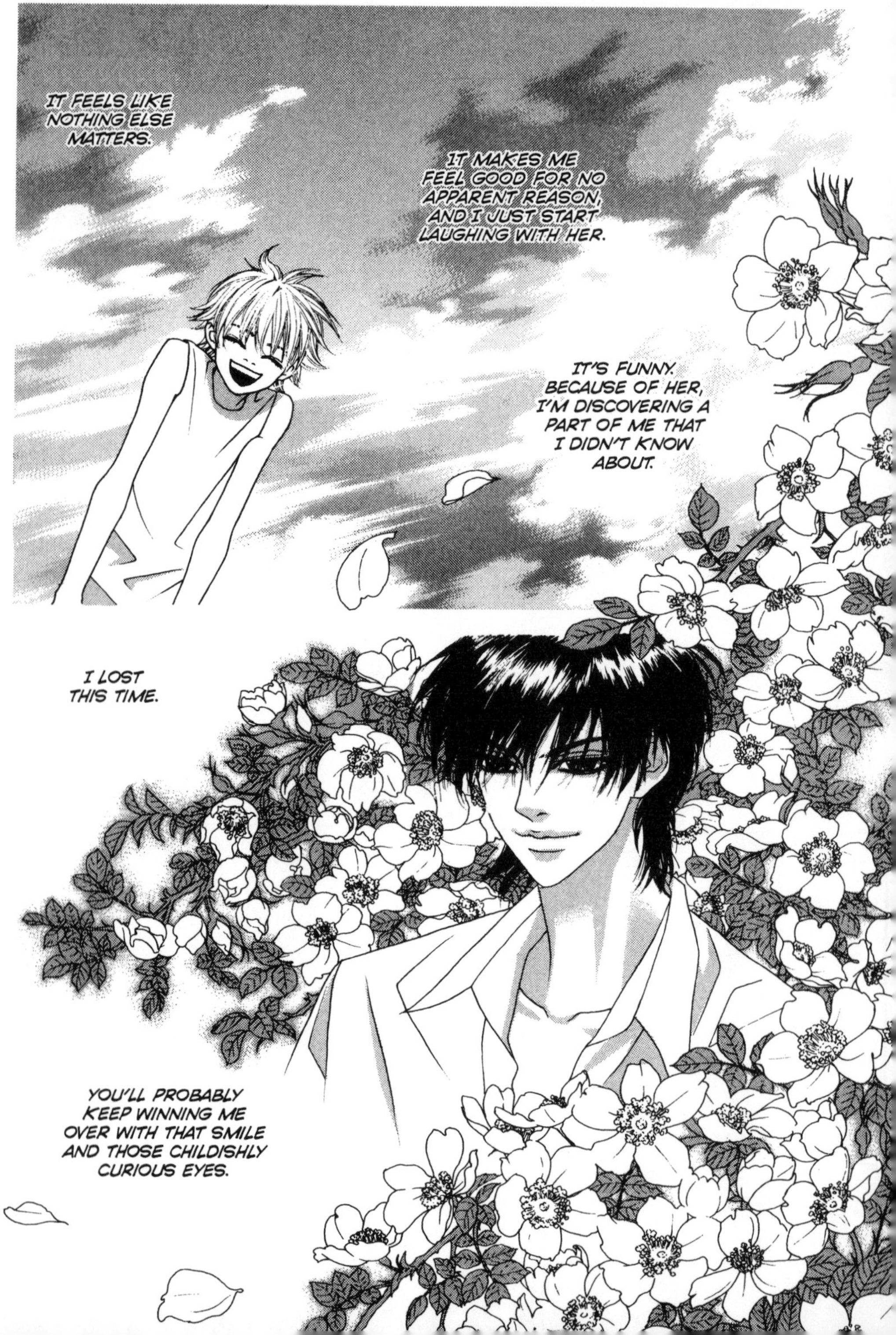
IT FEELS LIKE NOTHING ELSE MATTERS.
IT MAKES ME FEEL GOOD FOR NO APPARENT REASON, AND I JUST START LAUGHING WITH HER.
IT'S FUNNY. BECAUSE OF HER, I'M DISCOVERING A PART OF ME THAT I DIDN'T KNOW ABOUT.
I LOST THIS TIME.
YOU'LL PROBABLY KEEP WINNING ME OVER WITH THAT SMILE AND THOSE CHILDISHLY CURIOUS EYES.

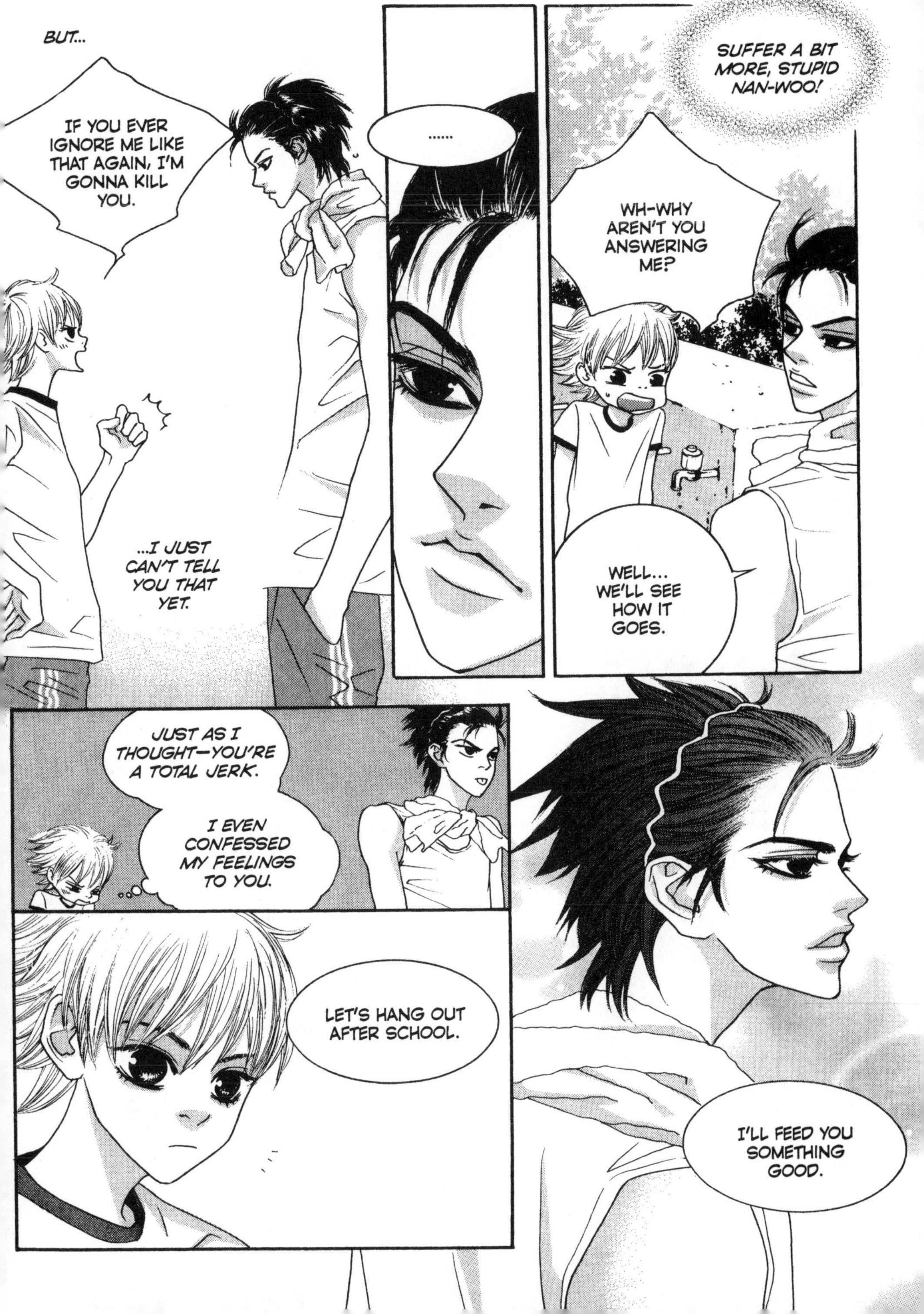
BUT...
IF YOU EVER IGNORE ME LIKE THAT AGAIN, I'M GONNA KILL YOU.
...I JUST CAN'T TELL YOU THAT YET.
......
SUFFER A BIT MORE, STUPID NAN-WOO!
WH-WHY AREN'T YOU ANSWERING ME?
WELL... WE'LL SEE HOW IT GOES.
JUST AS I THOUGHT—YOU'RE A TOTAL JERK.
I EVEN CONFESSED MY FEELINGS TO YOU.
LET'S HANG OUT AFTER SCHOOL.
I'LL FEED YOU SOMETHING GOOD.

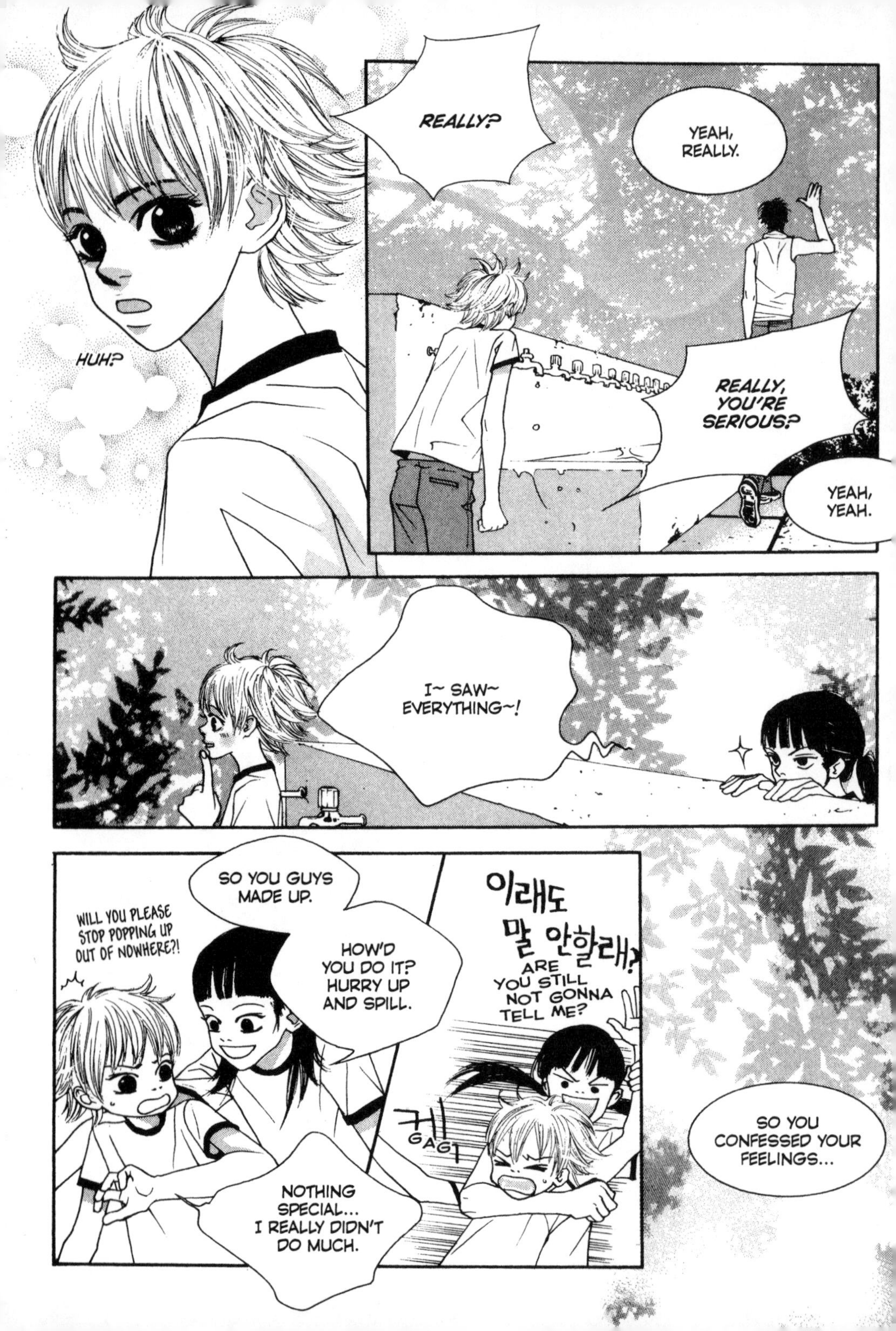
HUH?
REALLY?
YEAH, REALLY.
REALLY, YOU'RE SERIOUS?
YEAH, YEAH.
I~ SAW~ EVERYTHING~!
SO YOU GUYS MADE UP.
WILL YOU PLEASE STOP POPPING UP OUT OF NOWHERE?!
HOW'D YOU DO IT? HURRY UP AND SPILL.
NOTHING SPECIAL... I REALLY DIDN'T DO MUCH.
이래도 말 안할래?
ARE YOU STILL NOT GONNA TELL ME?
끼
GAGI
SO YOU CONFESSED YOUR FEELINGS...

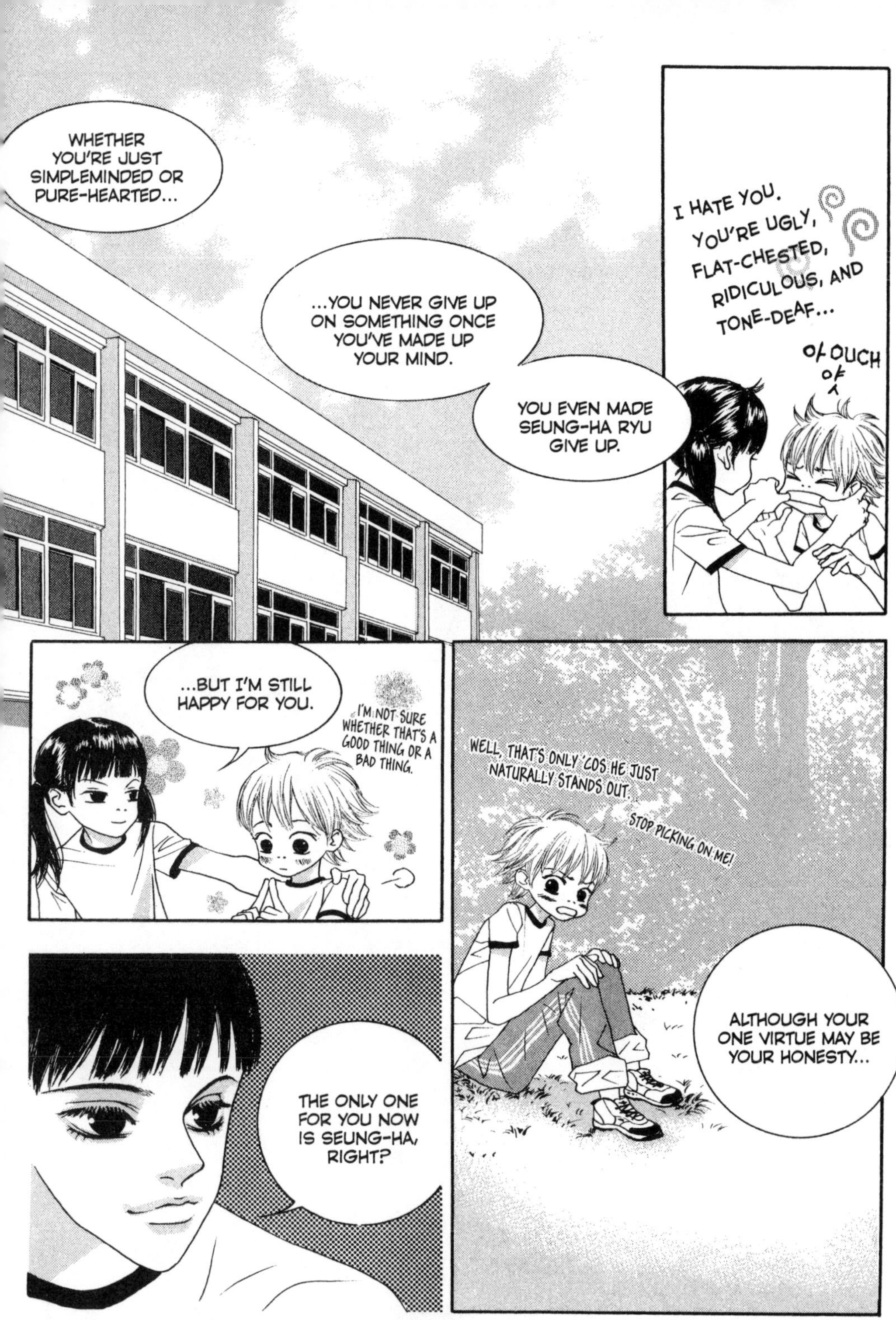
WHETHER YOU'RE JUST SIMPLEMINDED OR PURE-HEARTED...
...YOU NEVER GIVE UP ON SOMETHING ONCE YOU'VE MADE UP YOUR MIND.
YOU EVEN MADE SEUNG-HA RYU GIVE UP.
I HATE YOU. YOU'RE UGLY, FLAT-CHESTED, RIDICULOUS, AND TONE-DEAF...
아야 OUCH
...BUT I'M STILL HAPPY FOR YOU.
I'M NOT SURE WHETHER THAT'S A GOOD THING OR A BAD THING.
THE ONLY ONE FOR YOU NOW IS SEUNG-HA, RIGHT?
WELL, THAT'S ONLY 'COS HE JUST NATURALLY STANDS OUT.
STOP PICKING ON ME!
ALTHOUGH YOUR ONE VIRTUE MAY BE YOUR HONESTY...

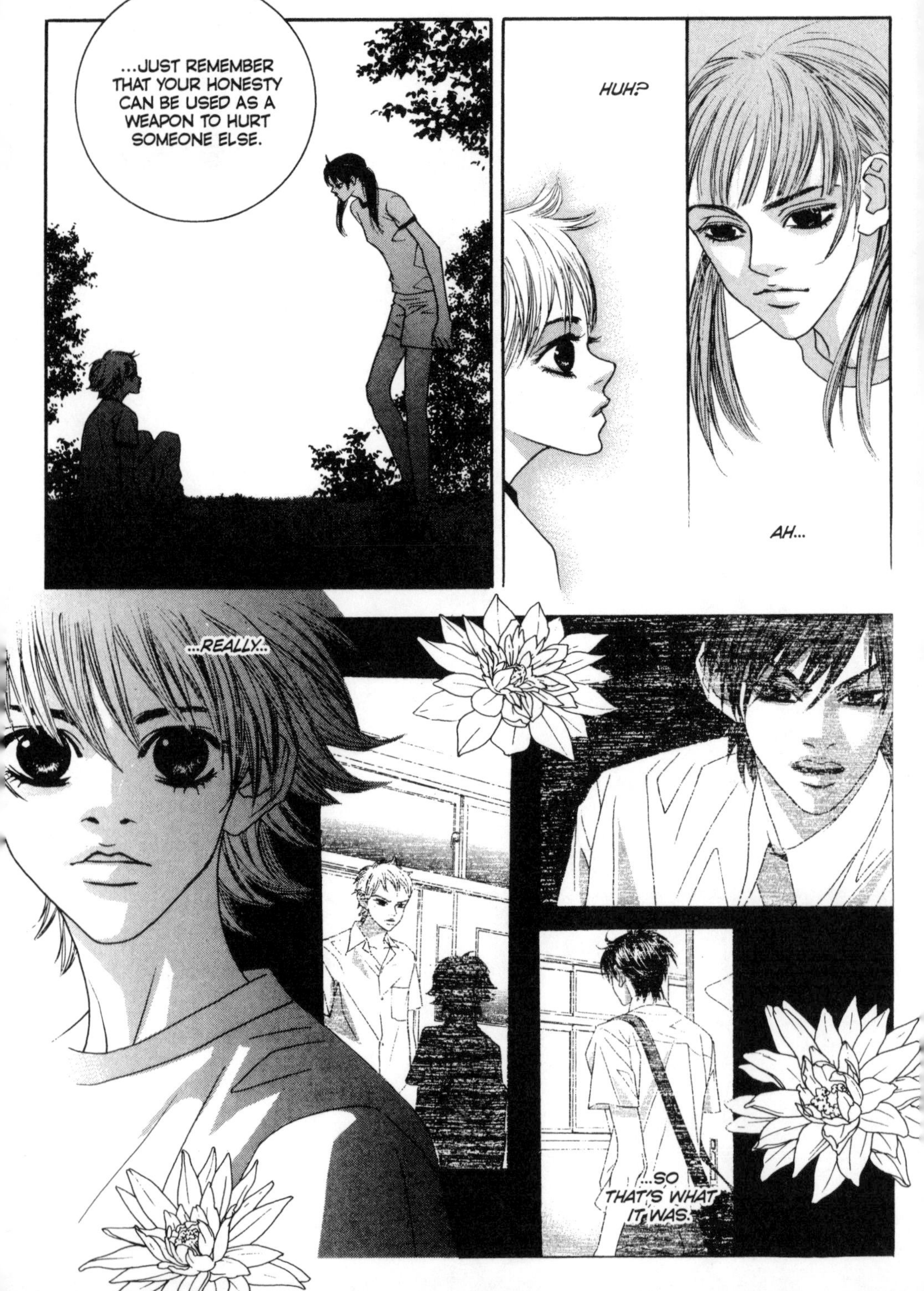
...JUST REMEMBER THAT YOUR HONESTY CAN BE USED AS A WEAPON TO HURT SOMEONE ELSE.
HUH?
AH...
...REALLY...
...SO THAT'S WHAT IT WAS.

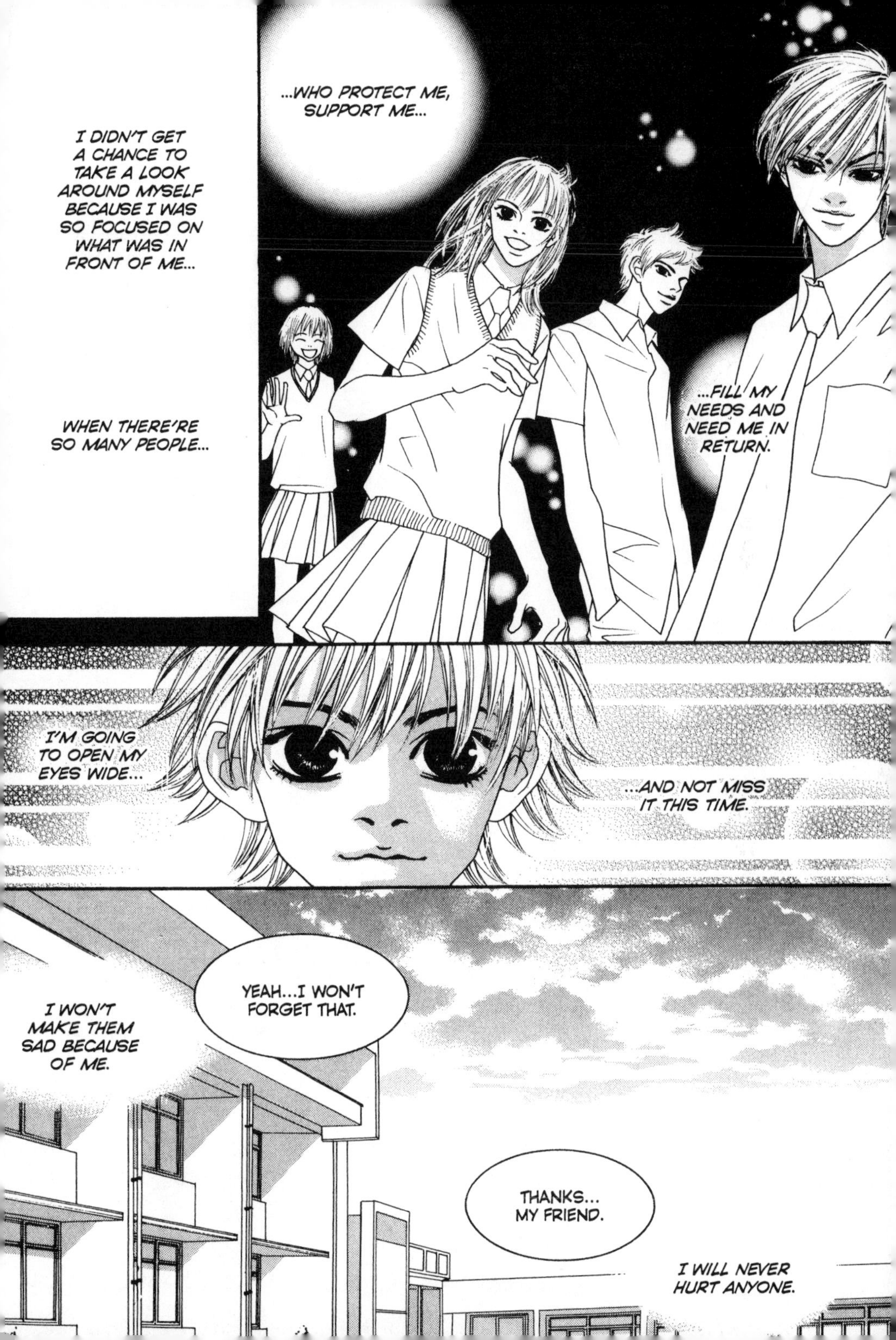
I DIDN'T GET A CHANCE TO TAKE A LOOK AROUND MYSELF BECAUSE I WAS SO FOCUSED ON WHAT WAS IN FRONT OF ME...
WHEN THERE'RE SO MANY PEOPLE...
...WHO PROTECT ME, SUPPORT ME...
...FILL MY NEEDS AND NEED ME IN RETURN.
I'M GOING TO OPEN MY EYES WIDE...
...AND NOT MISS IT THIS TIME.
I WON'T MAKE THEM SAD BECAUSE OF ME.
YEAH...I WON'T FORGET THAT.
THANKS... MY FRIEND.
I WILL NEVER HURT ANYONE.

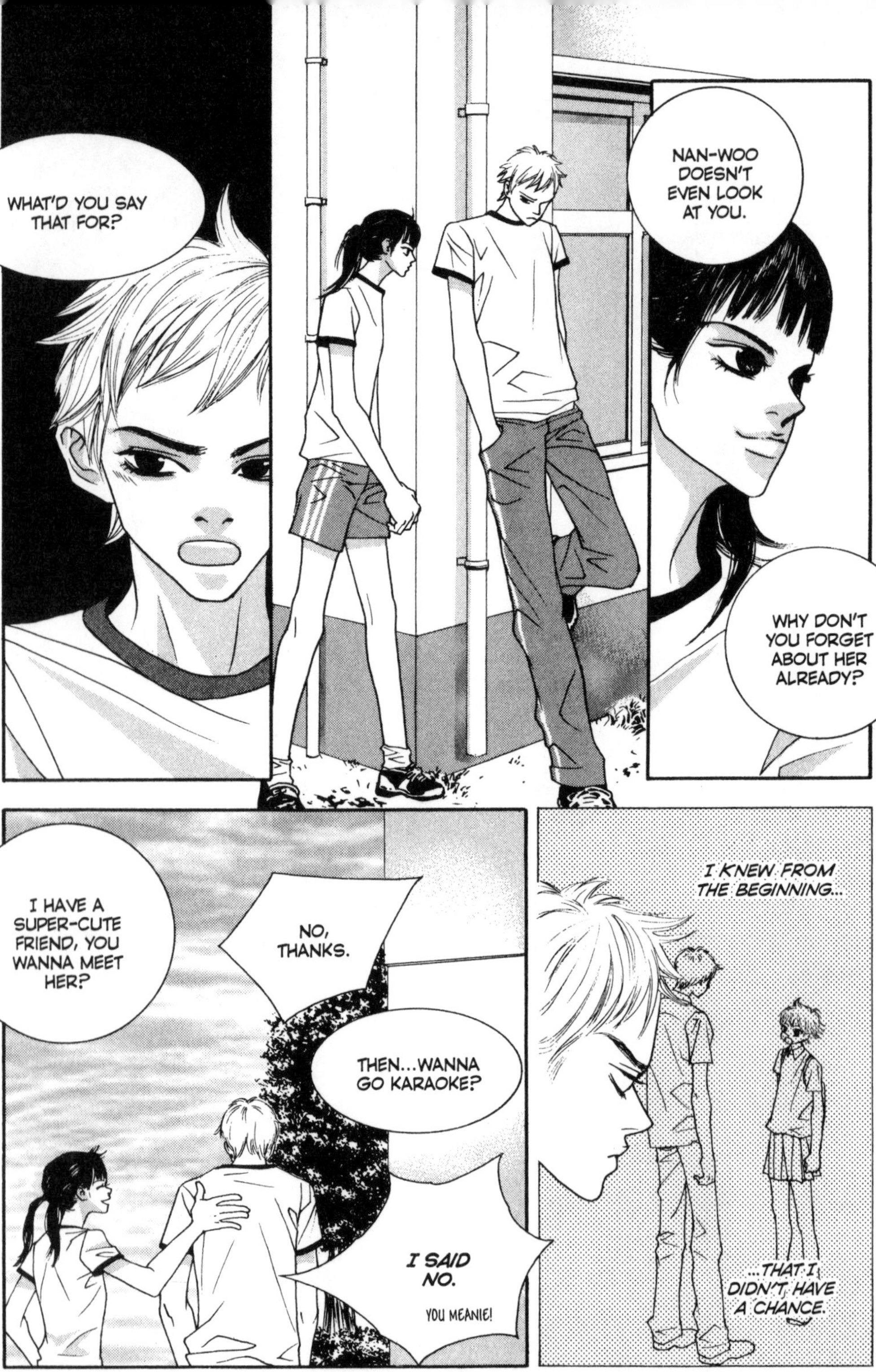
WHAT'D YOU SAY THAT FOR?
NAN-WOO DOESN'T EVEN LOOK AT YOU.
WHY DON'T YOU FORGET ABOUT HER ALREADY?
I HAVE A SUPER-CUTE FRIEND, YOU WANNA MEET HER?
NO, THANKS.
THEN...WANNA GO KARAOKE?
I SAID NO.
YOU MEANIE!
I KNEW FROM THE BEGINNING...
...THAT I DIDN'T HAVE A CHANCE.

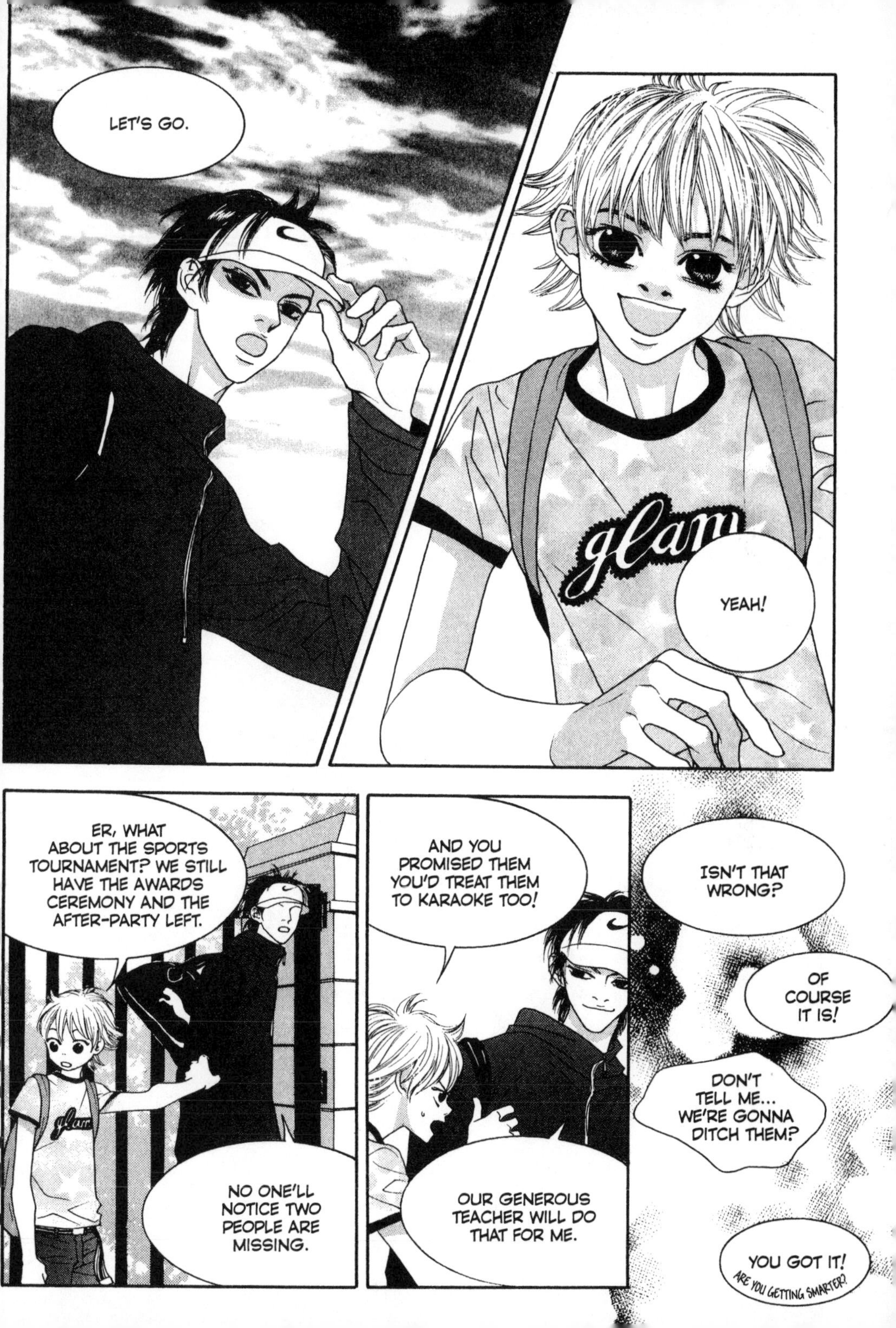
LET'S GO.
YEAH!
ER, WHAT ABOUT THE SPORTS TOURNAMENT? WE STILL HAVE THE AWARDS CEREMONY AND THE AFTER-PARTY LEFT.
NO ONE'LL NOTICE TWO PEOPLE ARE MISSING.
AND YOU PROMISED THEM YOU'D TREAT THEM TO KARAOKE TOO!
OUR GENEROUS TEACHER WILL DO THAT FOR ME.
ISN'T THAT WRONG?
OF COURSE IT IS!
DON'T TELL ME... WE'RE GONNA DITCH THEM?
YOU GOT IT!
ARE YOU GETTING SMARTER?

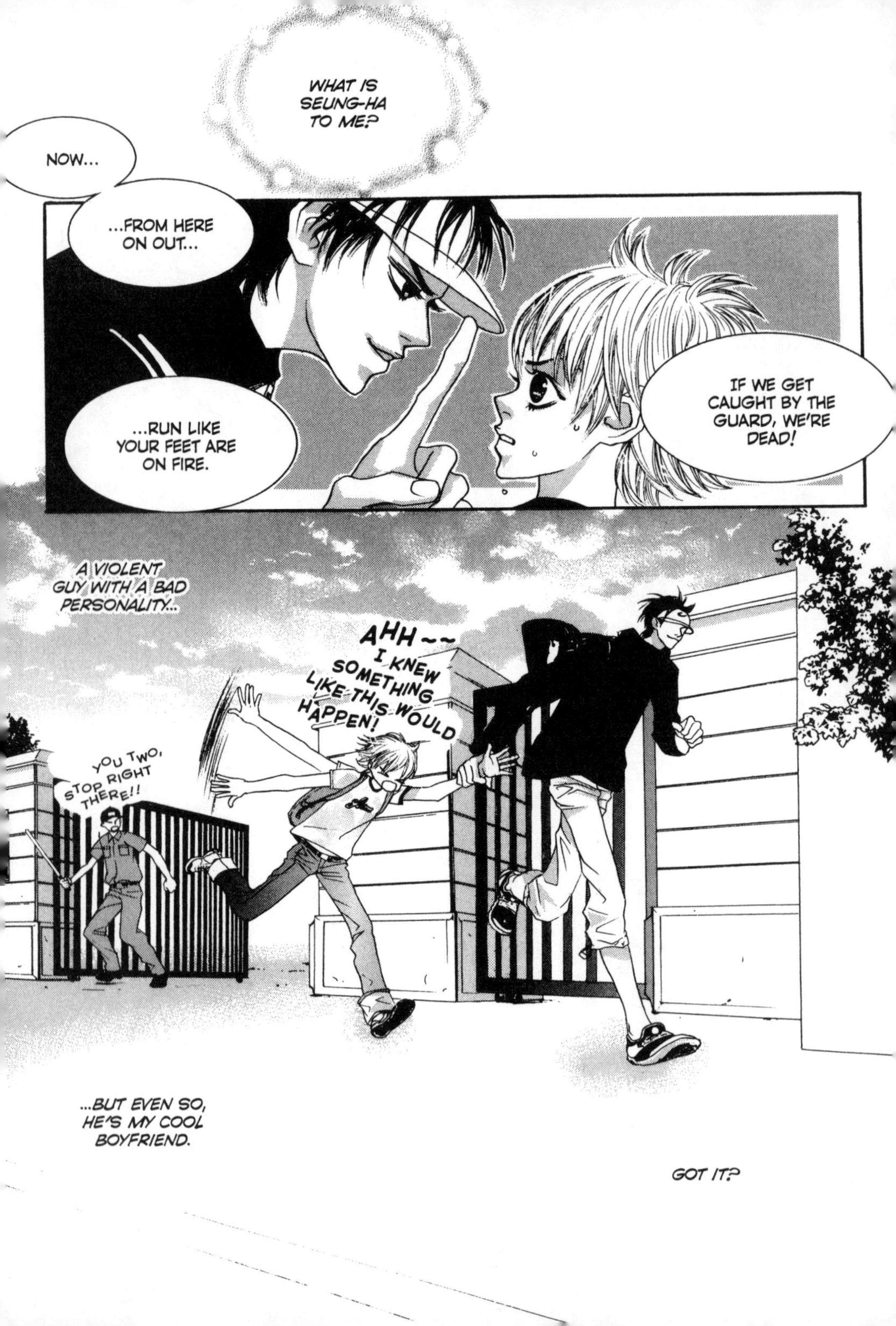
WHAT IS SEUNG-HA TO ME?
NOW...
...FROM HERE ON OUT...
...RUN LIKE YOUR FEET ARE ON FIRE.
IF WE GET CAUGHT BY THE GUARD, WE'RE DEAD!
A VIOLENT GUY WITH A BAD PERSONALITY...
YOU TWO, STOP RIGHT THERE!!
AHH~~ I KNEW SOMETHING LIKE THIS WOULD HAPPEN!
...BUT EVEN SO, HE'S MY COOL BOYFRIEND.
GOT IT?

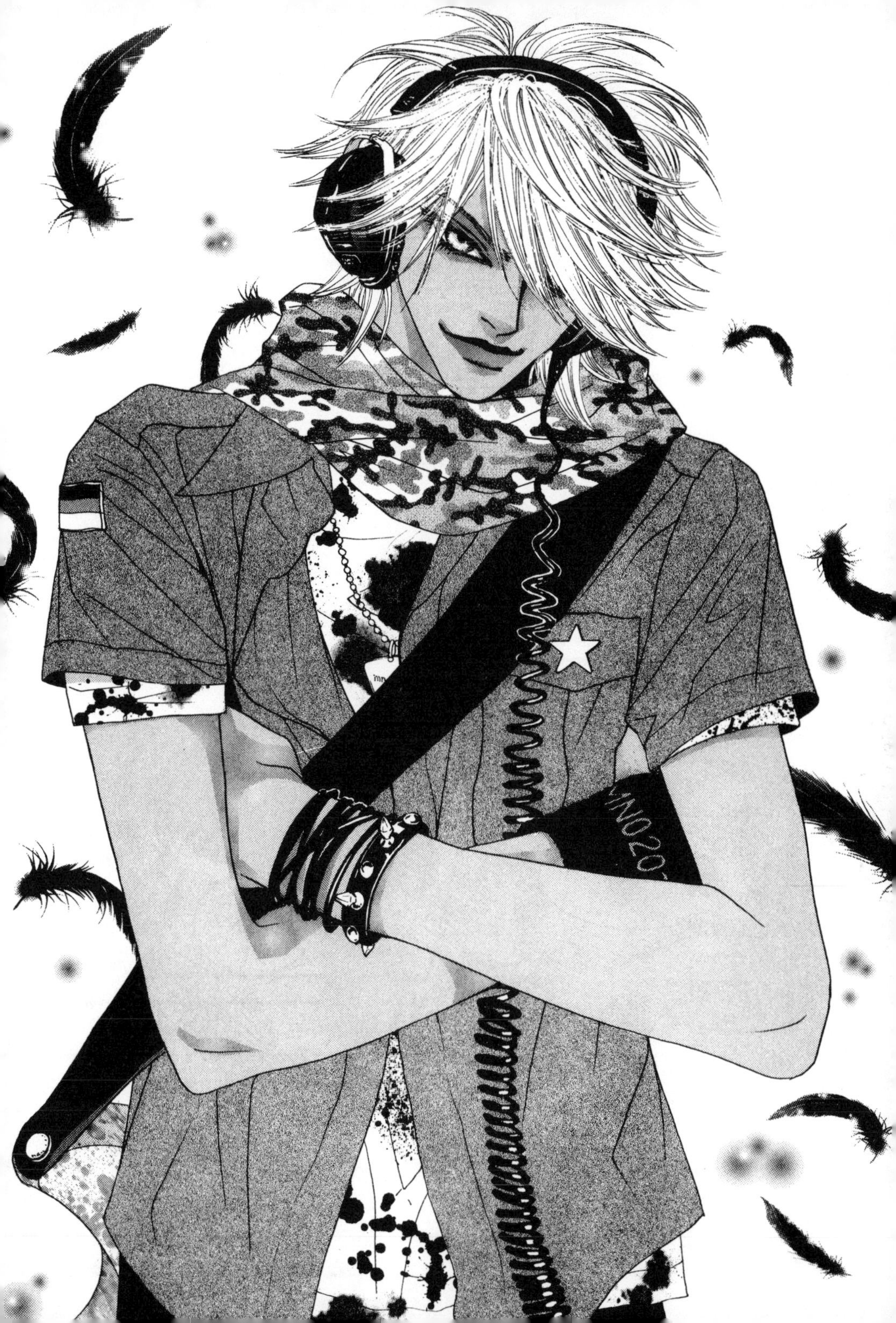

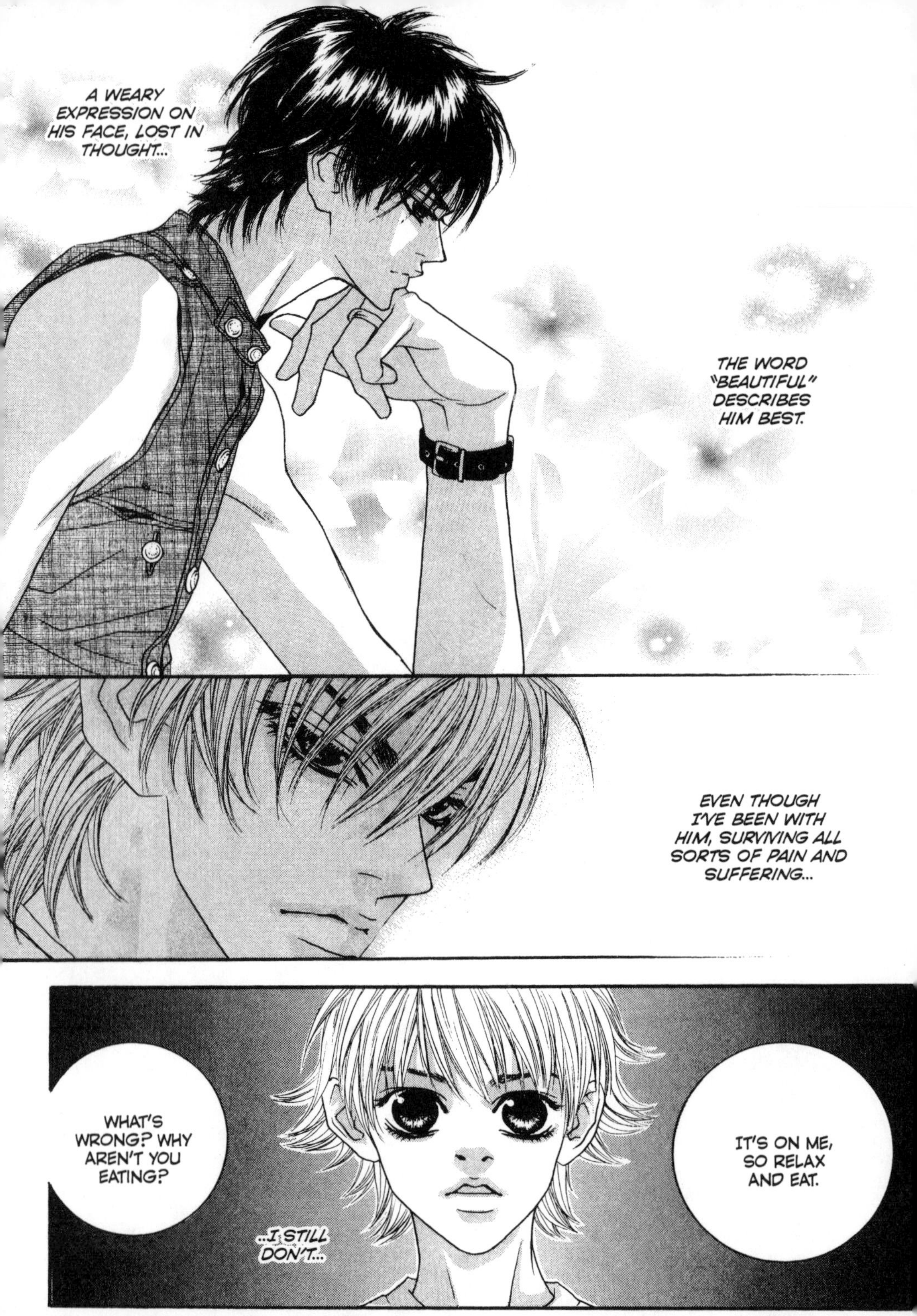
A WEARY EXPRESSION ON HIS FACE, LOST IN THOUGHT...
THE WORD "BEAUTIFUL" DESCRIBES HIM BEST.
EVEN THOUGH I'VE BEEN WITH HIM, SURVIVING ALL SORTS OF PAIN AND SUFFERING...
WHAT'S WRONG? WHY AREN'T YOU EATING?
...I STILL DON'T...
IT'S ON ME, SO RELAX AND EAT.

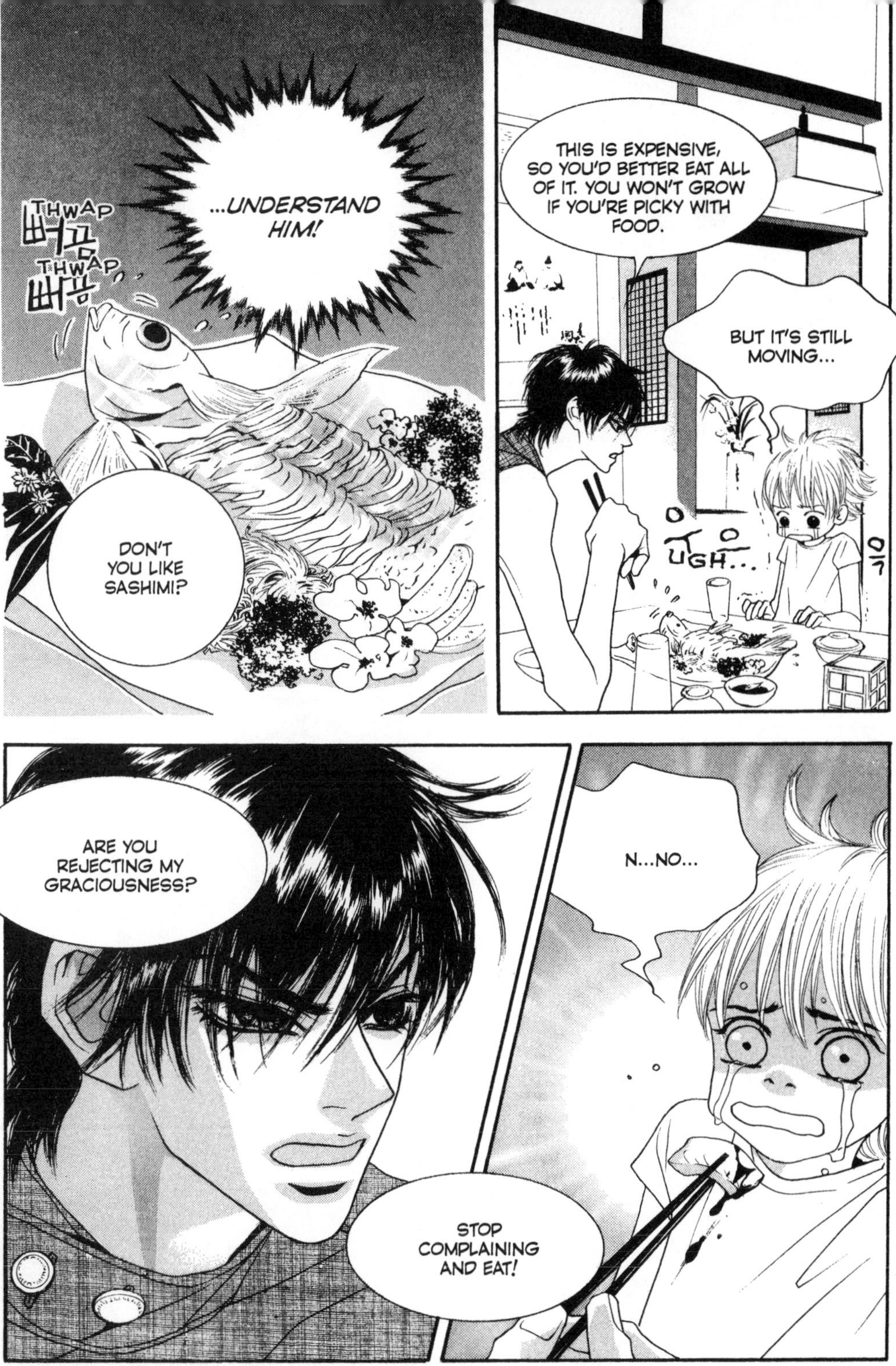
THWAP
THWAP
...UNDERSTAND HIM!
DON'T YOU LIKE SASHIMI?
THIS IS EXPENSIVE, SO YOU'D BETTER EAT ALL OF IT. YOU WON'T GROW IF YOU'RE PICKY WITH FOOD.
BUT IT'S STILL MOVING...
UGH...
ARE YOU REJECTING MY GRACIOUSNESS?
N...NO...
STOP COMPLAINING AND EAT!

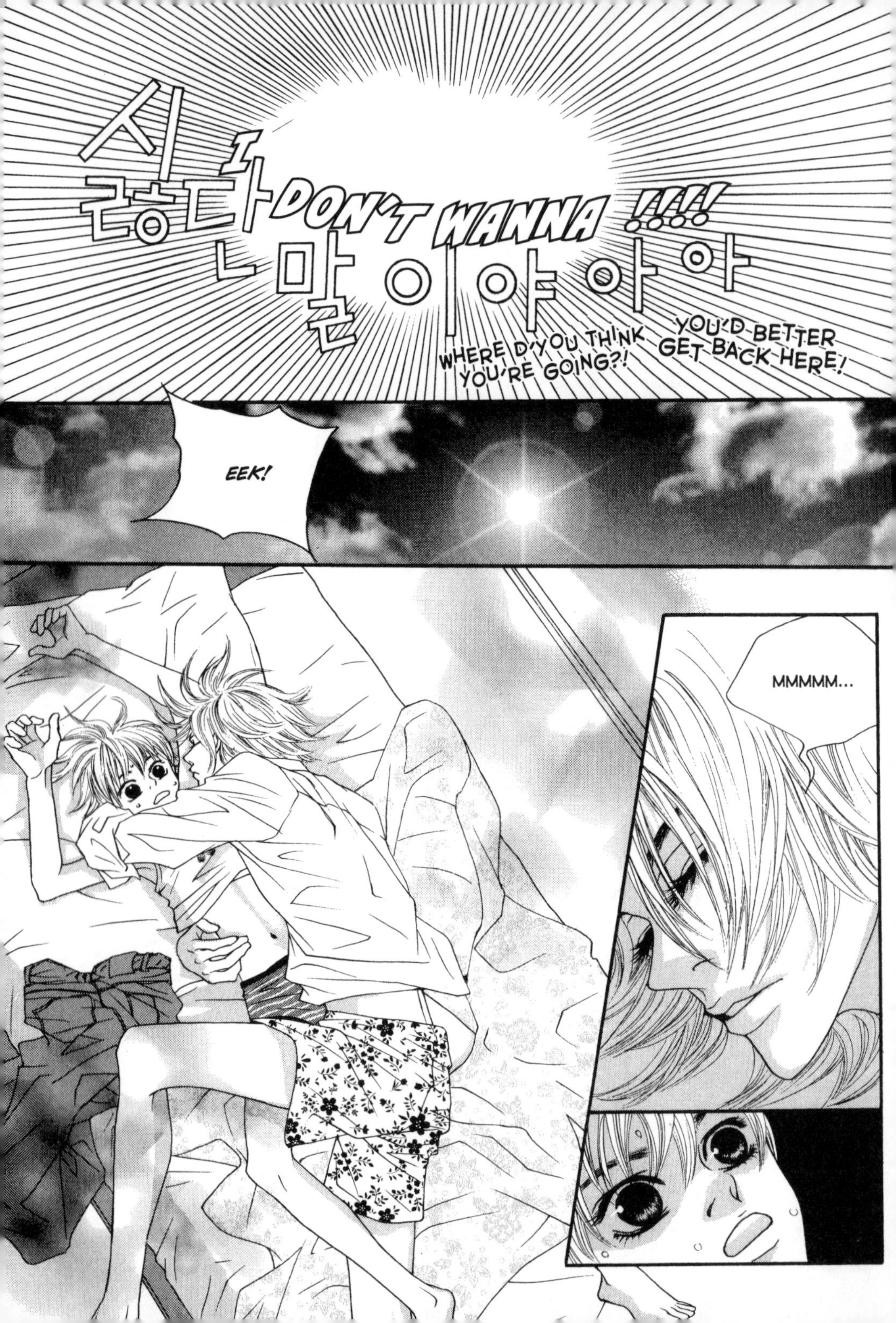
싫단 말이야아아
I DON'T WANNA !!!!
WHERE D'YOU THINK YOU'RE GOING?!
YOU'D BETTER GET BACK HERE!
EEK!
MMMMM...

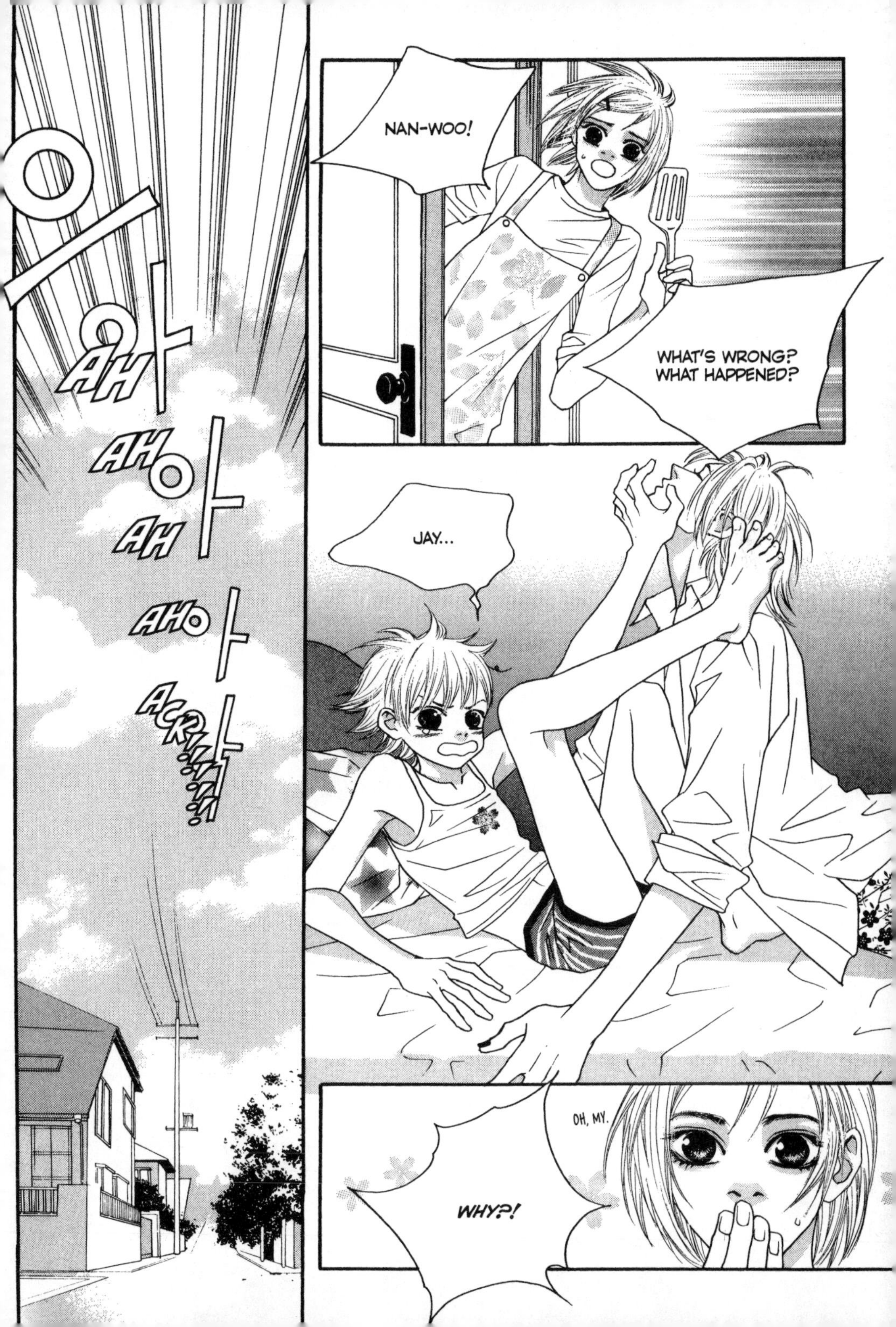

AH
AH
AH
AH
ACK!!!
NAN-WOO!
WHAT'S WRONG? WHAT HAPPENED?
JAY...
OH, MY.
WHY?!

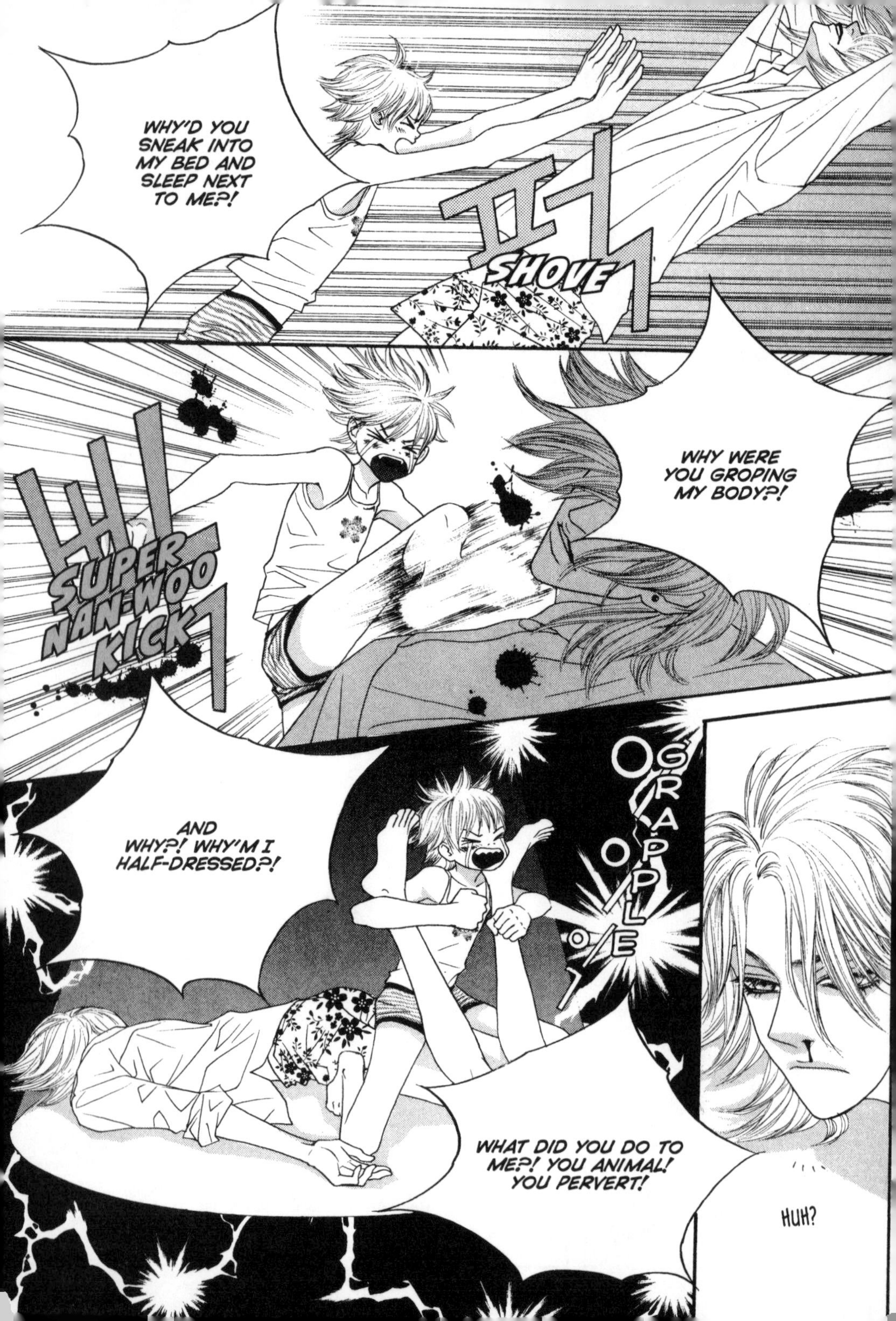
WHY'D YOU SNEAK INTO MY BED AND SLEEP NEXT TO ME?!
SHOVE
SUPER NAN-WOO KICK
WHY WERE YOU GROPING MY BODY?!
AND WHY?! WHY'M I HALF-DRESSED?!
GRAPPLE
WHAT DID YOU DO TO ME?! YOU ANIMAL! YOU PERVERT!
HUH?

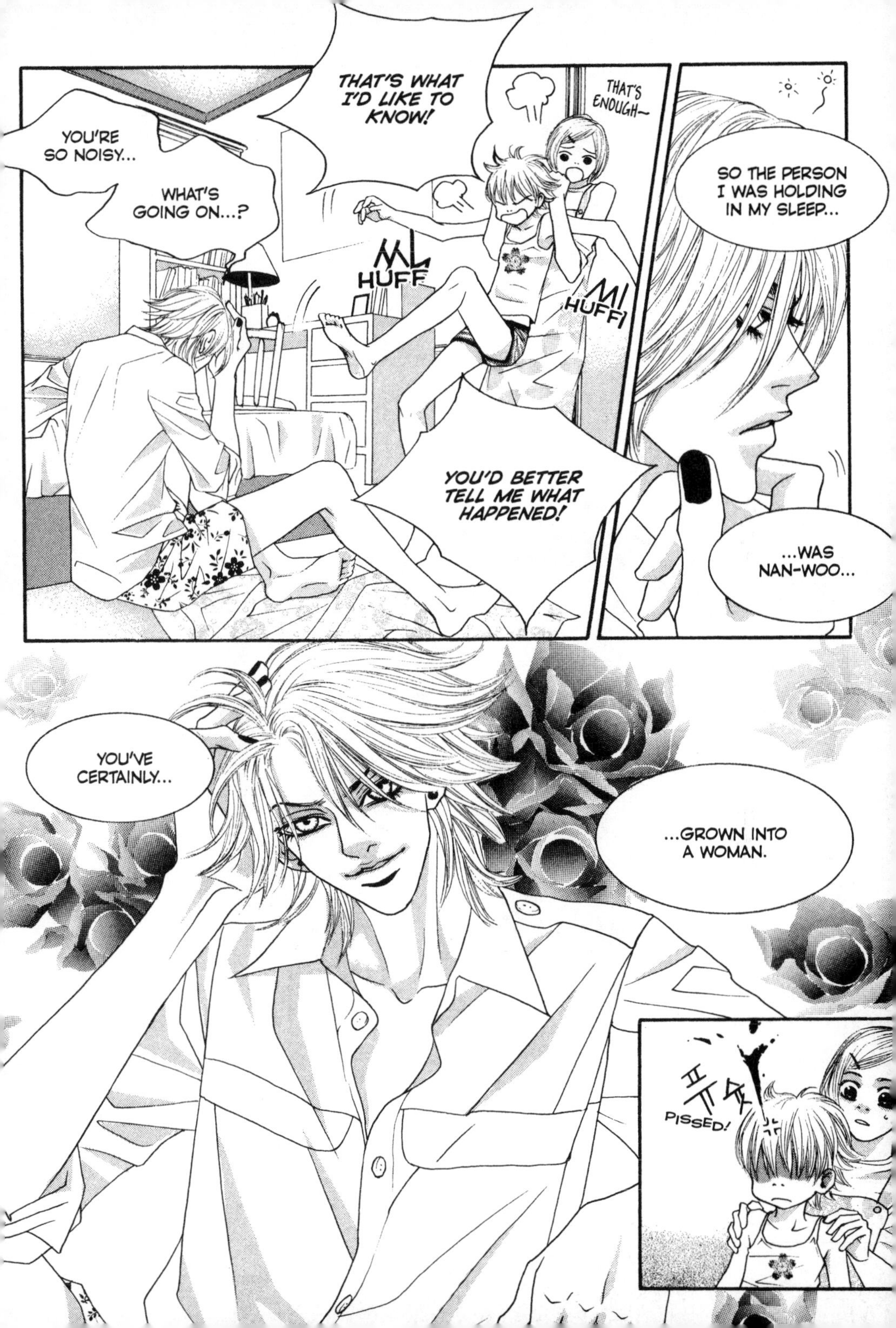
YOU'RE SO NOISY...
WHAT'S GOING ON...?
THAT'S WHAT I'D LIKE TO KNOW!
THAT'S ENOUGH~
HUFF
HUFF!
YOU'D BETTER TELL ME WHAT HAPPENED!
SO THE PERSON I WAS HOLDING IN MY SLEEP...
...WAS NAN-WOO...
YOU'VE CERTAINLY...
...GROWN INTO A WOMAN.
PISSED!

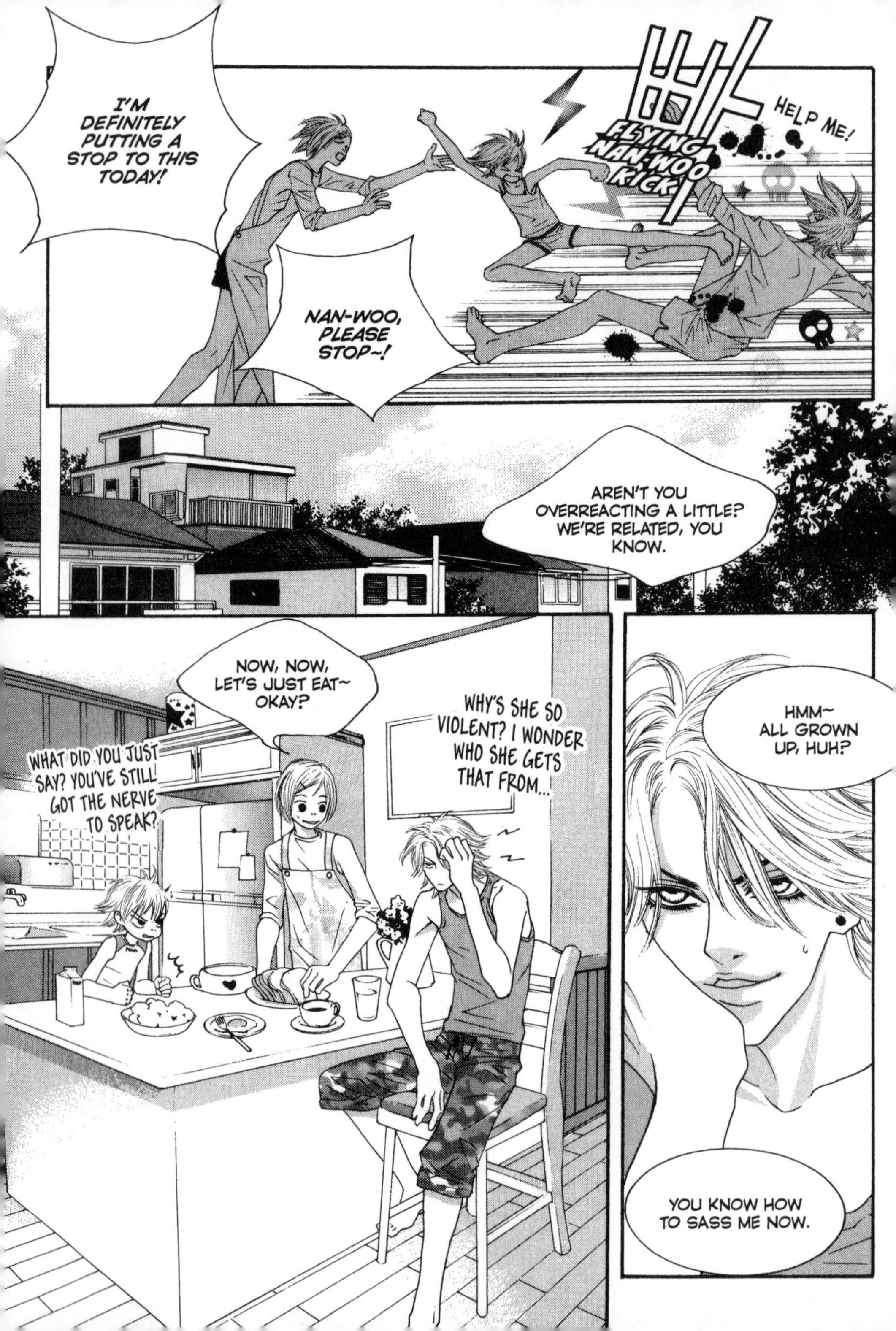
I'M DEFINITELY PUTTING A STOP TO THIS TODAY!
NAN-WOO, PLEASE STOP~!
FLYING NAN-WOO KICK
HELP ME!
AREN'T YOU OVERREACTING A LITTLE? WE'RE RELATED, YOU KNOW.
NOW, NOW, LET'S JUST EAT~ OKAY?
WHAT DID YOU JUST SAY? YOU'VE STILL GOT THE NERVE TO SPEAK?
WHY'S SHE SO VIOLENT? I WONDER WHO SHE GETS THAT FROM...
HMM~ ALL GROWN UP, HUH?
YOU KNOW HOW TO SASS ME NOW.

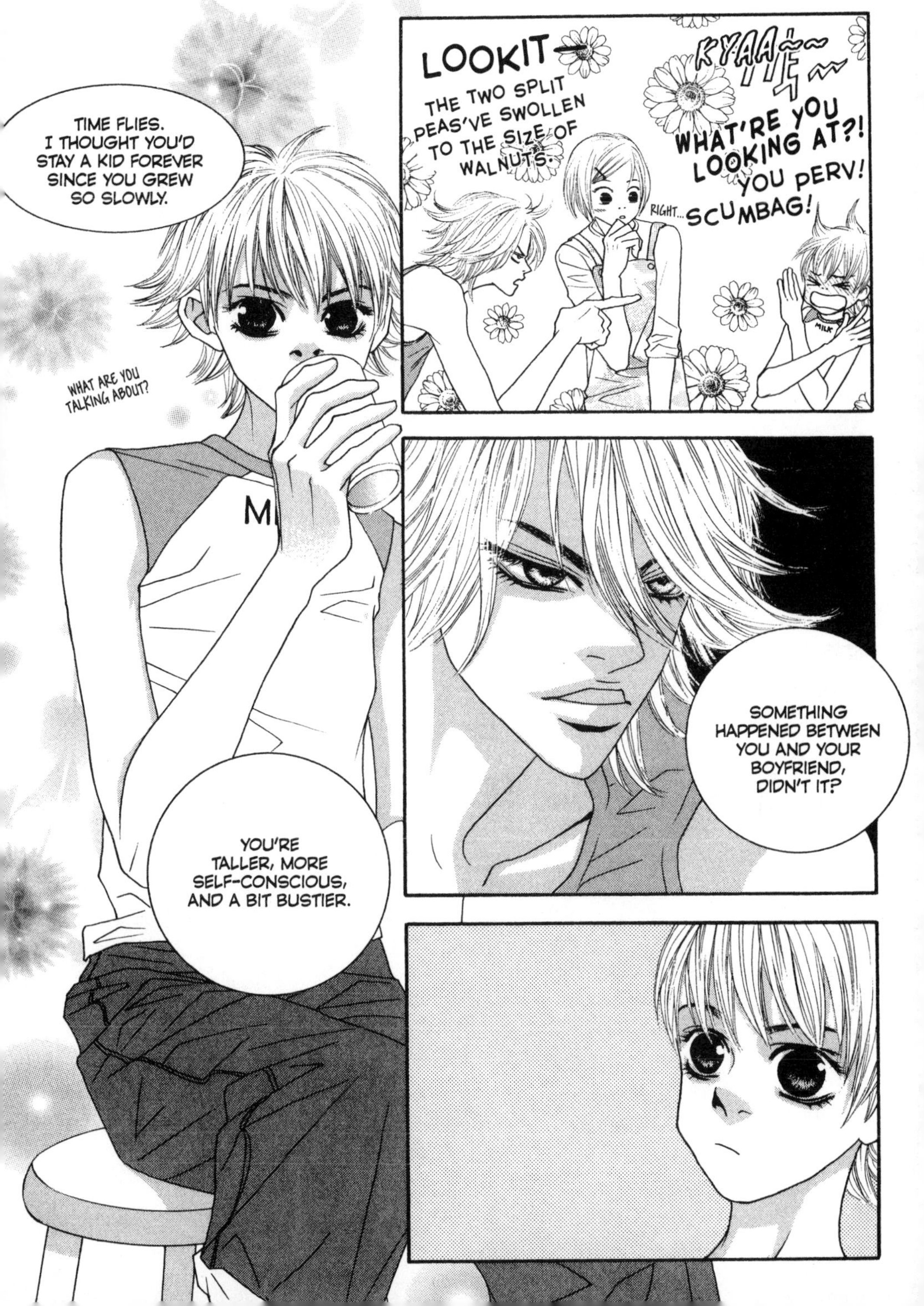
TIME FLIES. I THOUGHT YOU'D STAY A KID FOREVER SINCE YOU GREW SO SLOWLY.
WHAT ARE YOU TALKING ABOUT?
YOU'RE TALLER, MORE SELF-CONSCIOUS, AND A BIT BUSTIER.
LOOKIT—
THE TWO SPLIT PEAS'VE SWOLLEN TO THE SIZE OF WALNUTS.
KYAAA~~
WHAT'RE YOU LOOKING AT?! YOU PERV!
RIGHT...
SCUMBAG!
MILK
SOMETHING HAPPENED BETWEEN YOU AND YOUR BOYFRIEND, DIDN'T IT?

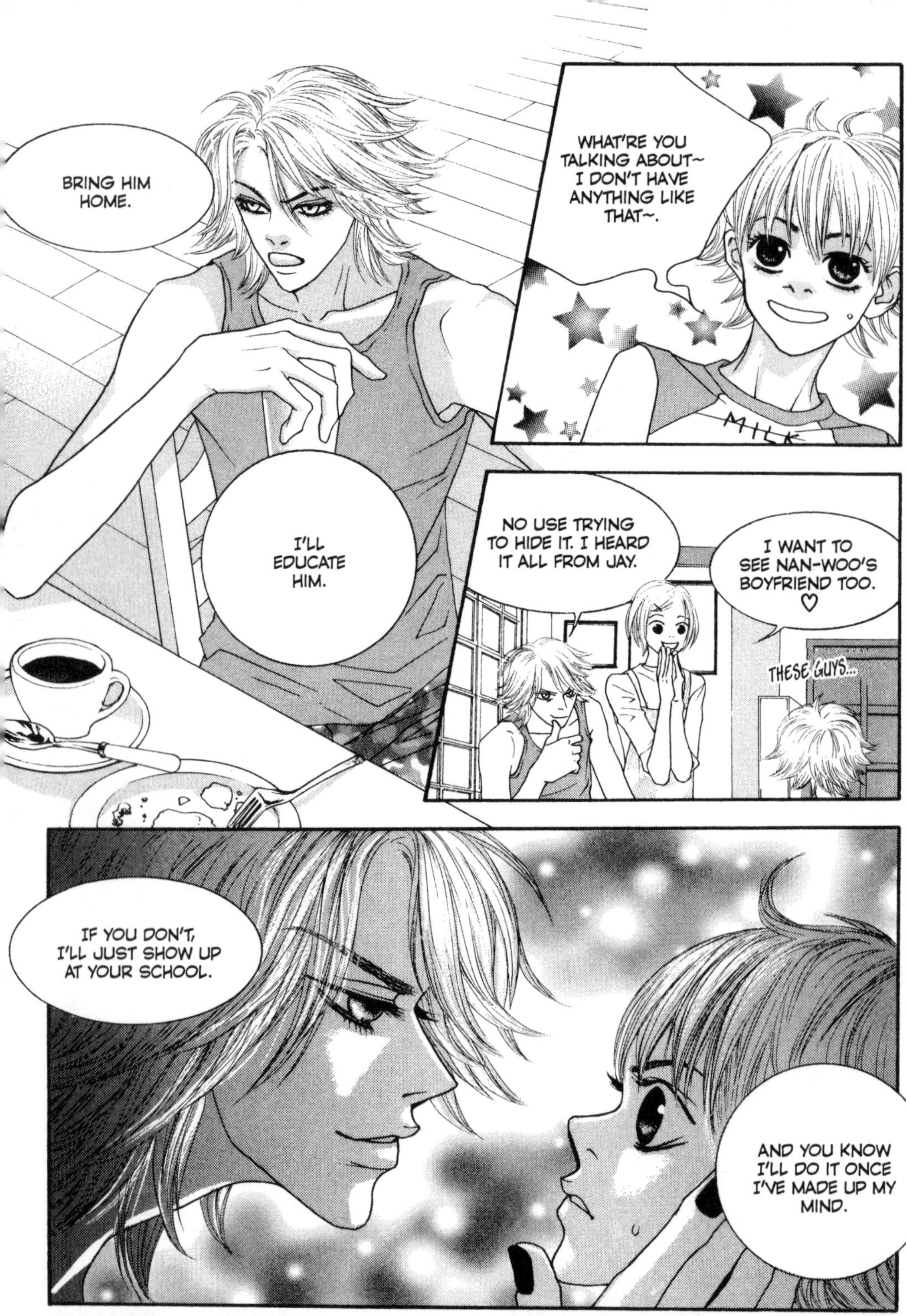
BRING HIM HOME.
I'LL EDUCATE HIM.
WHAT'RE YOU TALKING ABOUT~ I DON'T HAVE ANYTHING LIKE THAT~.
MILK
NO USE TRYING TO HIDE IT. I HEARD IT ALL FROM JAY.
I WANT TO SEE NAN-WOO'S BOYFRIEND TOO. ♡
THESE GUYS...
IF YOU DON'T, I'LL JUST SHOW UP AT YOUR SCHOOL.
AND YOU KNOW I'LL DO IT ONCE I'VE MADE UP MY MIND.

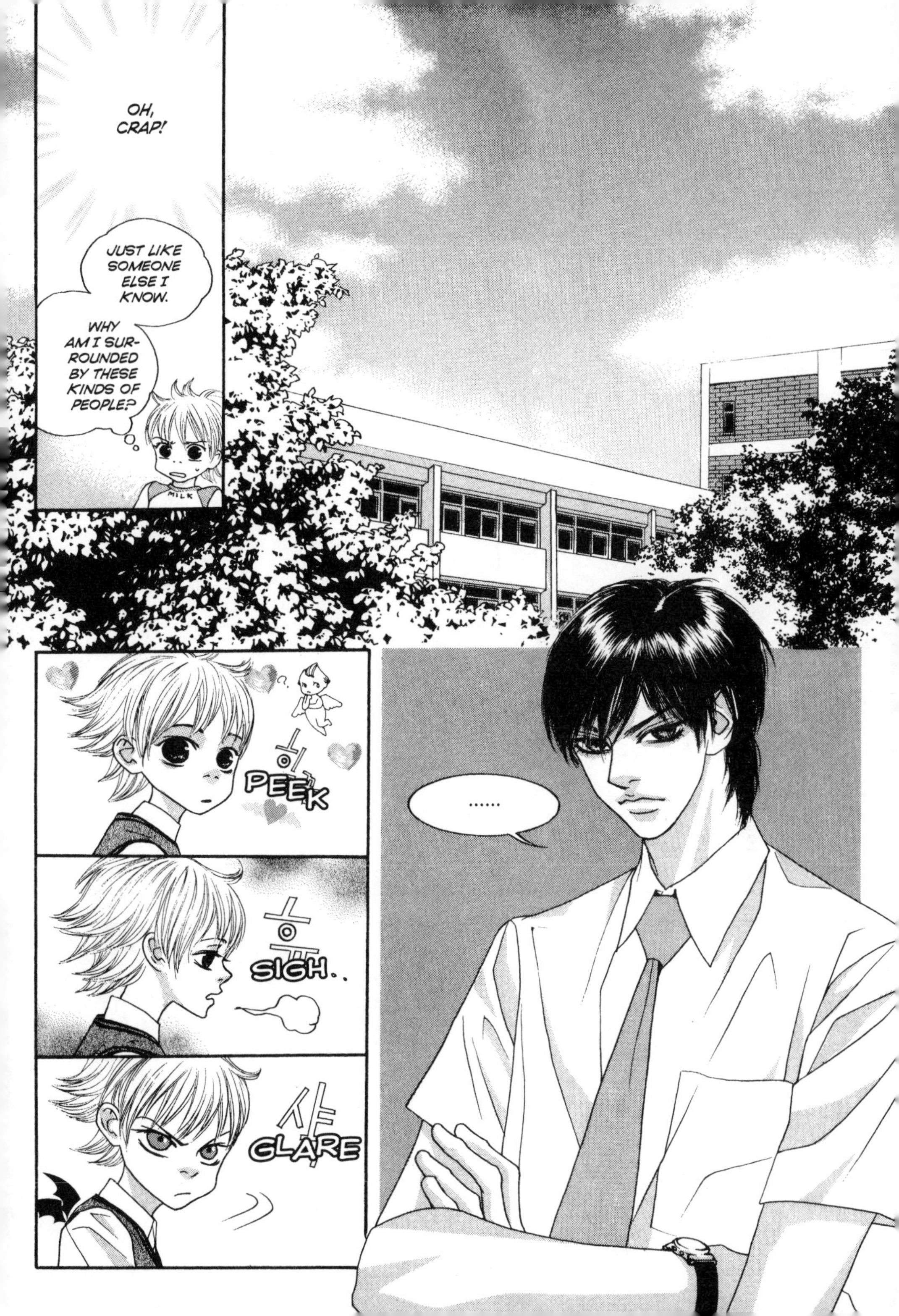
OH, CRAP!
JUST LIKE SOMEONE ELSE I KNOW.
WHY AM I SURROUNDED BY THESE KINDS OF PEOPLE?
PEEK
SIGH..
GLARE
......

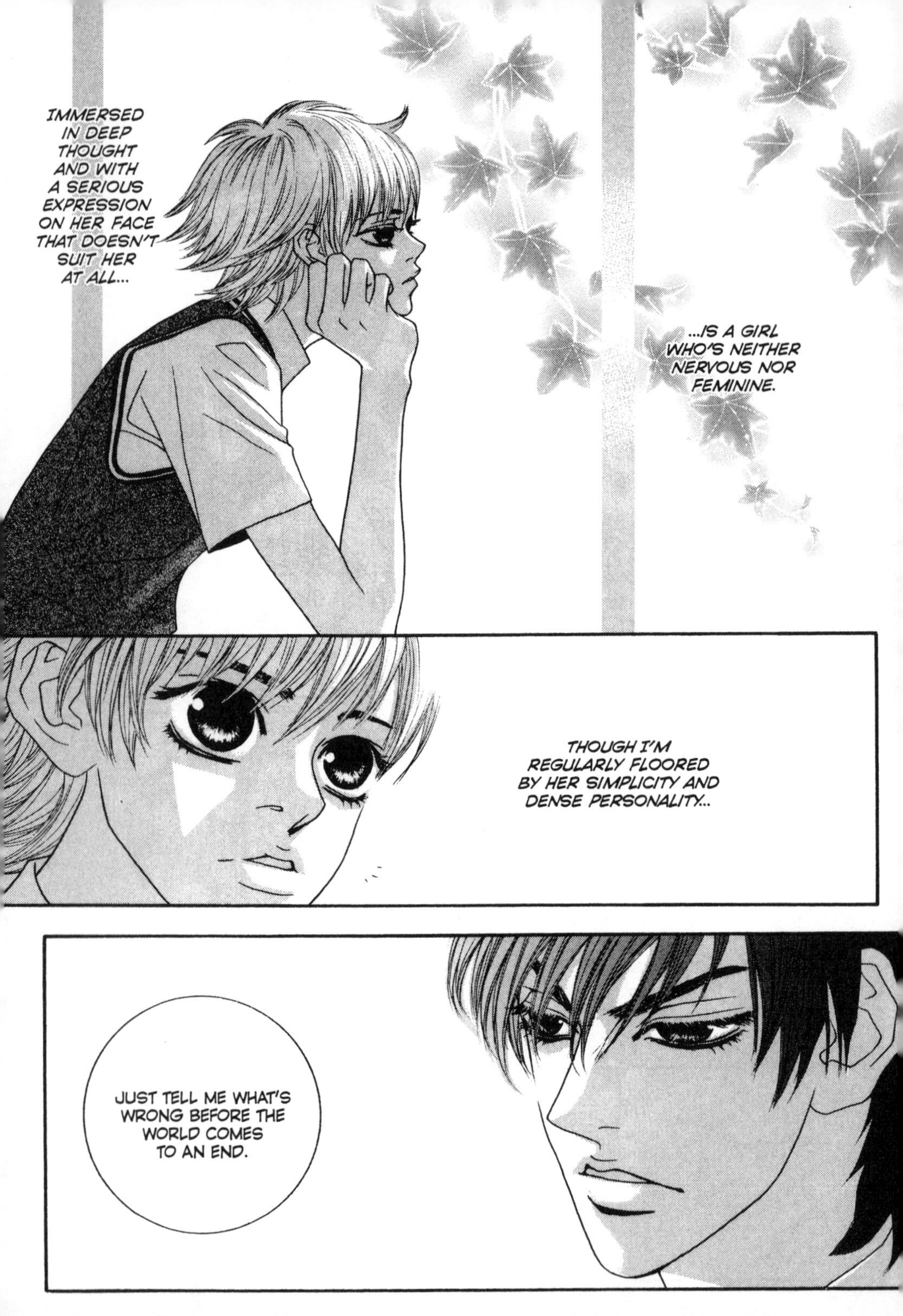
IMMERSED IN DEEP THOUGHT AND WITH A SERIOUS EXPRESSION ON HER FACE THAT DOESN'T SUIT HER AT ALL...
...IS A GIRL WHO'S NEITHER NERVOUS NOR FEMININE.
THOUGH I'M REGULARLY FLOORED BY HER SIMPLICITY AND DENSE PERSONALITY...
JUST TELL ME WHAT'S WRONG BEFORE THE WORLD COMES TO AN END.

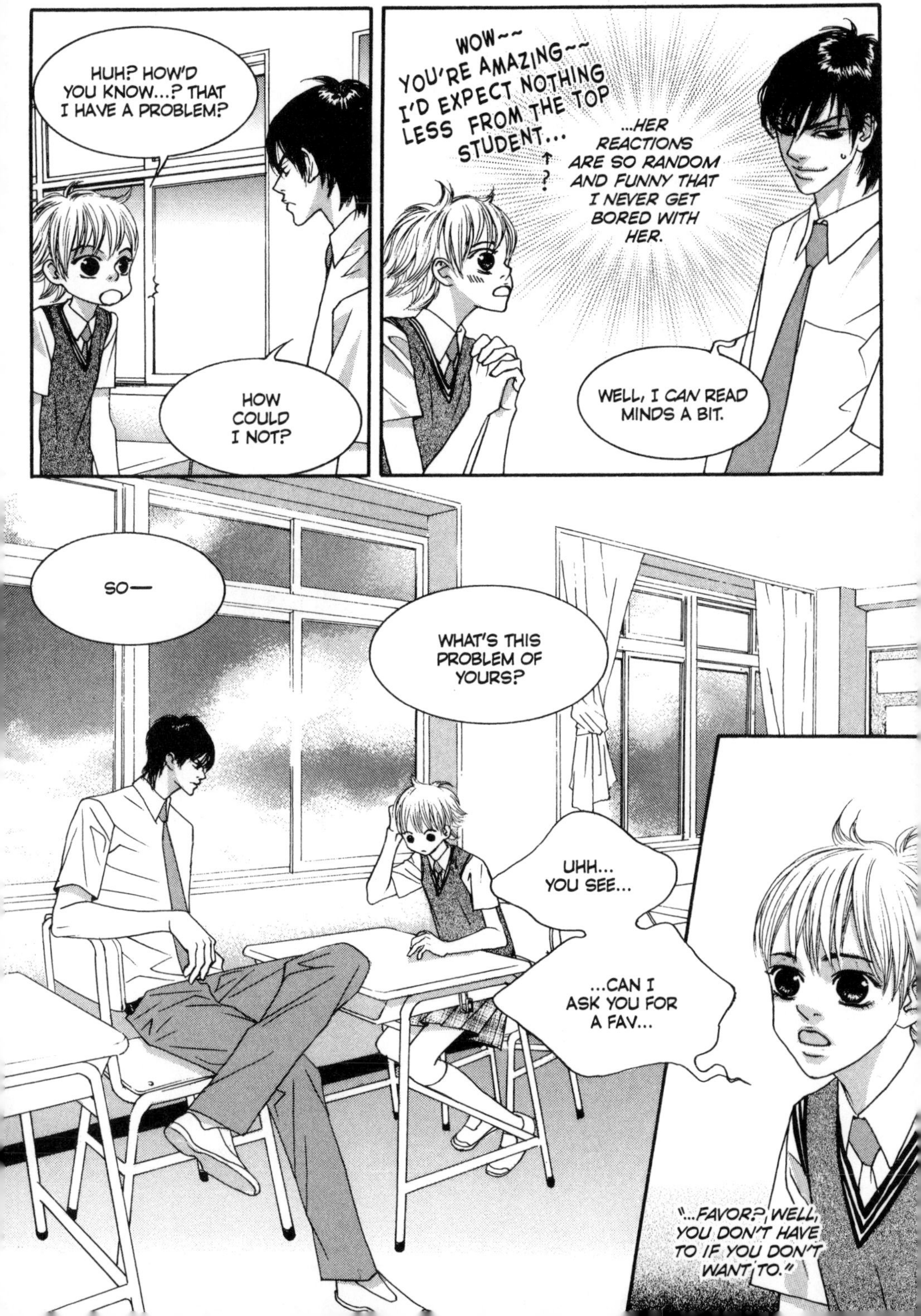
HUH? HOW'D YOU KNOW...? THAT I HAVE A PROBLEM?
HOW COULD I NOT?
WOW~~ YOU'RE AMAZING~~ I'D EXPECT NOTHING LESS FROM THE TOP STUDENT...
?
...HER REACTIONS ARE SO RANDOM AND FUNNY THAT I NEVER GET BORED WITH HER.
WELL, I CAN READ MINDS A BIT.
SO—
WHAT'S THIS PROBLEM OF YOURS?
UHH... YOU SEE...
...CAN I ASK YOU FOR A FAV...
"...FAVOR?, WELL, YOU DON'T HAVE TO IF YOU DON'T WANT TO."

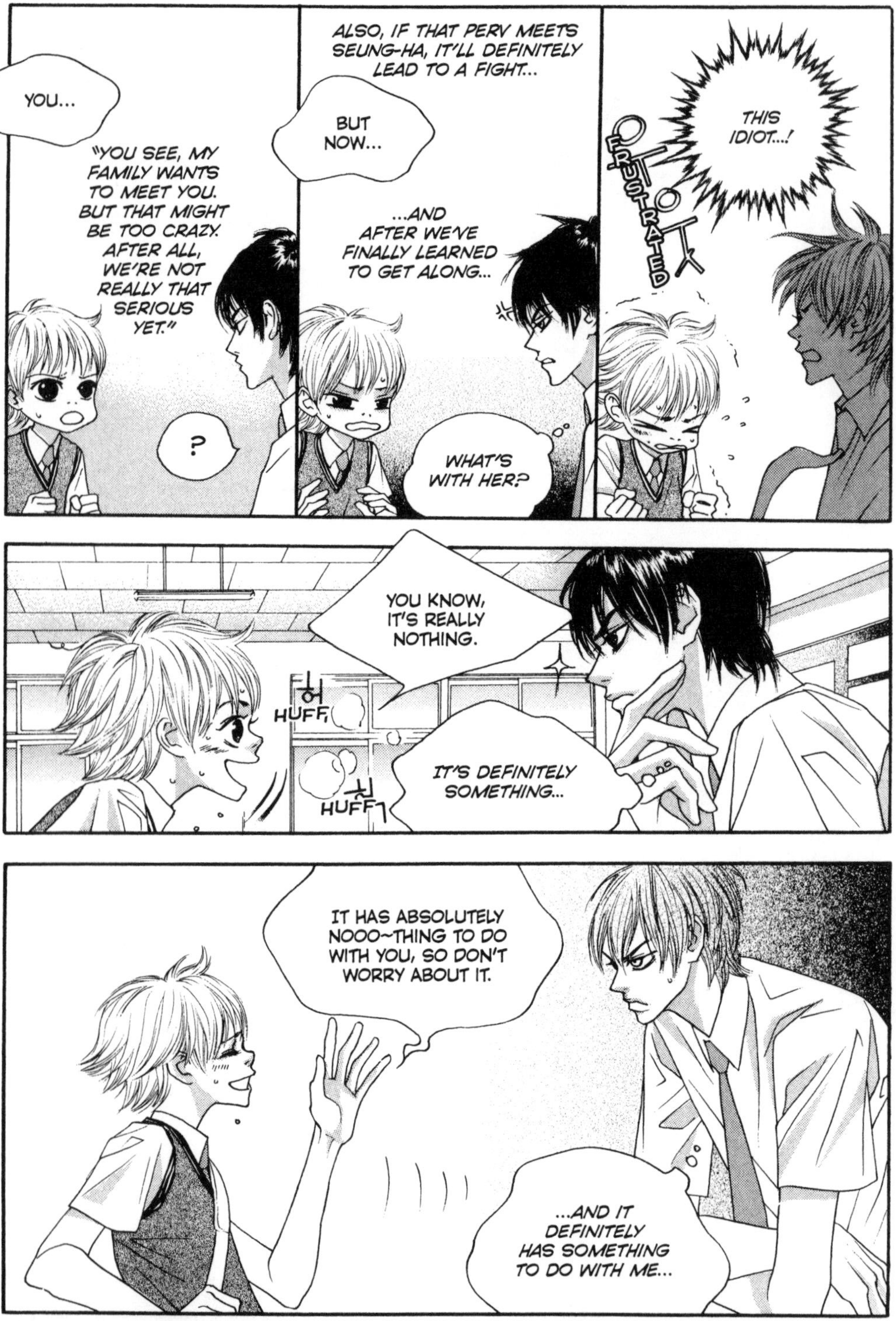
YOU...
"YOU SEE, MY FAMILY WANTS TO MEET YOU. BUT THAT MIGHT BE TOO CRAZY. AFTER ALL, WE'RE NOT REALLY THAT SERIOUS YET."
?
ALSO, IF THAT PERV MEETS SEUNG-HA, IT'LL DEFINITELY LEAD TO A FIGHT...
BUT NOW...
...AND AFTER WE'VE FINALLY LEARNED TO GET ALONG...
WHAT'S WITH HER?
FRUSTRATED
THIS IDIOT...!
YOU KNOW, IT'S REALLY NOTHING.
HUFF
HUFF
IT'S DEFINITELY SOMETHING...
IT HAS ABSOLUTELY NOOO~THING TO DO WITH YOU, SO DON'T WORRY ABOUT IT.
...AND IT DEFINITELY HAS SOMETHING TO DO WITH ME...

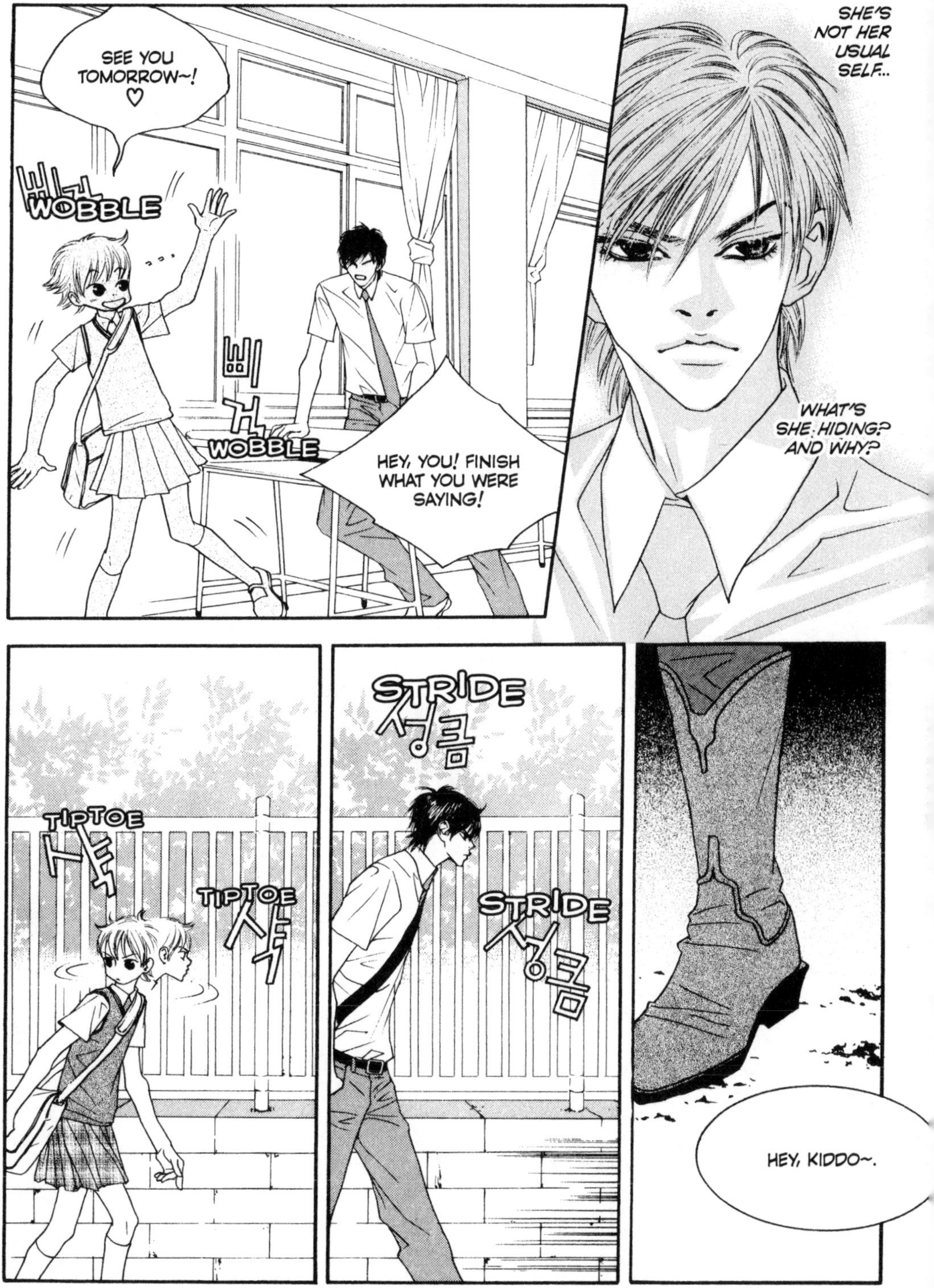

SEE YOU TOMORROW~! ♡
WOBBLE
...
WOBBLE
HEY, YOU! FINISH WHAT YOU WERE SAYING!
SHE'S NOT HER USUAL SELF...
WHAT'S SHE HIDING? AND WHY?
TIPTOE
TIPTOE
STRIDE
성큼
STRIDE
성큼
HEY, KIDDO~.

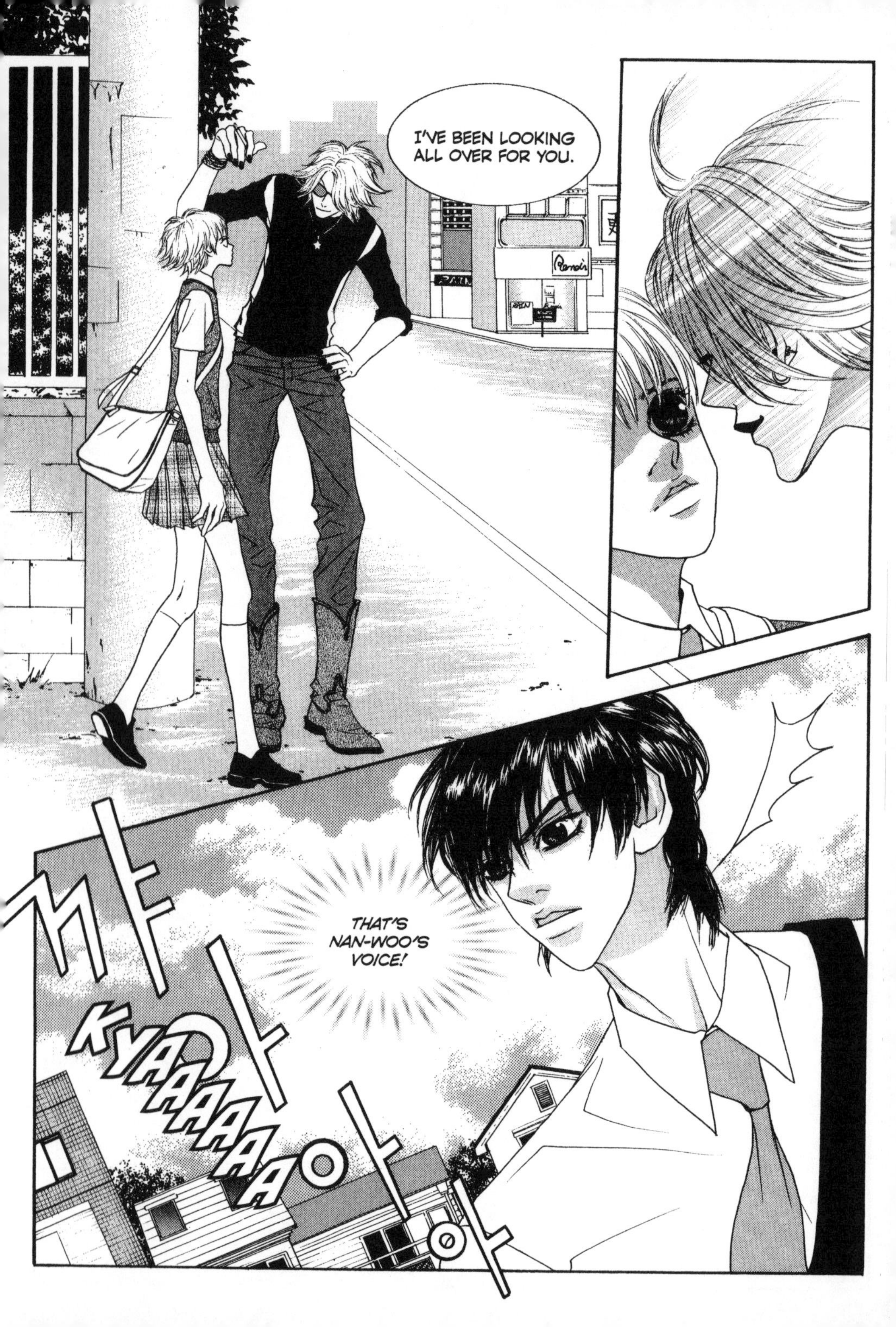
I'VE BEEN LOOKING ALL OVER FOR YOU.
THAT'S NAN-WOO'S VOICE!
KYAAAAAA

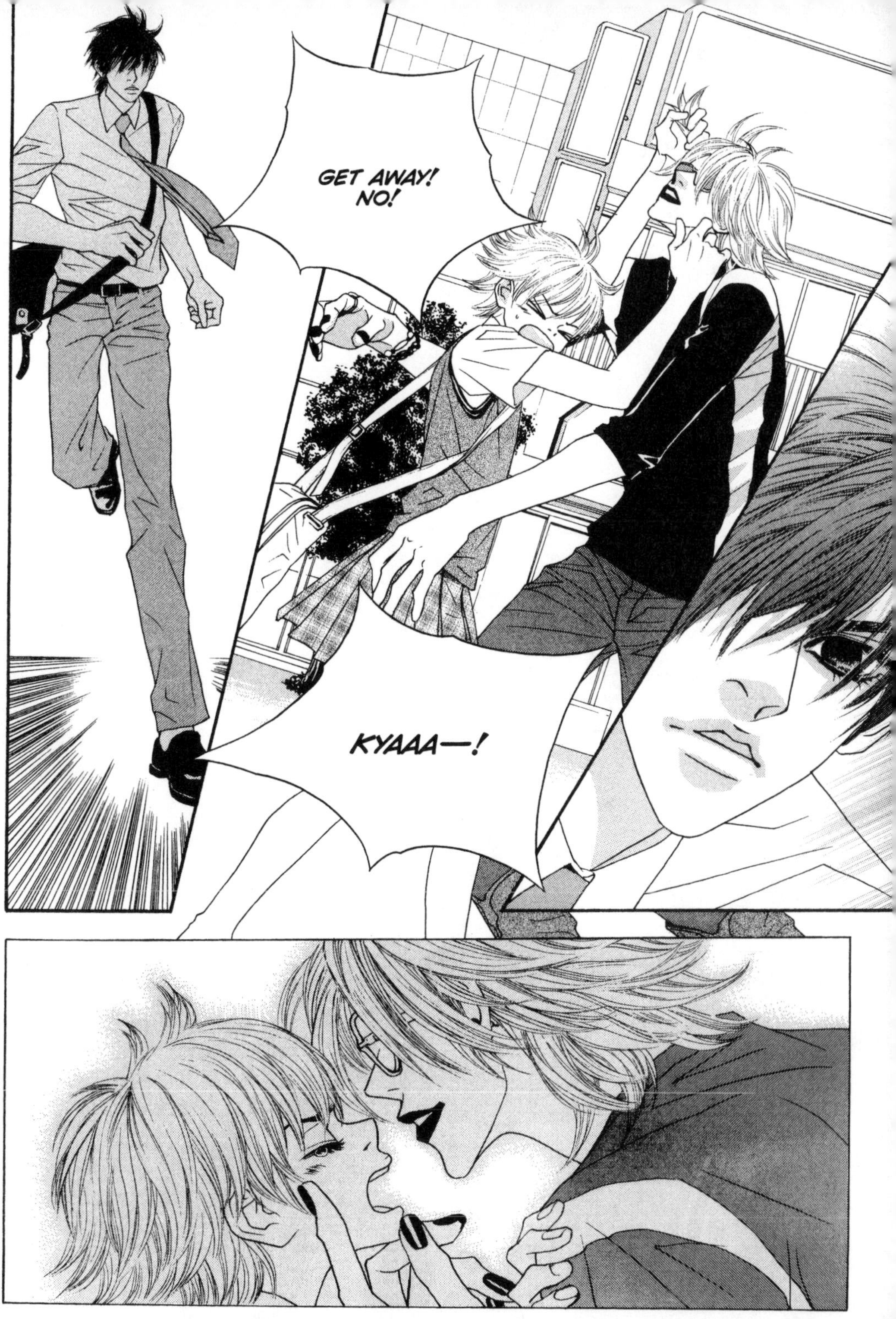
GET AWAY! NO!
KYAAA—!

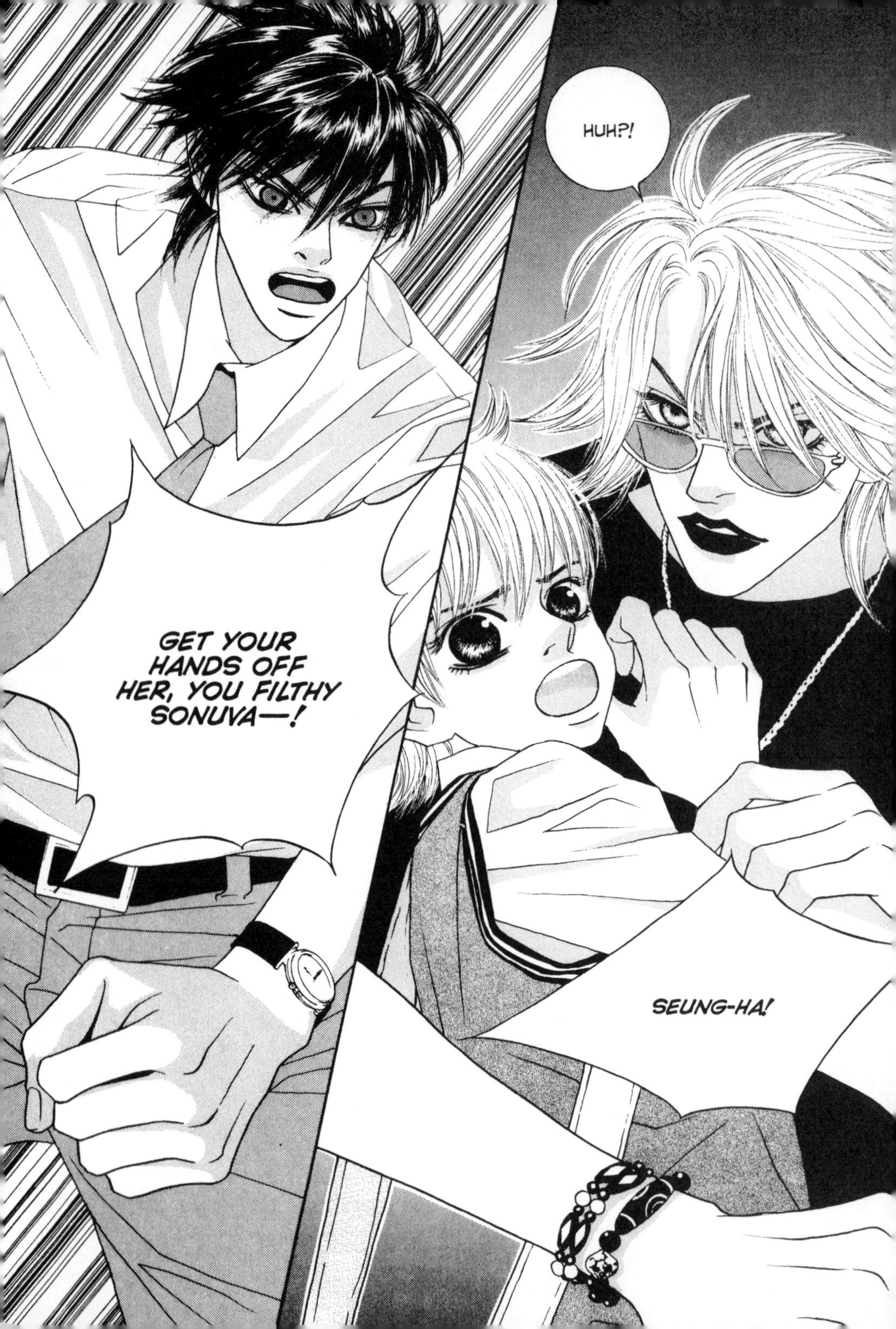
GET YOUR HANDS OFF HER, YOU FILTHY SONUVA—!
HUH?!
SEUNG-HA!

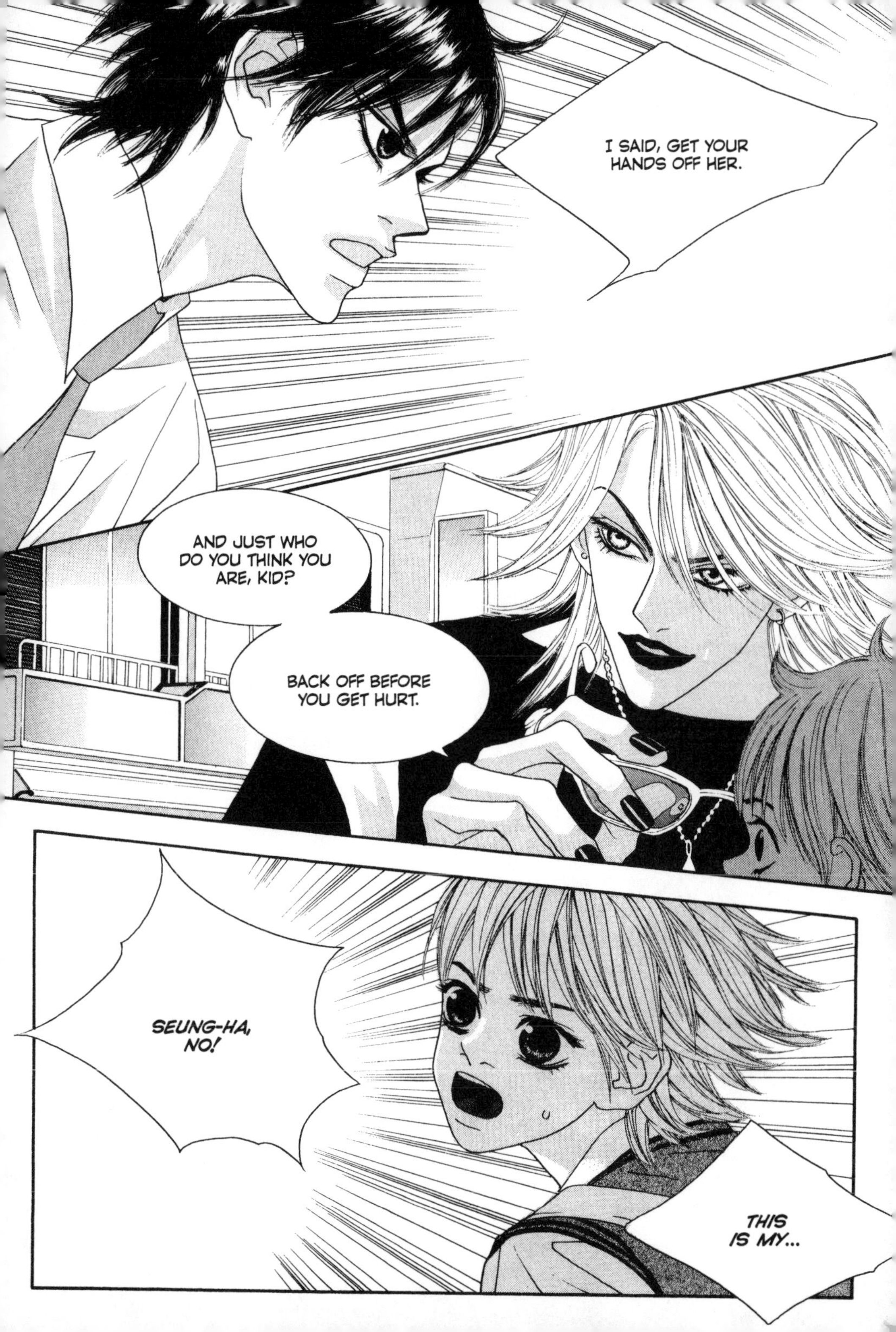
I SAID, GET YOUR HANDS OFF HER.
AND JUST WHO DO YOU THINK YOU ARE, KID?
BACK OFF BEFORE YOU GET HURT.
SEUNG-HA, NO!
THIS IS MY...

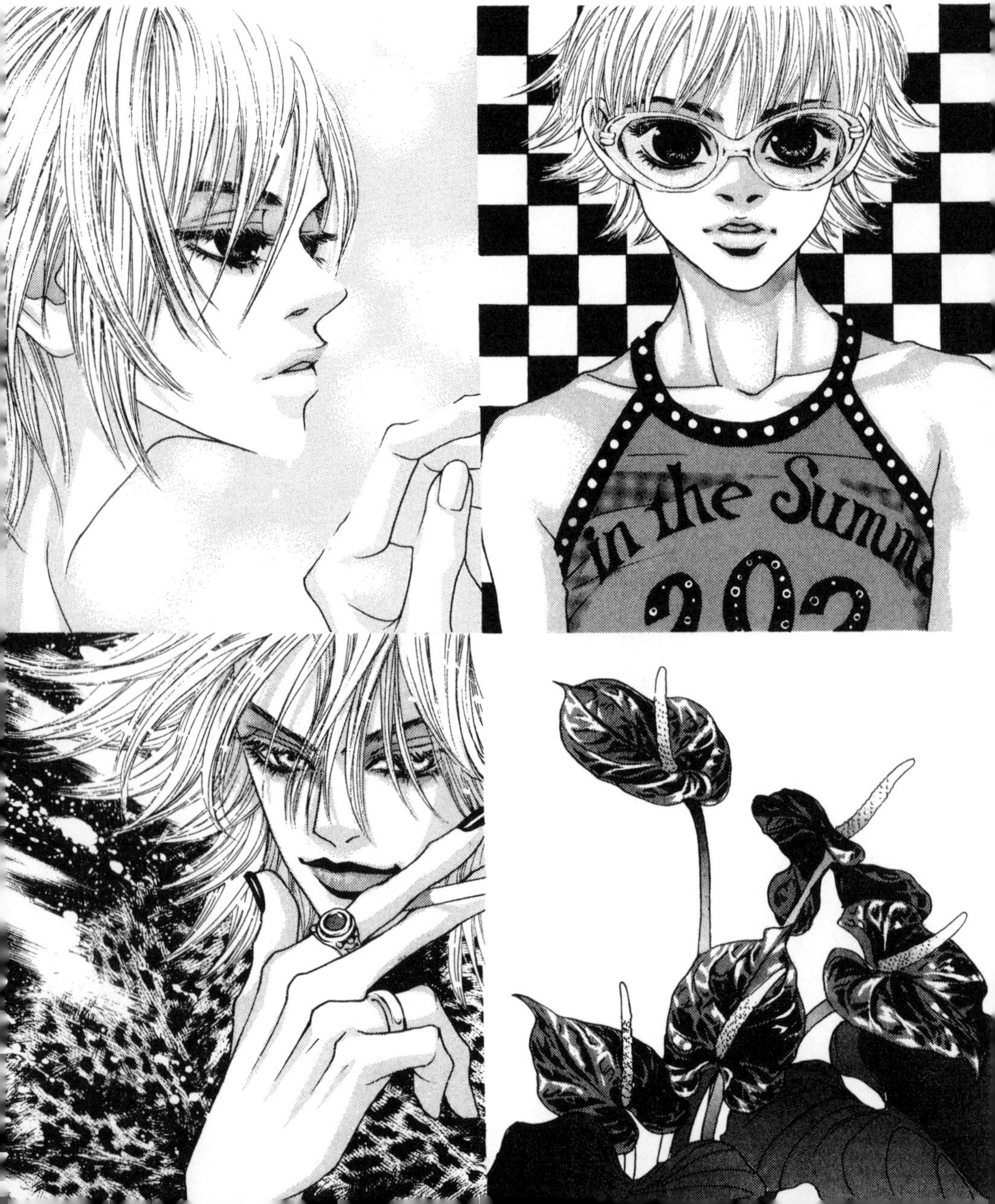
in the Summe

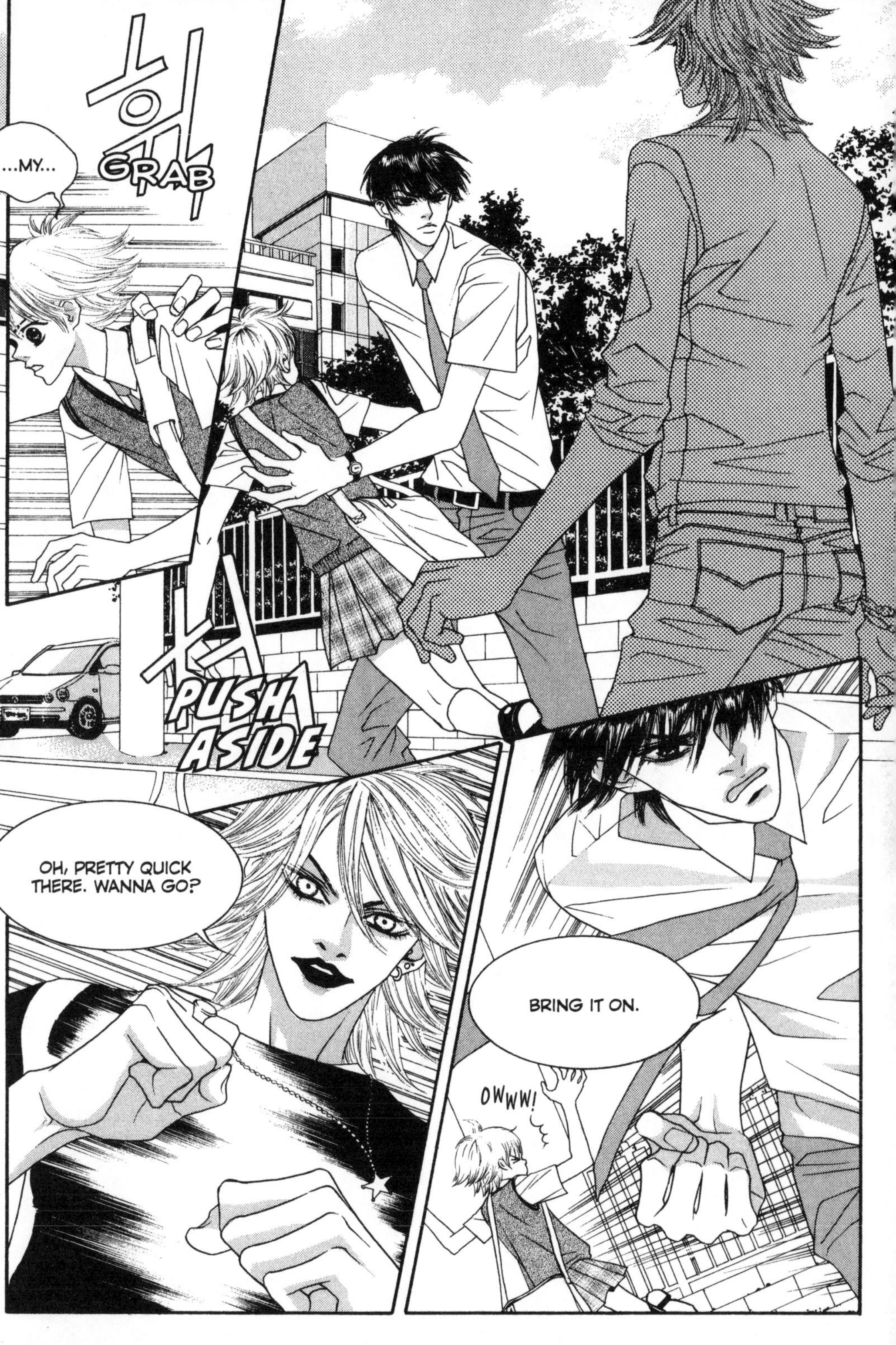
...MY...
GRAB
PUSH ASIDE
OH, PRETTY QUICK THERE. WANNA GO?
BRING IT ON.
OWWW!

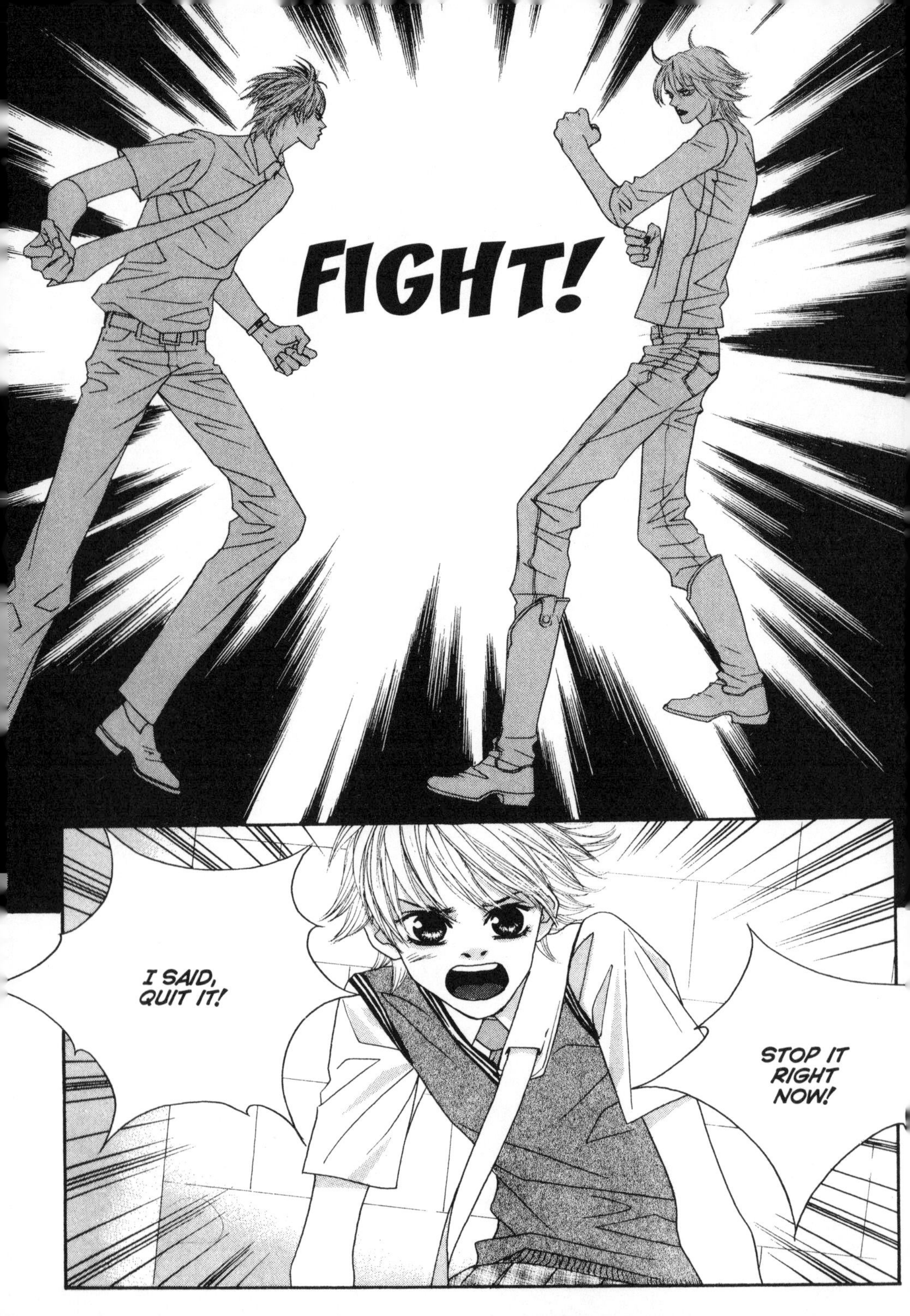
FIGHT!
I SAID, QUIT IT!
STOP IT RIGHT NOW!

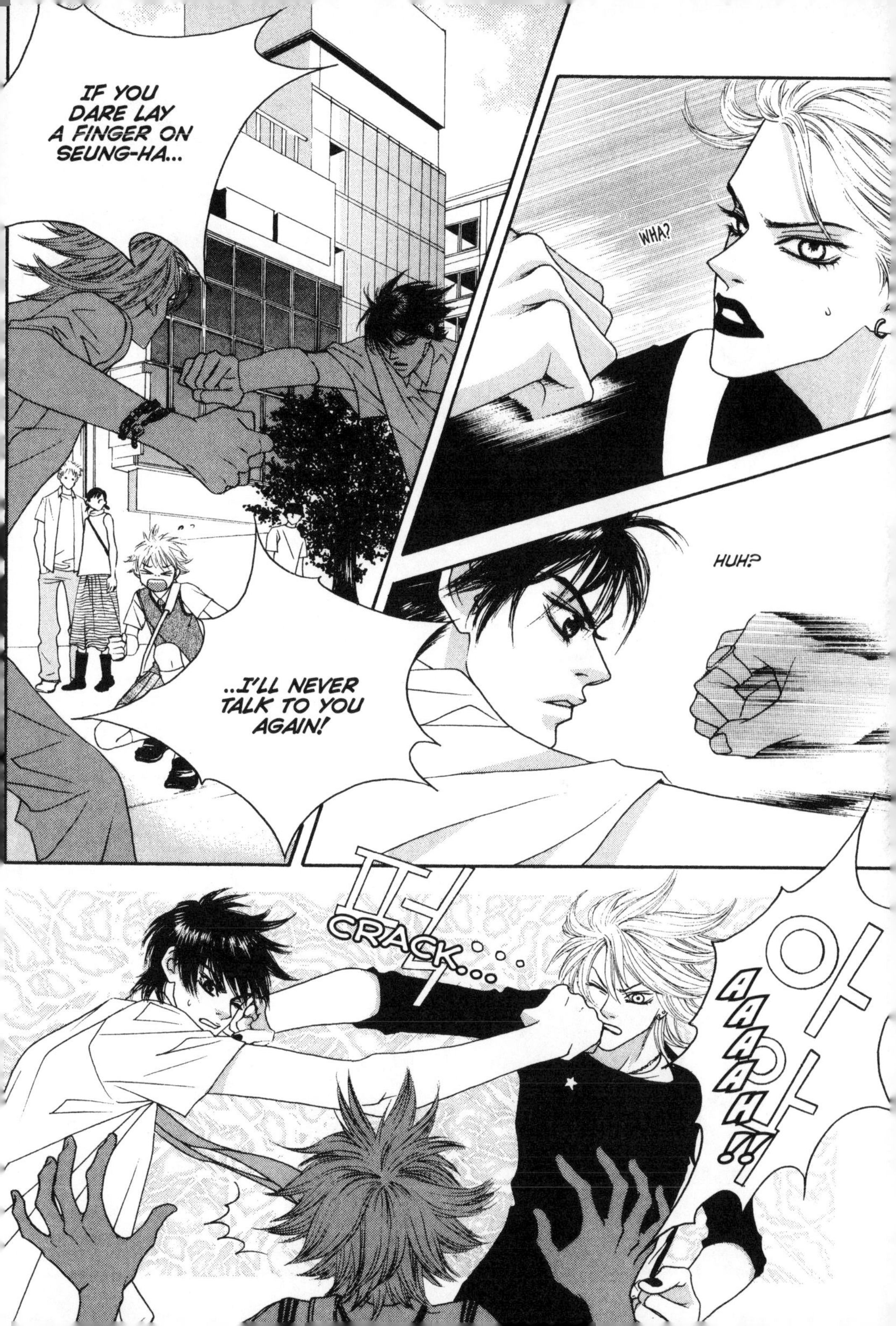
IF YOU DARE LAY A FINGER ON SEUNG-HA...
...I'LL NEVER TALK TO YOU AGAIN!
WHA?
HUH?
CRACK...
AAAAH!!

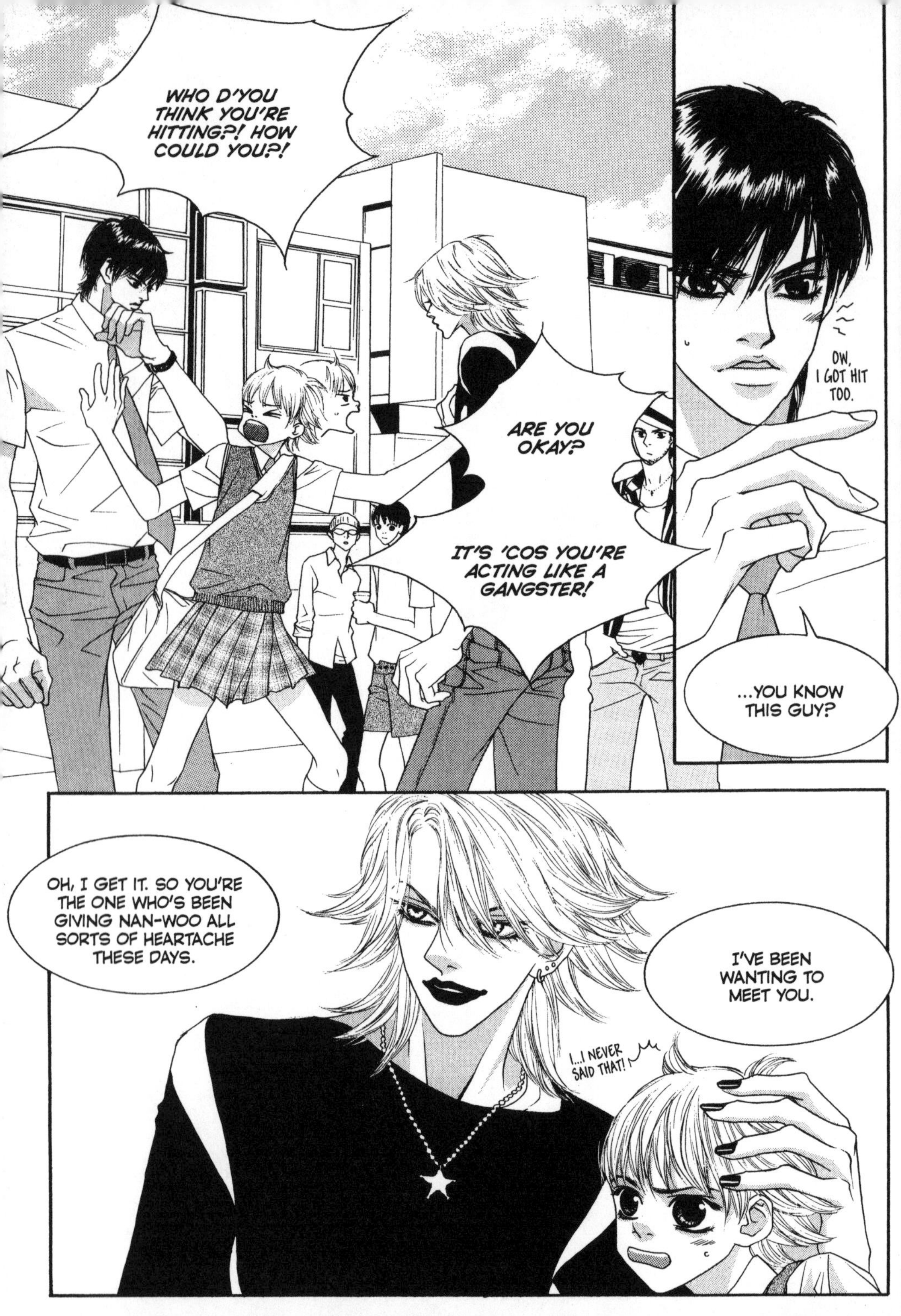
WHO D'YOU THINK YOU'RE HITTING?! HOW COULD YOU?!
ARE YOU OKAY?
IT'S 'COS YOU'RE ACTING LIKE A GANGSTER!
OW, I GOT HIT TOO.
...YOU KNOW THIS GUY?
OH, I GET IT. SO YOU'RE THE ONE WHO'S BEEN GIVING NAN-WOO ALL SORTS OF HEARTACHE THESE DAYS.
I'VE BEEN WANTING TO MEET YOU.
I...I NEVER SAID THAT!

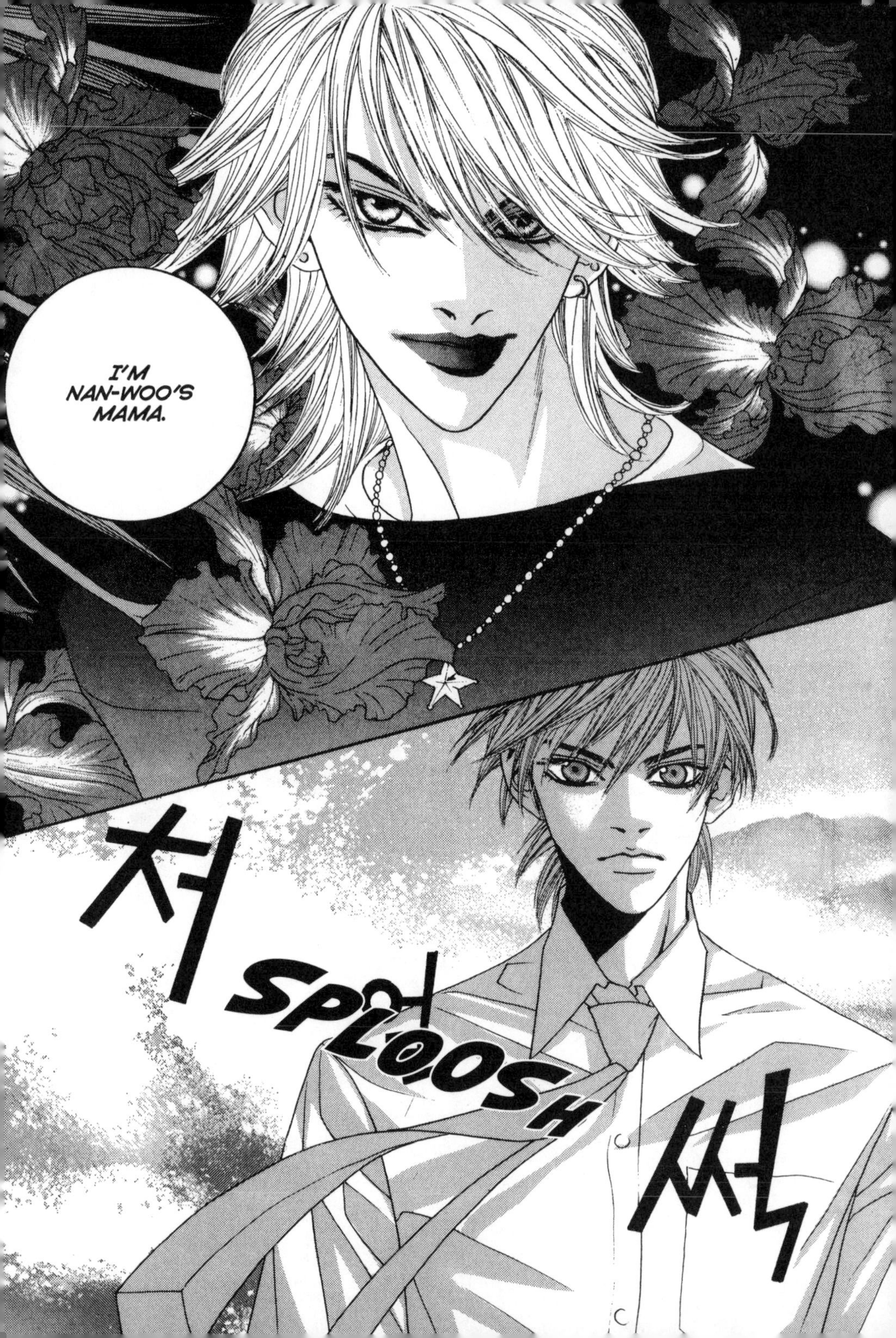
I'M NAN-WOO'S MAMA.
SPLOOSH

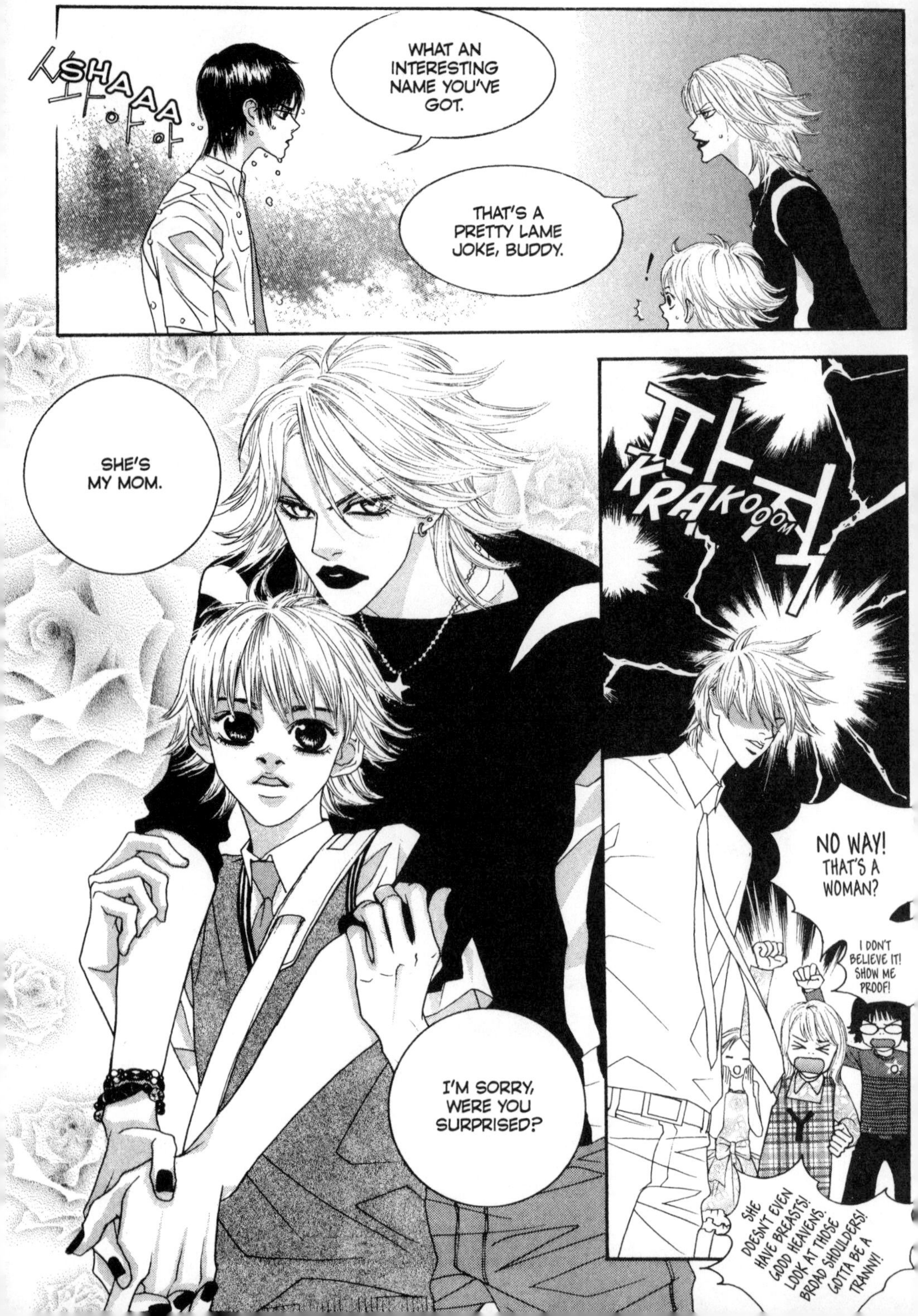
SHAAAA
WHAT AN INTERESTING NAME YOU'VE GOT.
THAT'S A PRETTY LAME JOKE, BUDDY.
SHE'S MY MOM.
I'M SORRY, WERE YOU SURPRISED?
KRAKOOOOM
NO WAY! THAT'S A WOMAN?
I DON'T BELIEVE IT! SHOW ME PROOF!
SHE DOESN'T EVEN HAVE BREASTS!
GOOD HEAVENS. LOOK AT THOSE BROAD SHOULDERS!
GOTTA BE A TRANNY!

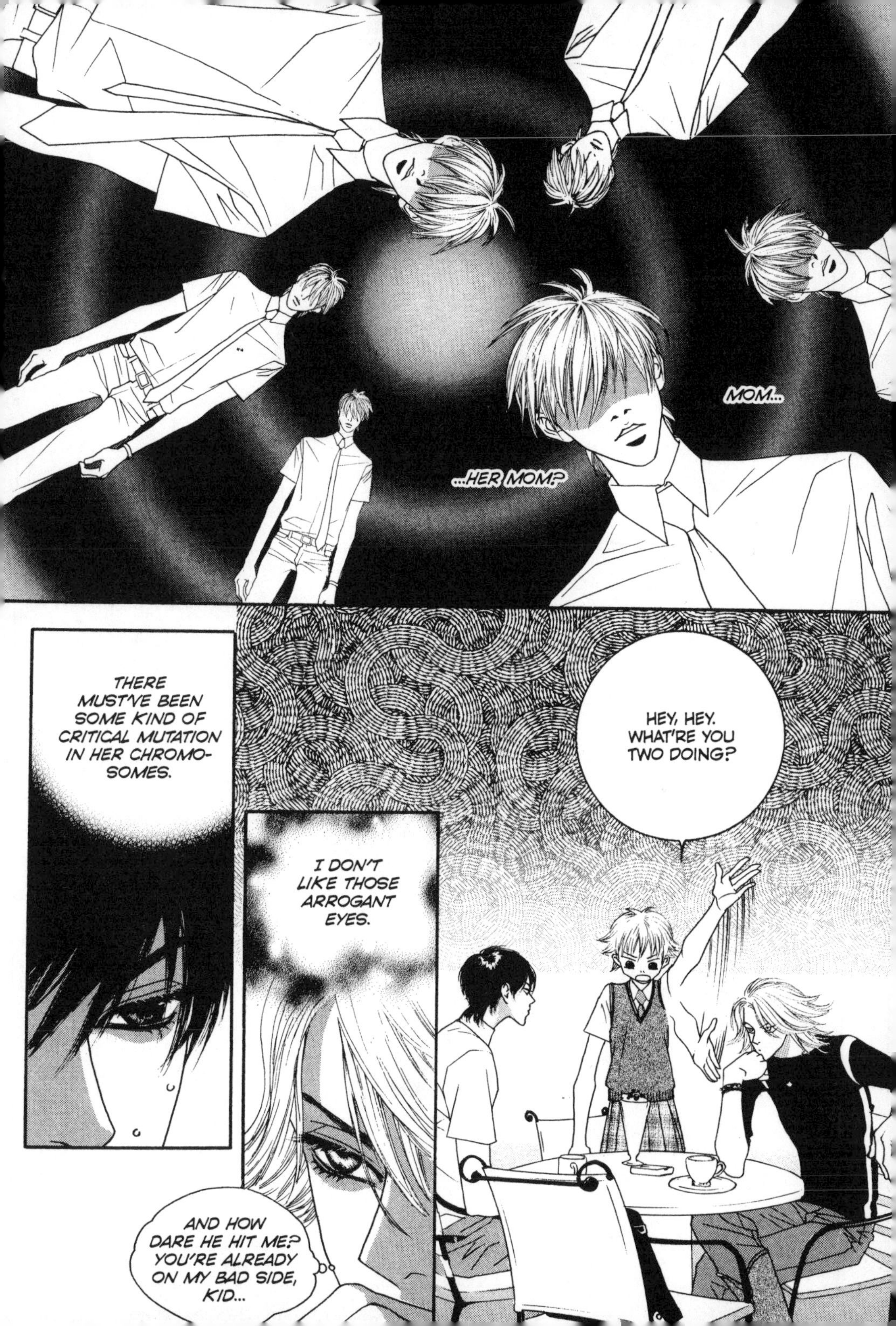
MOM...
...HER MOM?
THERE MUST'VE BEEN SOME KIND OF CRITICAL MUTATION IN HER CHROMO-SOMES.
I DON'T LIKE THOSE ARROGANT EYES.
AND HOW DARE HE HIT ME? YOU'RE ALREADY ON MY BAD SIDE, KID...
HEY, HEY. WHAT'RE YOU TWO DOING?

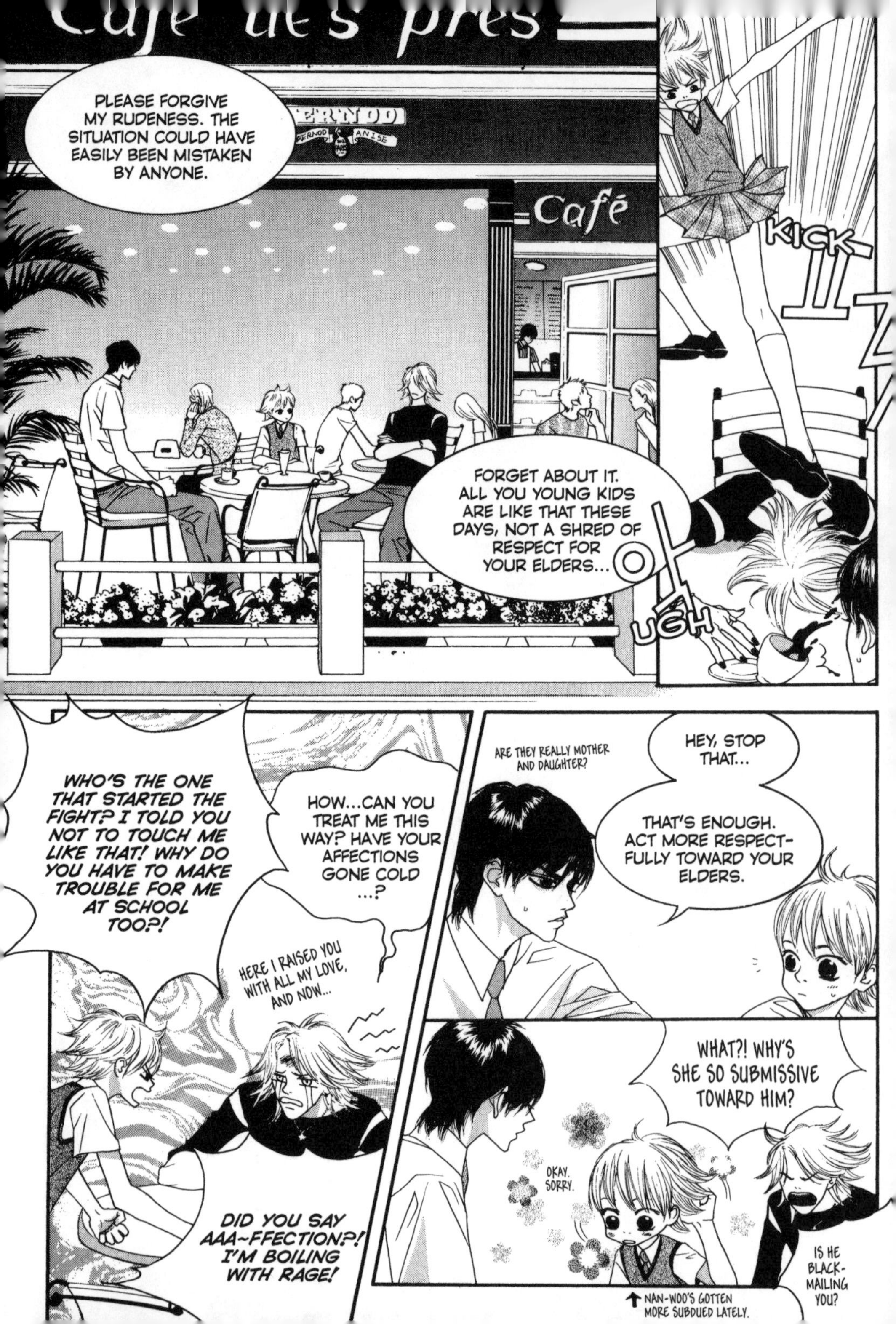
Café
PLEASE FORGIVE MY RUDENESS. THE SITUATION COULD HAVE EASILY BEEN MISTAKEN BY ANYONE.
FORGET ABOUT IT. ALL YOU YOUNG KIDS ARE LIKE THAT THESE DAYS, NOT A SHRED OF RESPECT FOR YOUR ELDERS...
KICK
UGH
WHO'S THE ONE THAT STARTED THE FIGHT? I TOLD YOU NOT TO TOUCH ME LIKE THAT! WHY DO YOU HAVE TO MAKE TROUBLE FOR ME AT SCHOOL TOO?!
HOW...CAN YOU TREAT ME THIS WAY? HAVE YOUR AFFECTIONS GONE COLD ...?
HERE I RAISED YOU WITH ALL MY LOVE, AND NOW...
DID YOU SAY AAA~FFECTION?! I'M BOILING WITH RAGE!
ARE THEY REALLY MOTHER AND DAUGHTER?
HEY, STOP THAT...
THAT'S ENOUGH. ACT MORE RESPECT-FULLY TOWARD YOUR ELDERS.
WHAT?! WHY'S SHE SO SUBMISSIVE TOWARD HIM?
OKAY. SORRY.
IS HE BLACK-MAILING YOU?
NAN-WOO'S GOTTEN MORE SUBDUED LATELY.

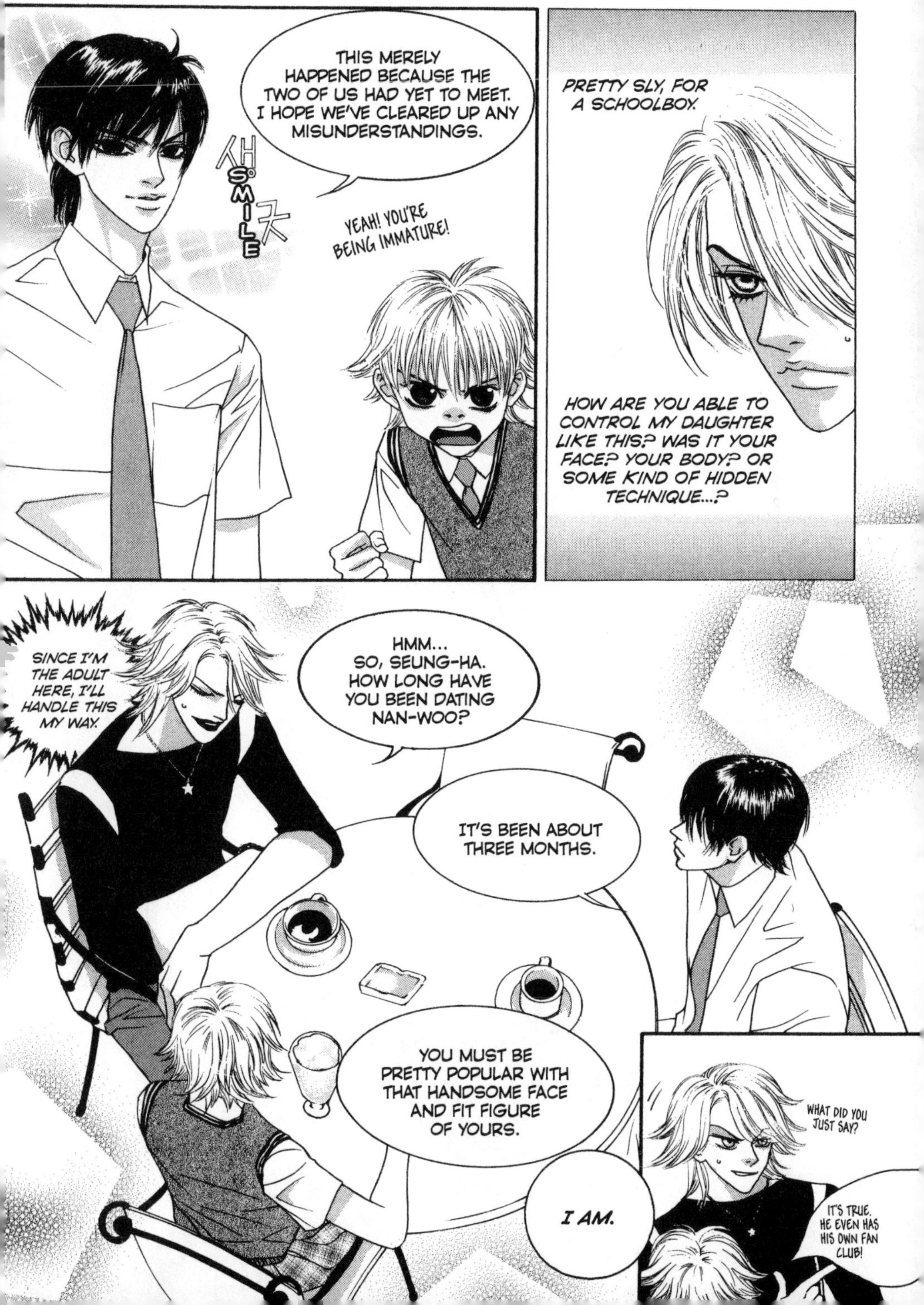

THIS MERELY HAPPENED BECAUSE THE TWO OF US HAD YET TO MEET. I HOPE WE'VE CLEARED UP ANY MISUNDERSTANDINGS.
SMILE
YEAH! YOU'RE BEING IMMATURE!
PRETTY SLY, FOR A SCHOOLBOY.
HOW ARE YOU ABLE TO CONTROL MY DAUGHTER LIKE THIS? WAS IT YOUR FACE? YOUR BODY? OR SOME KIND OF HIDDEN TECHNIQUE...?
SINCE I'M THE ADULT HERE, I'LL HANDLE THIS MY WAY.
HMM... SO, SEUNG-HA. HOW LONG HAVE YOU BEEN DATING NAN-WOO?
IT'S BEEN ABOUT THREE MONTHS.
YOU MUST BE PRETTY POPULAR WITH THAT HANDSOME FACE AND FIT FIGURE OF YOURS.
I AM.
WHAT DID YOU JUST SAY?
IT'S TRUE. HE EVEN HAS HIS OWN FAN CLUB!

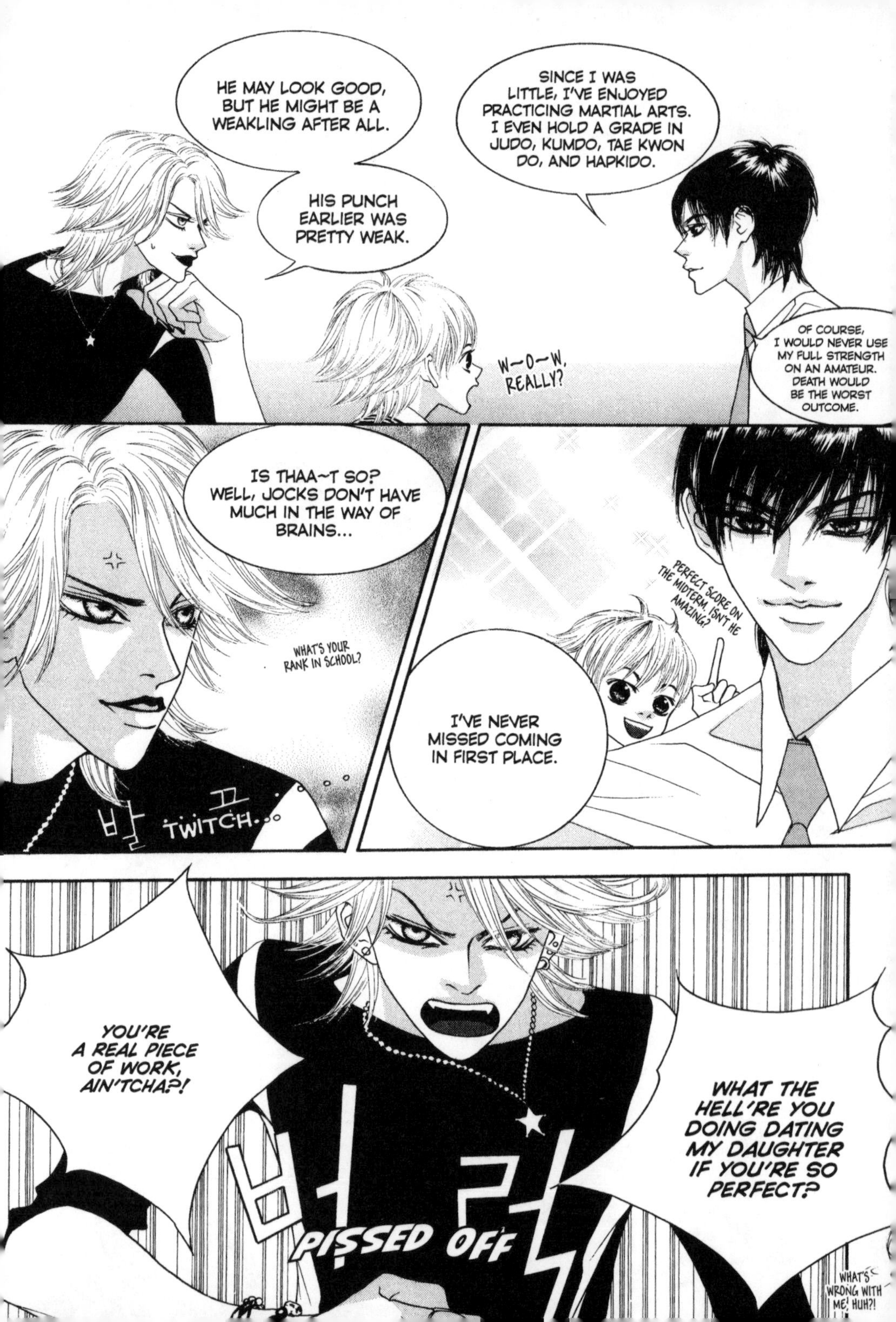
HE MAY LOOK GOOD, BUT HE MIGHT BE A WEAKLING AFTER ALL.
HIS PUNCH EARLIER WAS PRETTY WEAK.
SINCE I WAS LITTLE, I'VE ENJOYED PRACTICING MARTIAL ARTS. I EVEN HOLD A GRADE IN JUDO, KUMDO, TAE KWON DO, AND HAPKIDO.
W~O~W, REALLY?
OF COURSE, I WOULD NEVER USE MY FULL STRENGTH ON AN AMATEUR. DEATH WOULD BE THE WORST OUTCOME.
IS THAA~T SO? WELL, JOCKS DON'T HAVE MUCH IN THE WAY OF BRAINS...
WHAT'S YOUR RANK IN SCHOOL?
TWITCH...
PERFECT SCORE ON THE MIDTERM. ISN'T HE AMAZING?
I'VE NEVER MISSED COMING IN FIRST PLACE.
YOU'RE A REAL PIECE OF WORK, AIN'TCHA?!
WHAT THE HELL'RE YOU DOING DATING MY DAUGHTER IF YOU'RE SO PERFECT?
PISSED OFF
WHAT'S WRONG WITH ME, HUH?!

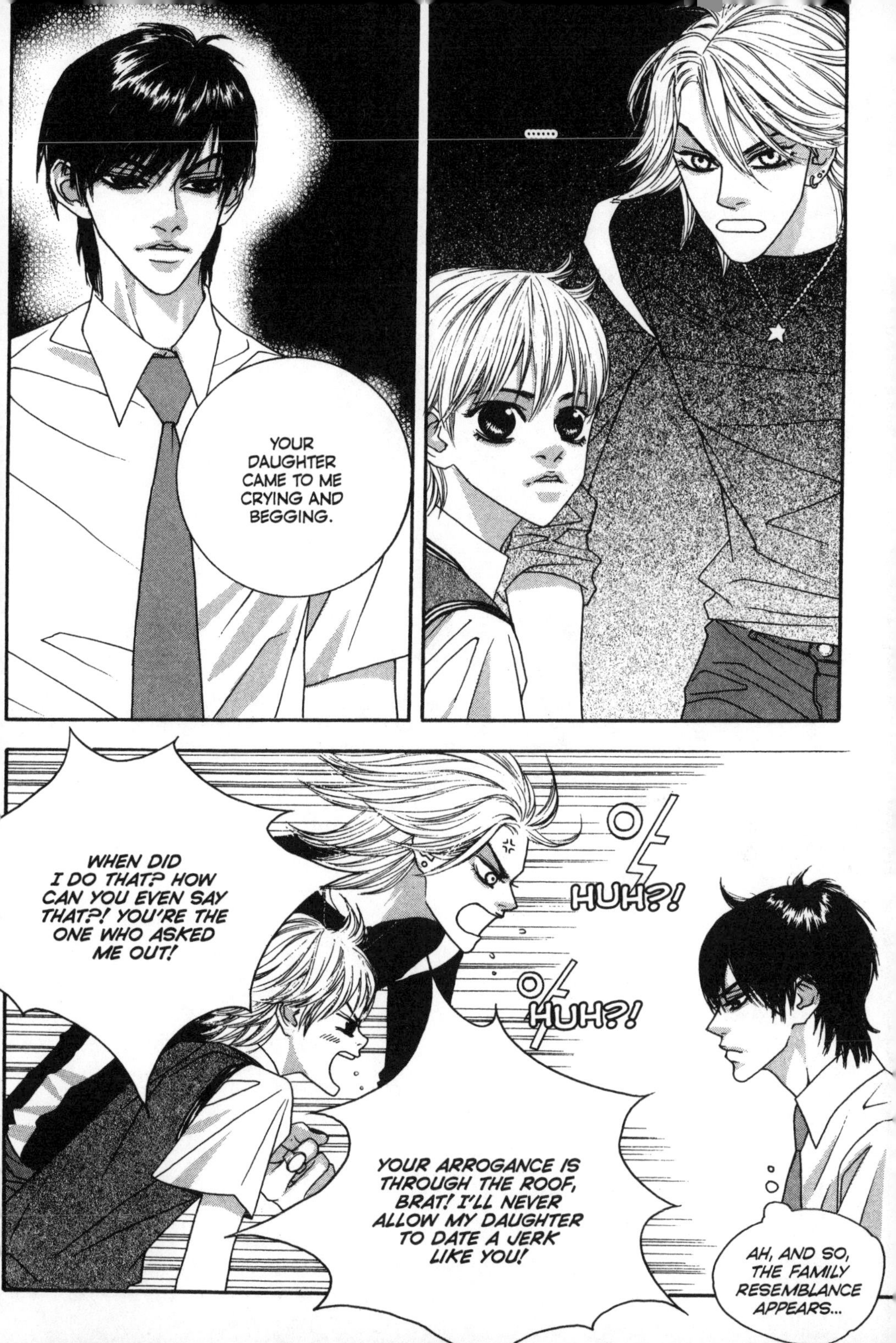

YOUR DAUGHTER CAME TO ME CRYING AND BEGGING.
......
WHEN DID I DO THAT? HOW CAN YOU EVEN SAY THAT?! YOU'RE THE ONE WHO ASKED ME OUT!
HUH?!
HUH?!
YOUR ARROGANCE IS THROUGH THE ROOF, BRAT! I'LL NEVER ALLOW MY DAUGHTER TO DATE A JERK LIKE YOU!
AH, AND SO, THE FAMILY RESEMBLANCE APPEARS...

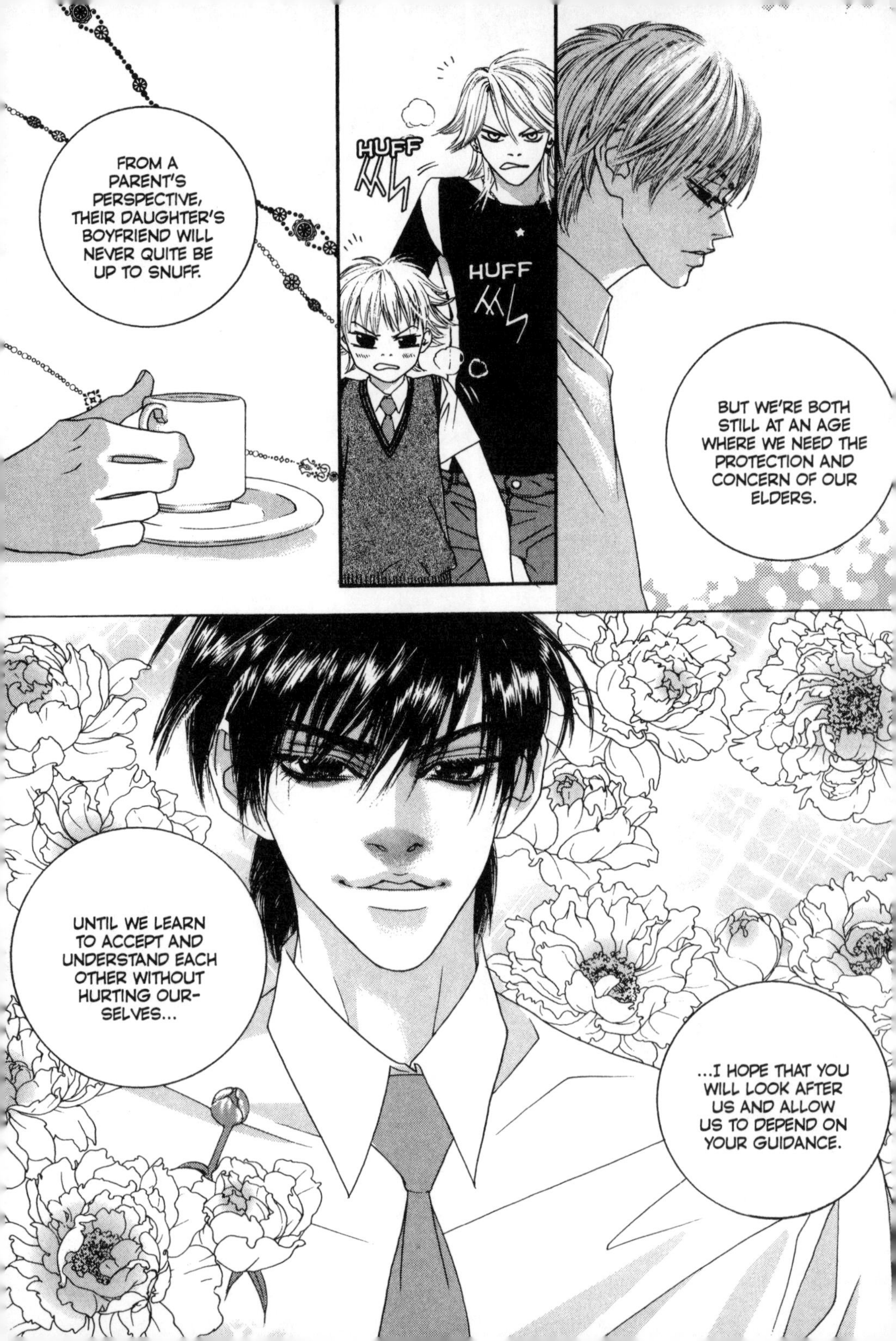
FROM A PARENT'S PERSPECTIVE, THEIR DAUGHTER'S BOYFRIEND WILL NEVER QUITE BE UP TO SNUFF.
HUFF
HUFF
BUT WE'RE BOTH STILL AT AN AGE WHERE WE NEED THE PROTECTION AND CONCERN OF OUR ELDERS.
UNTIL WE LEARN TO ACCEPT AND UNDERSTAND EACH OTHER WITHOUT HURTING OUR-SELVES...
...I HOPE THAT YOU WILL LOOK AFTER US AND ALLOW US TO DEPEND ON YOUR GUIDANCE.

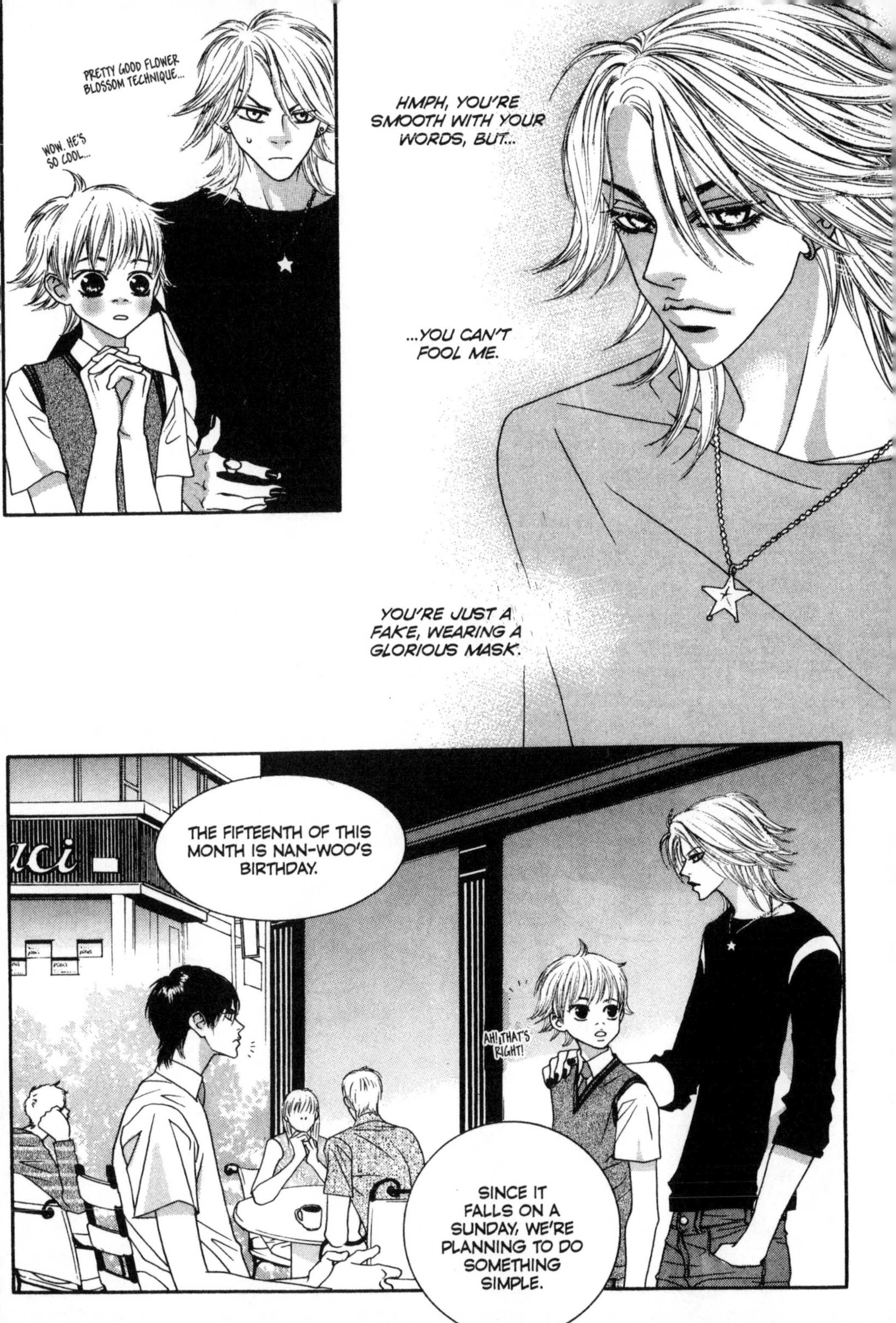
PRETTY GOOD FLOWER BLOSSOM TECHNIQUE...
WOW. HE'S SO COOL...
HMPH, YOU'RE SMOOTH WITH YOUR WORDS, BUT...
...YOU CAN'T FOOL ME.
YOU'RE JUST A FAKE, WEARING A GLORIOUS MASK.
THE FIFTEENTH OF THIS MONTH IS NAN-WOO'S BIRTHDAY.
AH! THAT'S RIGHT!
SINCE IT FALLS ON A SUNDAY, WE'RE PLANNING TO DO SOMETHING SIMPLE.

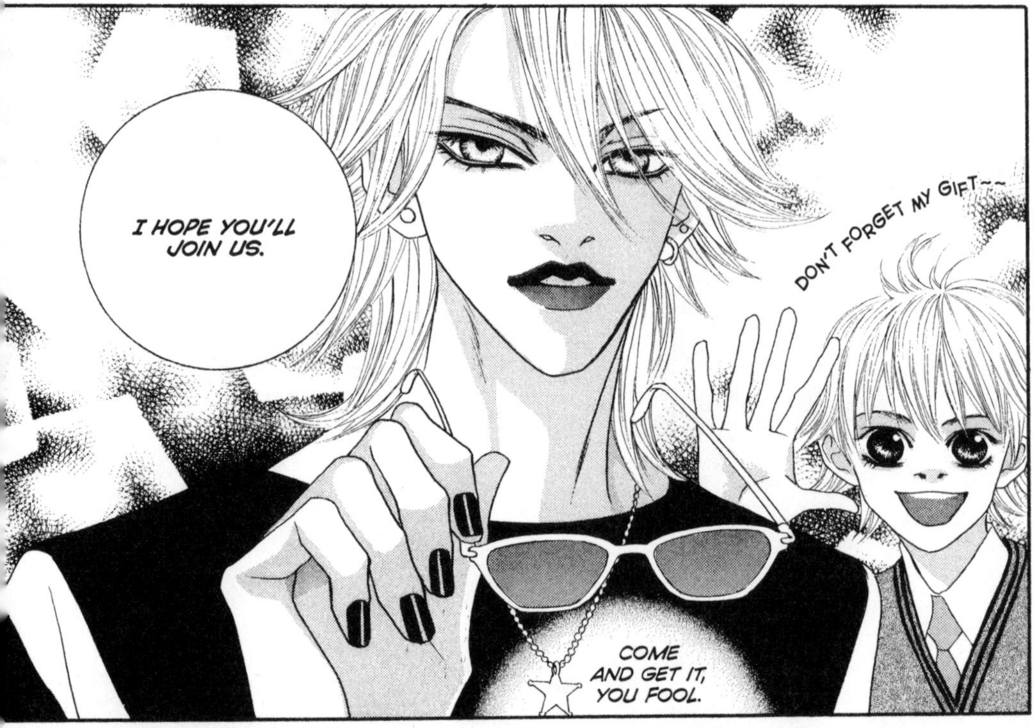
I HOPE YOU'LL JOIN US.
DON'T FORGET MY GIFT~~
COME AND GET IT, YOU FOOL.
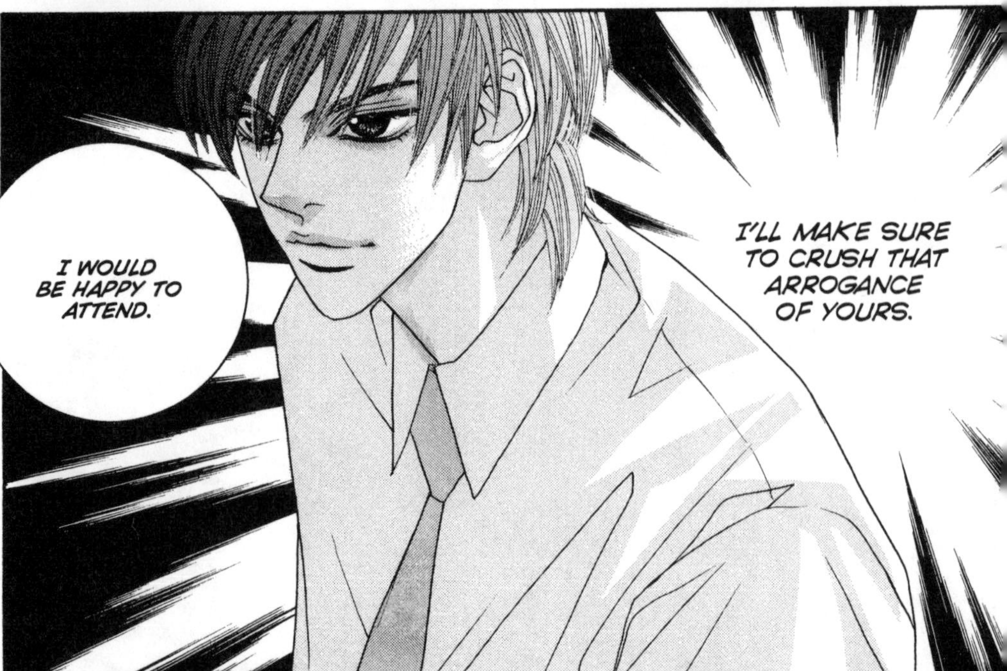
I WOULD BE HAPPY TO ATTEND.
I'LL MAKE SURE TO CRUSH THAT ARROGANCE OF YOURS.

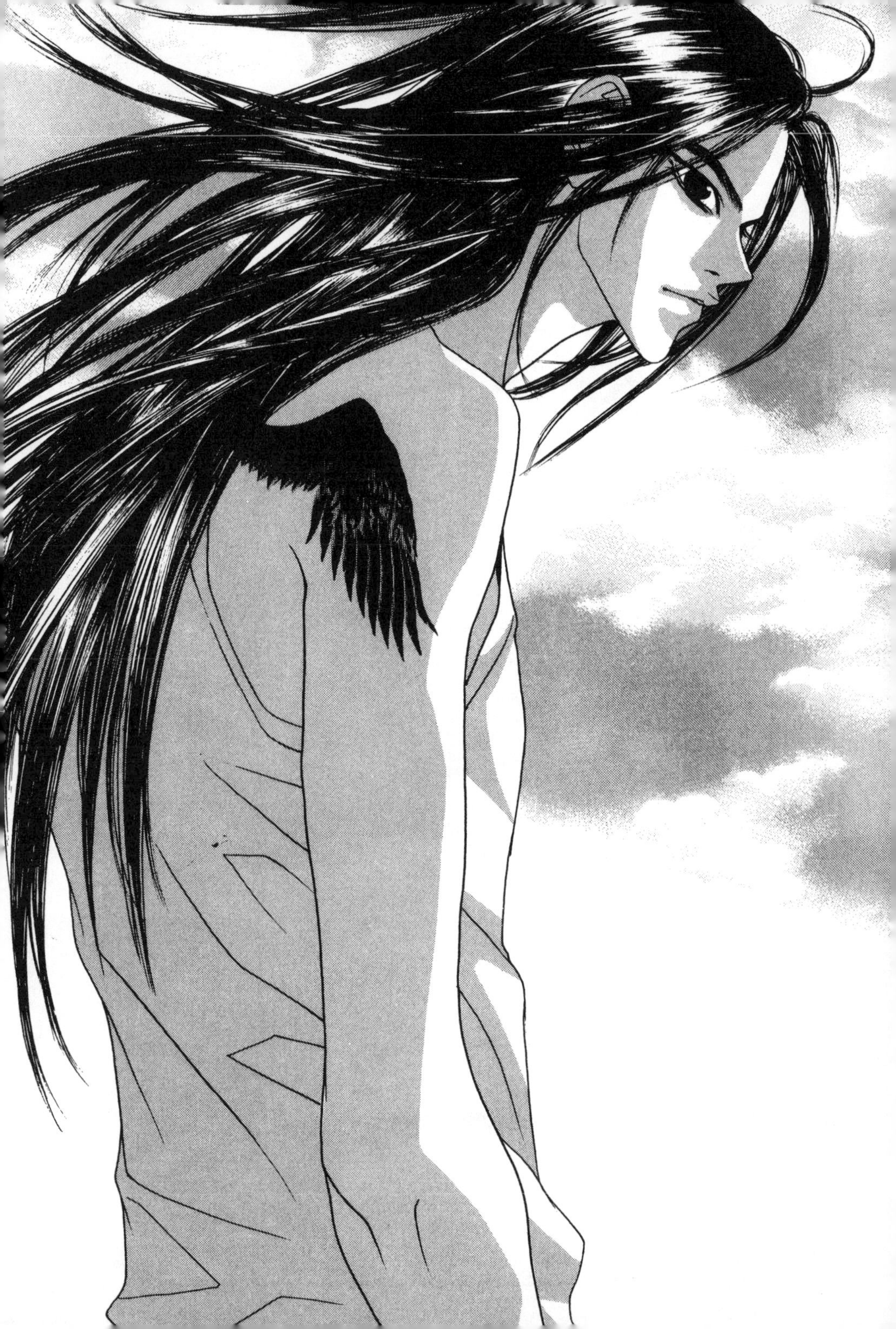

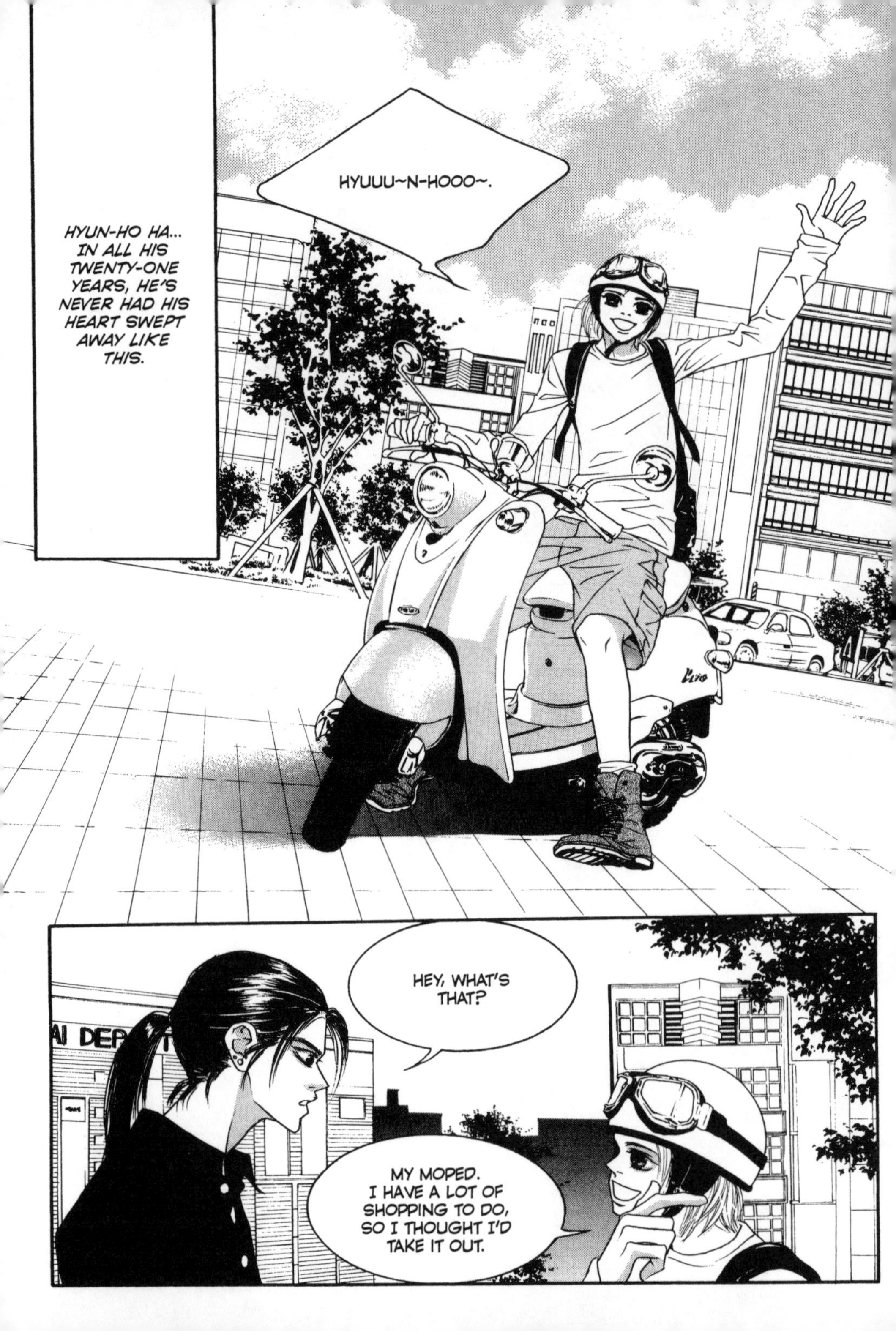
HYUN-HO HA... IN ALL HIS TWENTY-ONE YEARS, HE'S NEVER HAD HIS HEART SWEPT AWAY LIKE THIS.
HYUUU~N-HOOO~.
AI DEP
HEY, WHAT'S THAT?
MY MOPED. I HAVE A LOT OF SHOPPING TO DO, SO I THOUGHT I'D TAKE IT OUT.

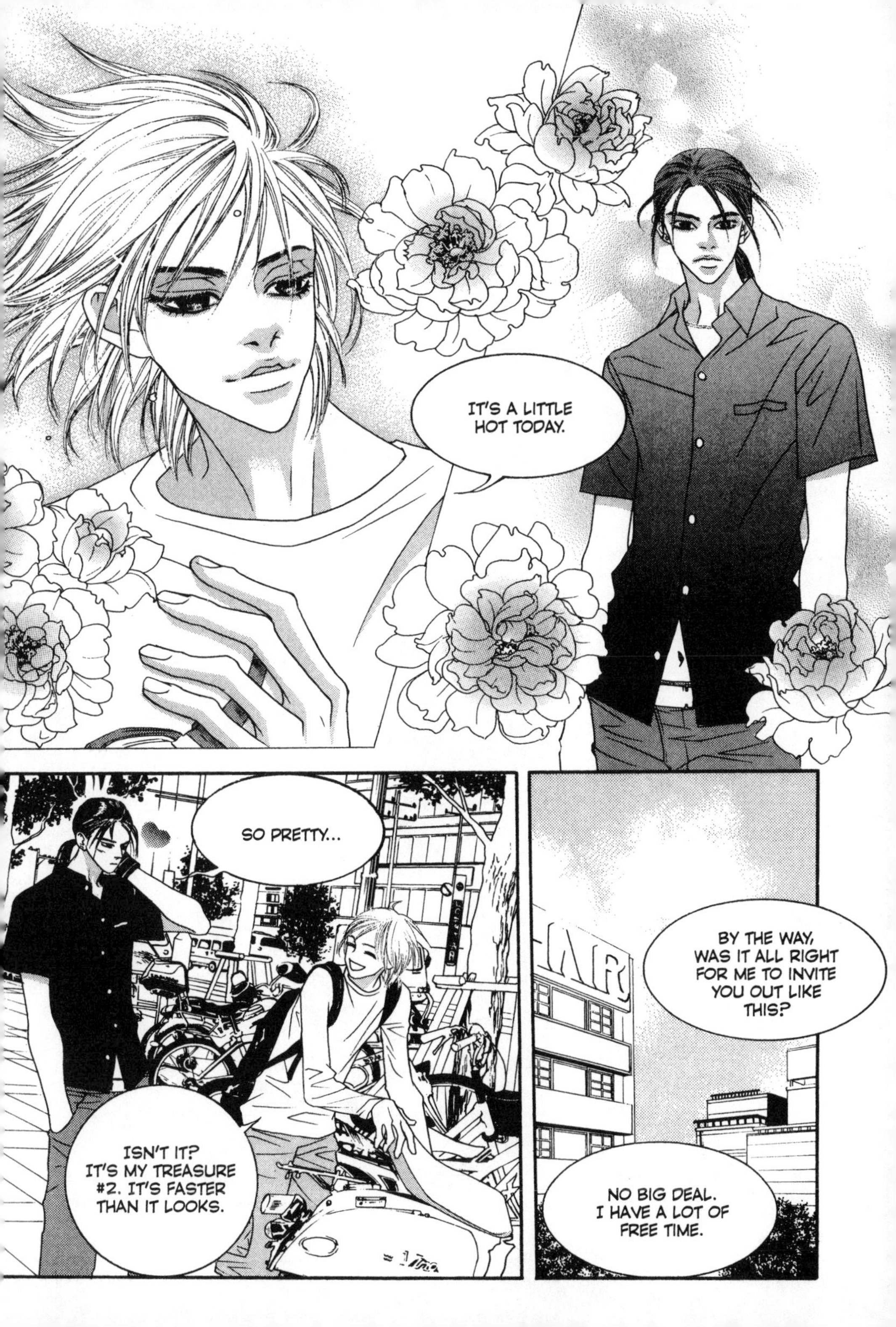
IT'S A LITTLE HOT TODAY.
SO PRETTY...
ISN'T IT? IT'S MY TREASURE #2. IT'S FASTER THAN IT LOOKS.
BY THE WAY, WAS IT ALL RIGHT FOR ME TO INVITE YOU OUT LIKE THIS?
NO BIG DEAL. I HAVE A LOT OF FREE TIME.

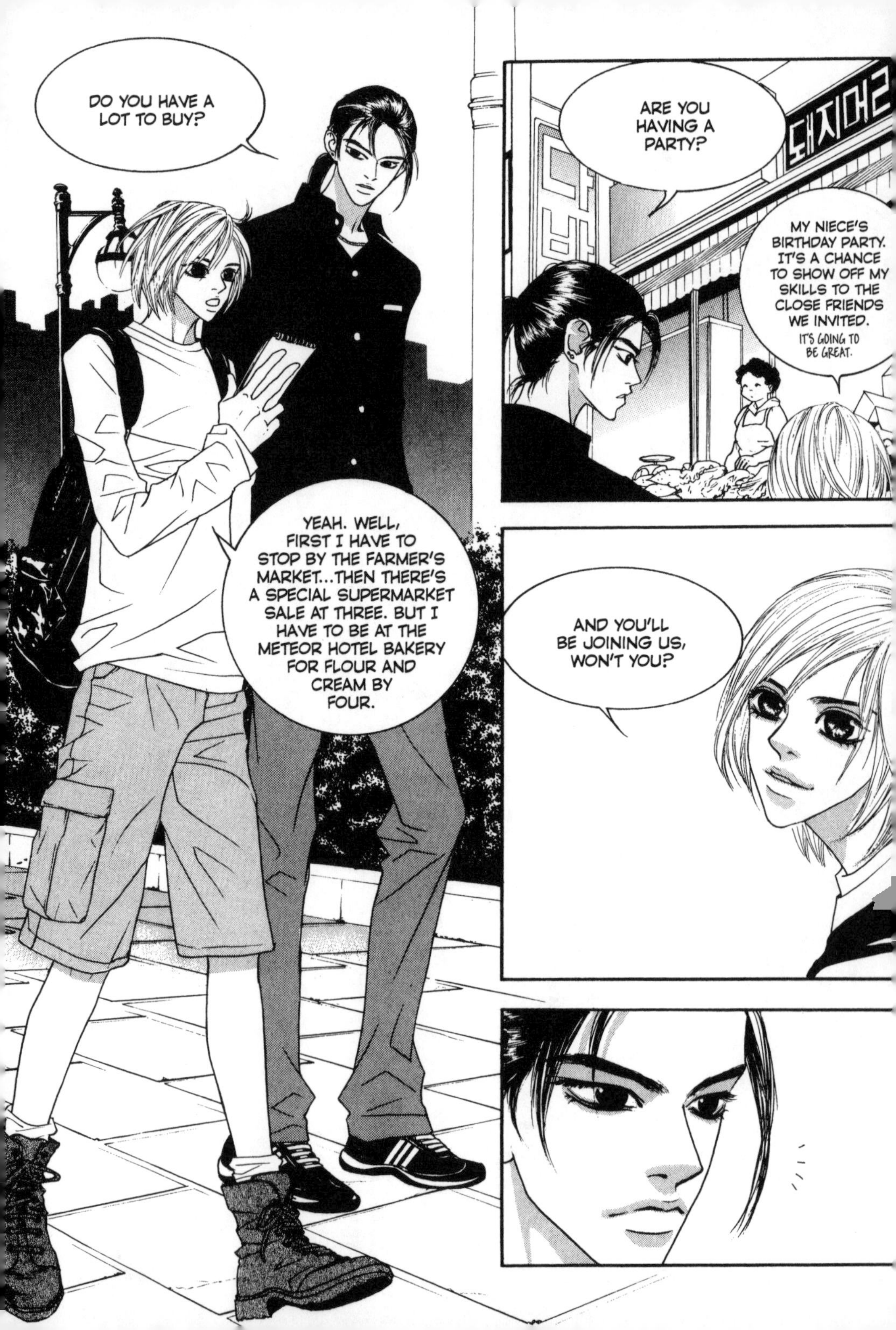
DO YOU HAVE A LOT TO BUY?
YEAH. WELL, FIRST I HAVE TO STOP BY THE FARMER'S MARKET...THEN THERE'S A SPECIAL SUPERMARKET SALE AT THREE. BUT I HAVE TO BE AT THE METEOR HOTEL BAKERY FOR FLOUR AND CREAM BY FOUR.
ARE YOU HAVING A PARTY?
MY NIECE'S BIRTHDAY PARTY. IT'S A CHANCE TO SHOW OFF MY SKILLS TO THE CLOSE FRIENDS WE INVITED.
IT'S GOING TO BE GREAT.
AND YOU'LL BE JOINING US, WON'T YOU?

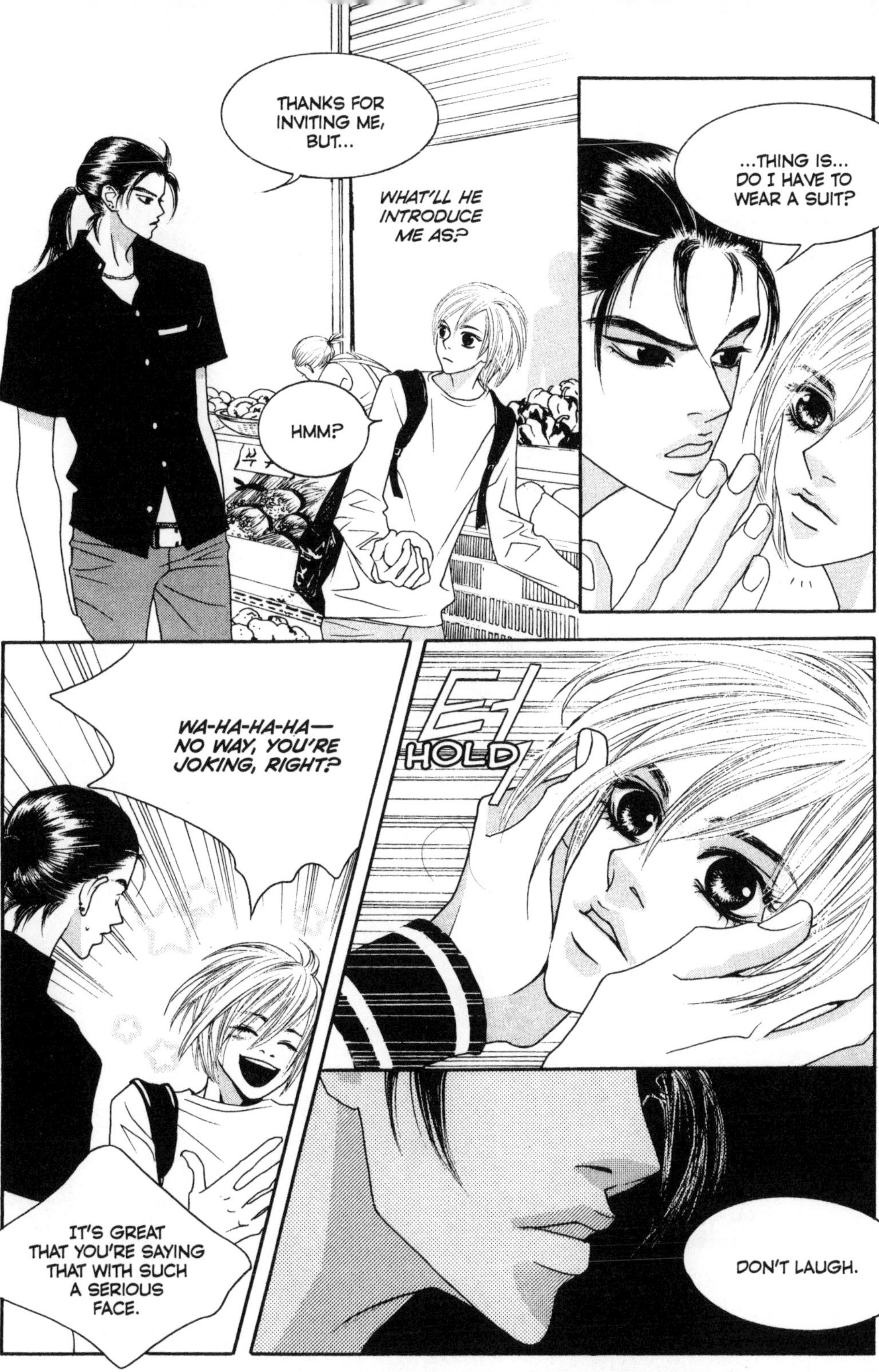
THANKS FOR INVITING ME, BUT...
WHAT'LL HE INTRODUCE ME AS?
HMM?
...THING IS... DO I HAVE TO WEAR A SUIT?
WA-HA-HA-HA— NO WAY, YOU'RE JOKING, RIGHT?
IT'S GREAT THAT YOU'RE SAYING THAT WITH SUCH A SERIOUS FACE.
HOLD
DON'T LAUGH.

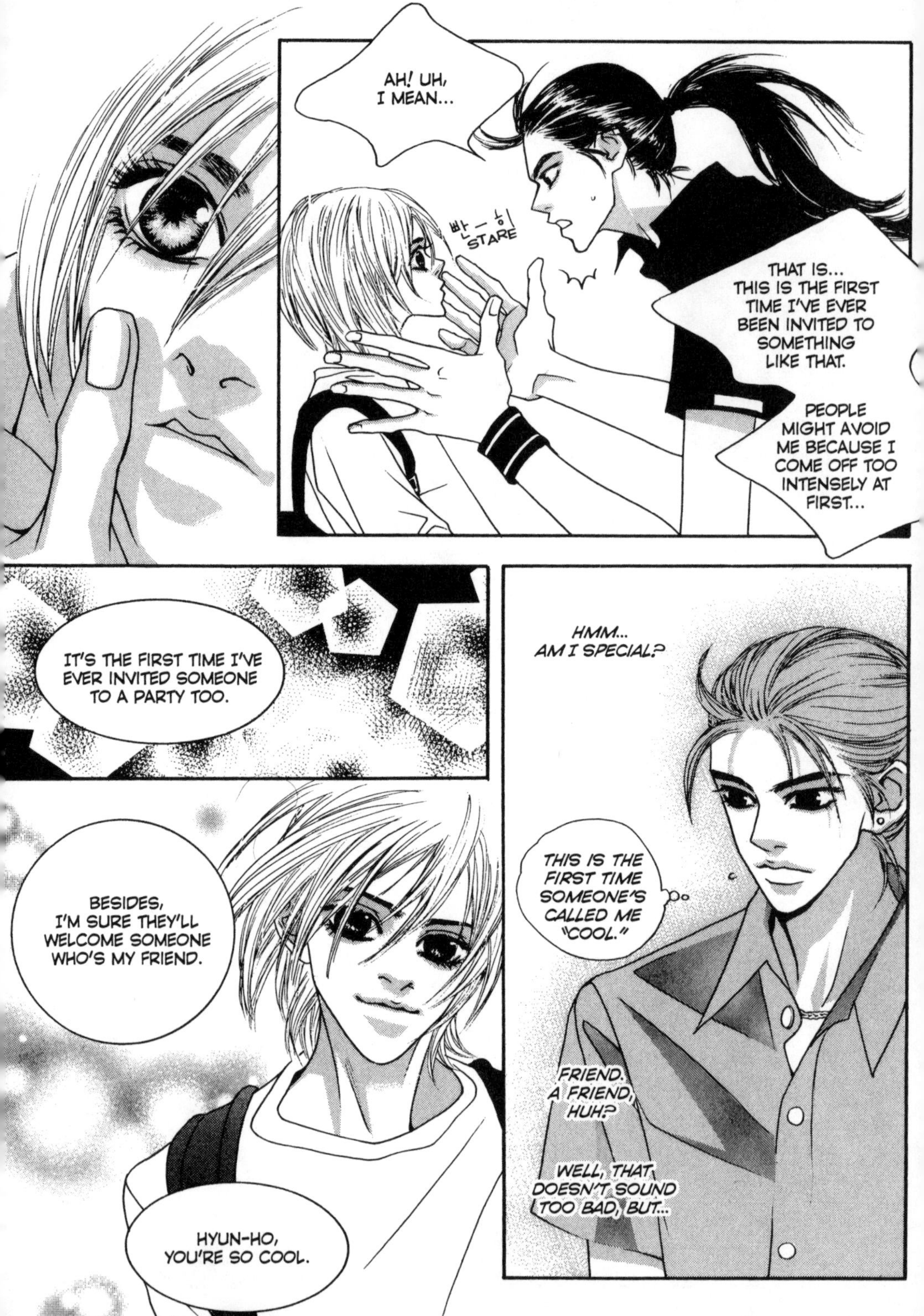

AH! UH, I MEAN...
빤―히
STARE
THAT IS... THIS IS THE FIRST TIME I'VE EVER BEEN INVITED TO SOMETHING LIKE THAT.
PEOPLE MIGHT AVOID ME BECAUSE I COME OFF TOO INTENSELY AT FIRST...
IT'S THE FIRST TIME I'VE EVER INVITED SOMEONE TO A PARTY TOO.
HMM... AM I SPECIAL?
BESIDES, I'M SURE THEY'LL WELCOME SOMEONE WHO'S MY FRIEND.
HYUN-HO, YOU'RE SO COOL.
THIS IS THE FIRST TIME SOMEONE'S CALLED ME "COOL."
FRIEND. A FRIEND, HUH?
WELL, THAT DOESN'T SOUND TOO BAD, BUT...

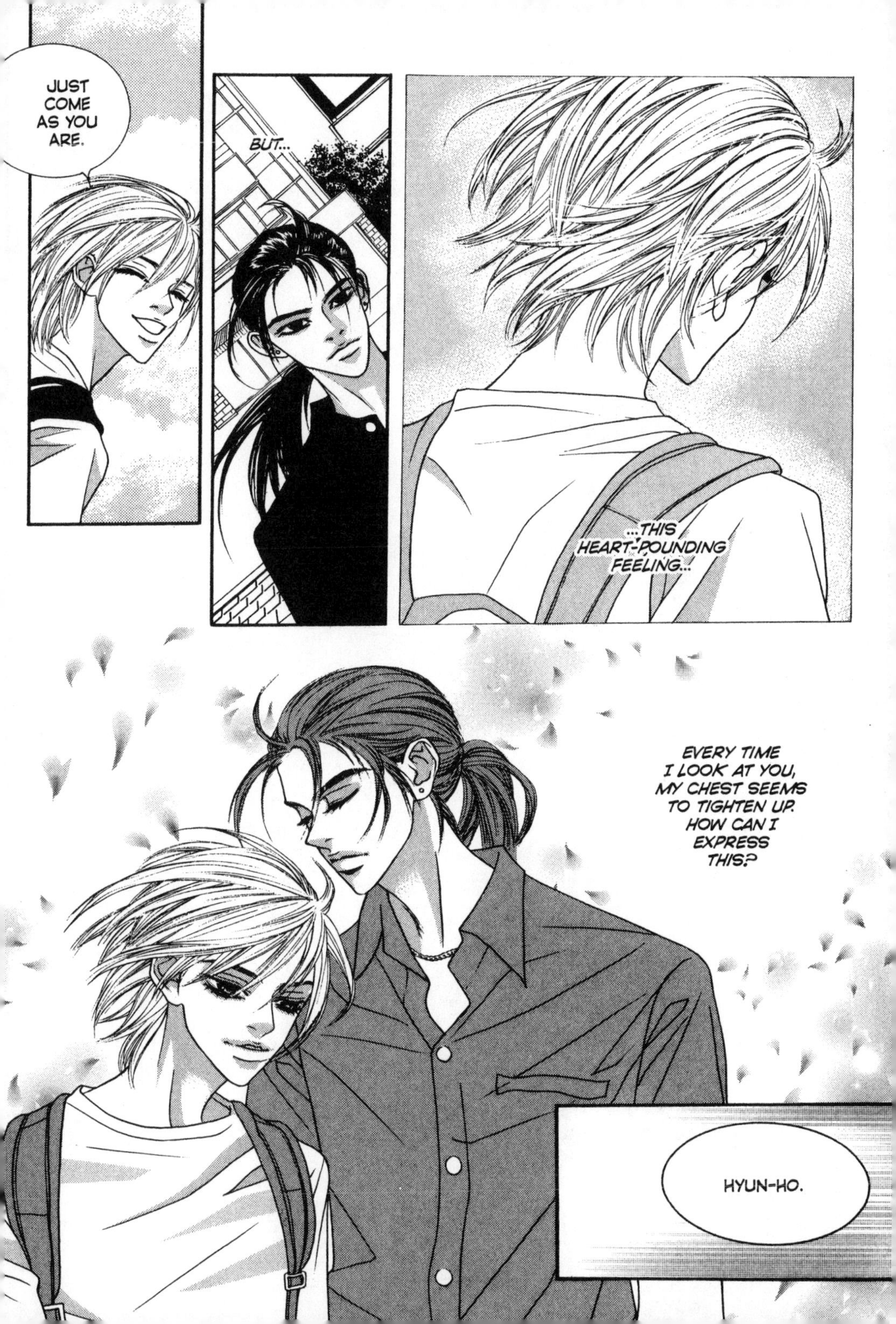
JUST COME AS YOU ARE.
BUT...
...THIS HEART-POUNDING FEELING...
EVERY TIME I LOOK AT YOU, MY CHEST SEEMS TO TIGHTEN UP. HOW CAN I EXPRESS THIS?
HYUN-HO.

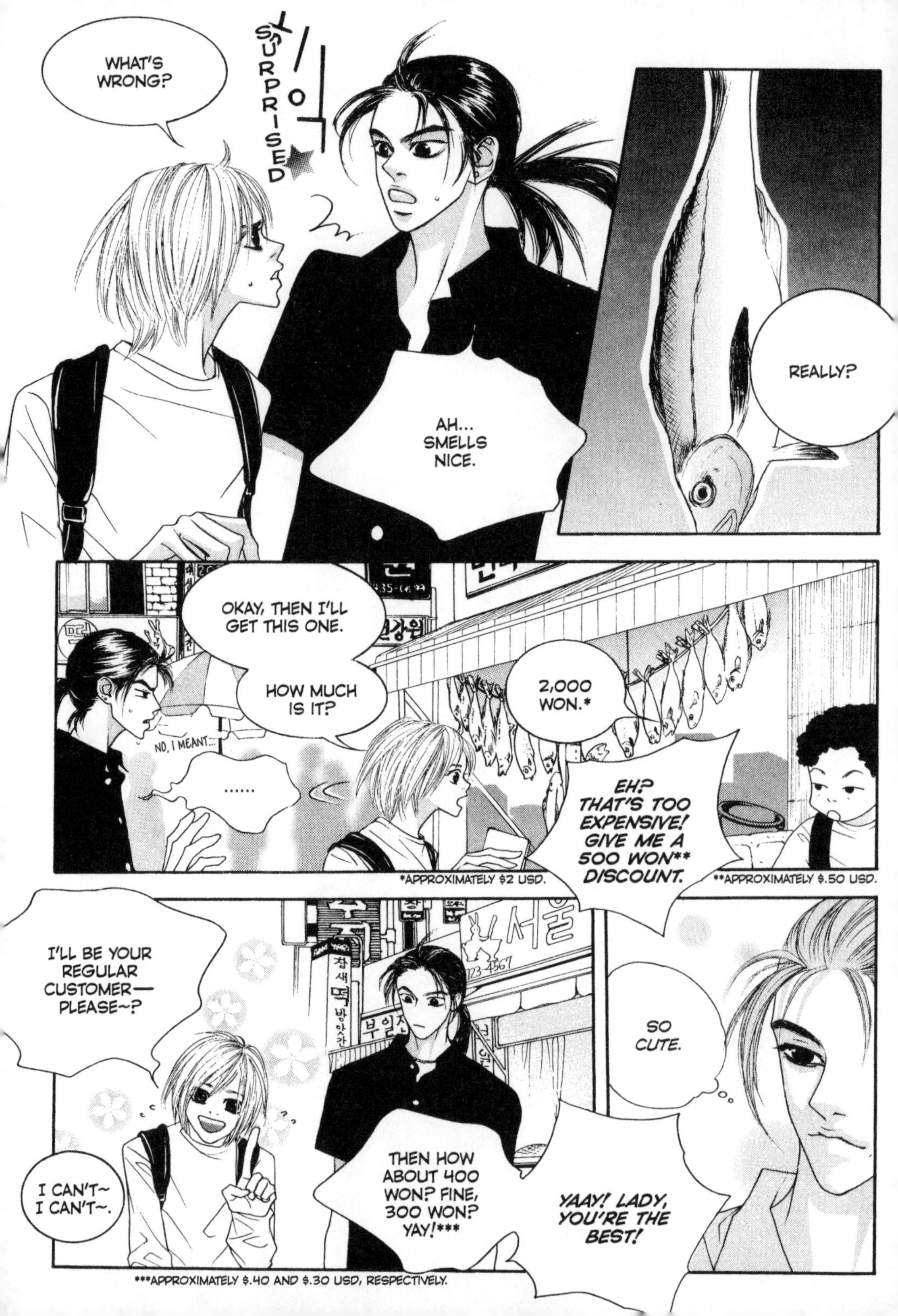
WHAT'S WRONG?
SURPRISED
AH... SMELLS NICE.
REALLY?
OKAY, THEN I'LL GET THIS ONE.
HOW MUCH IS IT?
NO, I MEANT...
......
2,000 WON.*
EH? THAT'S TOO EXPENSIVE! GIVE ME A 500 WON** DISCOUNT.
*APPROXIMATELY $2 USD.
**APPROXIMATELY $.50 USD.
I'LL BE YOUR REGULAR CUSTOMER— PLEASE~?
I CAN'T~ I CAN'T~.
THEN HOW ABOUT 400 WON? FINE, 300 WON? YAY!***
YAAY! LADY, YOU'RE THE BEST!
SO CUTE.
***APPROXIMATELY $.40 AND $.30 USD, RESPECTIVELY.

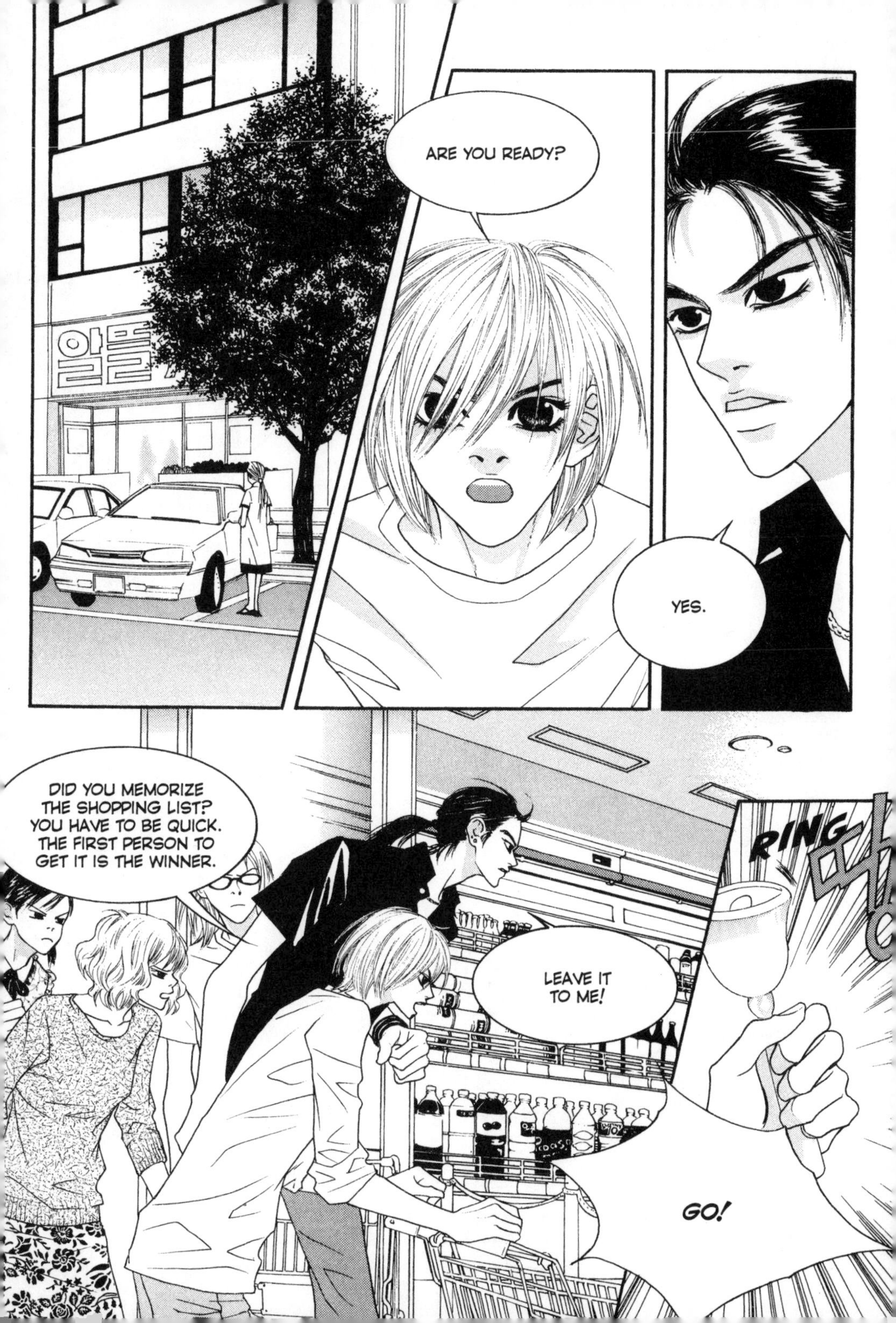
ARE YOU READY?
YES.
DID YOU MEMORIZE THE SHOPPING LIST? YOU HAVE TO BE QUICK. THE FIRST PERSON TO GET IT IS THE WINNER.
LEAVE IT TO ME!
RING
GO!

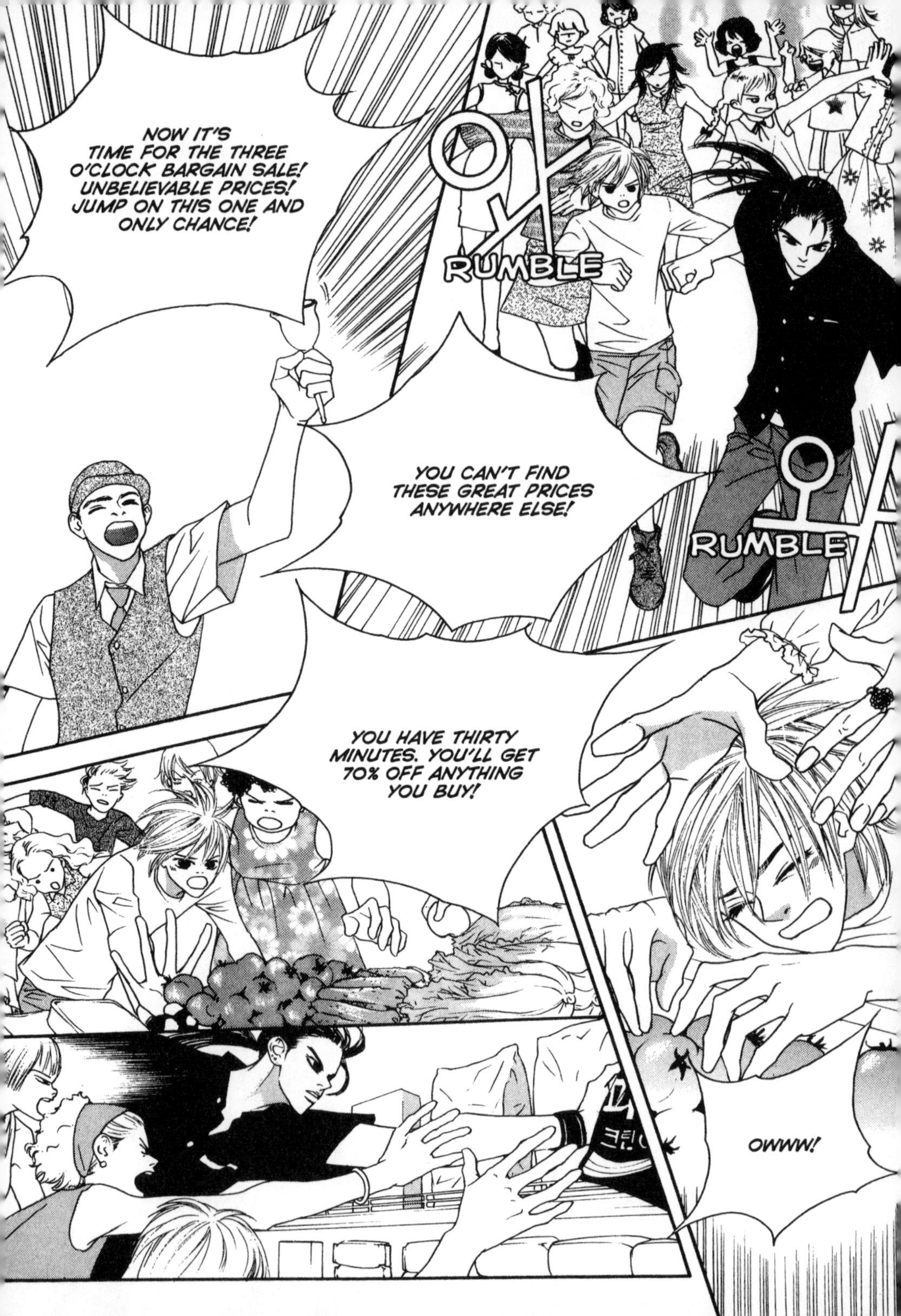
NOW IT'S TIME FOR THE THREE O'CLOCK BARGAIN SALE! UNBELIEVABLE PRICES! JUMP ON THIS ONE AND ONLY CHANCE!
RUMBLE
YOU CAN'T FIND THESE GREAT PRICES ANYWHERE ELSE!
RUMBLE
YOU HAVE THIRTY MINUTES. YOU'LL GET 70% OFF ANYTHING YOU BUY!
OWWW!

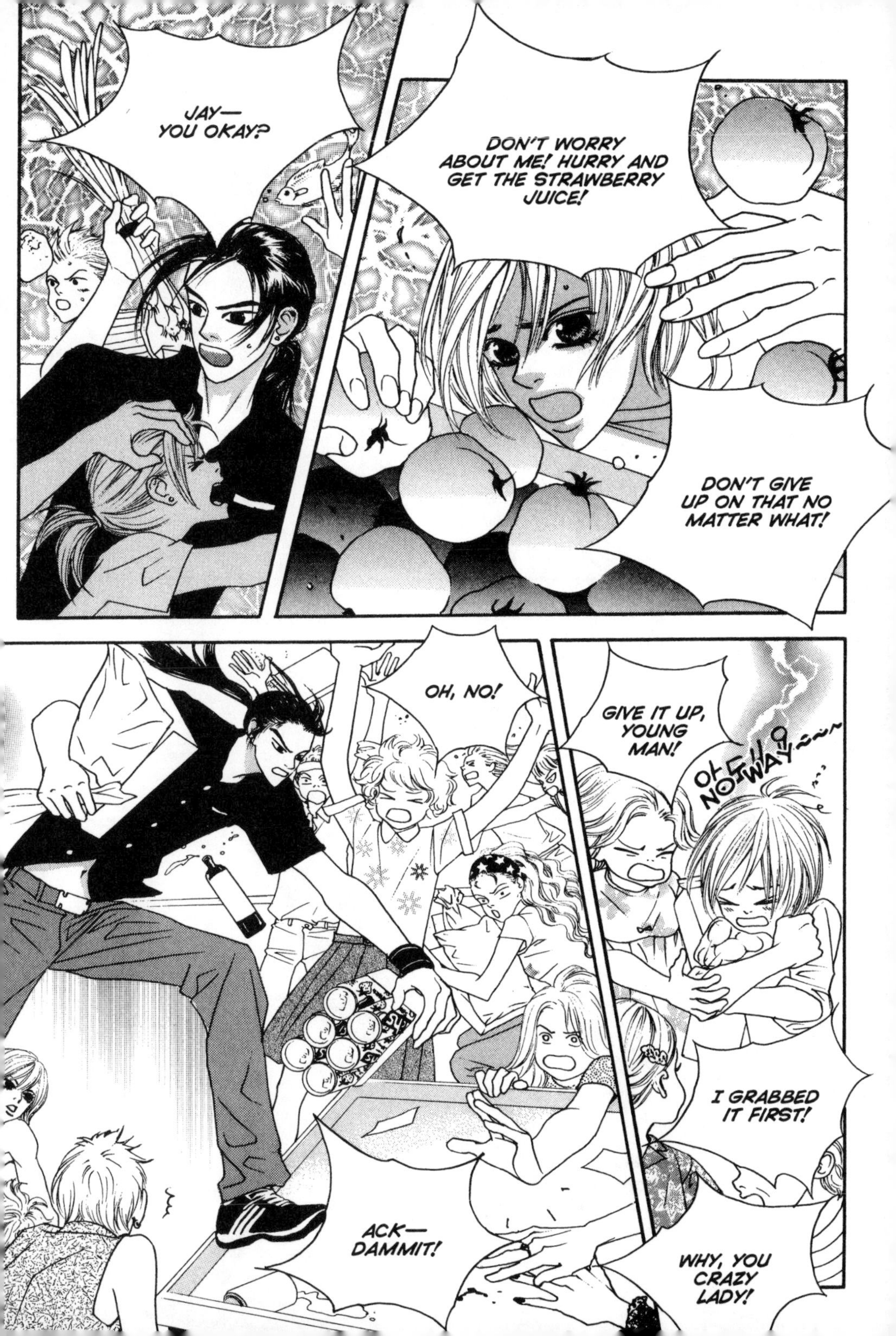
JAY— YOU OKAY?
DON'T WORRY ABOUT ME! HURRY AND GET THE STRAWBERRY JUICE!
DON'T GIVE UP ON THAT NO MATTER WHAT!
OH, NO!
ACK— DAMMIT!
GIVE IT UP, YOUNG MAN!
OH NO WAY
I GRABBED IT FIRST!
WHY, YOU CRAZY LADY!

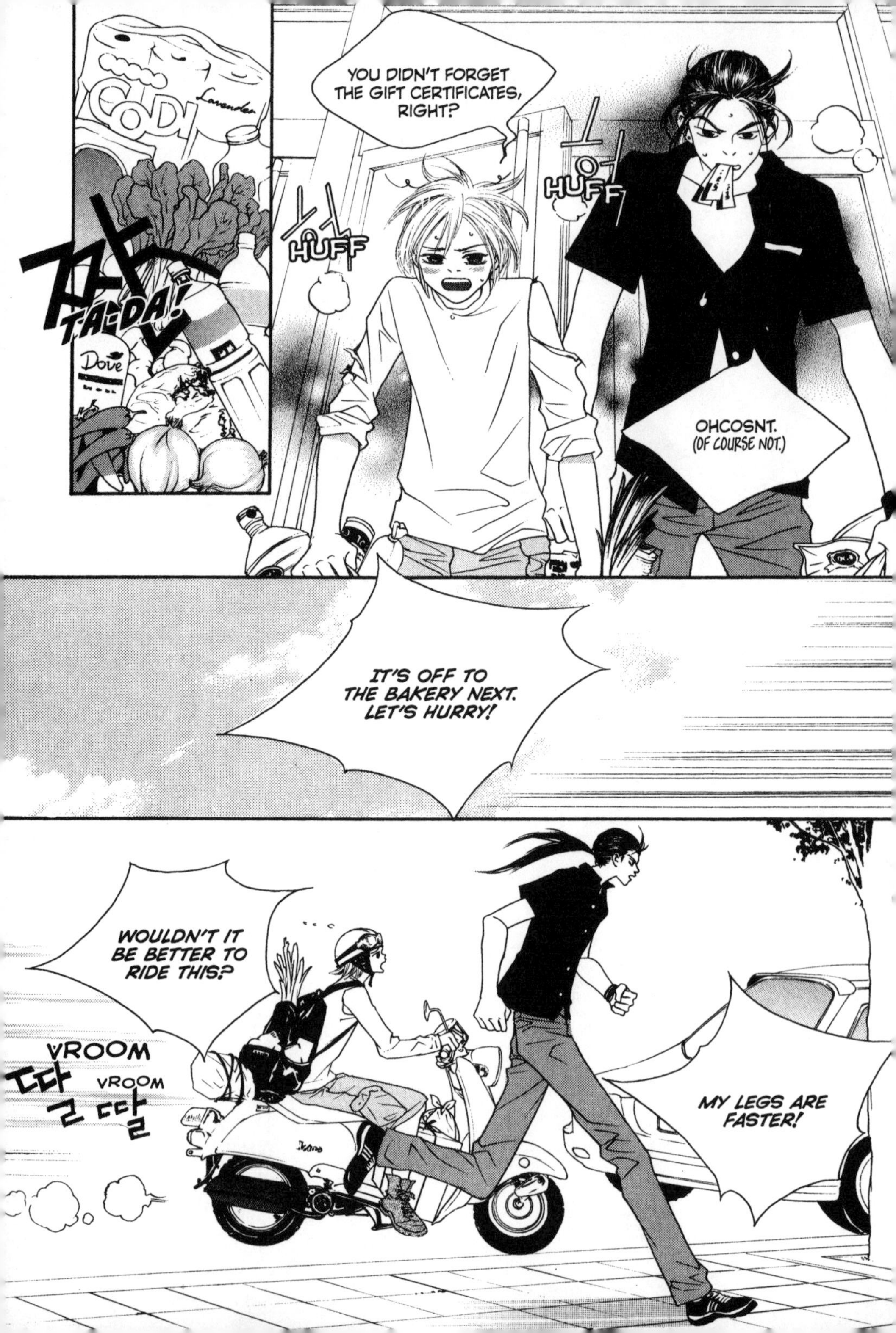
CODI
Lavender
Dove
TA-DA!
YOU DIDN'T FORGET THE GIFT CERTIFICATES, RIGHT?
HUFF
HUFF
OHCOSNT.
(OF COURSE NOT.)
IT'S OFF TO THE BAKERY NEXT. LET'S HURRY!
WOULDN'T IT BE BETTER TO RIDE THIS?
VROOM
VROOM
MY LEGS ARE FASTER!

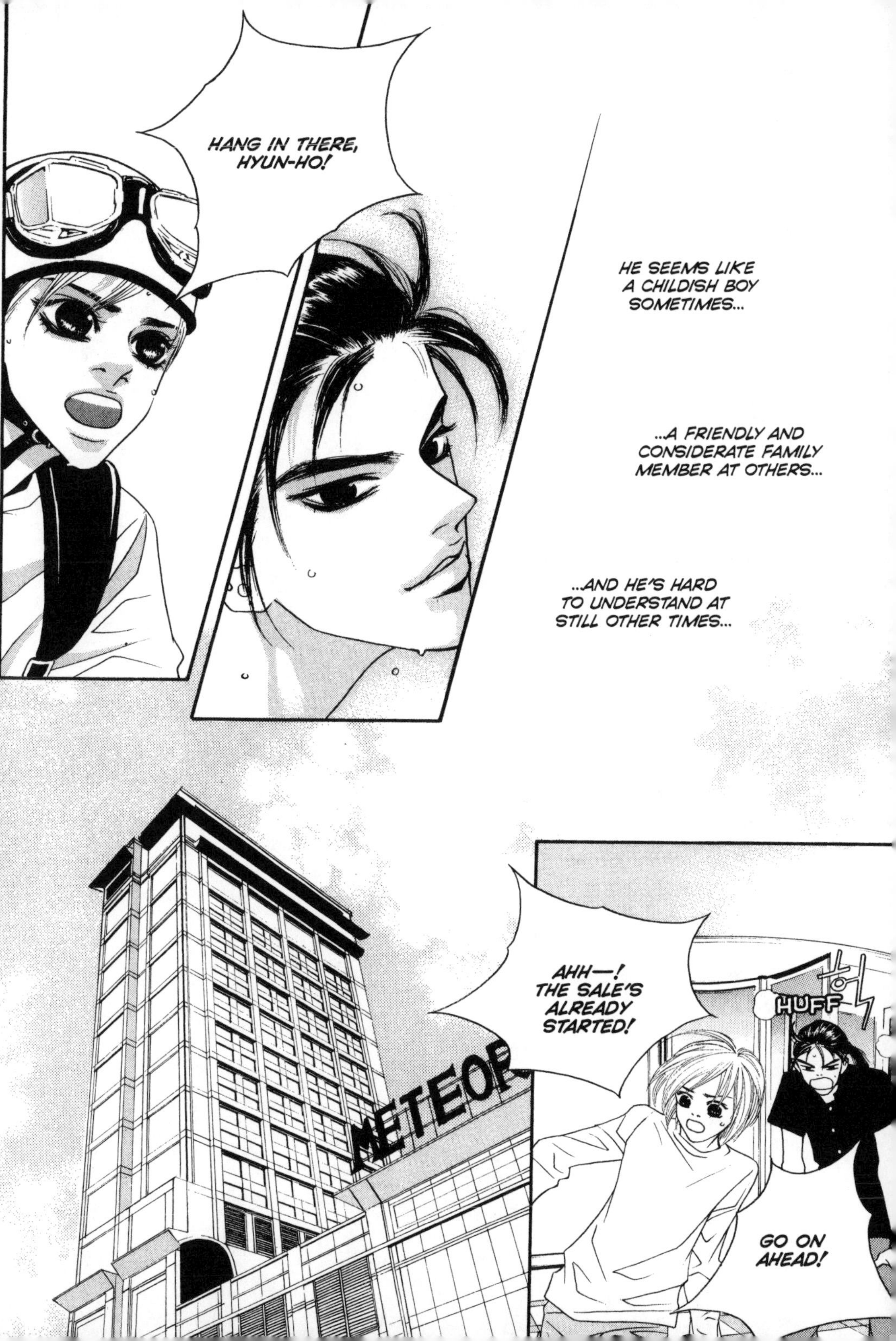
HANG IN THERE, HYUN-HO!
HE SEEMS LIKE A CHILDISH BOY SOMETIMES...
...A FRIENDLY AND CONSIDERATE FAMILY MEMBER AT OTHERS...
...AND HE'S HARD TO UNDERSTAND AT STILL OTHER TIMES...
METEOR
AHH—! THE SALE'S ALREADY STARTED!
HUFF
GO ON AHEAD!

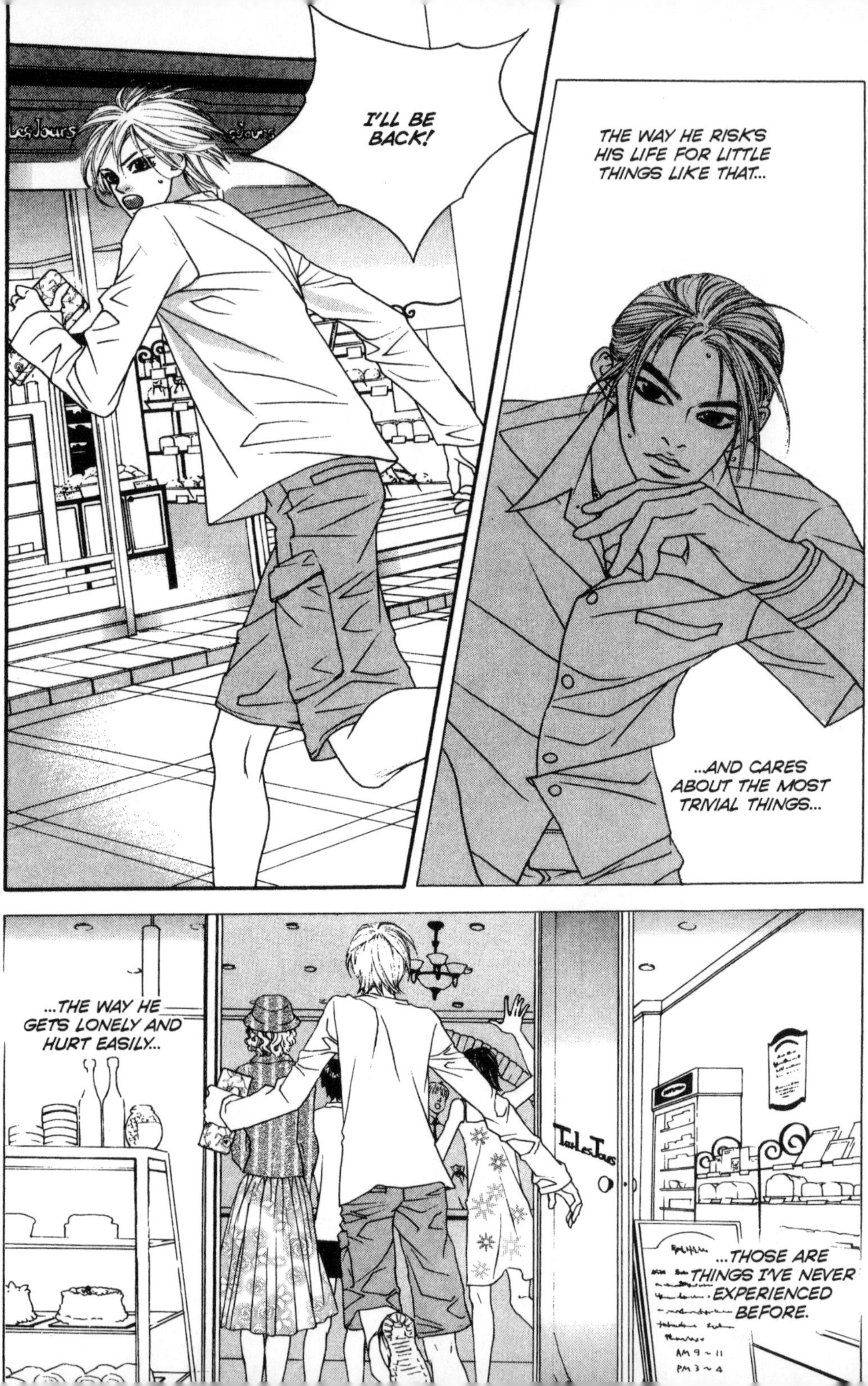
I'LL BE BACK!
THE WAY HE RISKS HIS LIFE FOR LITTLE THINGS LIKE THAT...
...AND CARES ABOUT THE MOST TRIVIAL THINGS...
...THE WAY HE GETS LONELY AND HURT EASILY...
...THOSE ARE THINGS I'VE NEVER EXPERIENCED BEFORE.

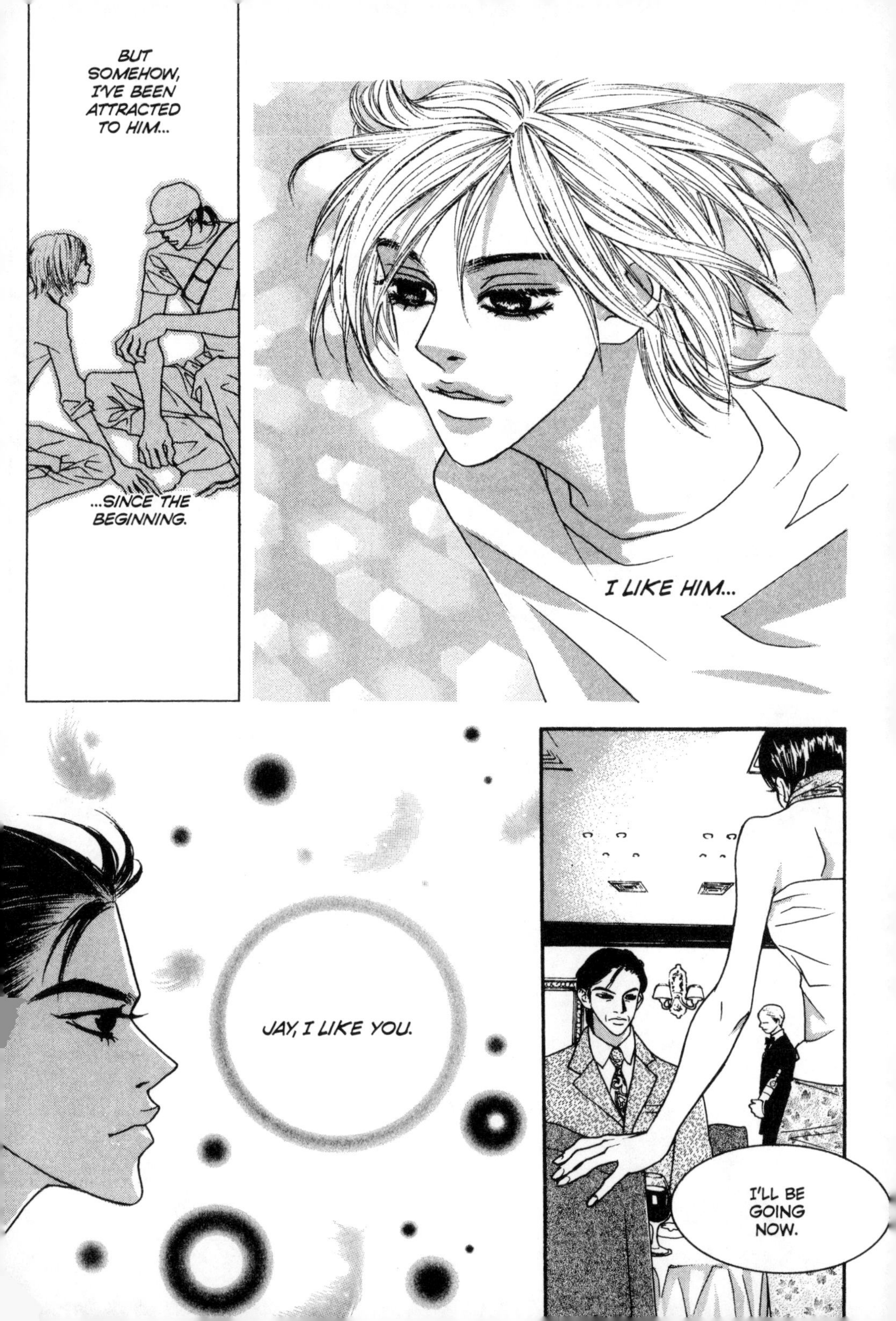
BUT SOMEHOW, I'VE BEEN ATTRACTED TO HIM...
...SINCE THE BEGINNING.
I LIKE HIM...
JAY, I LIKE YOU.
I'LL BE GOING NOW.

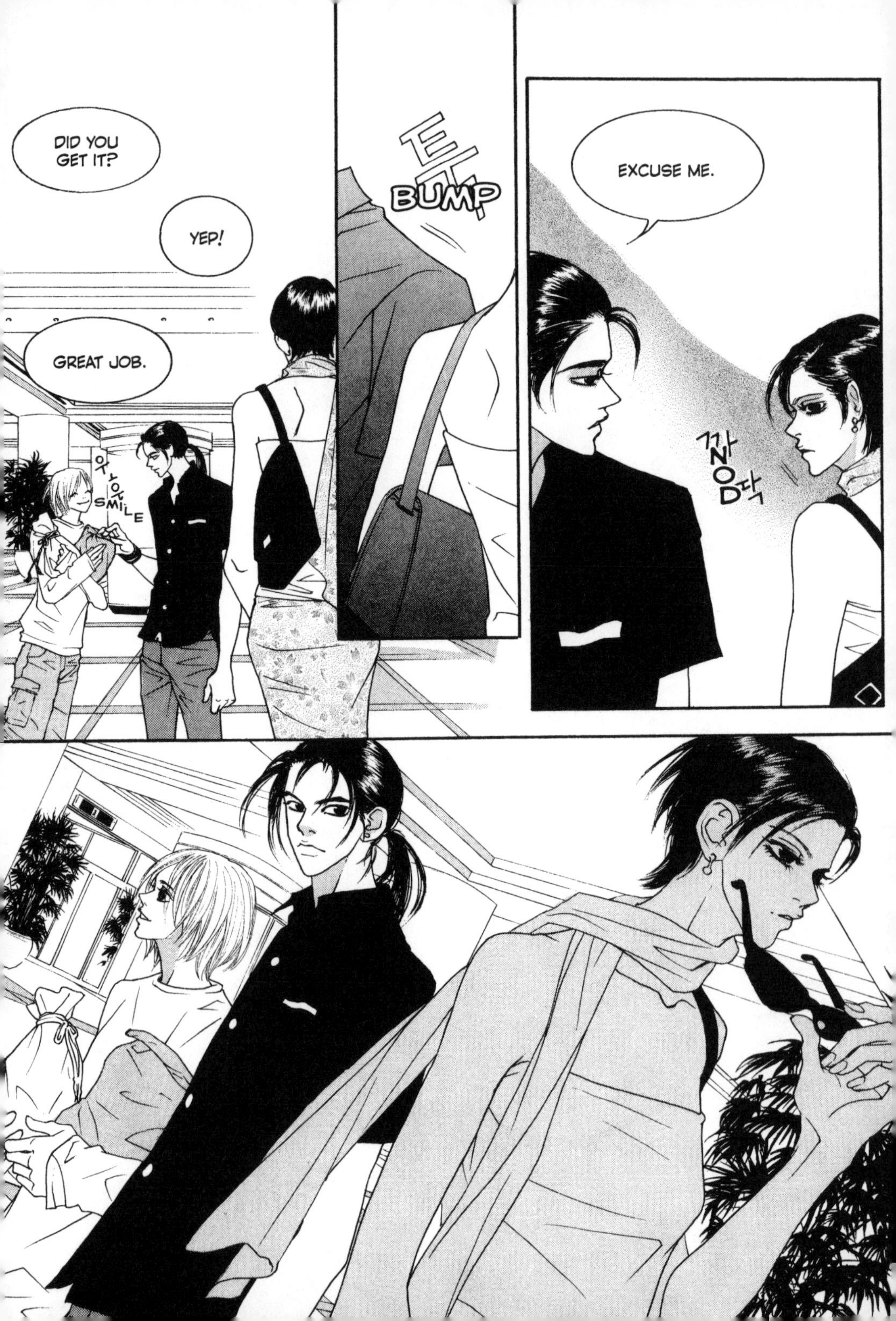

DID YOU GET IT?
YEP!
GREAT JOB.
SMILE
BUMP
EXCUSE ME.
NOD

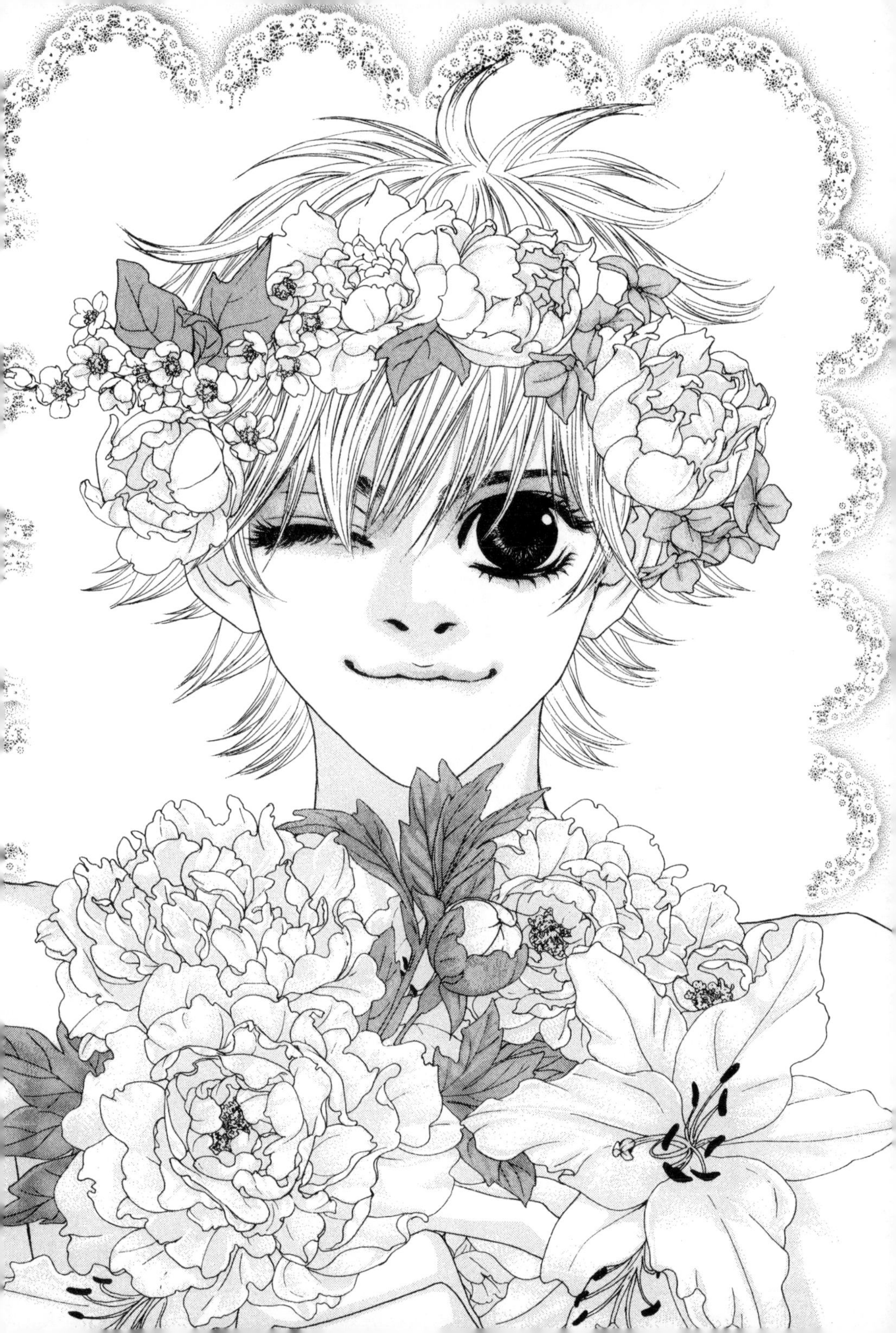

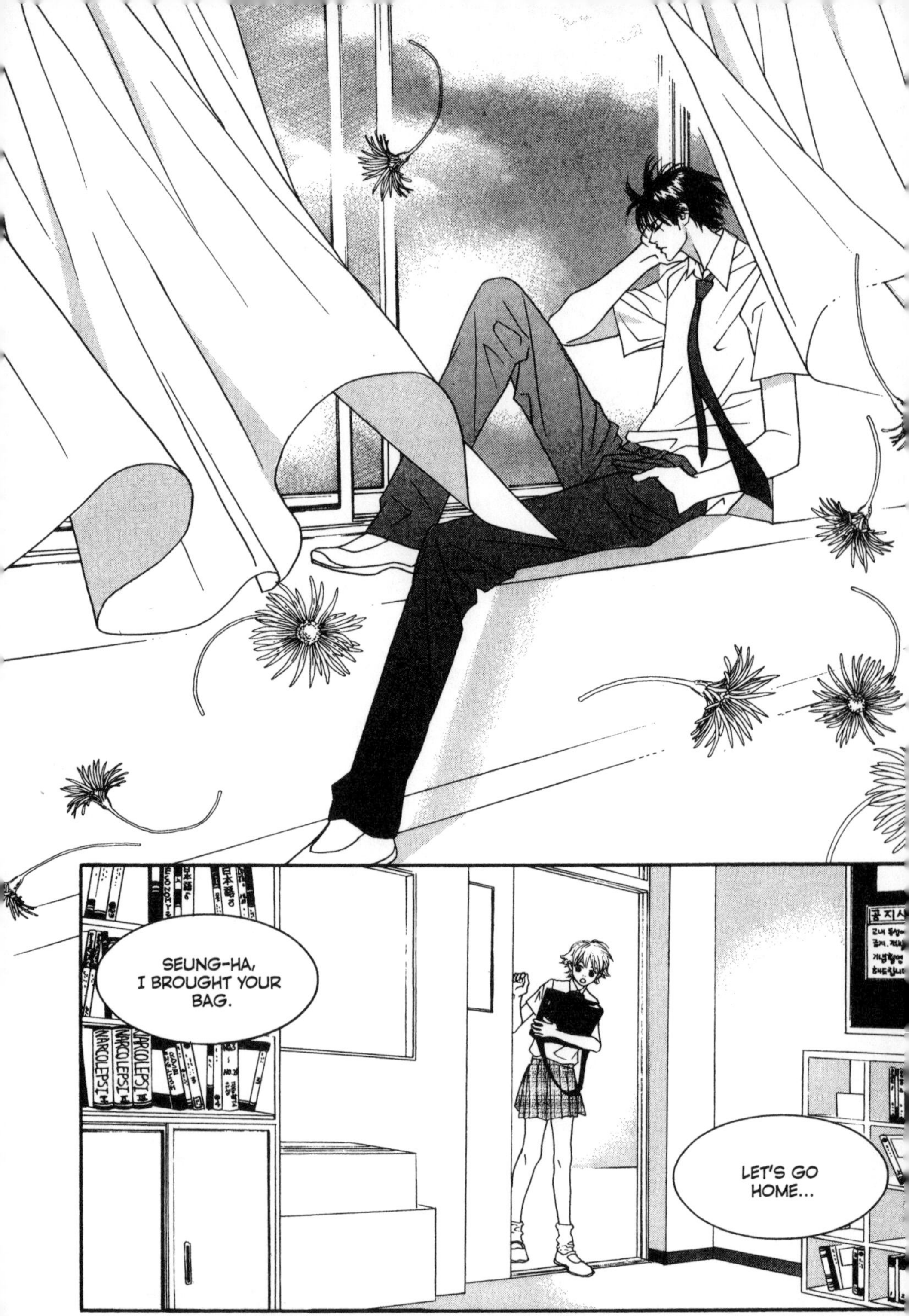
SEUNG-HA, I BROUGHT YOUR BAG.
LET'S GO HOME...

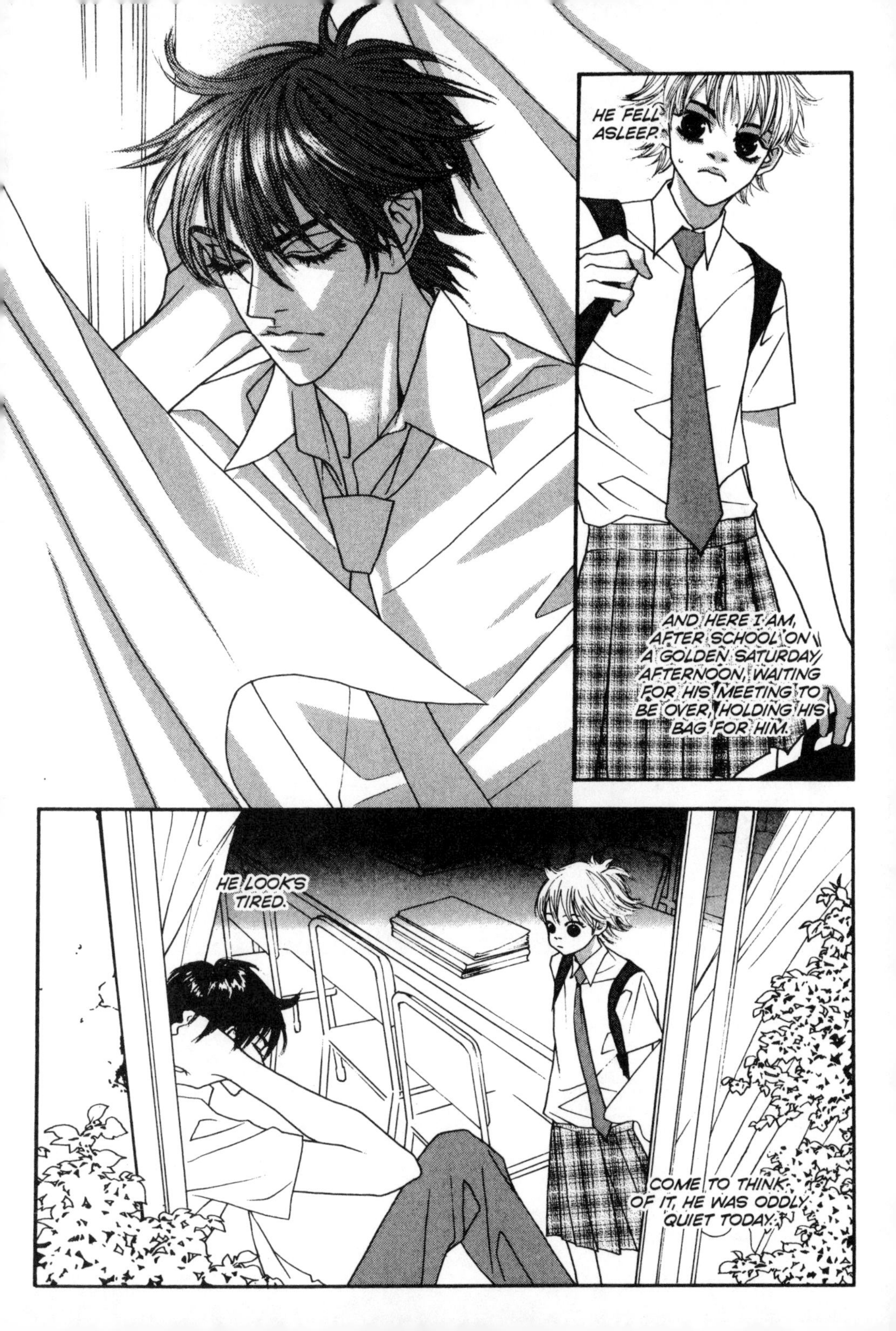
HE FELL ASLEEP.
AND HERE I AM, AFTER SCHOOL ON A GOLDEN SATURDAY AFTERNOON, WAITING FOR HIS MEETING TO BE OVER, HOLDING HIS BAG FOR HIM.
HE LOOKS TIRED.
COME TO THINK OF IT, HE WAS ODDLY QUIET TODAY.

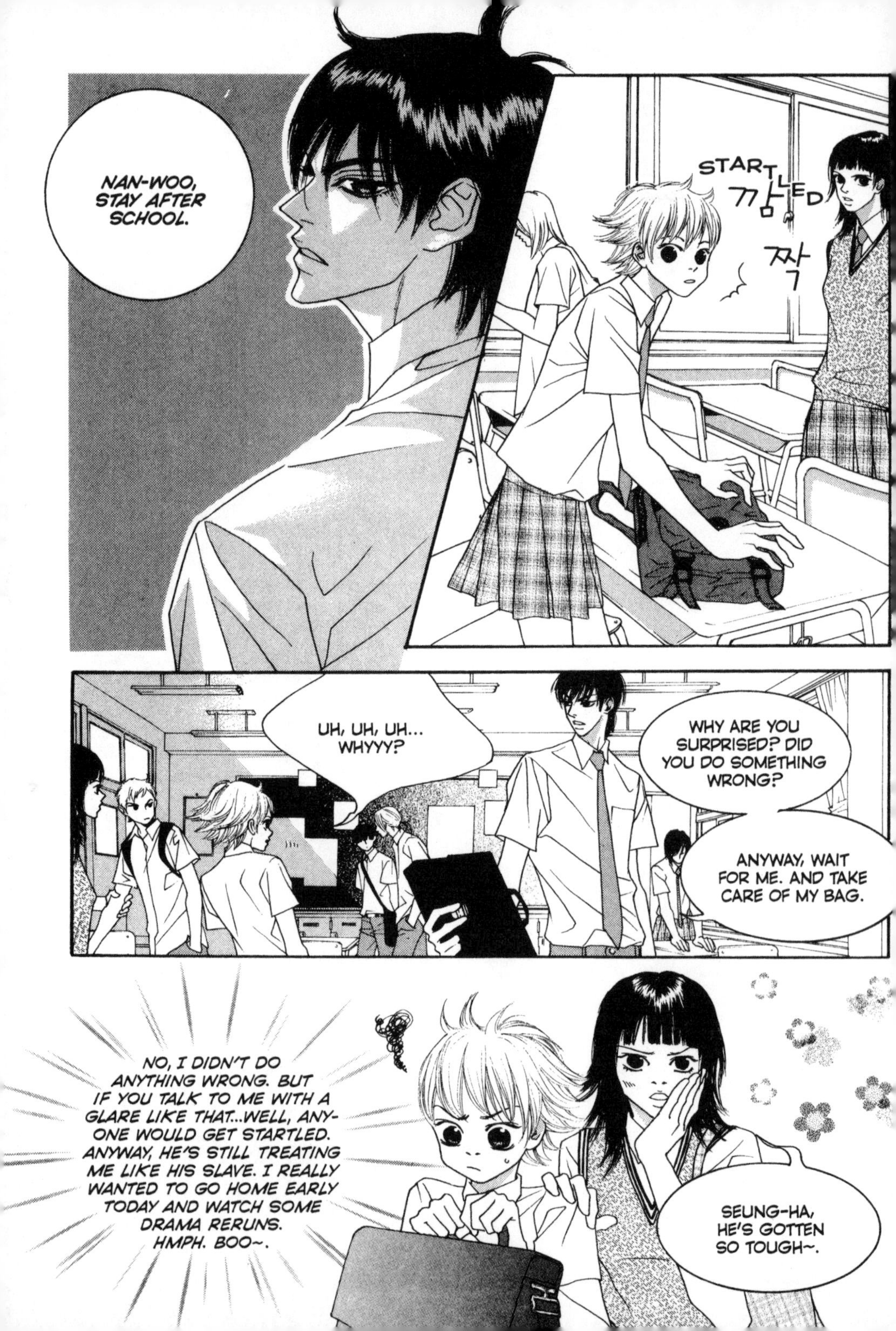
NAN-WOO, STAY AFTER SCHOOL.
STARTLED
깜짝
UH, UH, UH... WHYYY?
WHY ARE YOU SURPRISED? DID YOU DO SOMETHING WRONG?
ANYWAY, WAIT FOR ME. AND TAKE CARE OF MY BAG.
NO, I DIDN'T DO ANYTHING WRONG. BUT IF YOU TALK TO ME WITH A GLARE LIKE THAT...WELL, ANYONE WOULD GET STARTLED. ANYWAY, HE'S STILL TREATING ME LIKE HIS SLAVE. I REALLY WANTED TO GO HOME EARLY TODAY AND WATCH SOME DRAMA RERUNS. HMPH. BOO~.
SEUNG-HA, HE'S GOTTEN SO TOUGH~.

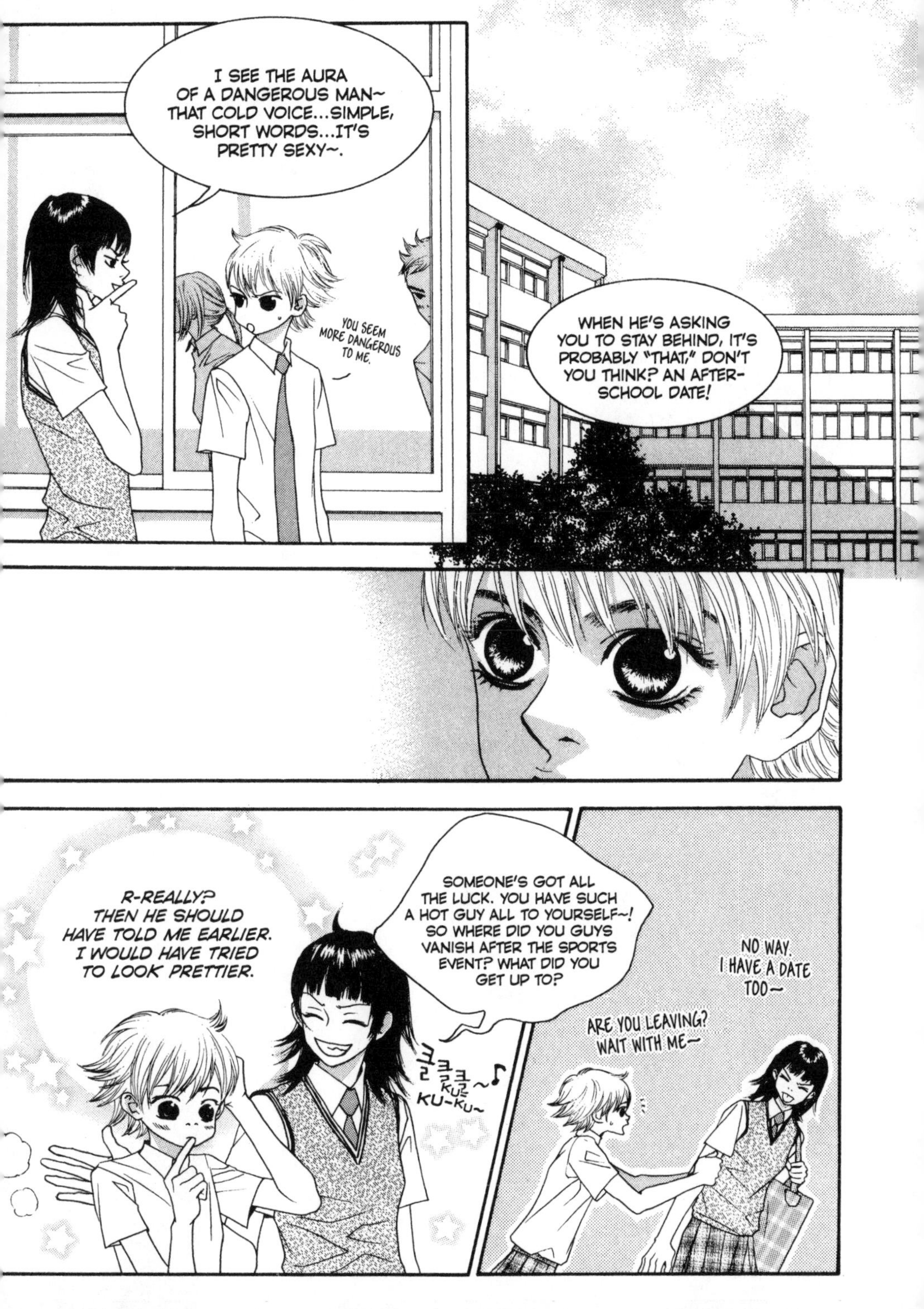

I SEE THE AURA OF A DANGEROUS MAN~ THAT COLD VOICE...SIMPLE, SHORT WORDS...IT'S PRETTY SEXY~.
YOU SEEM MORE DANGEROUS TO ME.
WHEN HE'S ASKING YOU TO STAY BEHIND, IT'S PROBABLY "THAT," DON'T YOU THINK? AN AFTER-SCHOOL DATE!
R-REALLY? THEN HE SHOULD HAVE TOLD ME EARLIER. I WOULD HAVE TRIED TO LOOK PRETTIER.
SOMEONE'S GOT ALL THE LUCK. YOU HAVE SUCH A HOT GUY ALL TO YOURSELF~! SO WHERE DID YOU GUYS VANISH AFTER THE SPORTS EVENT? WHAT DID YOU GET UP TO?
KU-KU~
NO WAY. I HAVE A DATE TOO~
ARE YOU LEAVING? WAIT WITH ME~

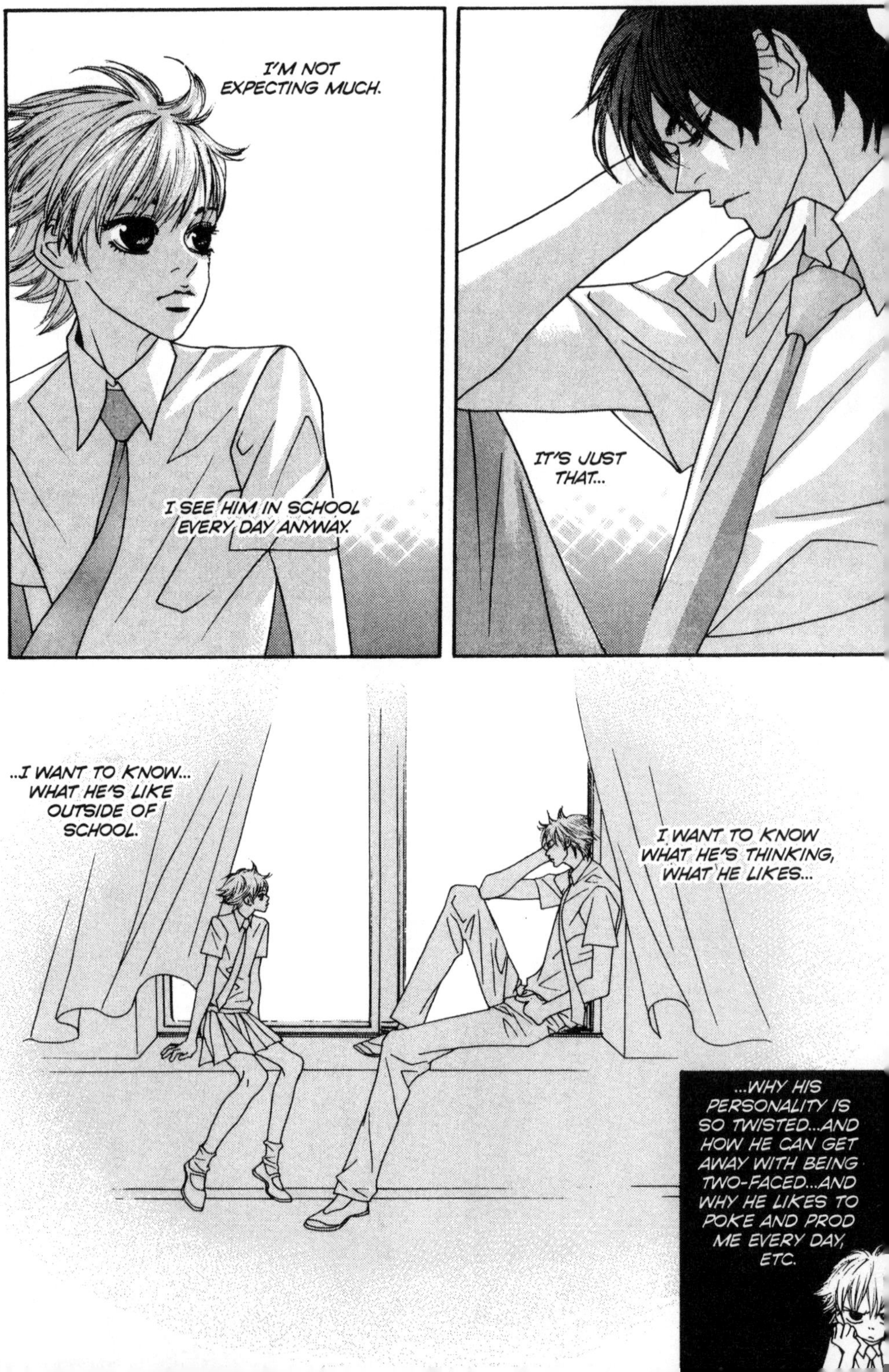
I'M NOT EXPECTING MUCH.
I SEE HIM IN SCHOOL EVERY DAY ANYWAY.
IT'S JUST THAT...
...I WANT TO KNOW... WHAT HE'S LIKE OUTSIDE OF SCHOOL.
I WANT TO KNOW WHAT HE'S THINKING, WHAT HE LIKES...
...WHY HIS PERSONALITY IS SO TWISTED...AND HOW HE CAN GET AWAY WITH BEING TWO-FACED...AND WHY HE LIKES TO POKE AND PROD ME EVERY DAY, ETC.

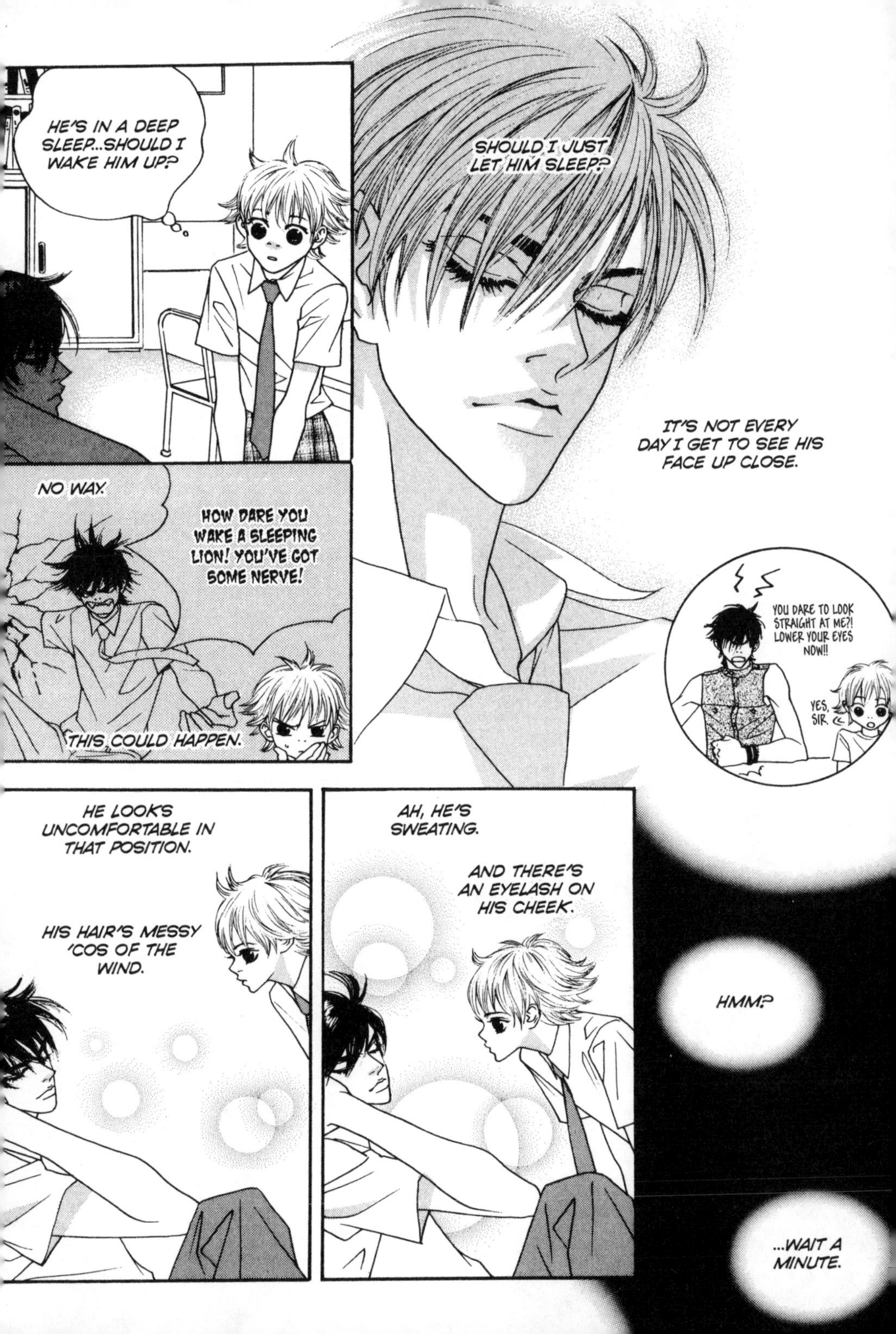
HE'S IN A DEEP SLEEP...SHOULD I WAKE HIM UP?
NO WAY.
HOW DARE YOU WAKE A SLEEPING LION! YOU'VE GOT SOME NERVE!
THIS COULD HAPPEN.
SHOULD I JUST LET HIM SLEEP?
IT'S NOT EVERY DAY I GET TO SEE HIS FACE UP CLOSE.
YOU DARE TO LOOK STRAIGHT AT ME?! LOWER YOUR EYES NOW!!
YES, SIR.
HE LOOKS UNCOMFORTABLE IN THAT POSITION.
HIS HAIR'S MESSY 'COS OF THE WIND.
AH, HE'S SWEATING.
AND THERE'S AN EYELASH ON HIS CHEEK.
HMM?
...WAIT A MINUTE.

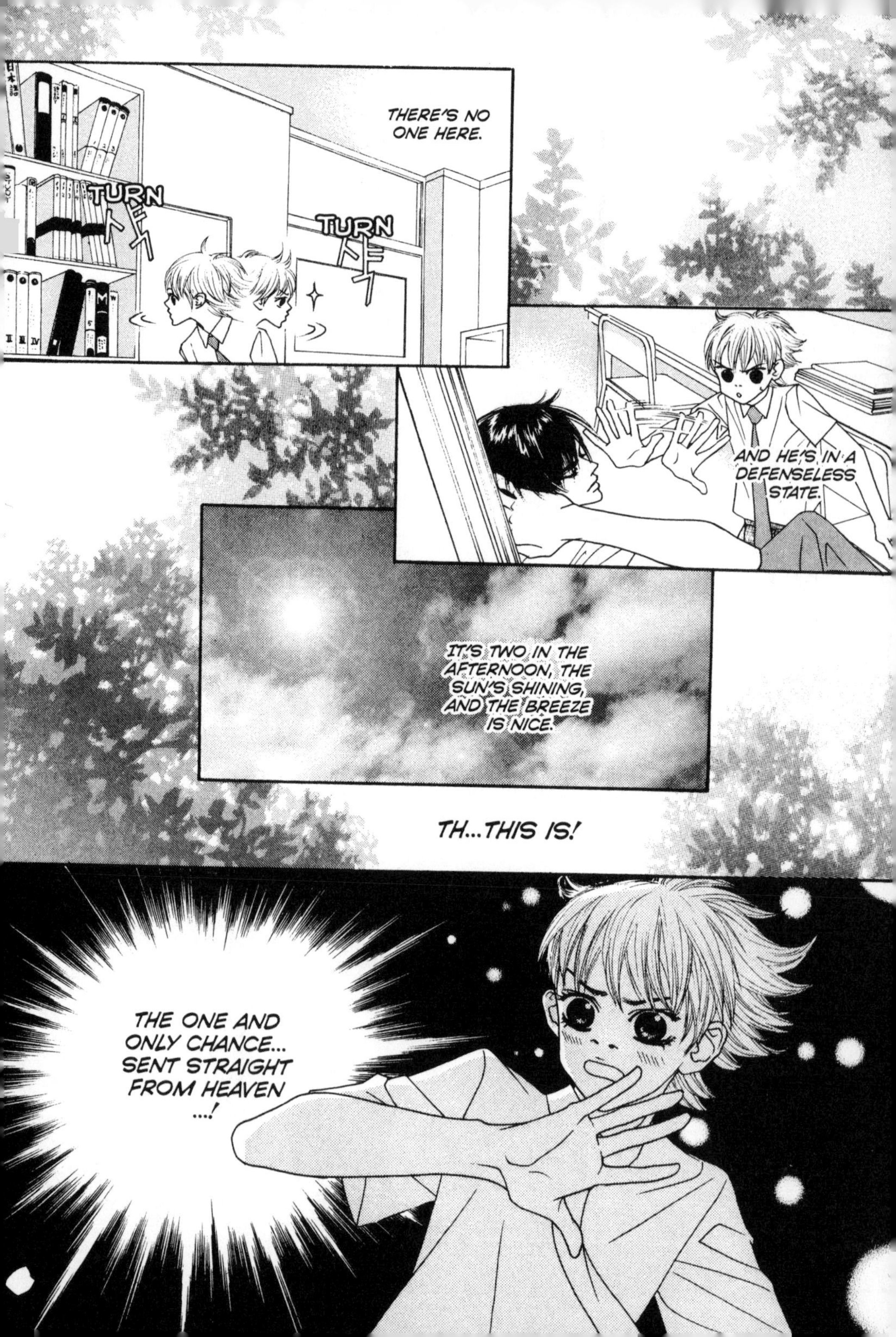
THERE'S NO ONE HERE.
TURN
TURN
AND HE'S IN A DEFENSELESS STATE.
IT'S TWO IN THE AFTERNOON, THE SUN'S SHINING, AND THE BREEZE IS NICE.
TH...THIS IS!
THE ONE AND ONLY CHANCE... SENT STRAIGHT FROM HEAVEN ...!

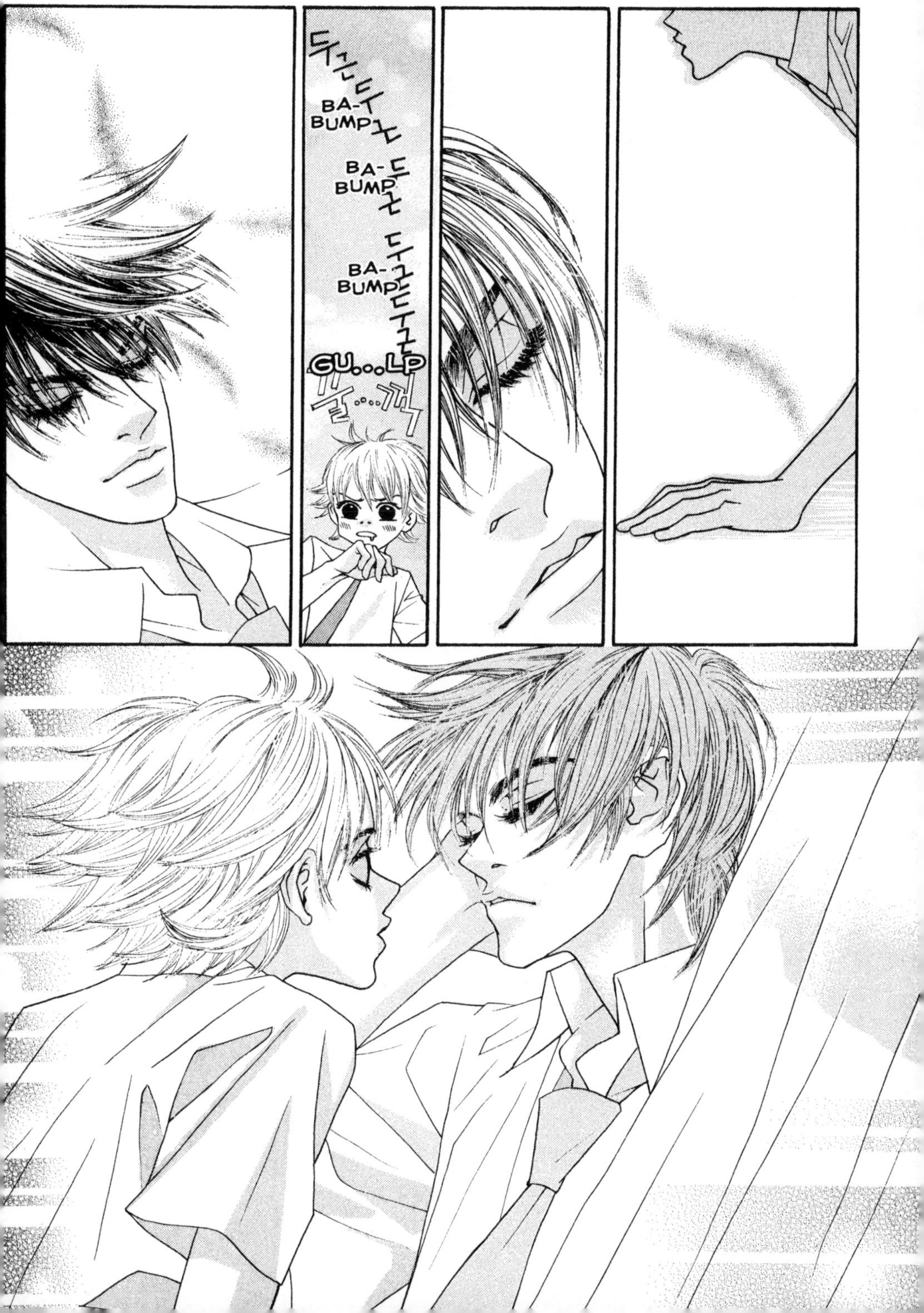
BA-BUMP
BA-BUMP
BA-BUMP
GU...LP
꿀...꺽

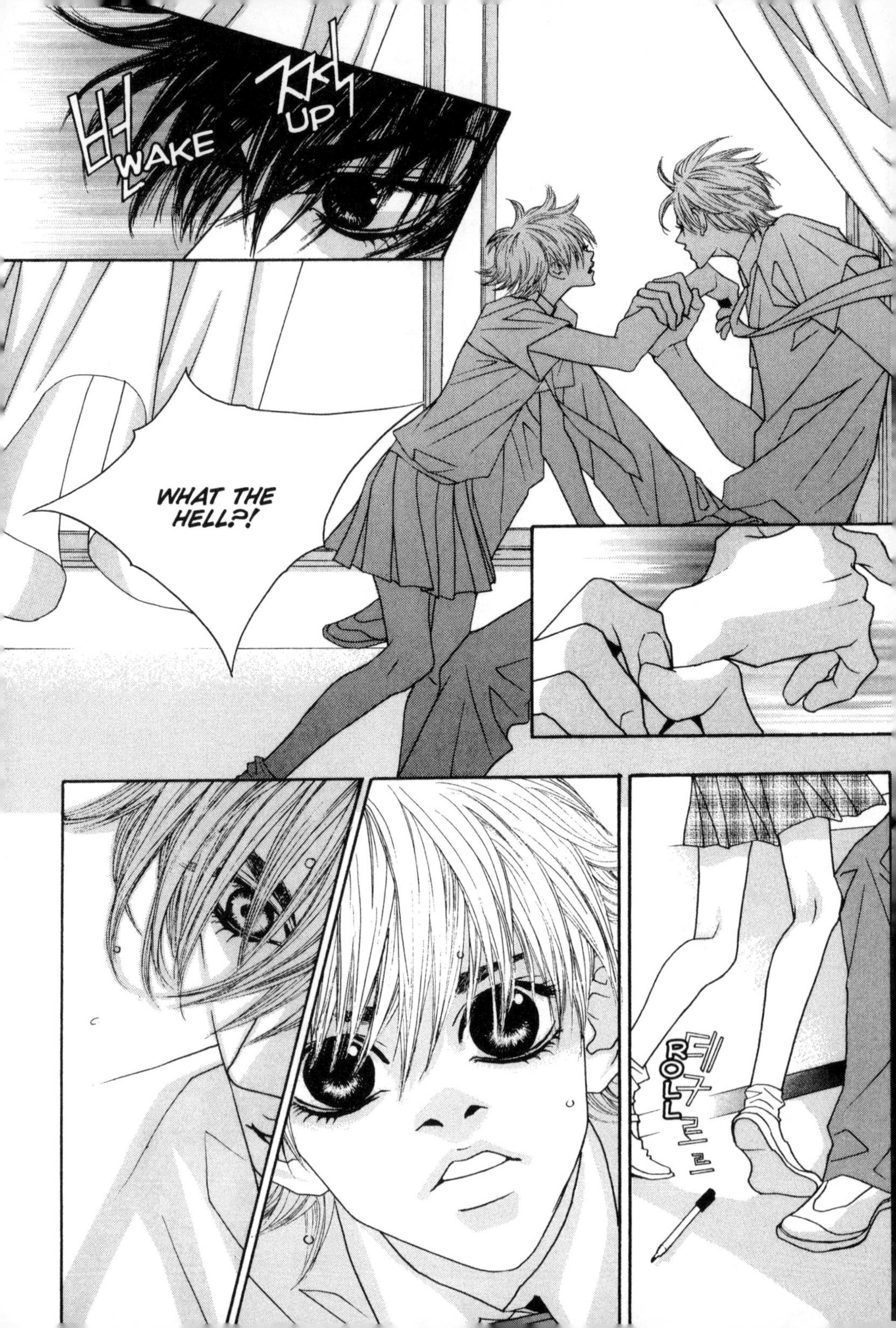

번쩍
WAKE UP
WHAT THE HELL?!
데구르르
ROLL

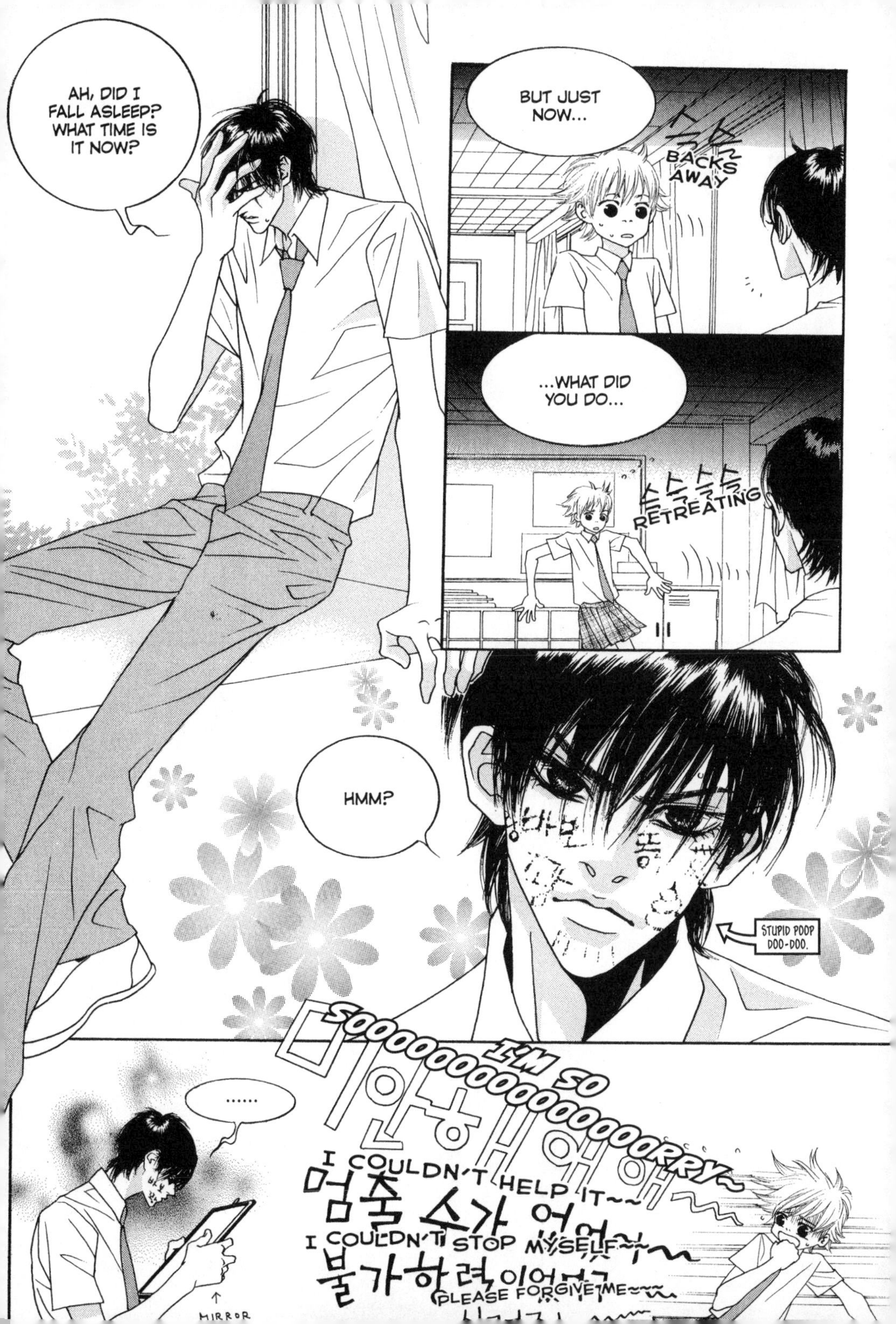

AH, DID I FALL ASLEEP? WHAT TIME IS IT NOW?
BUT JUST NOW...
BACKS AWAY
...WHAT DID YOU DO...
RETREATING
HMM?
STUPID POOP DOO-DOO.
......
MIRROR
I'M SO SOOOOOOOOOOOOOOORRY~
I COULDN'T HELP IT~~
I COULDN'T STOP MYSELF~~
PLEASE FORGIVE ME~~~

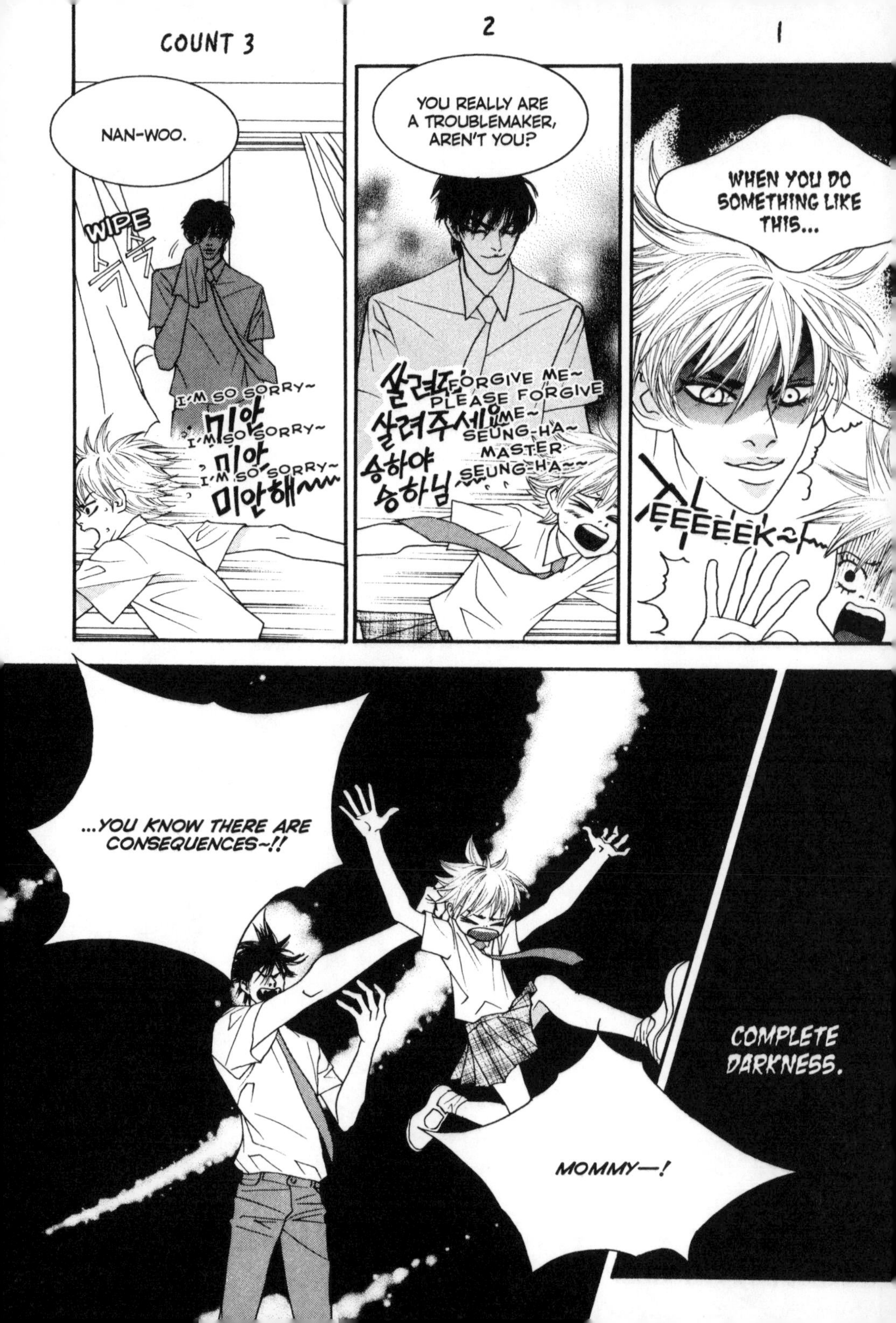
COUNT 3
NAN-WOO.
WIPE
I'M SO SORRY~
미안
I'M SO SORRY~
미안
I'M SO SORRY~
미안해
2
YOU REALLY ARE A TROUBLEMAKER, AREN'T YOU?
FORGIVE ME~
PLEASE FORGIVE ME~
살려주세요
SEUNG-HA~
승하야
MASTER SEUNG-HA~~
승하님
1
WHEN YOU DO SOMETHING LIKE THIS...
EEEEEK
...YOU KNOW THERE ARE CONSEQUENCES~!!
MOMMY—!
COMPLETE DARKNESS.

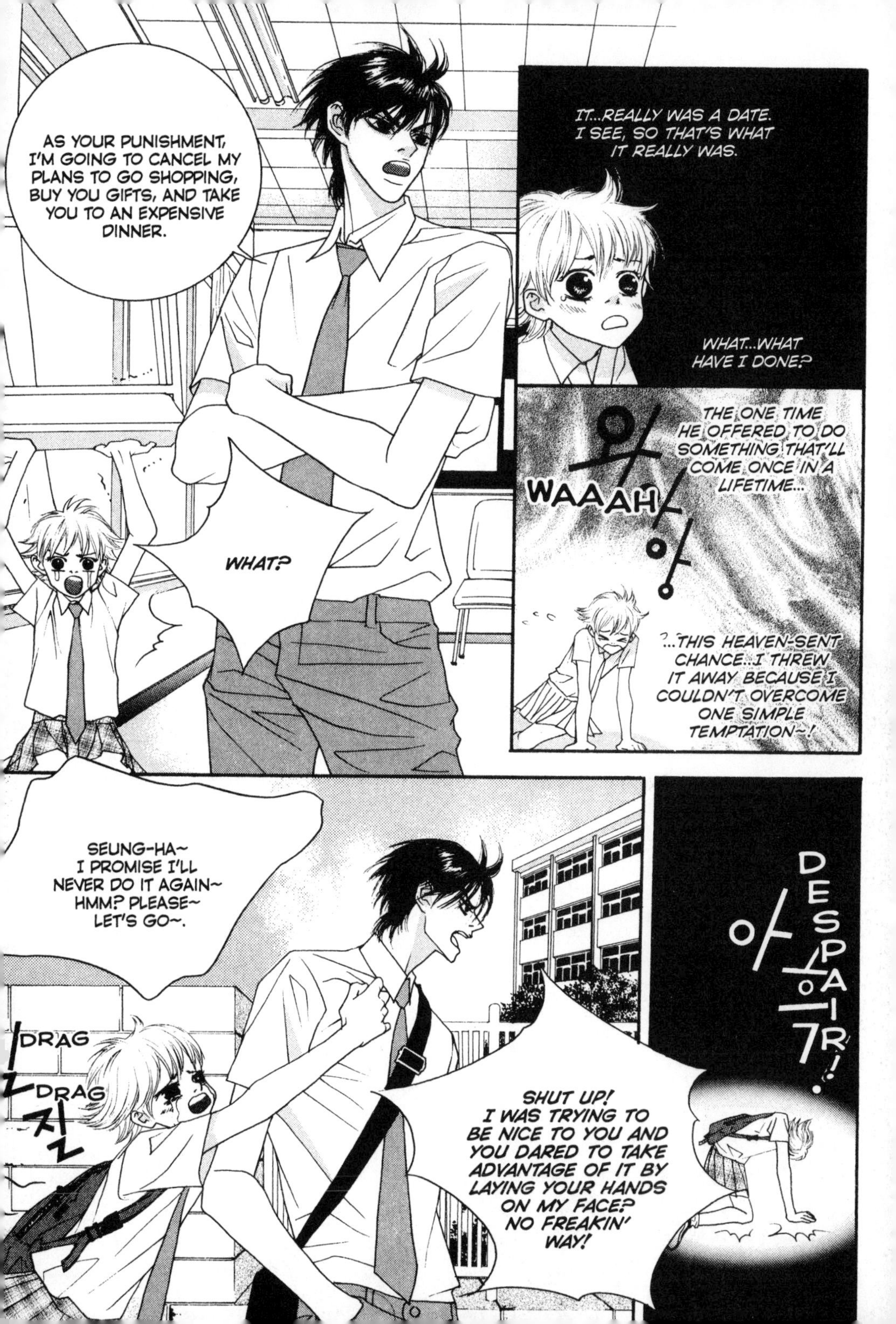

AS YOUR PUNISHMENT, I'M GOING TO CANCEL MY PLANS TO GO SHOPPING, BUY YOU GIFTS, AND TAKE YOU TO AN EXPENSIVE DINNER.
WHAT?
IT...REALLY WAS A DATE. I SEE, SO THAT'S WHAT IT REALLY WAS.
WHAT...WHAT HAVE I DONE?
THE ONE TIME HE OFFERED TO DO SOMETHING THAT'LL COME ONCE IN A LIFETIME...
와앙
WAAAH
...THIS HEAVEN-SENT CHANCE...I THREW IT AWAY BECAUSE I COULDN'T OVERCOME ONE SIMPLE TEMPTATION~!
SEUNG-HA~ I PROMISE I'LL NEVER DO IT AGAIN~ HMM? PLEASE~ LET'S GO~.
DRAG
DRAG
SHUT UP! I WAS TRYING TO BE NICE TO YOU AND YOU DARED TO TAKE ADVANTAGE OF IT BY LAYING YOUR HANDS ON MY FACE? NO FREAKIN' WAY!
DESPAIR!

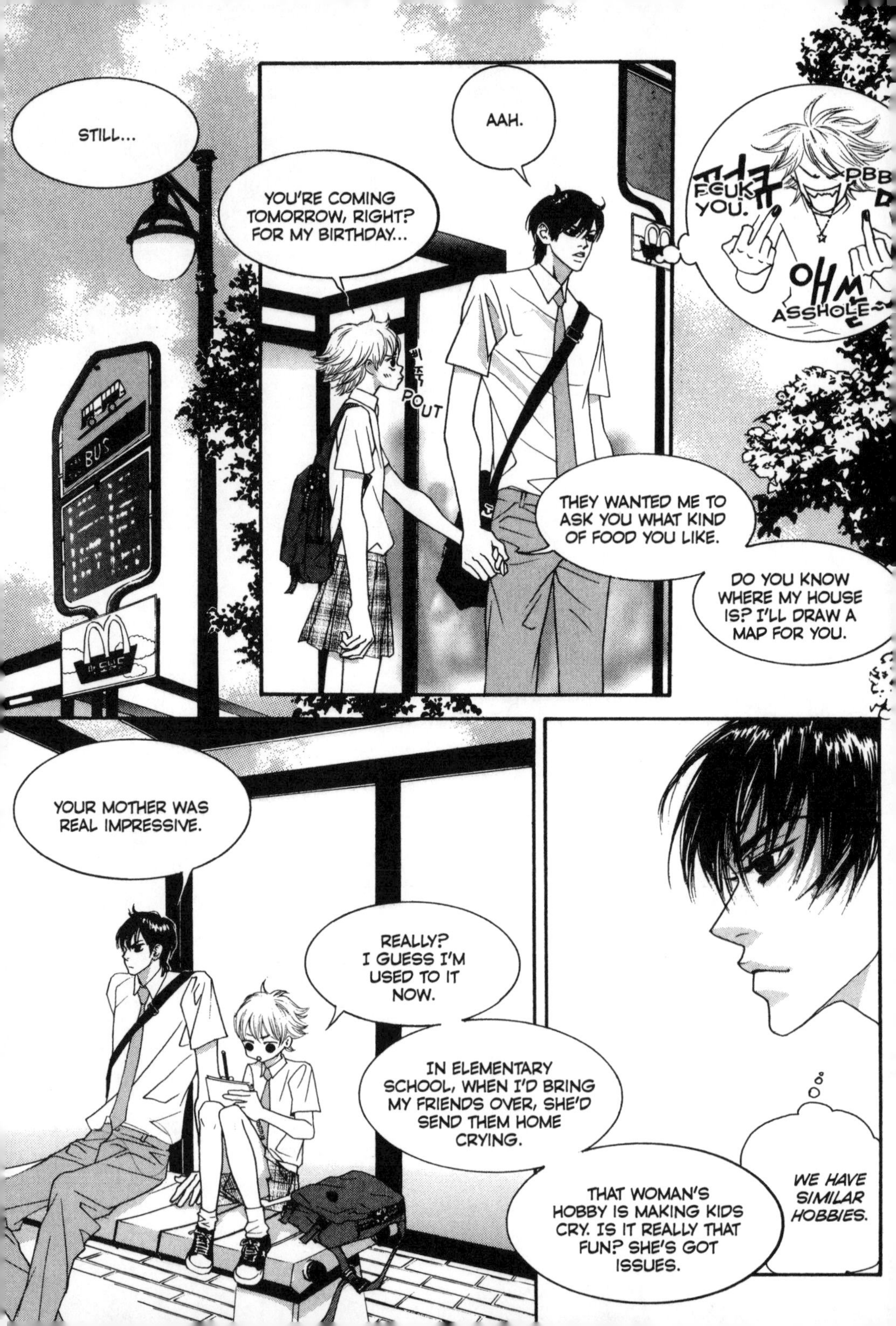
STILL...
YOU'RE COMING TOMORROW, RIGHT? FOR MY BIRTHDAY...
AAH.
FCUK YOU.
ASSHOLE~
POUT
THEY WANTED ME TO ASK YOU WHAT KIND OF FOOD YOU LIKE.
DO YOU KNOW WHERE MY HOUSE IS? I'LL DRAW A MAP FOR YOU.
YOUR MOTHER WAS REAL IMPRESSIVE.
REALLY? I GUESS I'M USED TO IT NOW.
IN ELEMENTARY SCHOOL, WHEN I'D BRING MY FRIENDS OVER, SHE'D SEND THEM HOME CRYING.
THAT WOMAN'S HOBBY IS MAKING KIDS CRY. IS IT REALLY THAT FUN? SHE'S GOT ISSUES.
WE HAVE SIMILAR HOBBIES.

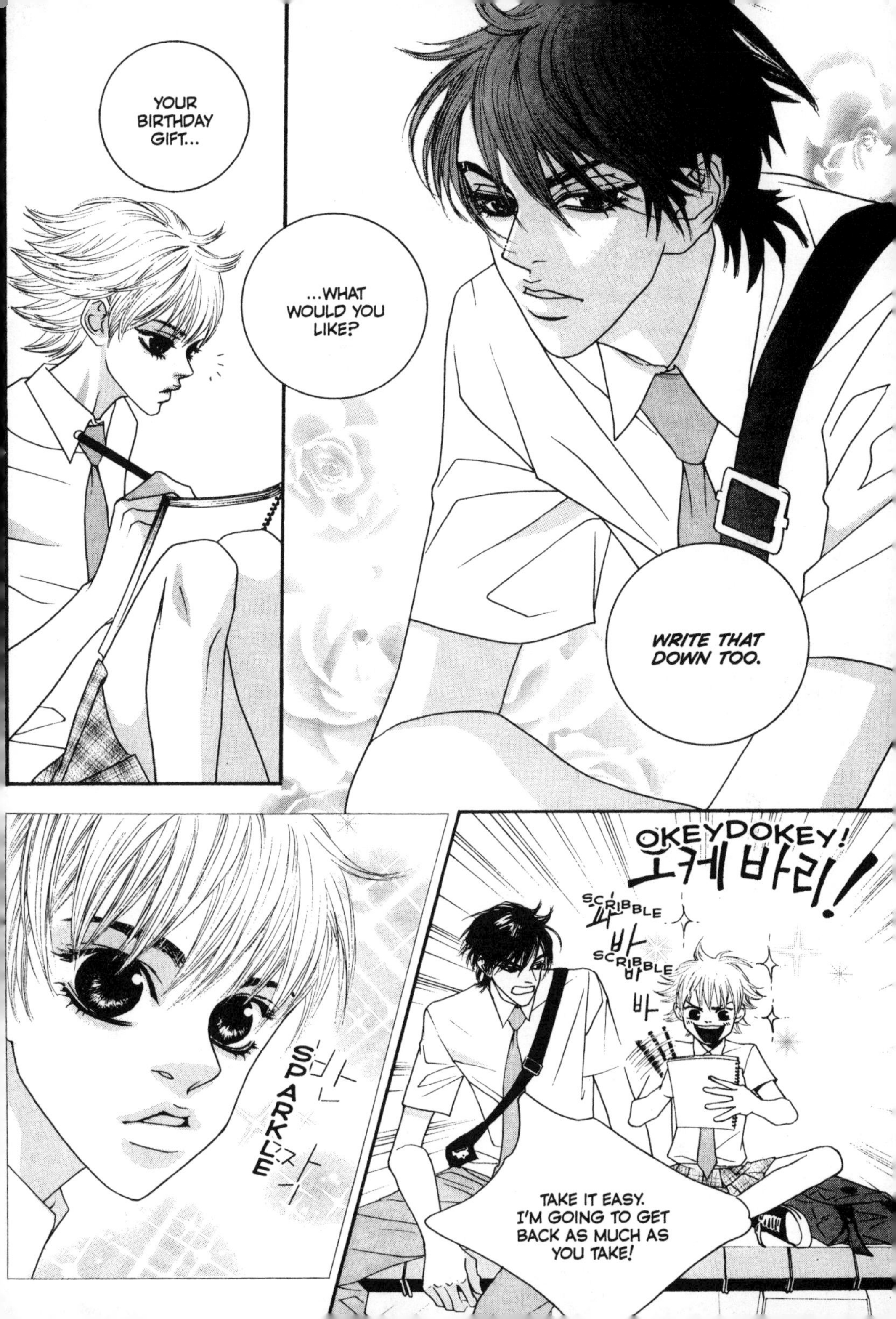
YOUR BIRTHDAY GIFT...
...WHAT WOULD YOU LIKE?
WRITE THAT DOWN TOO.
SPARKLE
OKEYDOKEY!
오케 바리!
SCRIBBLE
SCRIBBLE
TAKE IT EASY. I'M GOING TO GET BACK AS MUCH AS YOU TAKE!

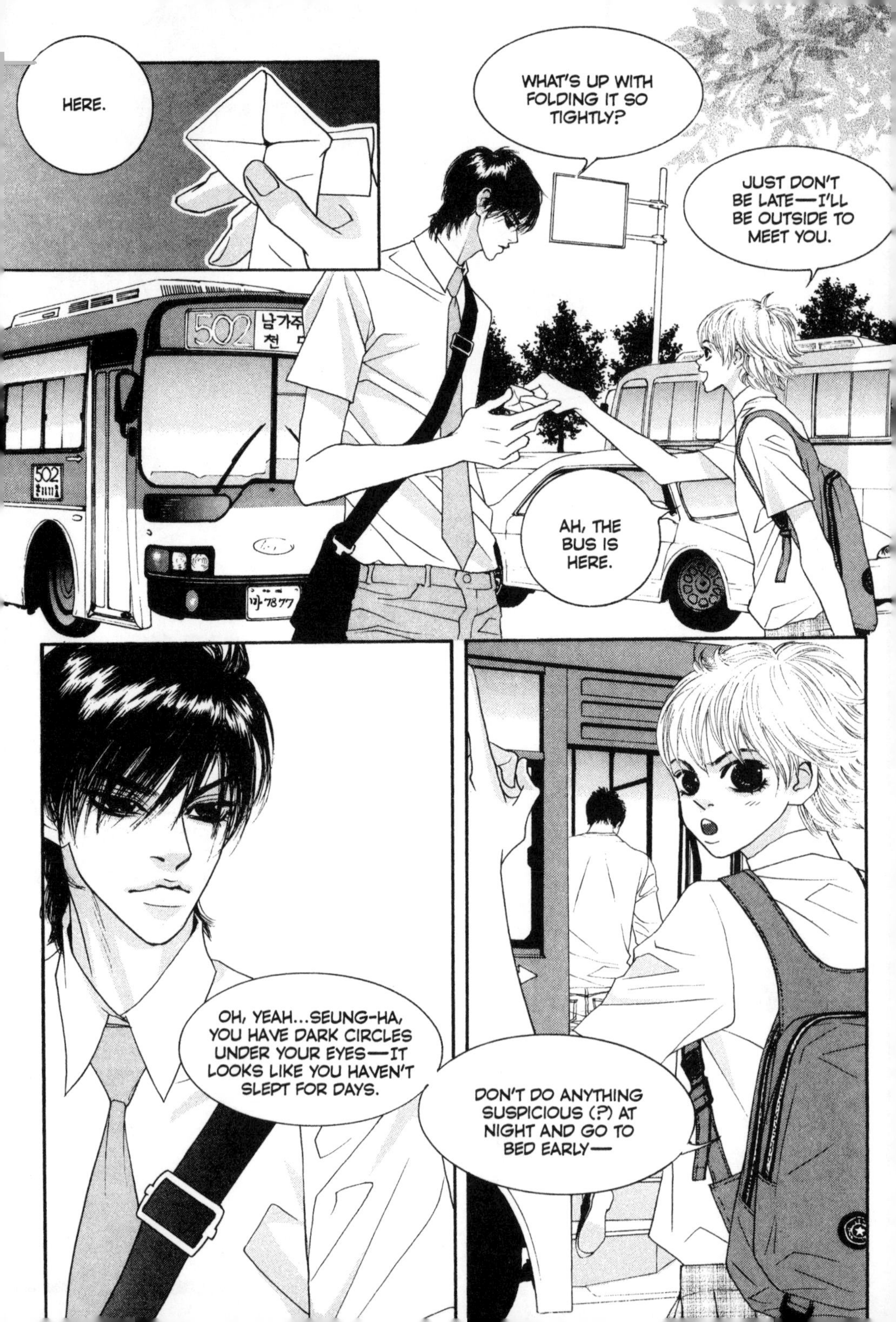
HERE.
WHAT'S UP WITH FOLDING IT SO TIGHTLY?
JUST DON'T BE LATE—I'LL BE OUTSIDE TO MEET YOU.
AH, THE BUS IS HERE.
OH, YEAH...SEUNG-HA, YOU HAVE DARK CIRCLES UNDER YOUR EYES—IT LOOKS LIKE YOU HAVEN'T SLEPT FOR DAYS.
DON'T DO ANYTHING SUSPICIOUS (?) AT NIGHT AND GO TO BED EARLY—

SEE YOU TOMORROW—

I'VE BEEN HAVING A HARD TIME FALLING ASLEEP EVER SINCE I MET NAN-WOO'S MOTHER.

I KEEP THINKING OF THINGS I'VE BEEN TRYING TO FORGET FOR A LONG TIME.

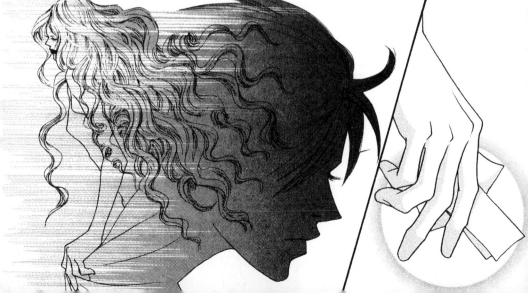

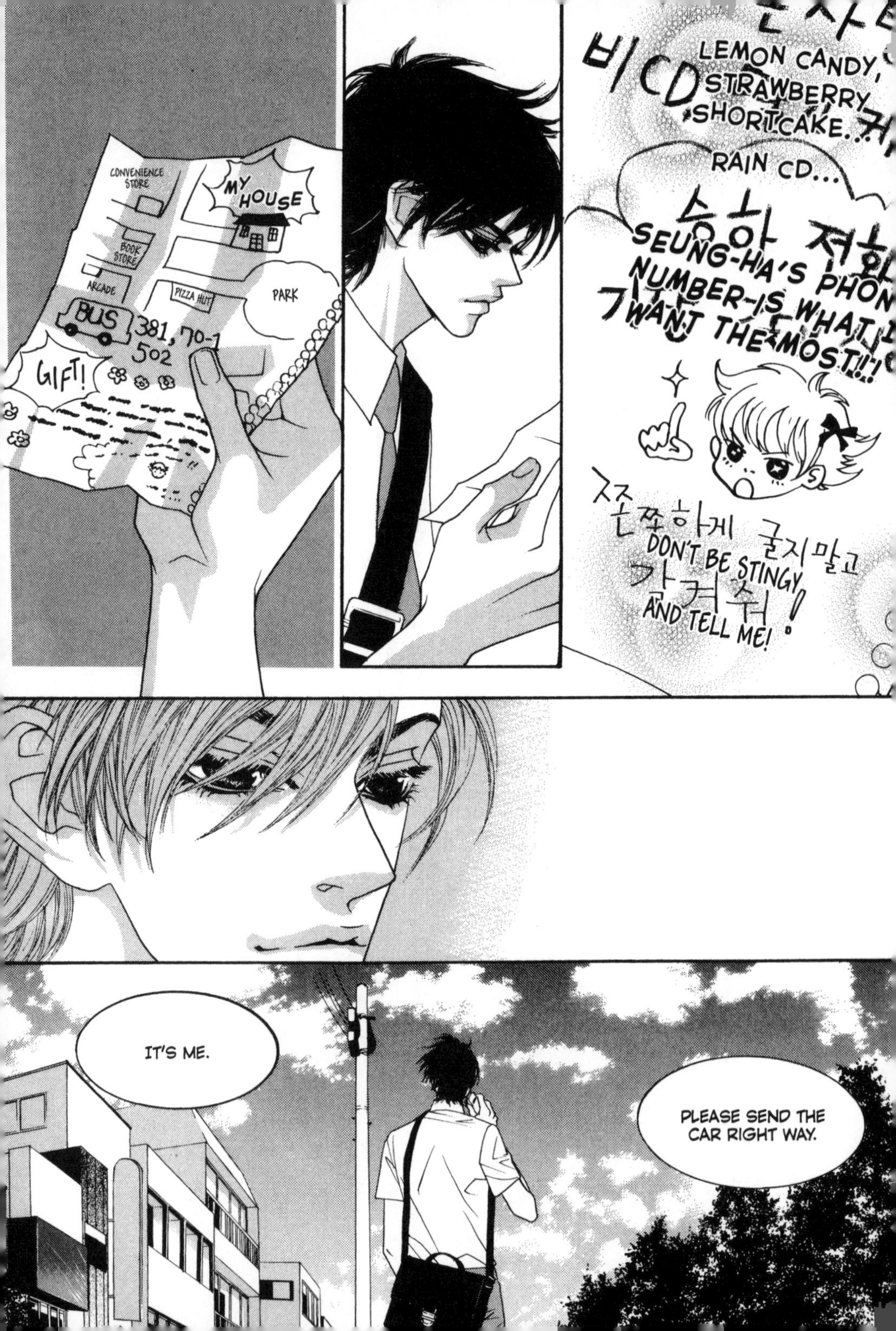
CONVENIENCE STORE
MY HOUSE
BOOK STORE
ARCADE
PIZZA HUT
PARK
BUS
381, 70-1
502
GIFT!
LEMON CANDY, STRAWBERRY SHORTCAKE...
RAIN CD...
SEUNG-HA'S PHON NUMBER IS WHAT I WANT THE MOST!!!
DON'T BE STINGY AND TELL ME!
IT'S ME.
PLEASE SEND THE CAR RIGHT WAY.

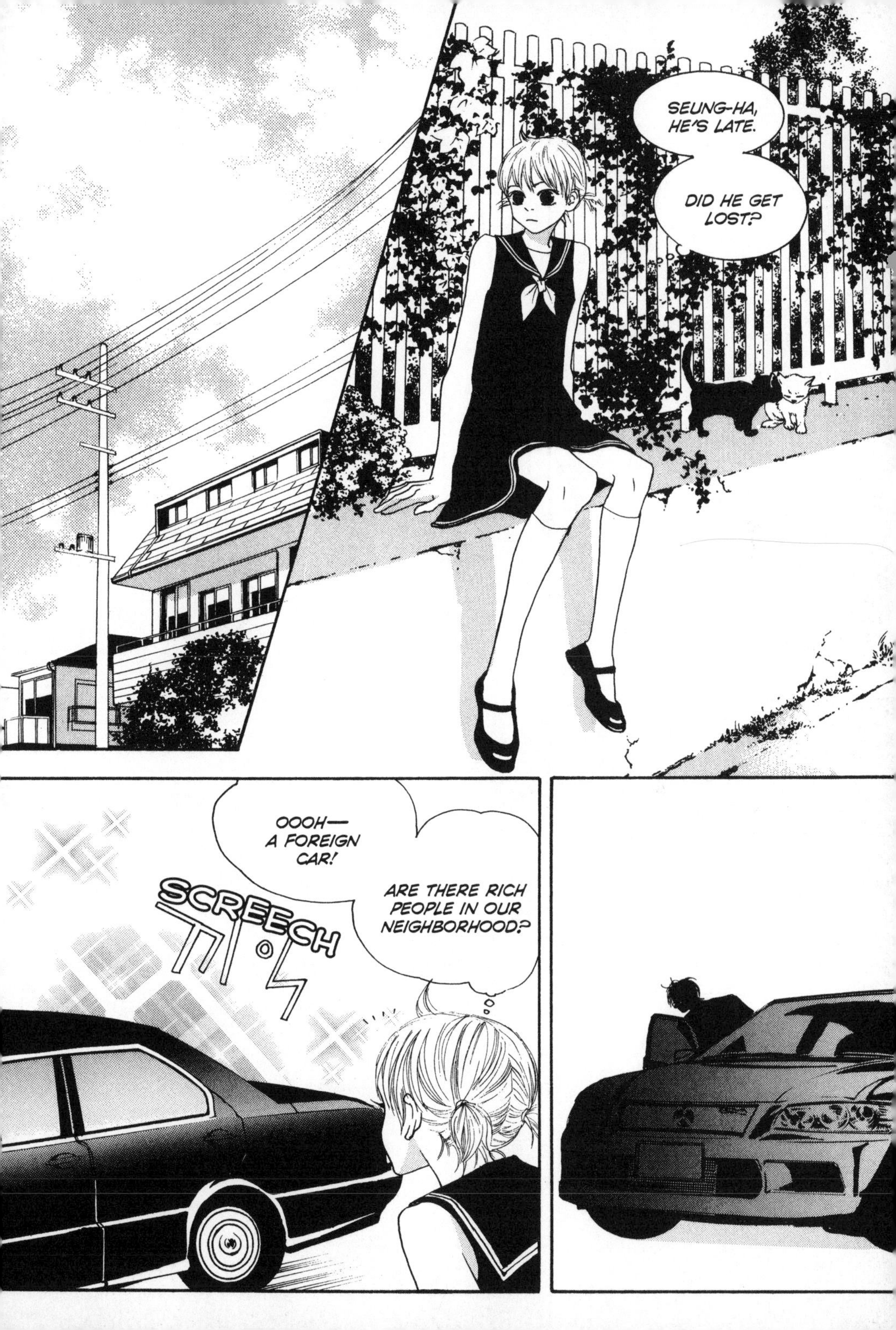
SEUNG-HA, HE'S LATE.
DID HE GET LOST?
OOOH— A FOREIGN CAR!
SCREECH
ARE THERE RICH PEOPLE IN OUR NEIGHBORHOOD?

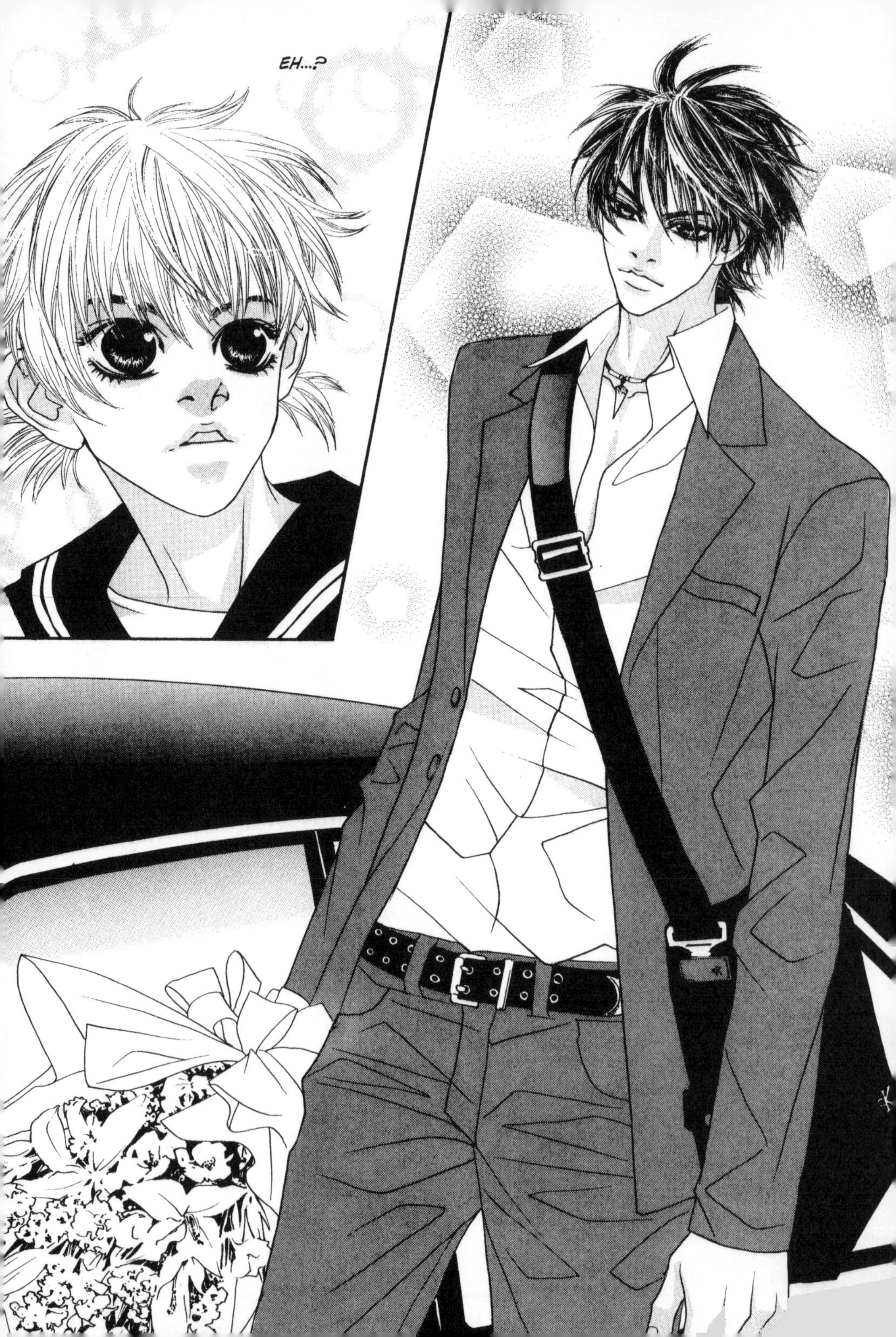
EH...?

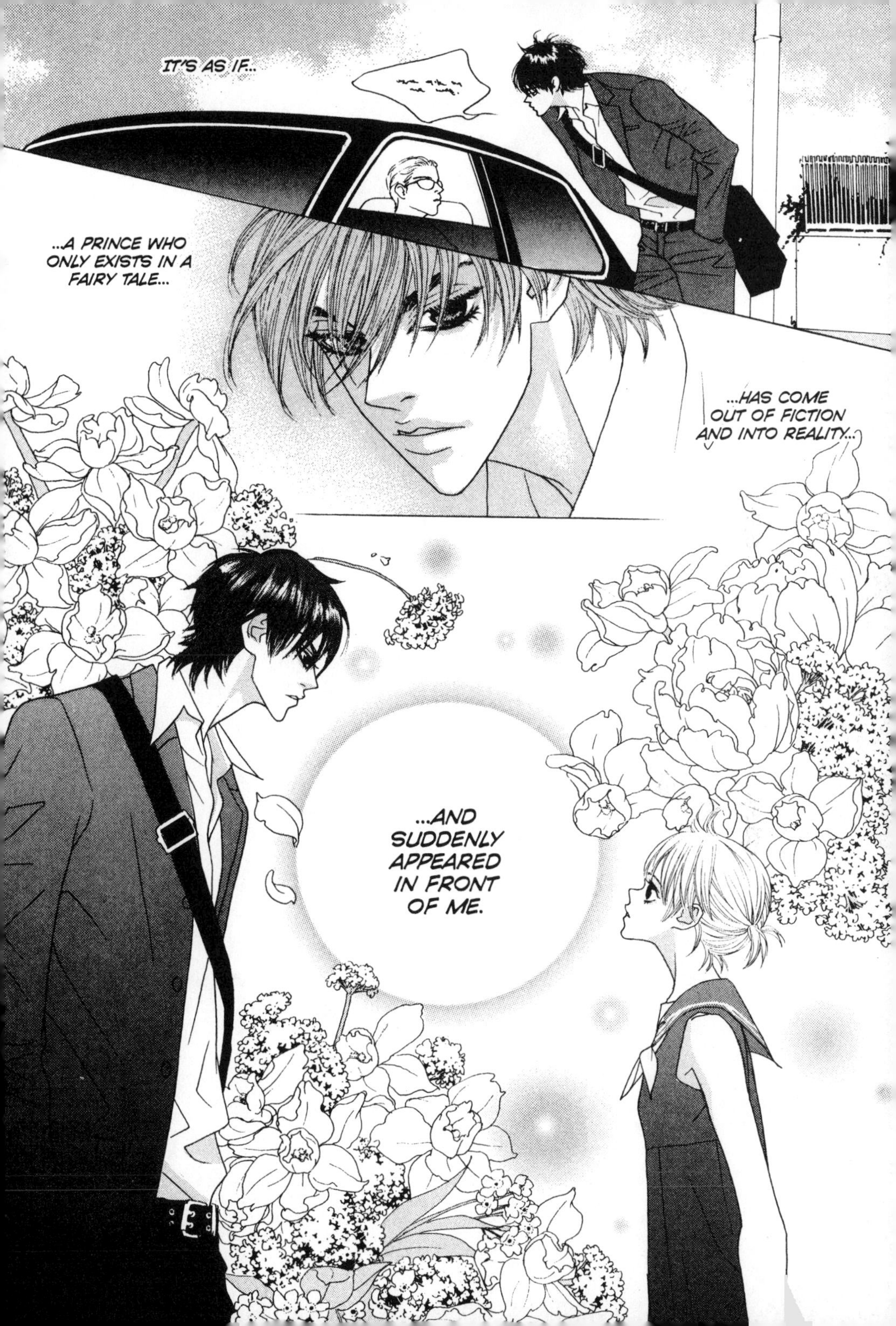
IT'S AS IF...
...A PRINCE WHO ONLY EXISTS IN A FAIRY TALE...
...HAS COME OUT OF FICTION AND INTO REALITY...
...AND SUDDENLY APPEARED IN FRONT OF ME.

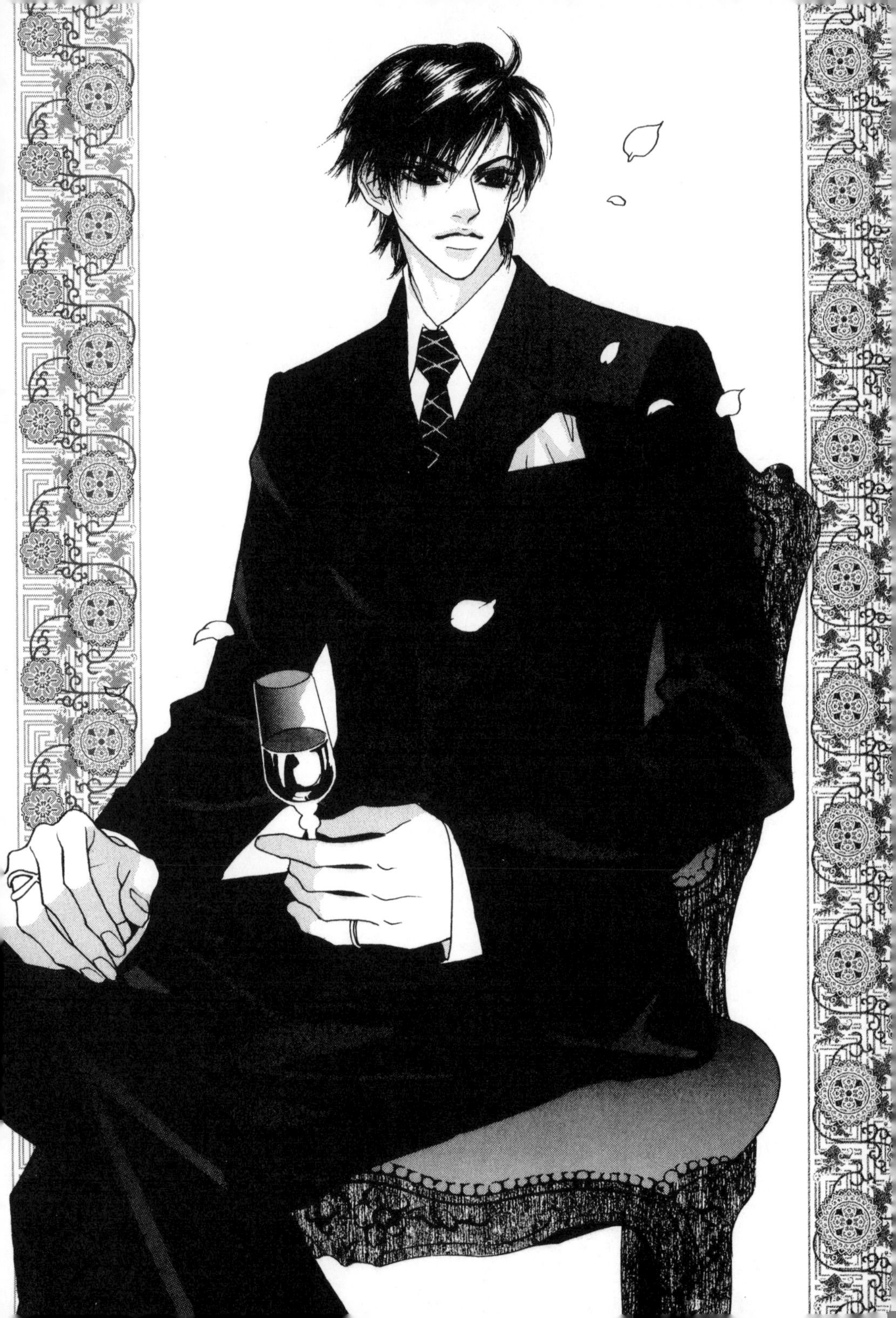

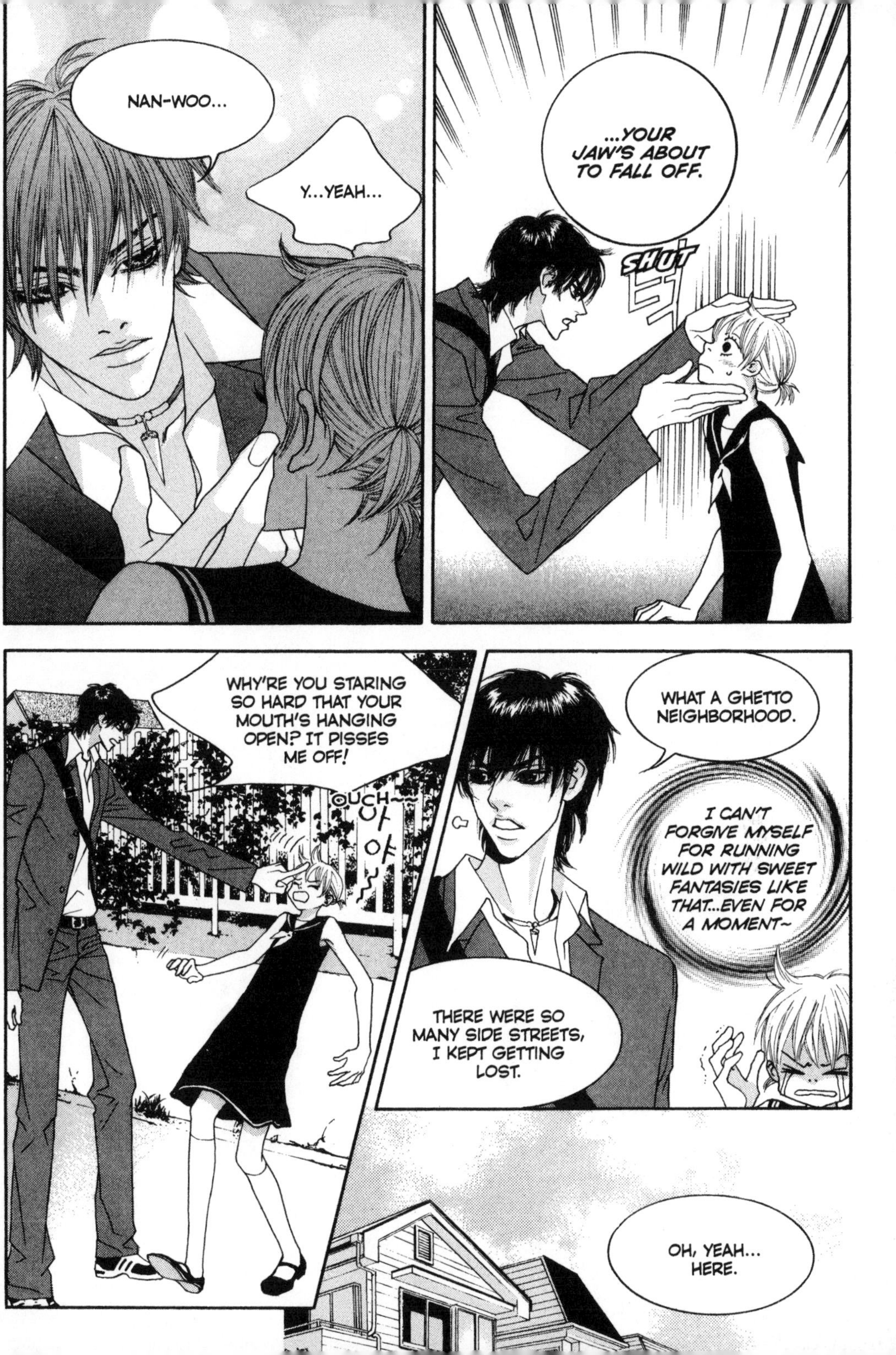
NAN-WOO...
Y...YEAH...
...YOUR JAW'S ABOUT TO FALL OFF.
SHUT
WHY'RE YOU STARING SO HARD THAT YOUR MOUTH'S HANGING OPEN? IT PISSES ME OFF!
OUCH~~
WHAT A GHETTO NEIGHBORHOOD.
I CAN'T FORGIVE MYSELF FOR RUNNING WILD WITH SWEET FANTASIES LIKE THAT...EVEN FOR A MOMENT~
THERE WERE SO MANY SIDE STREETS, I KEPT GETTING LOST.
OH, YEAH... HERE.

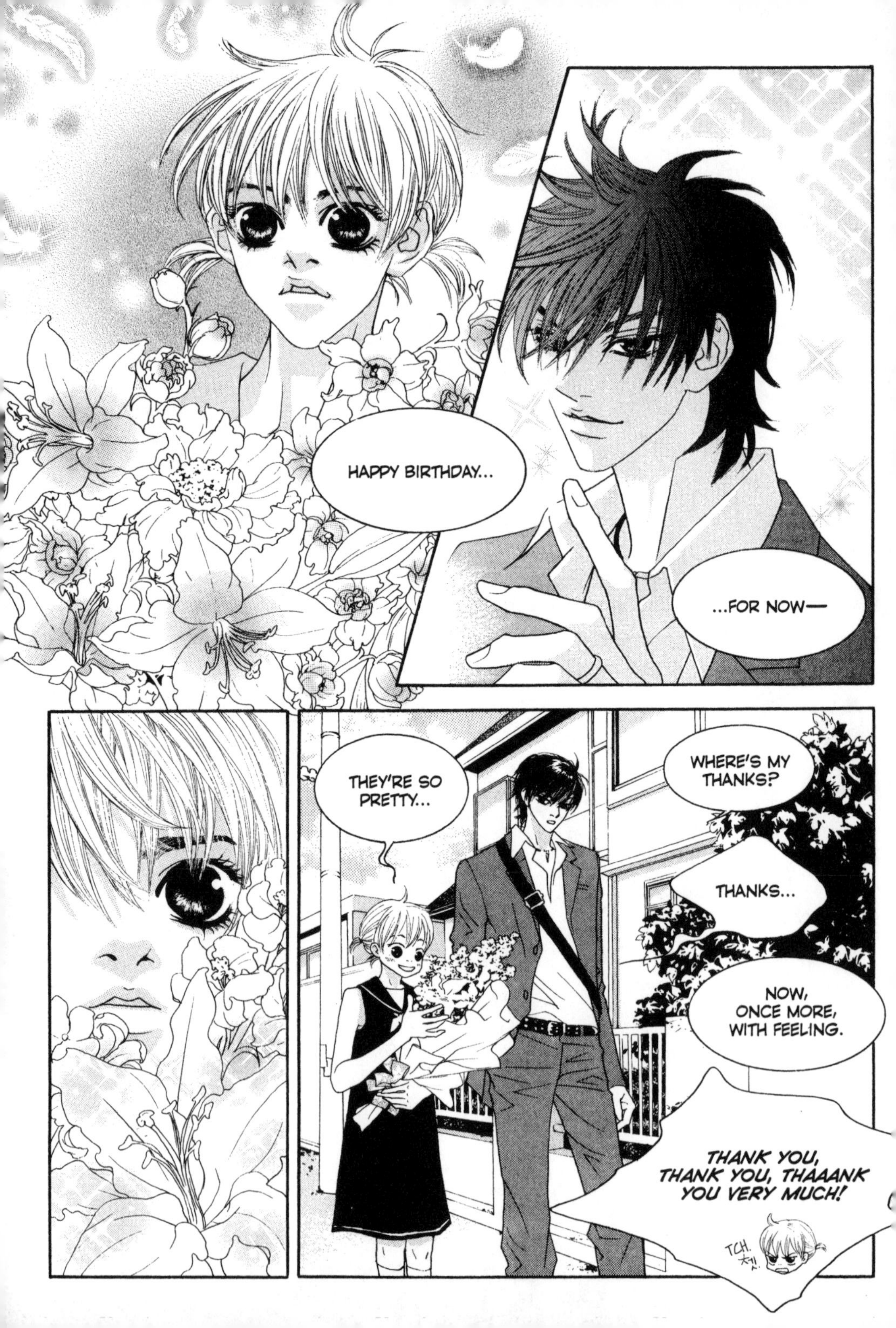
HAPPY BIRTHDAY...
...FOR NOW—
THEY'RE SO PRETTY...
WHERE'S MY THANKS?
THANKS...
NOW, ONCE MORE, WITH FEELING.
THANK YOU, THANK YOU, THAAANK YOU VERY MUCH!
TCH.

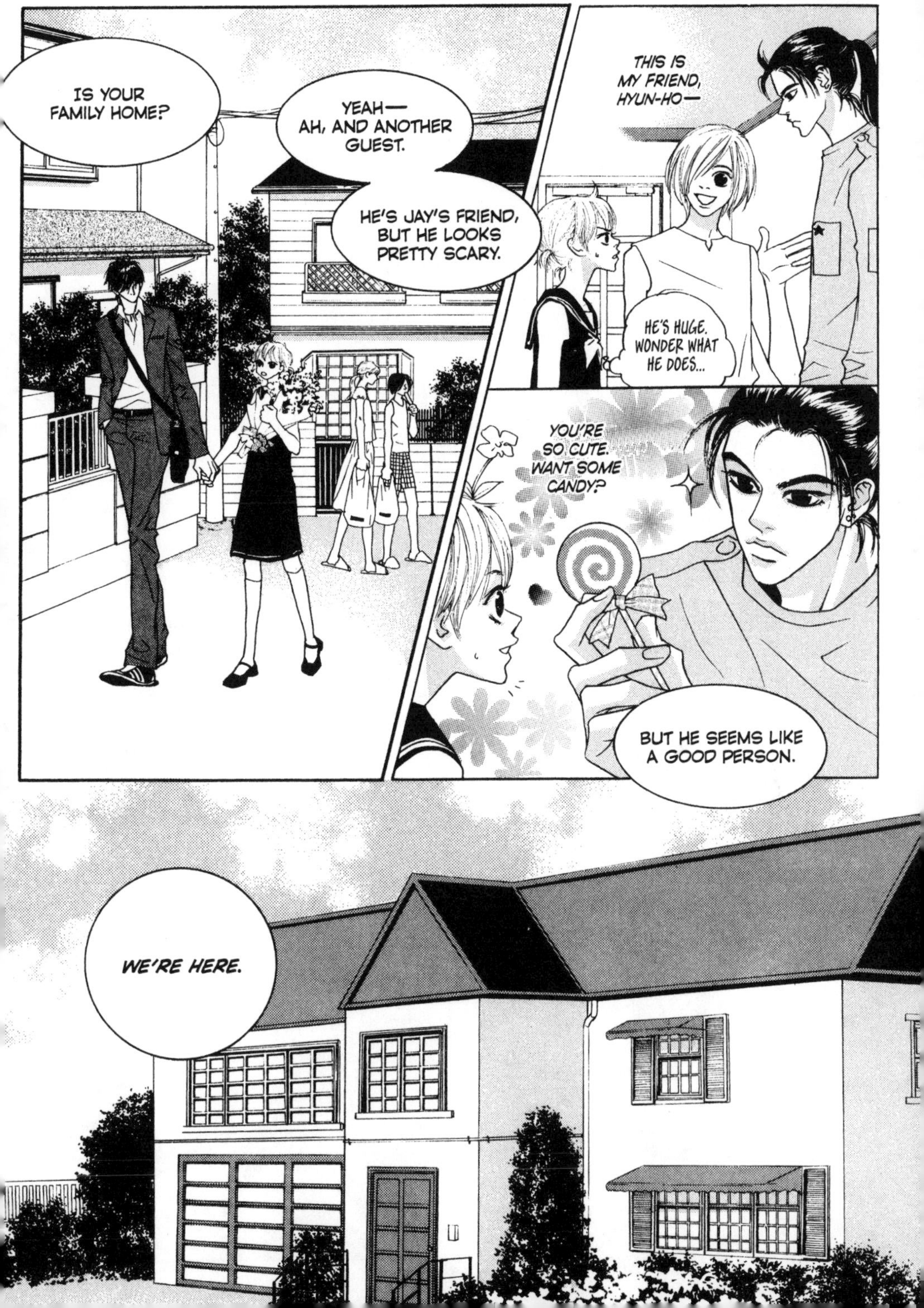
IS YOUR FAMILY HOME?
YEAH— AH, AND ANOTHER GUEST.
HE'S JAY'S FRIEND, BUT HE LOOKS PRETTY SCARY.
THIS IS MY FRIEND, HYUN-HO—
HE'S HUGE. WONDER WHAT HE DOES...
YOU'RE SO CUTE. WANT SOME CANDY?
BUT HE SEEMS LIKE A GOOD PERSON.
WE'RE HERE.

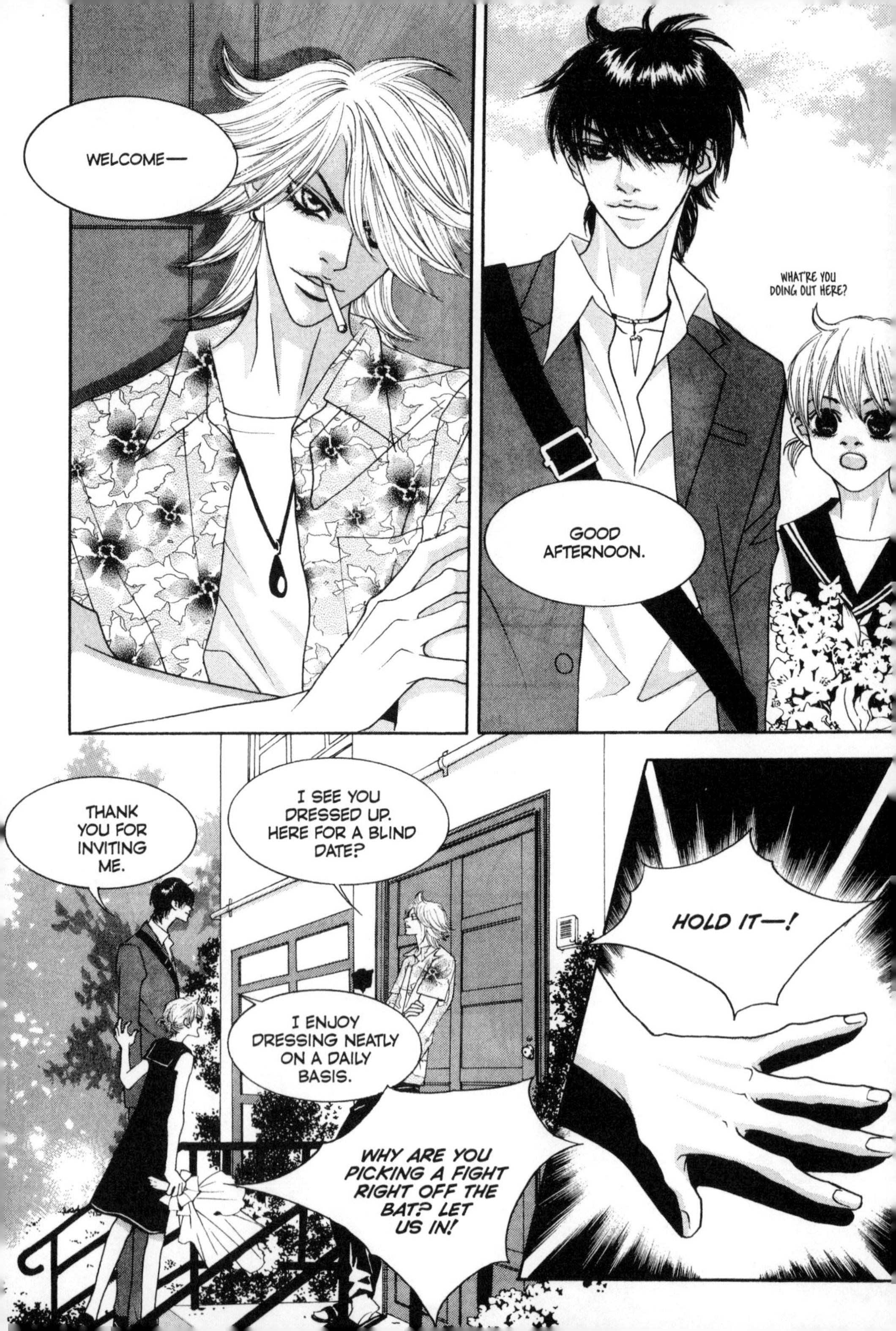

WELCOME—
WHAT'RE YOU DOING OUT HERE?
GOOD AFTERNOON.
THANK YOU FOR INVITING ME.
I SEE YOU DRESSED UP. HERE FOR A BLIND DATE?
I ENJOY DRESSING NEATLY ON A DAILY BASIS.
HOLD IT—!
WHY ARE YOU PICKING A FIGHT RIGHT OFF THE BAT? LET US IN!

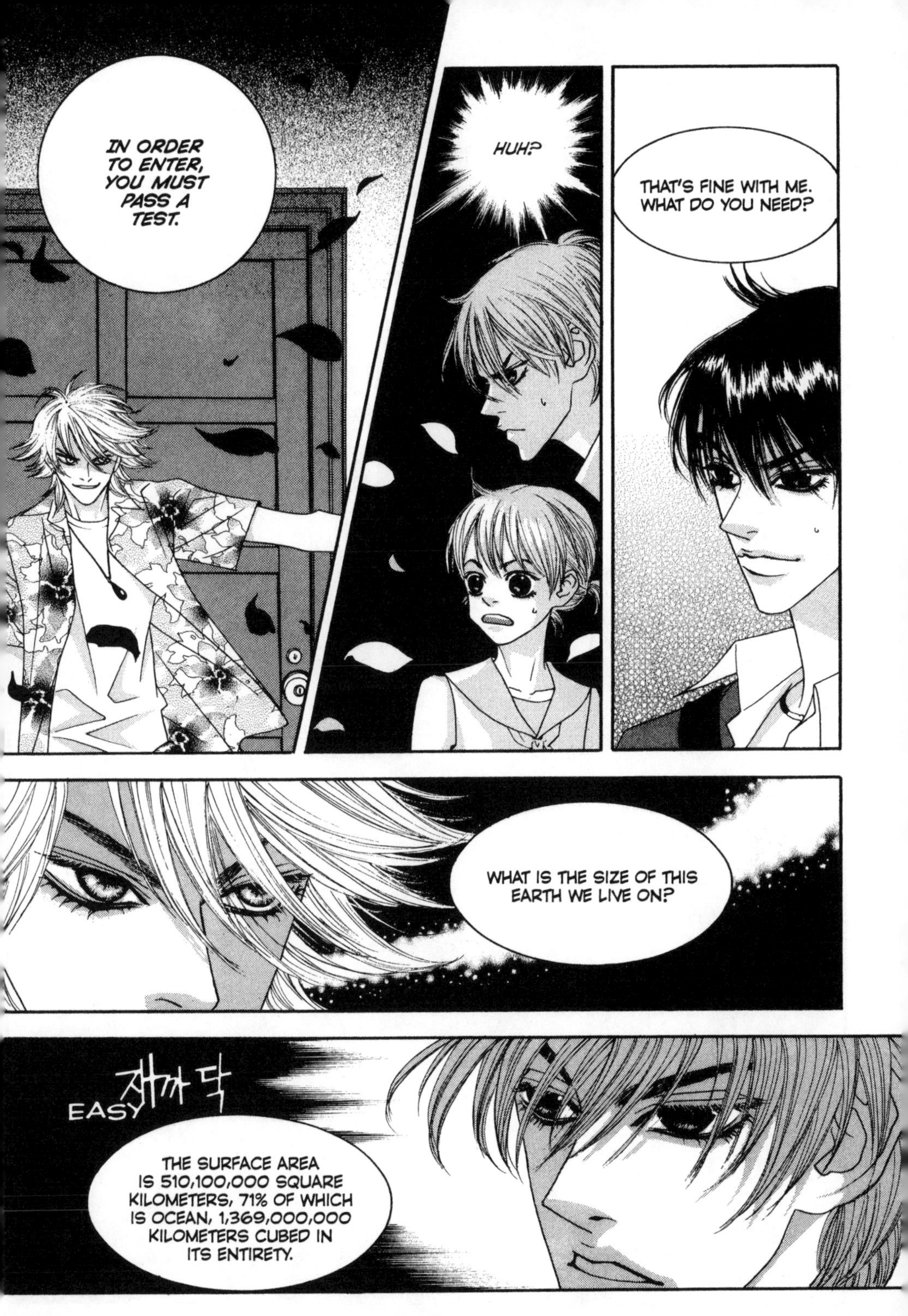
IN ORDER TO ENTER, YOU MUST PASS A TEST.
HUH?
THAT'S FINE WITH ME. WHAT DO YOU NEED?
WHAT IS THE SIZE OF THIS EARTH WE LIVE ON?
EASY
THE SURFACE AREA IS 510,100,000 SQUARE KILOMETERS, 71% OF WHICH IS OCEAN, 1,369,000,000 KILOMETERS CUBED IN ITS ENTIRETY.

THE HEIGHT OF MOUNT BAEK-DU?

ALTITUDE: 2,750 KILO-METERS.

3,598 × 4,412 ÷ 350 − 72 = ?

45,283.36.

WHOA.....

DIZZY~

WHO RECEIVED THE 1916 NOBEL PRIZE IN LITERATURE?

CARL GUSTAF VERNER VON HEIDENSTAM.

TH-THEN... WHAT'S THE NAME OF TETSURO HOSHINO'S FATHER FROM *GALAXY EXPRESS 999*?

FAUST!

*A CELEBRATED JAPANESE MANGA SERIES BY LEIJI MATSUMOTO WHICH WAS ALSO MADE INTO SEVERAL ANIME TV SERIES AND FILMS.

MAY I COME IN NOW?

all clear

NAN-WOO! YOU TOLD HIM ALL THE ANSWERS, DIDN'T YOU! YOU TRAITOR! HOW COULD YOU?

HOW CAN I TELL HIM SOMETHING I DON'T EVEN KNOW?

BY THE WAY, DID YOU COME HERE EMPTY-HANDED?

NO, HERE—

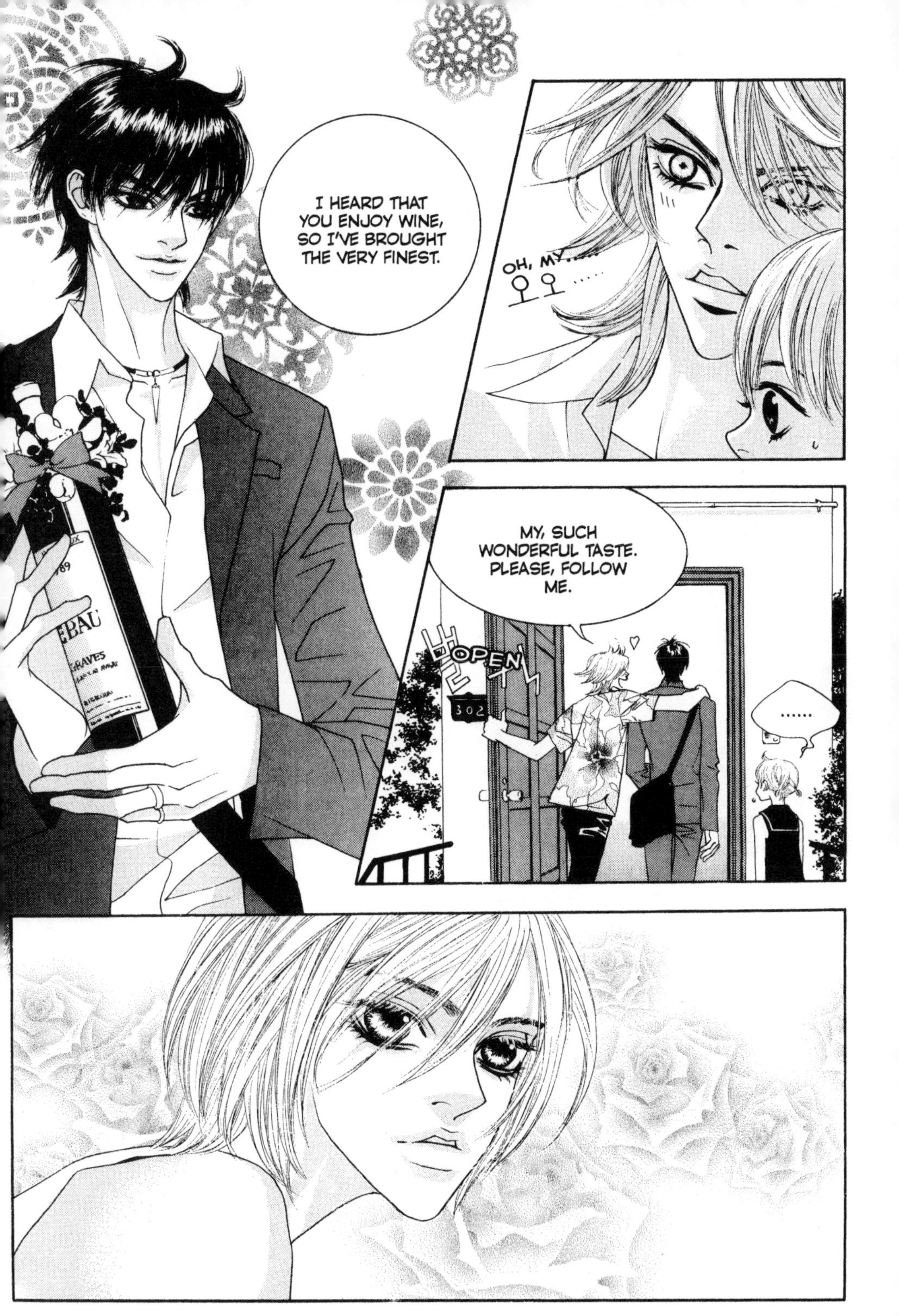
I HEARD THAT YOU ENJOY WINE, SO I'VE BROUGHT THE VERY FINEST.
OH, MY......
MY, SUCH WONDERFUL TASTE. PLEASE, FOLLOW ME.
OPEN
......

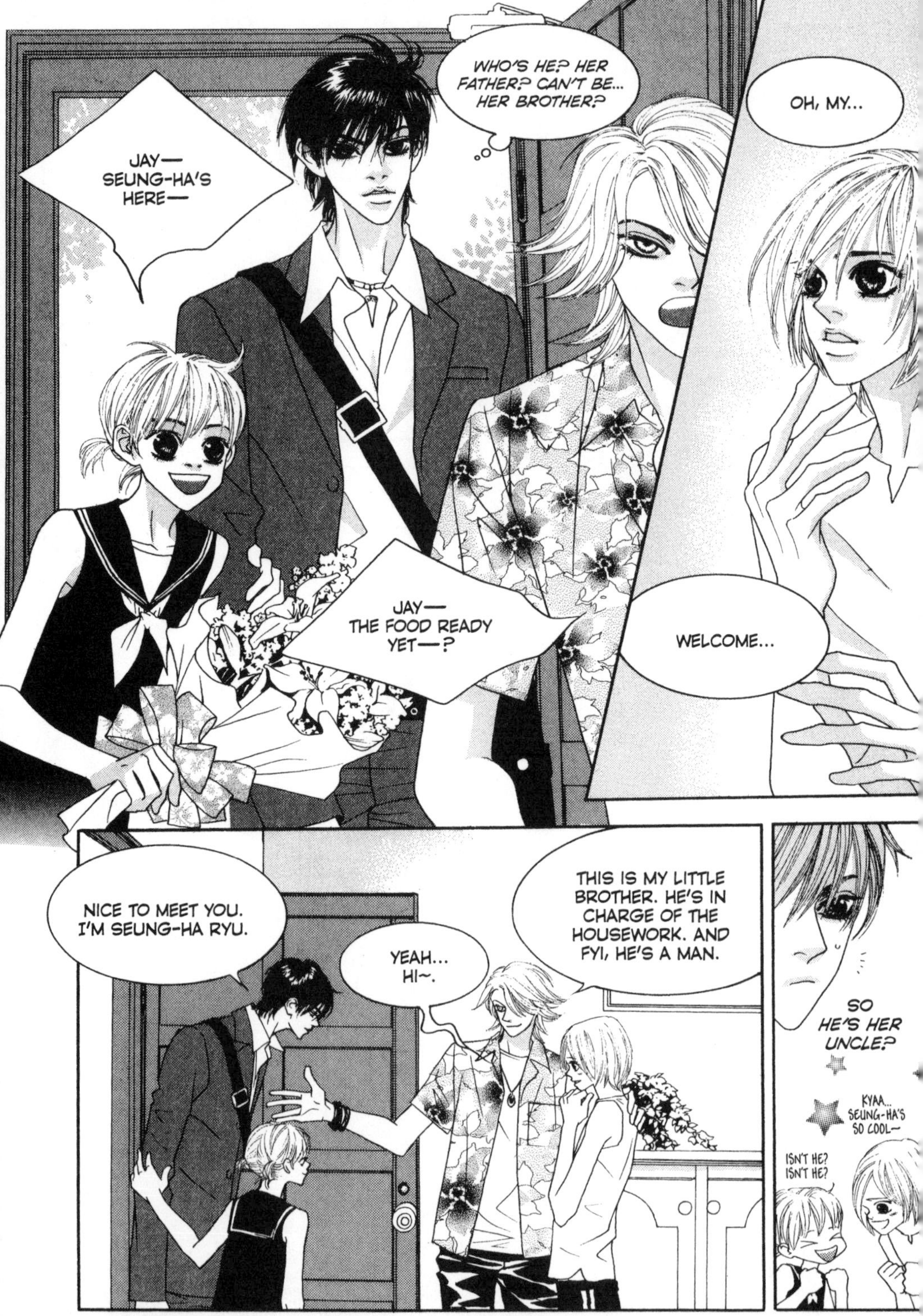
JAY— SEUNG-HA'S HERE—
WHO'S HE? HER FATHER? CAN'T BE... HER BROTHER?
JAY— THE FOOD READY YET—?
OH, MY...
WELCOME...
NICE TO MEET YOU. I'M SEUNG-HA RYU.
YEAH... HI~.
THIS IS MY LITTLE BROTHER. HE'S IN CHARGE OF THE HOUSEWORK. AND FYI, HE'S A MAN.
SO HE'S HER UNCLE?
KYAA... SEUNG-HA'S SO COOL~
ISN'T HE? ISN'T HE?

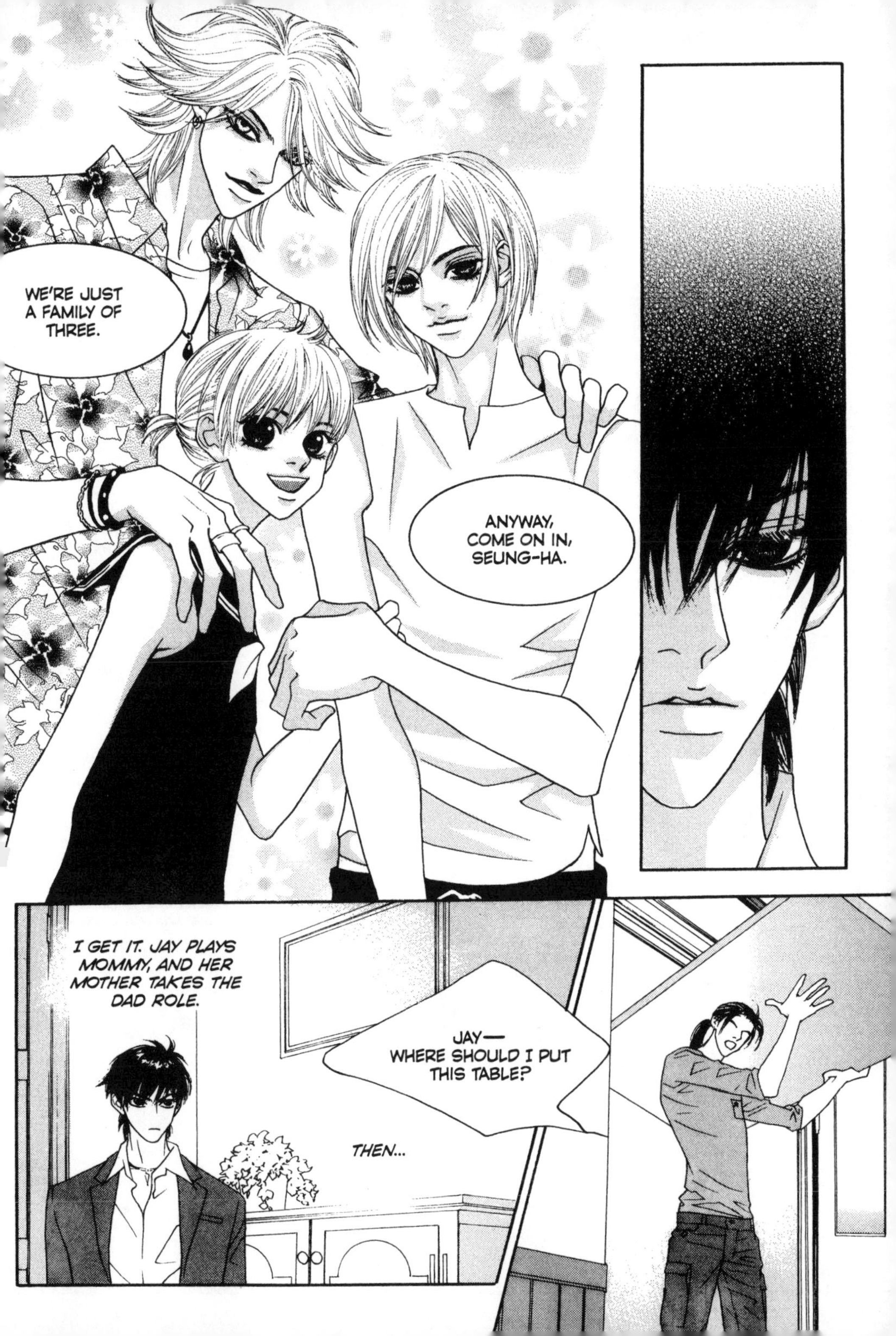
WE'RE JUST A FAMILY OF THREE.
ANYWAY, COME ON IN, SEUNG-HA.
I GET IT. JAY PLAYS MOMMY, AND HER MOTHER TAKES THE DAD ROLE.
JAY— WHERE SHOULD I PUT THIS TABLE?
THEN...

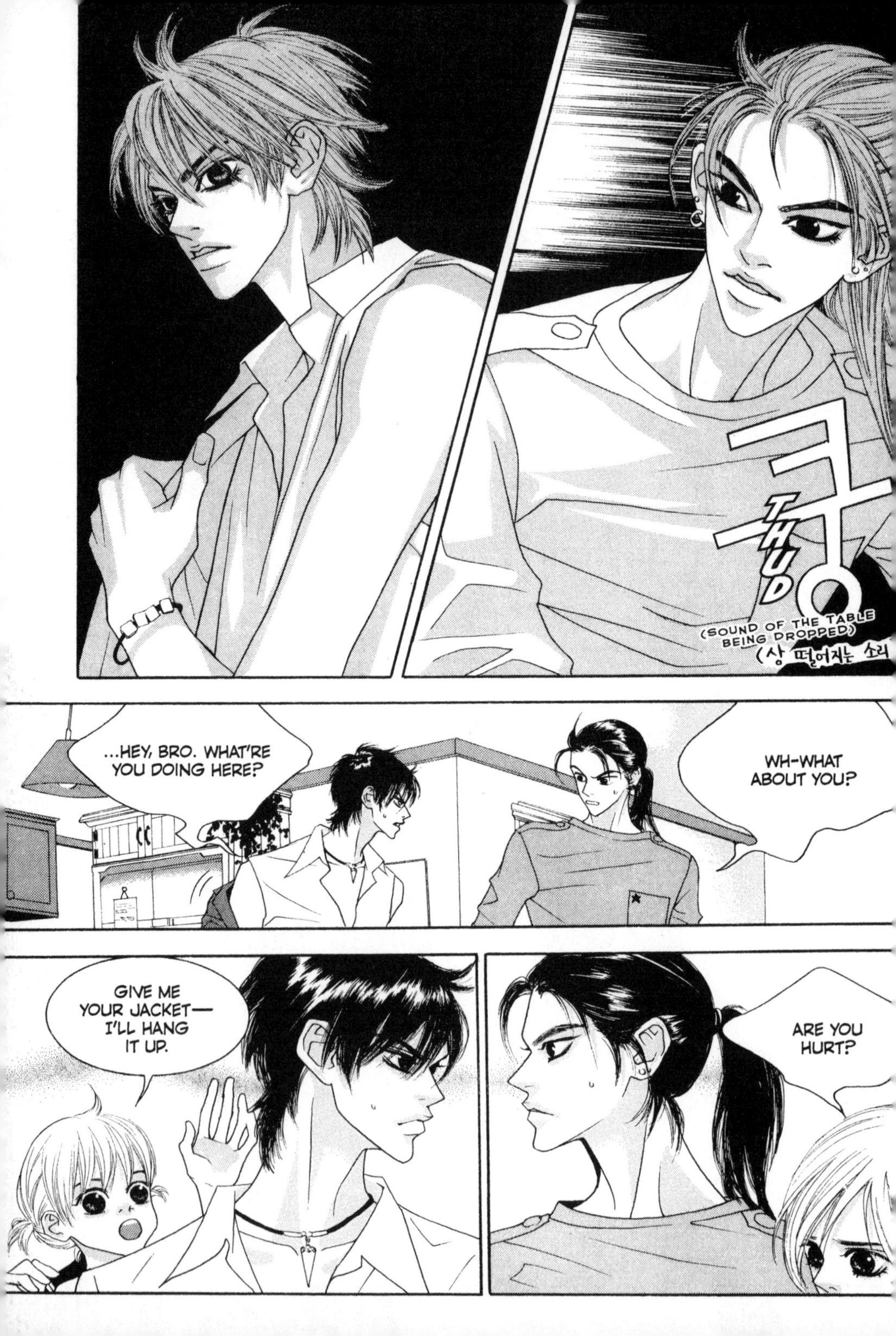
THUD
(SOUND OF THE TABLE BEING DROPPED)
(상 떨어지는 소리
...HEY, BRO. WHAT'RE YOU DOING HERE?
WH-WHAT ABOUT YOU?
GIVE ME YOUR JACKET— I'LL HANG IT UP.
ARE YOU HURT?

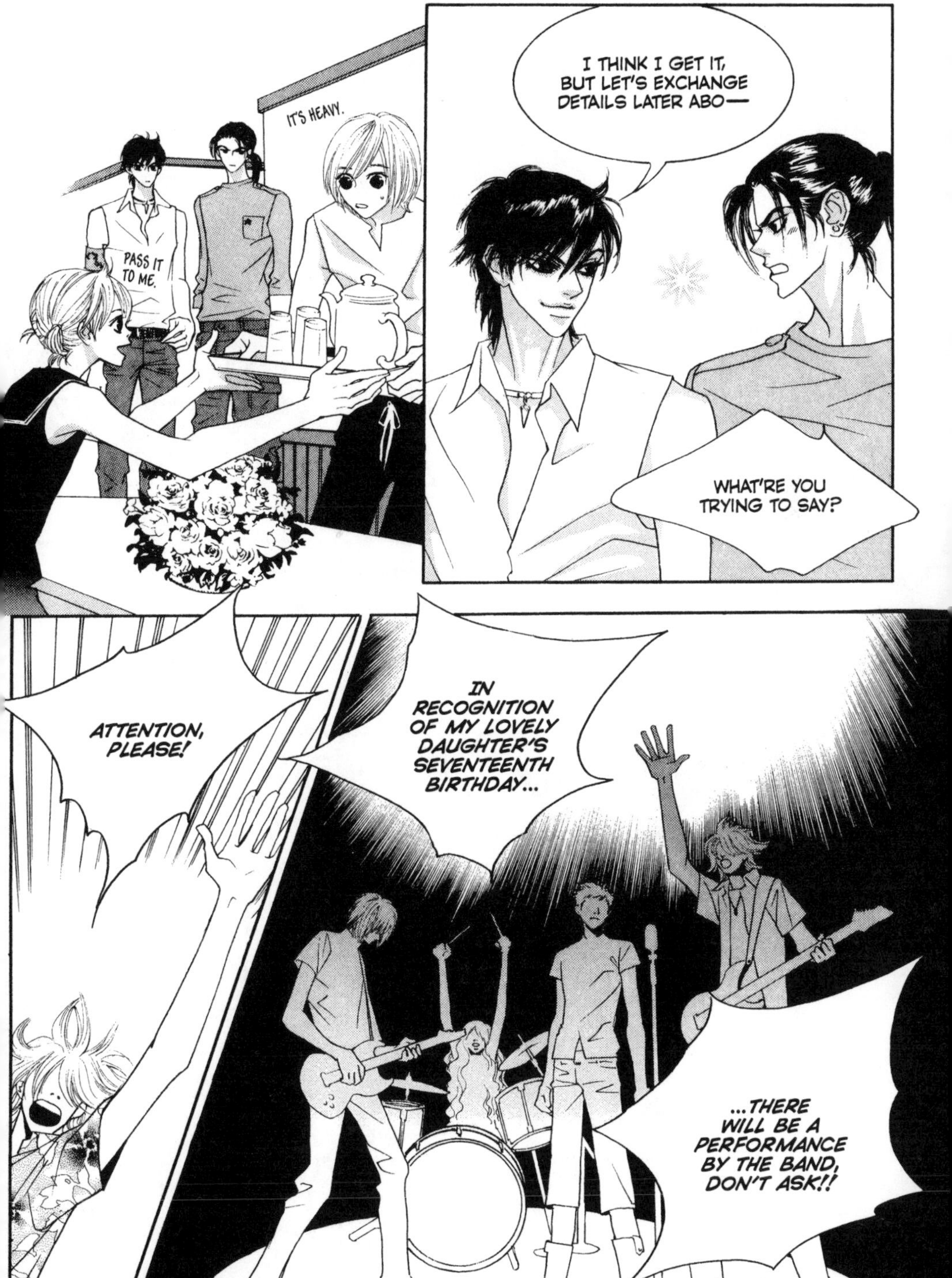
IT'S HEAVY.
PASS IT TO ME.
I THINK I GET IT, BUT LET'S EXCHANGE DETAILS LATER ABO—
WHAT'RE YOU TRYING TO SAY?
ATTENTION, PLEASE!
IN RECOGNITION OF MY LOVELY DAUGHTER'S SEVENTEENTH BIRTHDAY...
...THERE WILL BE A PERFORMANCE BY THE BAND, DON'T ASK!!

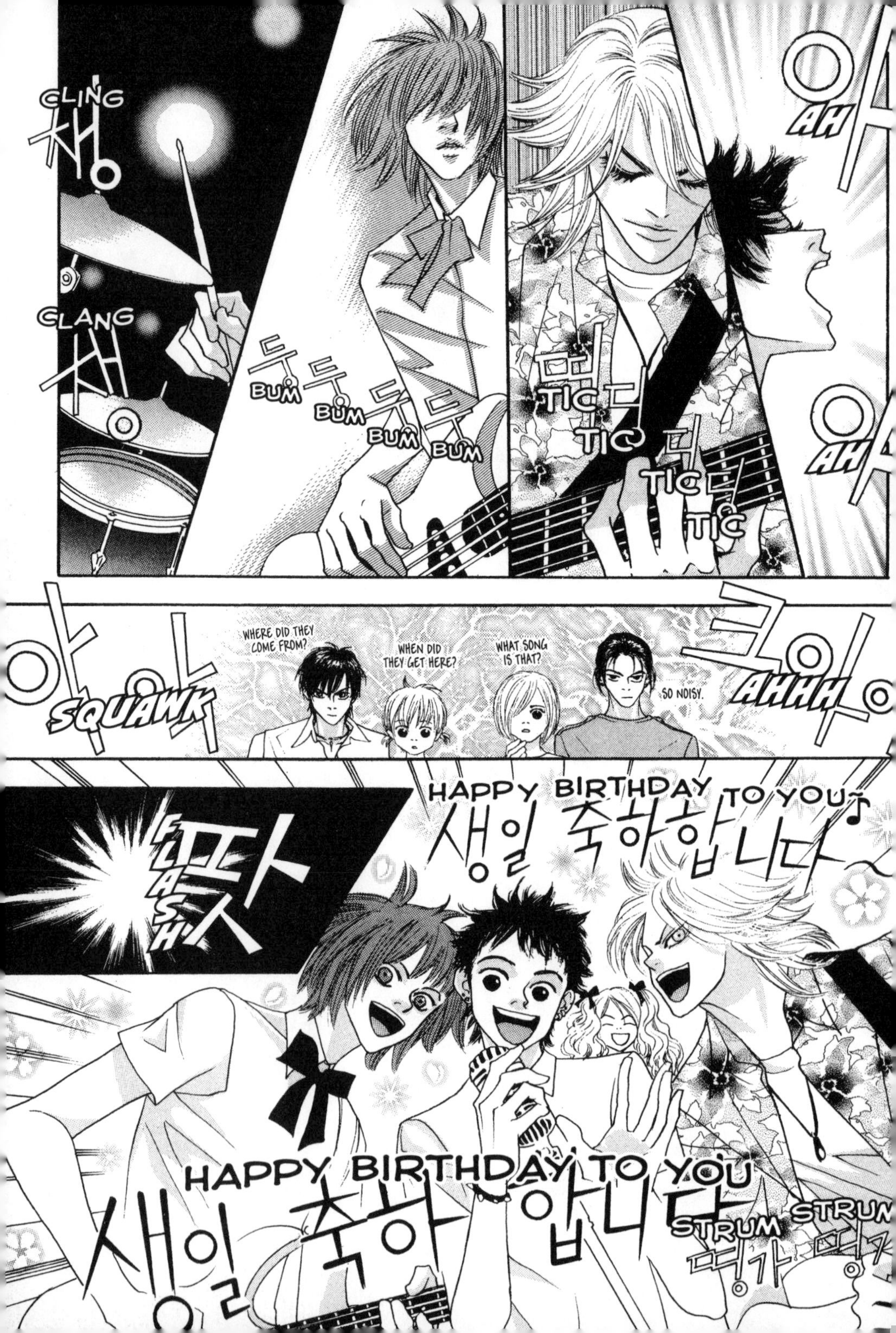

CLING
CLANG
BUM BUM BUM BUM
TIC TIC TIC TIC
AH
AH
SQUAWK
WHERE DID THEY COME FROM?
WHEN DID THEY GET HERE?
WHAT SONG IS THAT?
SO NOISY.
AHHH
FLASH
HAPPY BIRTHDAY TO YOU♪
생일 축하합니다
HAPPY BIRTHDAY TO YOU
생일 축하합니다
STRUM STRUM

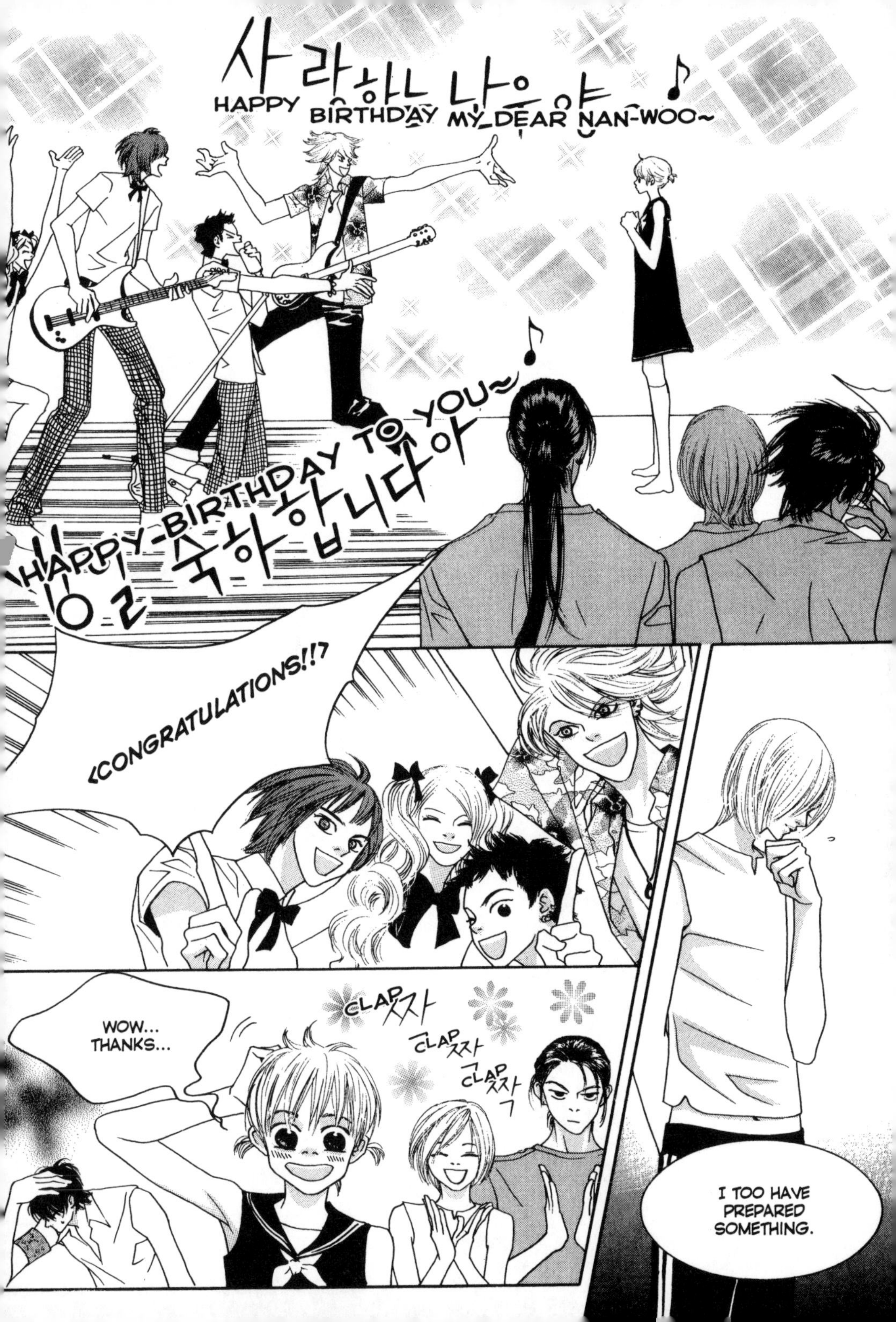
HAPPY BIRTHDAY MY DEAR NAN-WOO~
HAPPY-BIRTHDAY TO YOU~
‹CONGRATULATIONS!!›
WOW... THANKS...
CLAP
CLAP
CLAP
I TOO HAVE PREPARED SOMETHING.

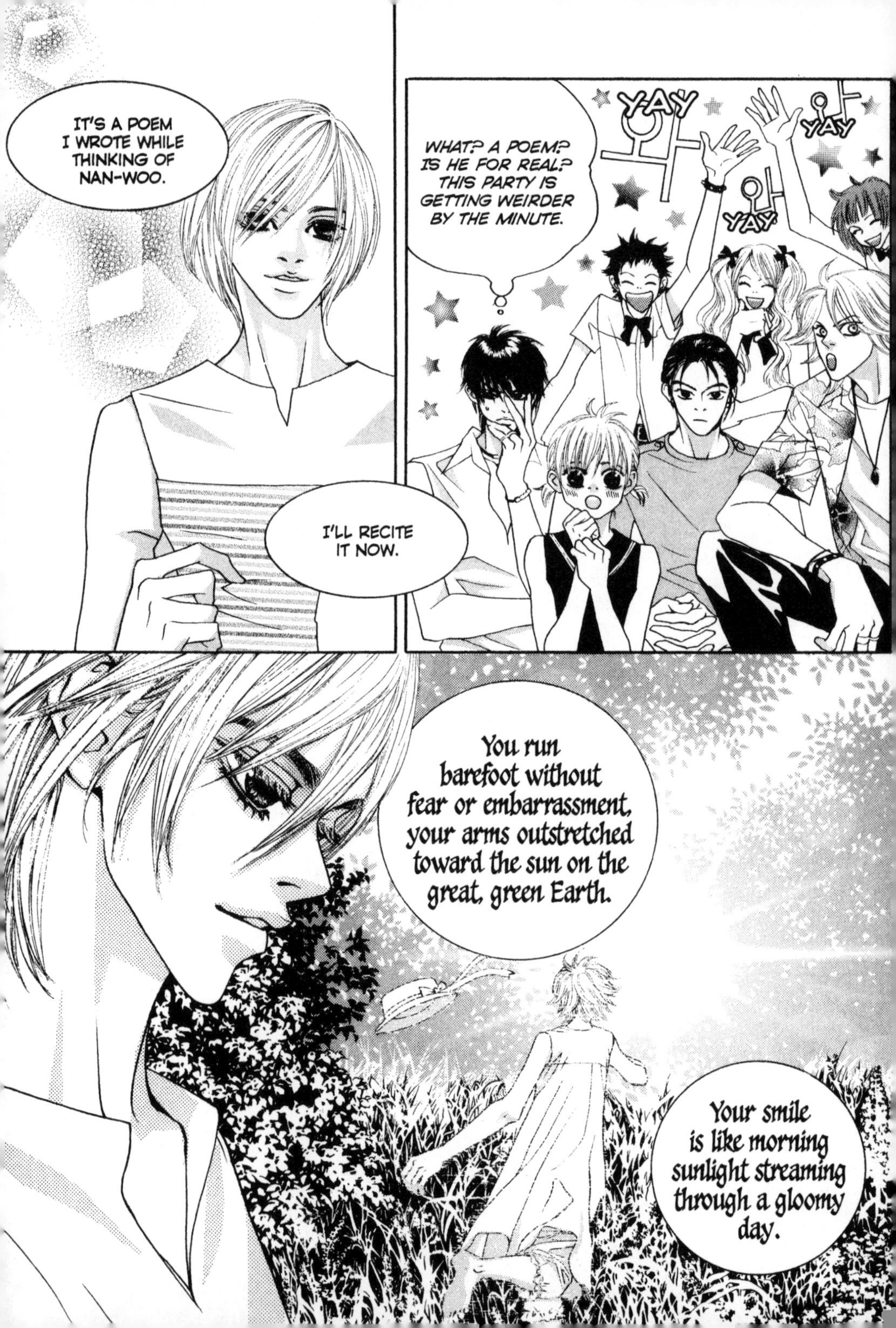

IT'S A POEM I WROTE WHILE THINKING OF NAN-WOO.
WHAT? A POEM? IS HE FOR REAL? THIS PARTY IS GETTING WEIRDER BY THE MINUTE.
YAY
YAY
YAY
I'LL RECITE IT NOW.
You run barefoot without fear or embarrassment, your arms outstretched toward the sun on the great, green Earth.
Your smile is like morning sunlight streaming through a gloomy day.

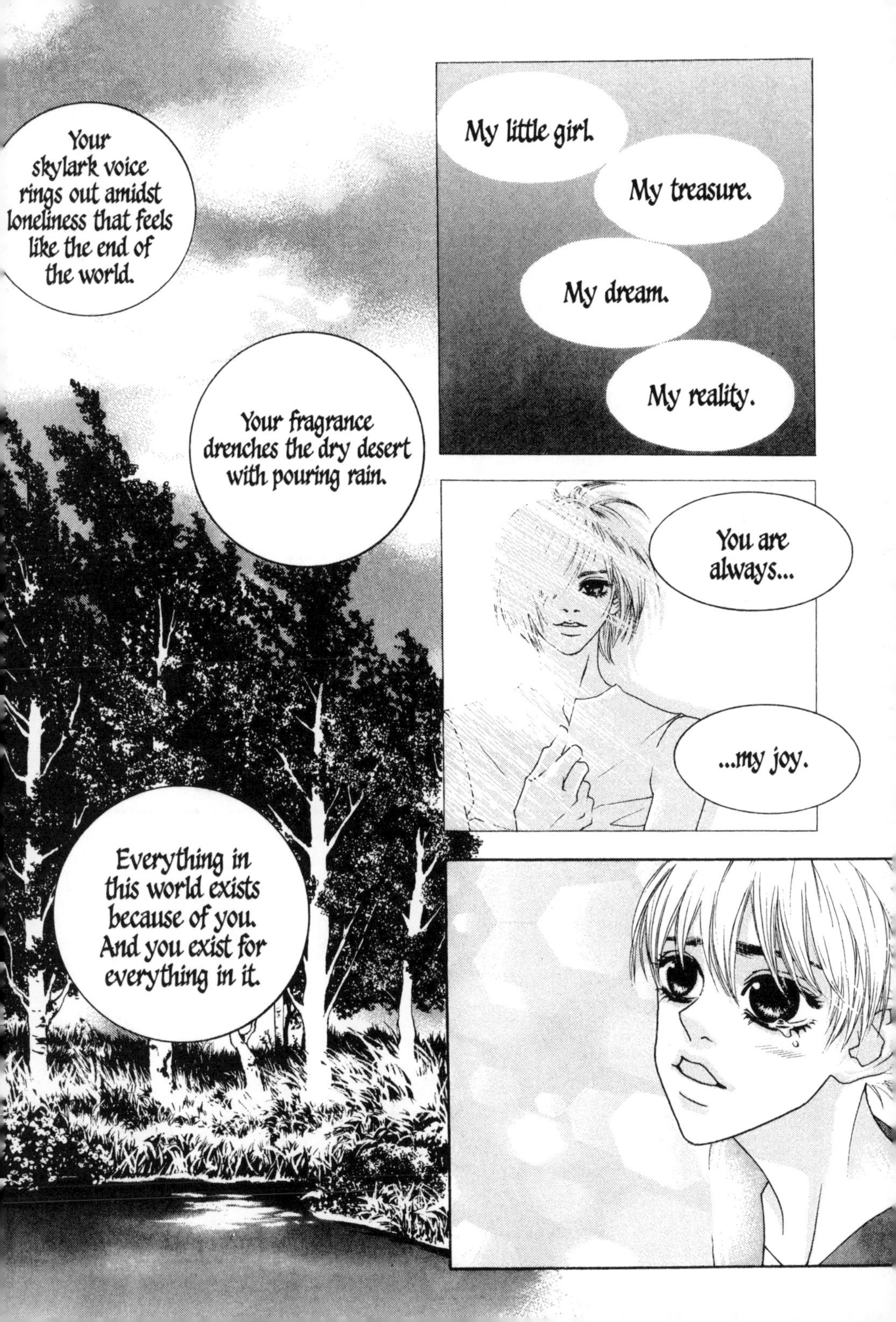
Your skylark voice rings out amidst loneliness that feels like the end of the world.
Your fragrance drenches the dry desert with pouring rain.
Everything in this world exists because of you. And you exist for everything in it.
My little girl.
My treasure.
My dream.
My reality.
You are always...
...my joy.

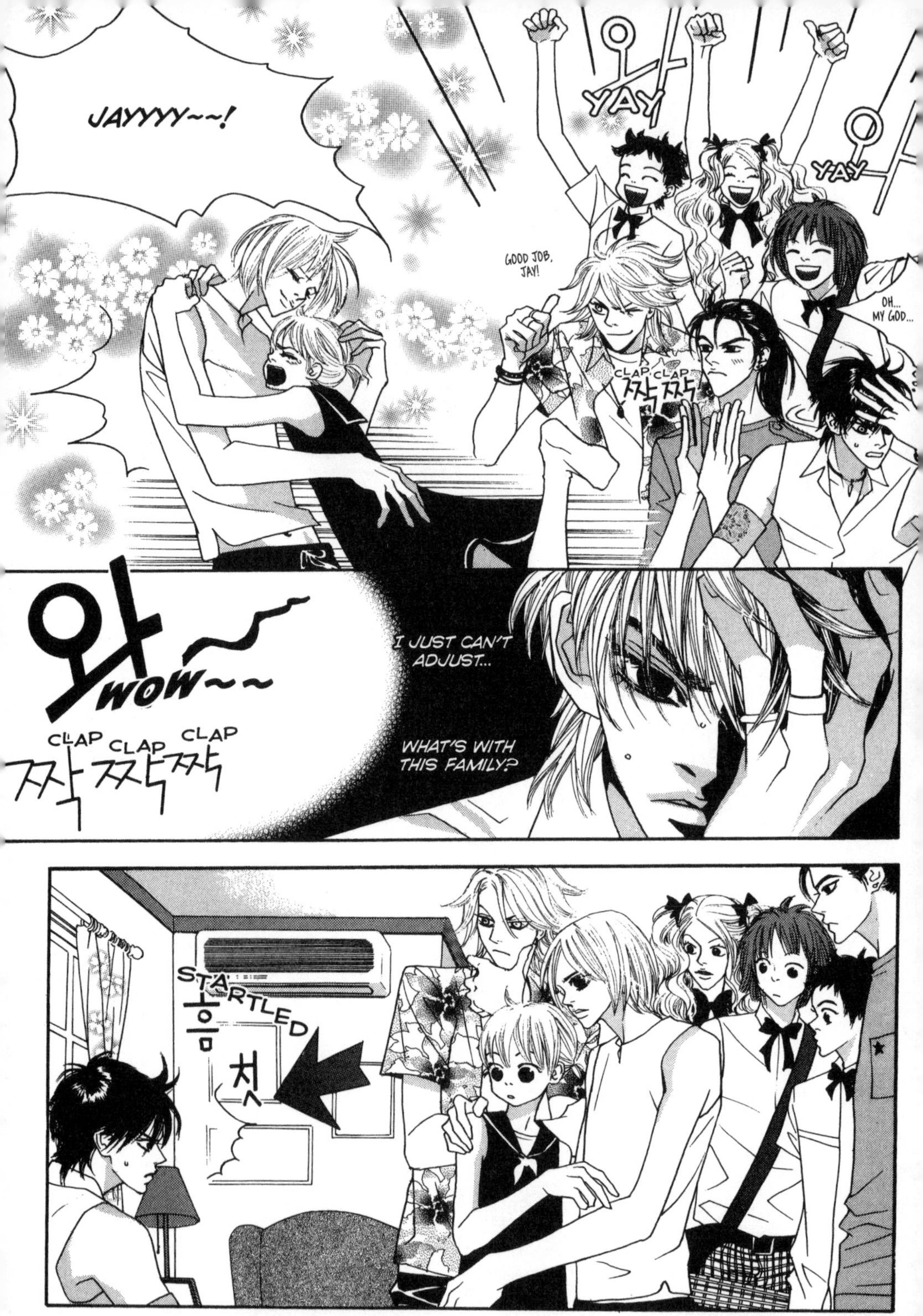
JAYYYY~~!
와 YAY
와 YAY
GOOD JOB, JAY!
CLAP CLAP 짝짝
OH... MY GOD...
와 WOW~~
CLAP CLAP CLAP 짝짝짝
I JUST CAN'T ADJUST...
WHAT'S WITH THIS FAMILY?
STARTLED 흠칫

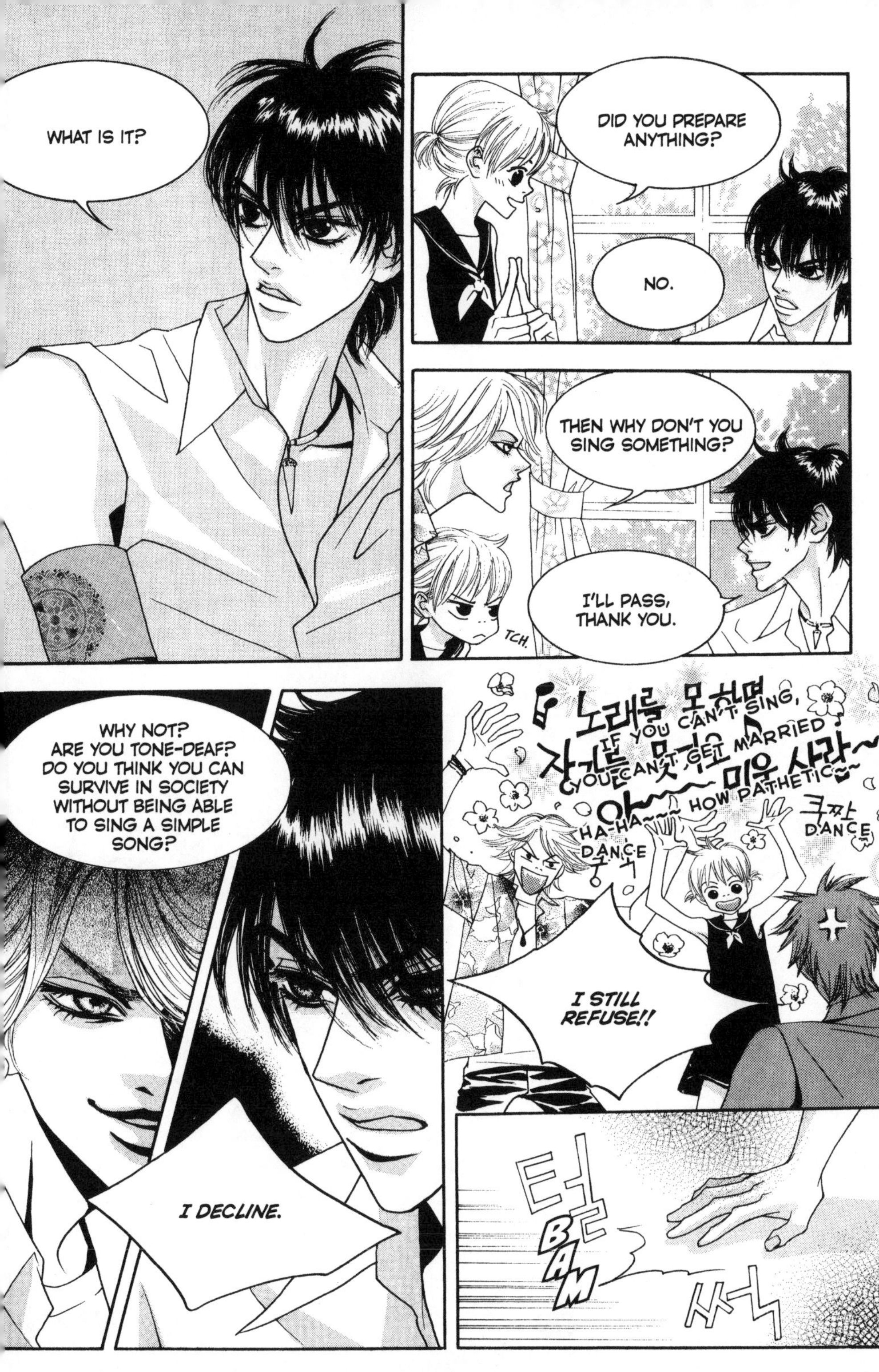
WHAT IS IT?
DID YOU PREPARE ANYTHING?
NO.
THEN WHY DON'T YOU SING SOMETHING?
I'LL PASS, THANK YOU.
TCH.
WHY NOT? ARE YOU TONE-DEAF? DO YOU THINK YOU CAN SURVIVE IN SOCIETY WITHOUT BEING ABLE TO SING A SIMPLE SONG?
I DECLINE.
노래를 못하면
IF YOU CAN'T SING,
장가를 못가요
YOU CAN'T GET MARRIED
아~~ 미운 사람~~
HA-HA~~ HOW PATHETIC~~
쿵짝
DANCE
DANCE
I STILL REFUSE!!
털
BAM
쓱

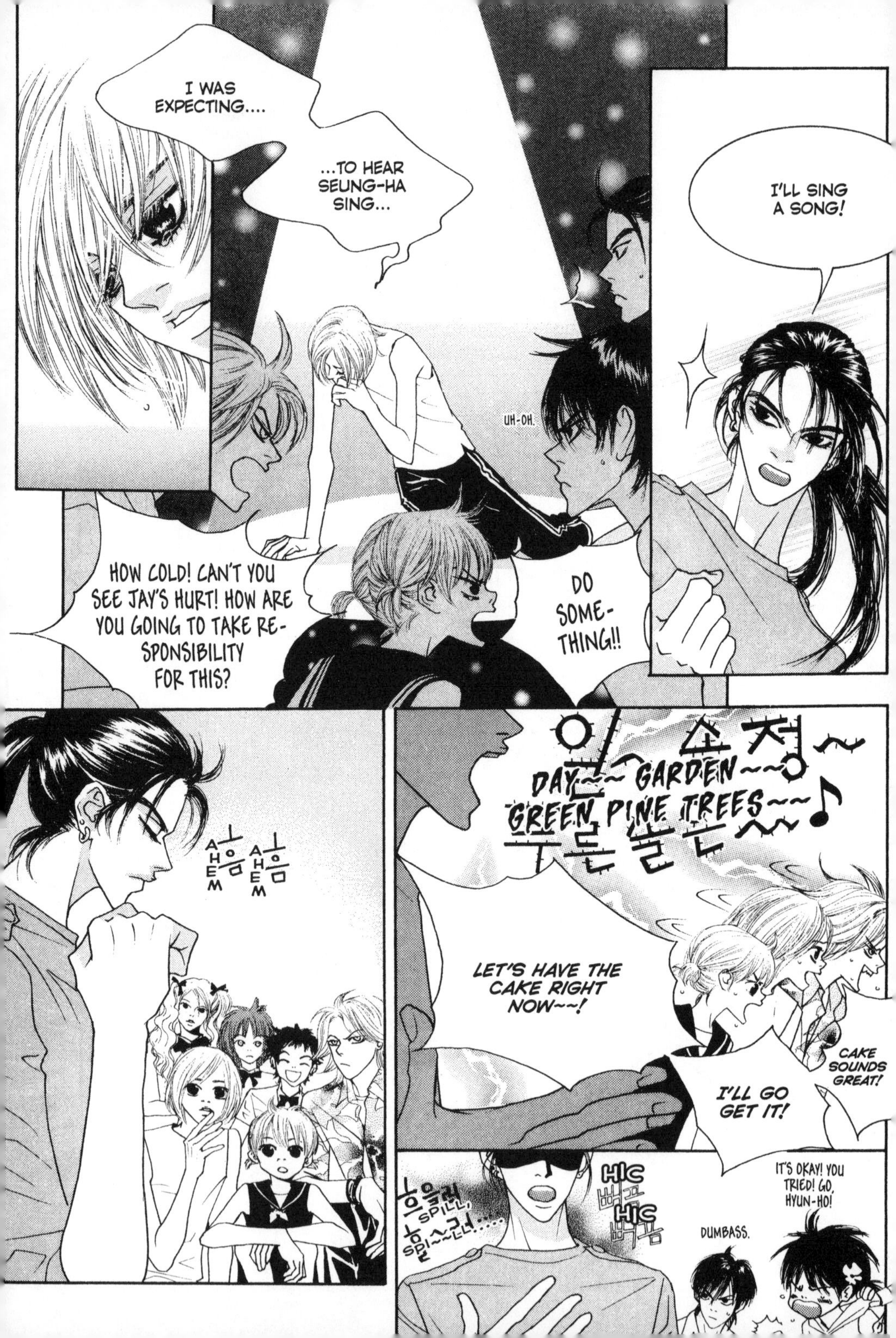
I WAS EXPECTING....
...TO HEAR SEUNG-HA SING...
UH-OH.
HOW COLD! CAN'T YOU SEE JAY'S HURT! HOW ARE YOU GOING TO TAKE RE-SPONSIBILITY FOR THIS?
DO SOME-THING!!
I'LL SING A SONG!
AHEM AHEM
DAY~~ GARDEN~~~ GREEN PINE TREES~~~♪
LET'S HAVE THE CAKE RIGHT NOW~~!
CAKE SOUNDS GREAT!
I'LL GO GET IT!
SPILL, SPILL~~....
HIC HIC
IT'S OKAY! YOU TRIED! GO, HYUN-HO!
DUMBASS.

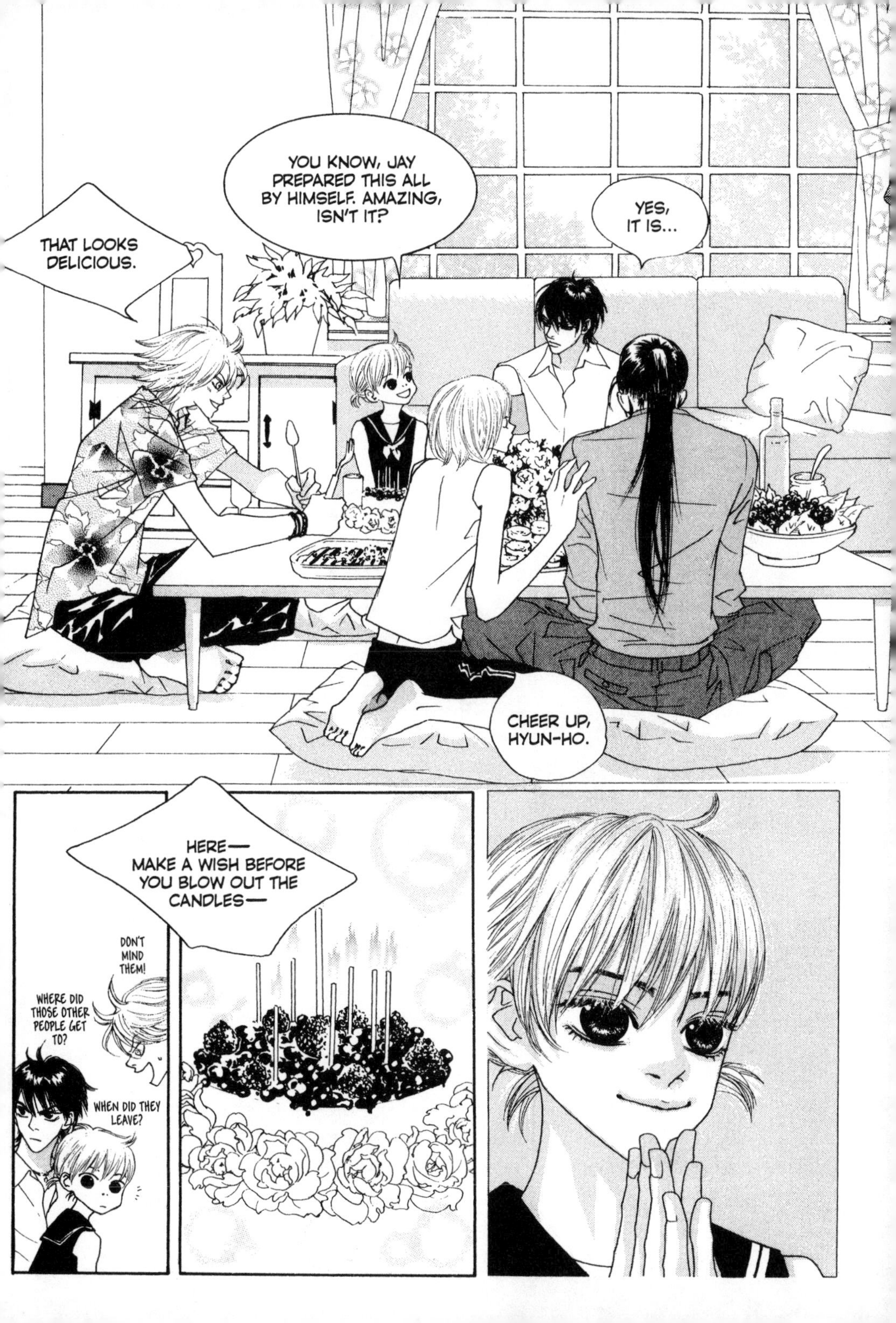
THAT LOOKS DELICIOUS.
YOU KNOW, JAY PREPARED THIS ALL BY HIMSELF. AMAZING, ISN'T IT?
YES, IT IS...
CHEER UP, HYUN-HO.
WHERE DID THOSE OTHER PEOPLE GET TO?
DON'T MIND THEM!
WHEN DID THEY LEAVE?
HERE— MAKE A WISH BEFORE YOU BLOW OUT THE CANDLES—

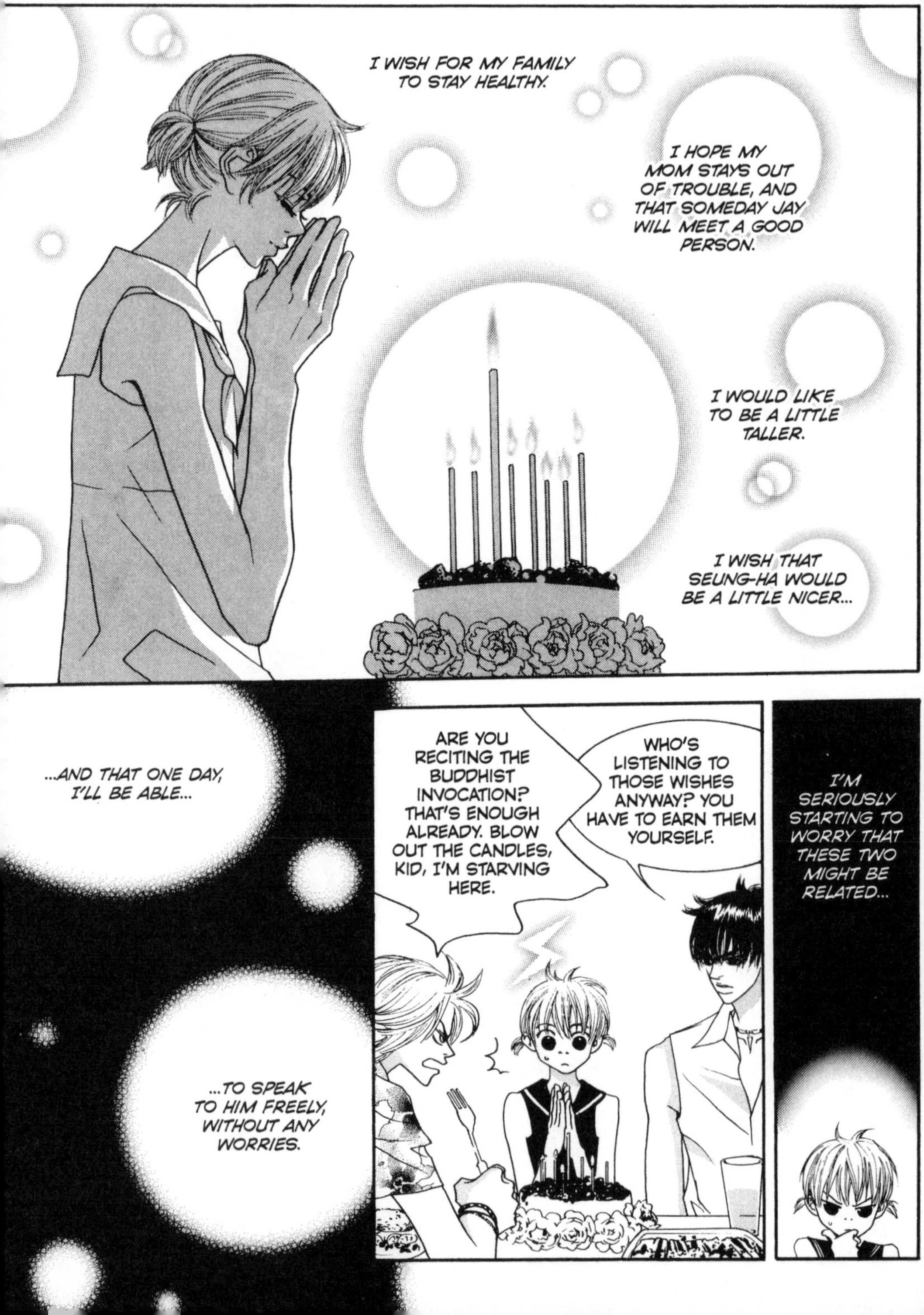
I WISH FOR MY FAMILY TO STAY HEALTHY.
I HOPE MY MOM STAYS OUT OF TROUBLE, AND THAT SOMEDAY JAY WILL MEET A GOOD PERSON.
I WOULD LIKE TO BE A LITTLE TALLER.
I WISH THAT SEUNG-HA WOULD BE A LITTLE NICER...
...AND THAT ONE DAY, I'LL BE ABLE...
...TO SPEAK TO HIM FREELY, WITHOUT ANY WORRIES.
ARE YOU RECITING THE BUDDHIST INVOCATION? THAT'S ENOUGH ALREADY. BLOW OUT THE CANDLES, KID, I'M STARVING HERE.
WHO'S LISTENING TO THOSE WISHES ANYWAY? YOU HAVE TO EARN THEM YOURSELF.
I'M SERIOUSLY STARTING TO WORRY THAT THESE TWO MIGHT BE RELATED...

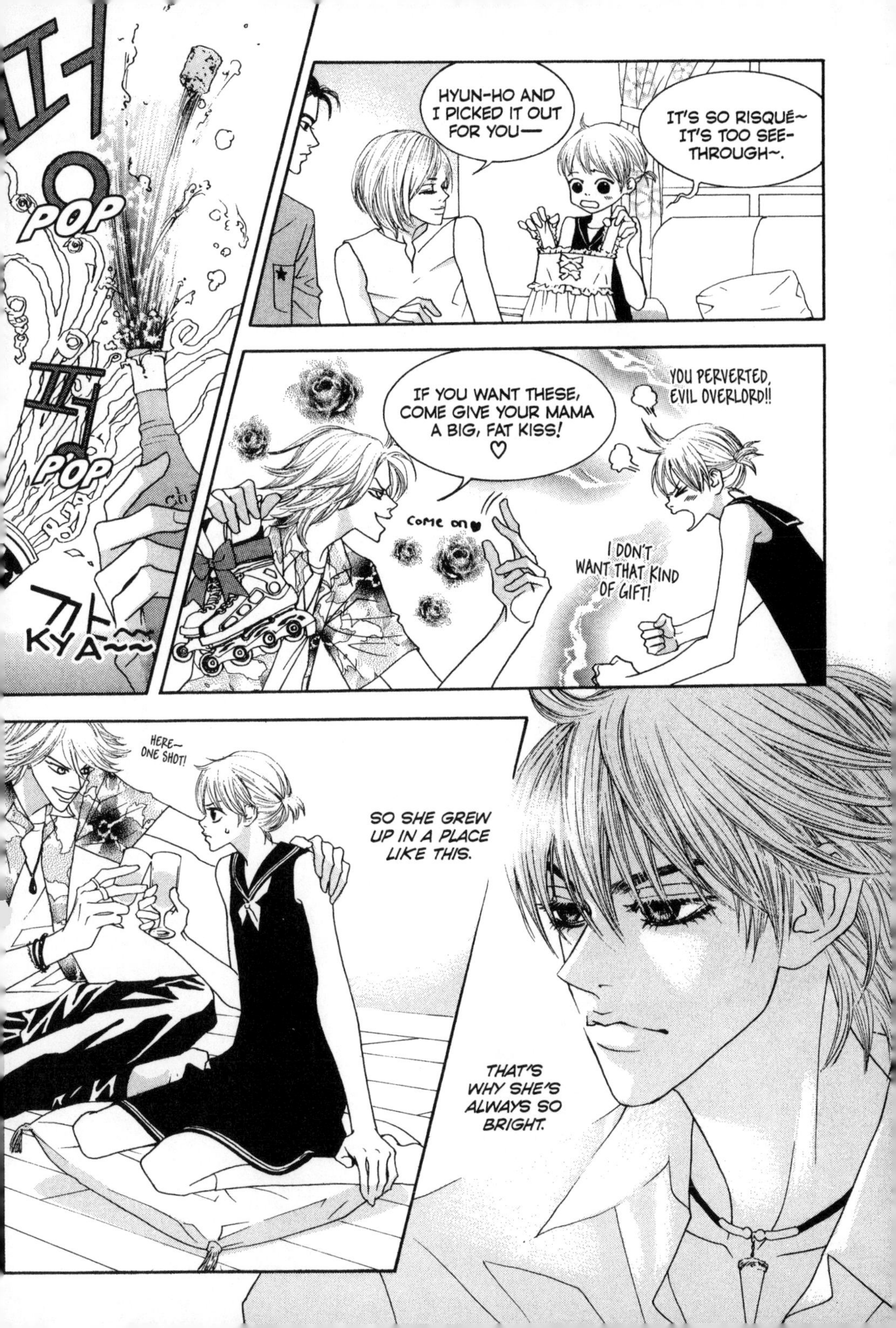

POP
POP
KYA~~~
HYUN-HO AND I PICKED IT OUT FOR YOU—
IT'S SO RISQUÉ~ IT'S TOO SEE-THROUGH~.
IF YOU WANT THESE, COME GIVE YOUR MAMA A BIG, FAT KISS! ♡
Come on♥
YOU PERVERTED, EVIL OVERLORD!!
I DON'T WANT THAT KIND OF GIFT!
HERE~ ONE SHOT!
SO SHE GREW UP IN A PLACE LIKE THIS.
THAT'S WHY SHE'S ALWAYS SO BRIGHT.

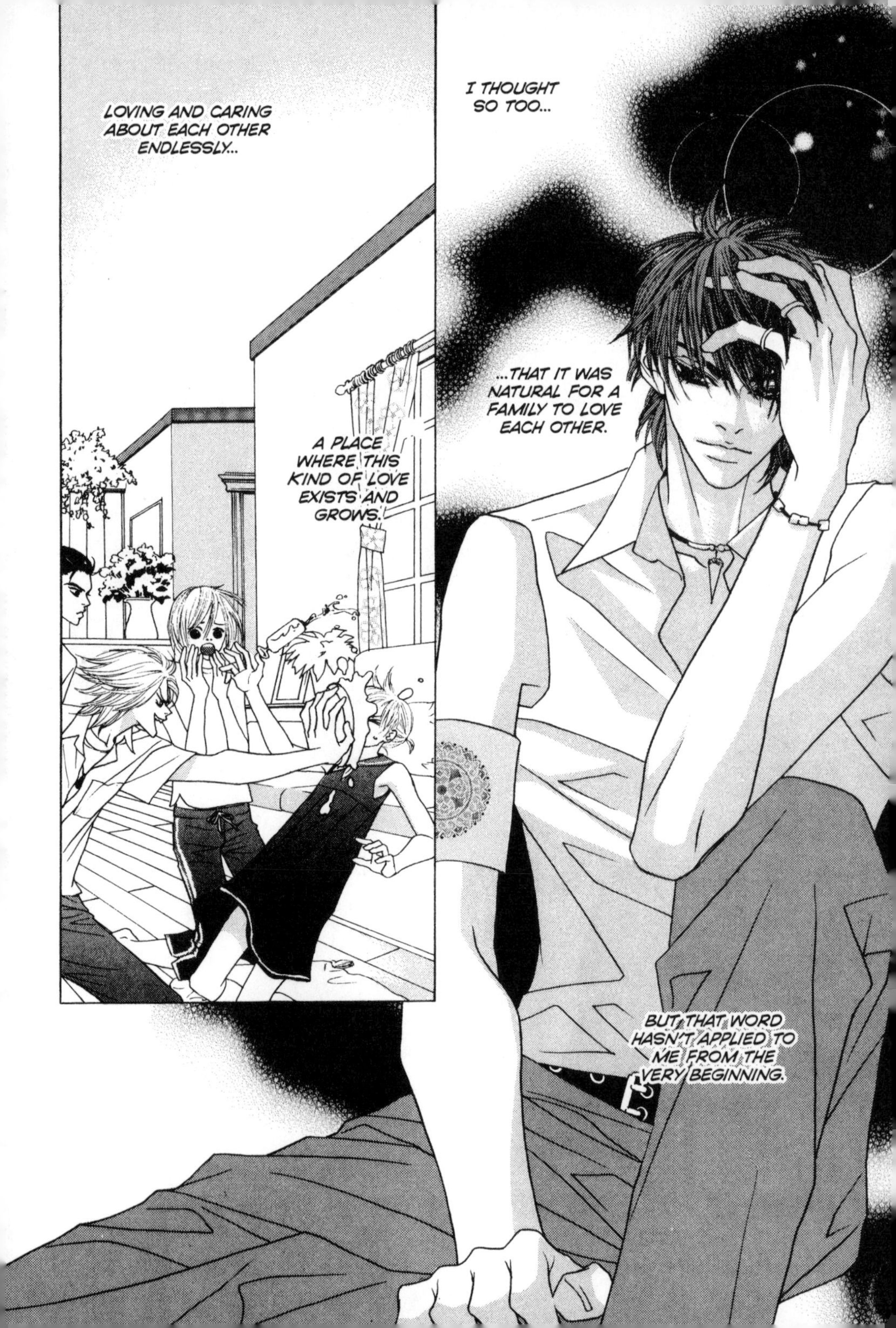
LOVING AND CARING ABOUT EACH OTHER ENDLESSLY...
A PLACE WHERE THIS KIND OF LOVE EXISTS AND GROWS.
I THOUGHT SO TOO...
...THAT IT WAS NATURAL FOR A FAMILY TO LOVE EACH OTHER.
BUT THAT WORD HASN'T APPLIED TO ME FROM THE VERY BEGINNING.

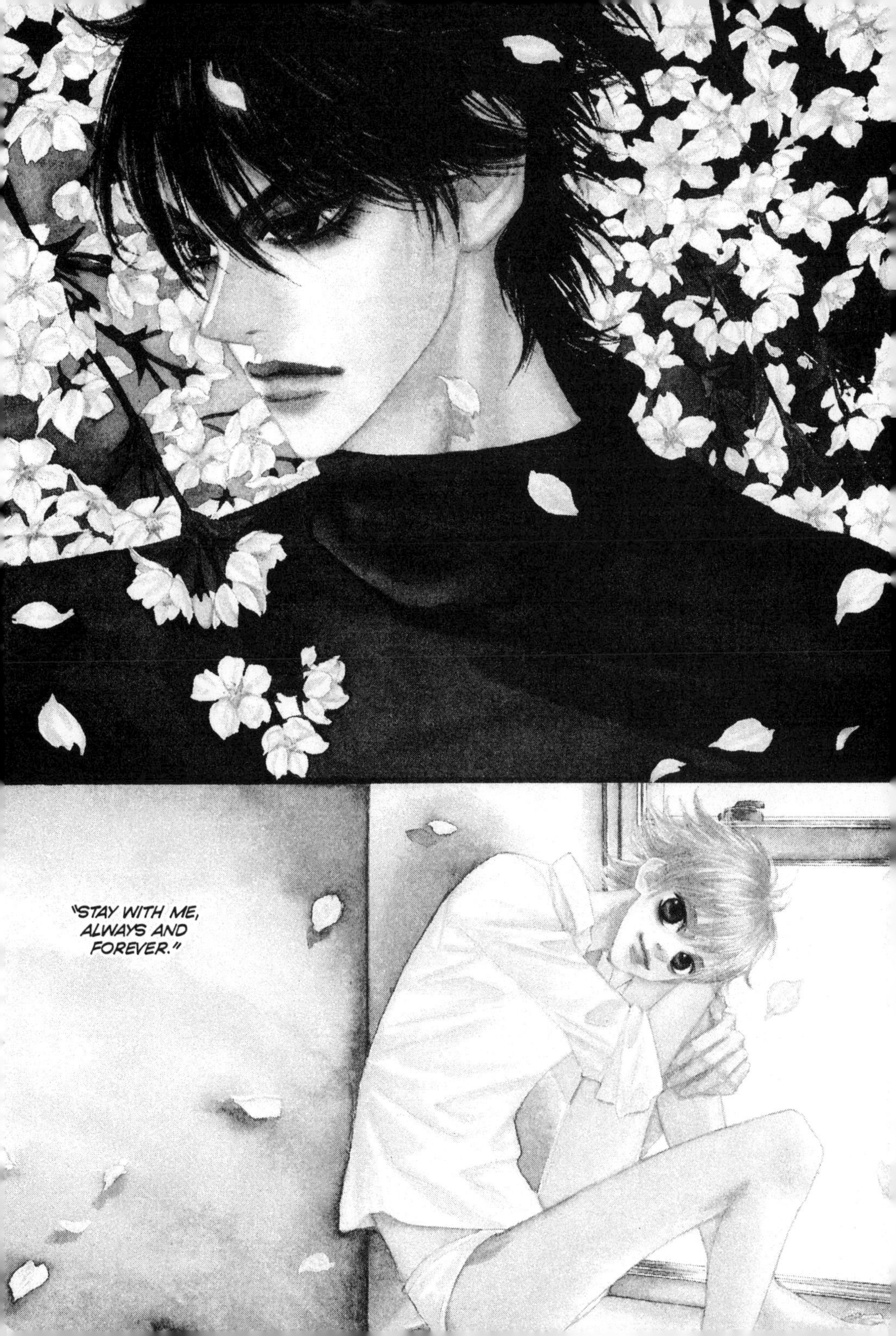
"STAY WITH ME, ALWAYS AND FOREVER."

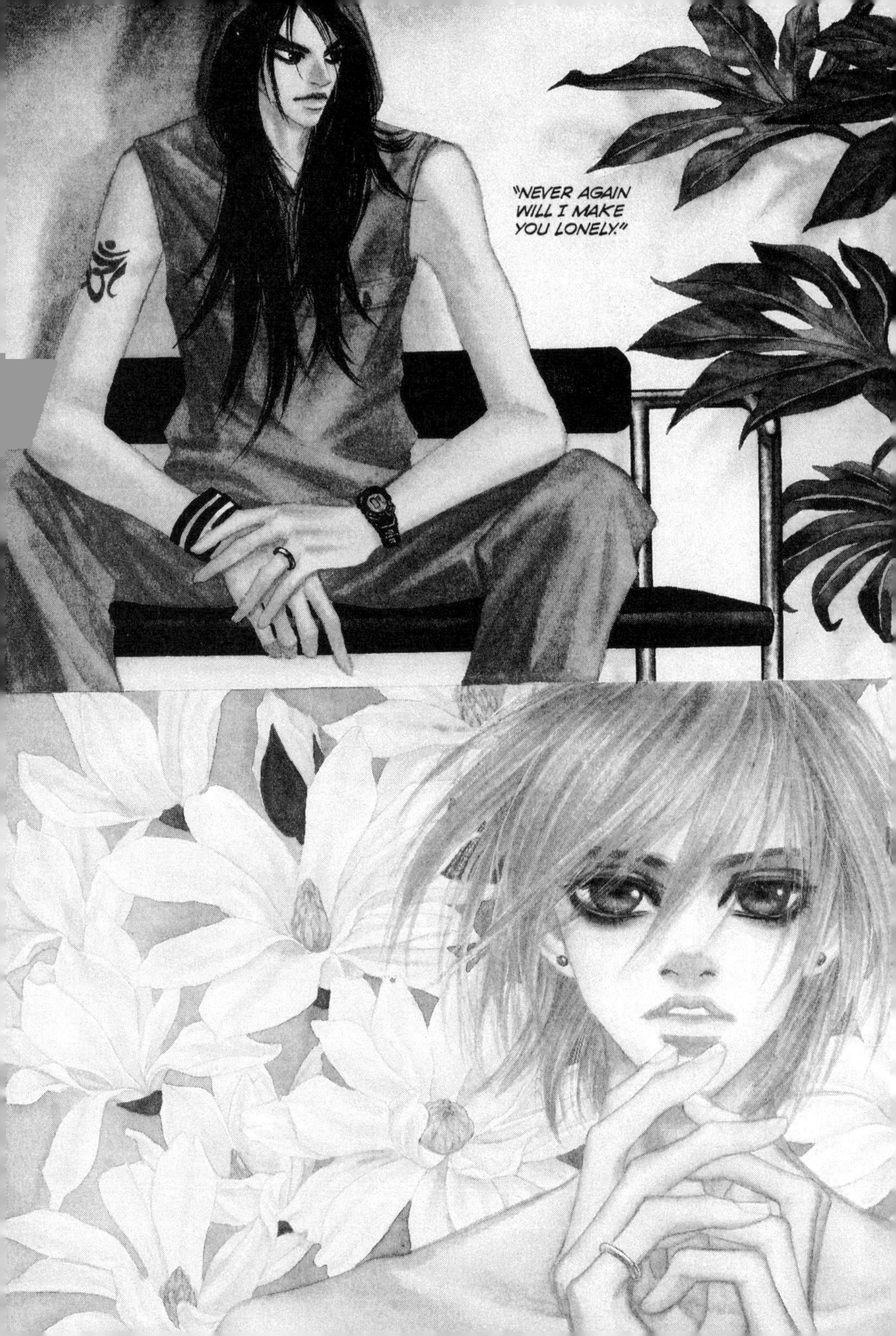
"NEVER AGAIN WILL I MAKE YOU LONELY."

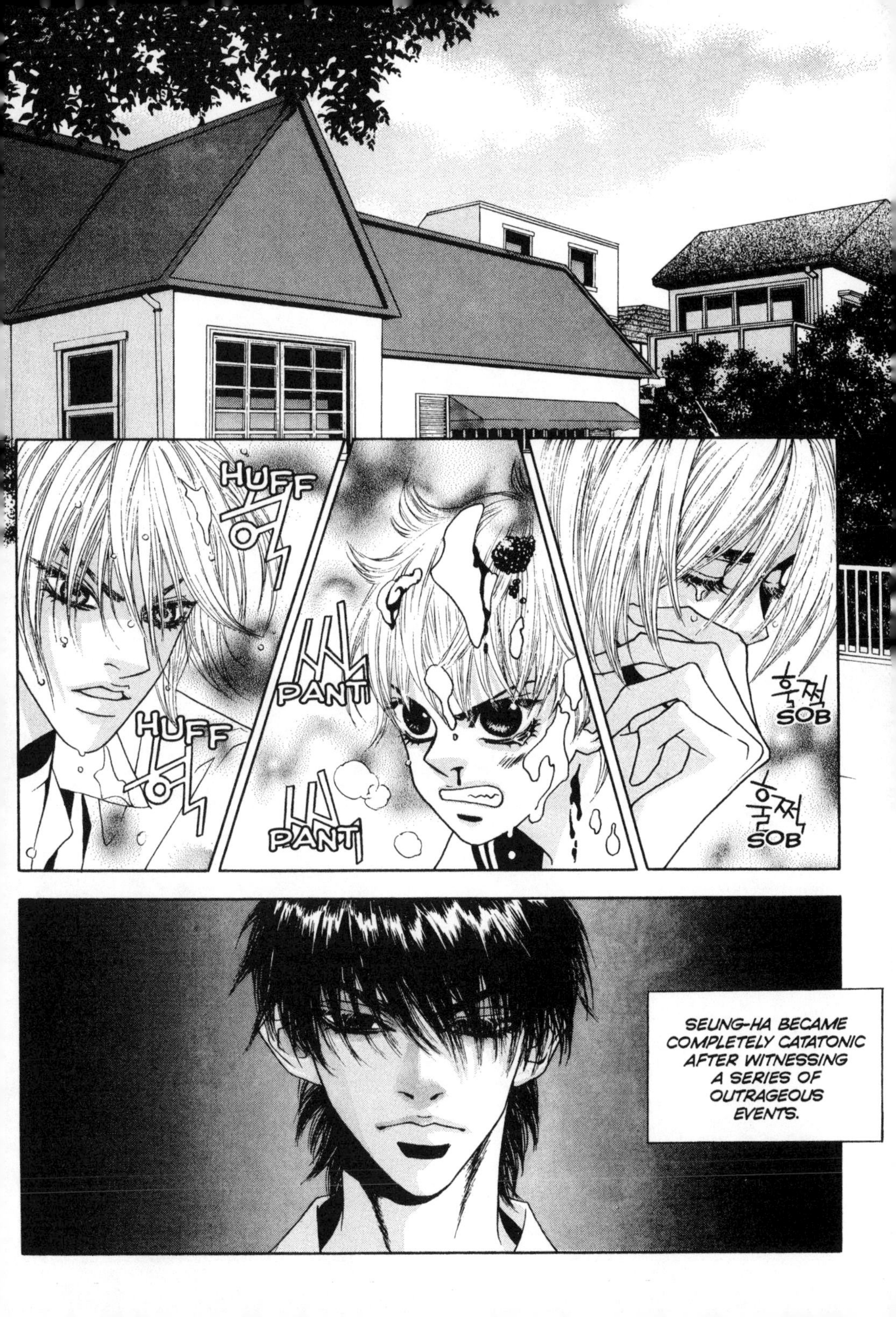
HUFF
헉
HUFF
헉
PANT
씨
PANT
씨
훌쩍
SOB
훌쩍
SOB
SEUNG-HA BECAME COMPLETELY CATATONIC AFTER WITNESSING A SERIES OF OUTRAGEOUS EVENTS.

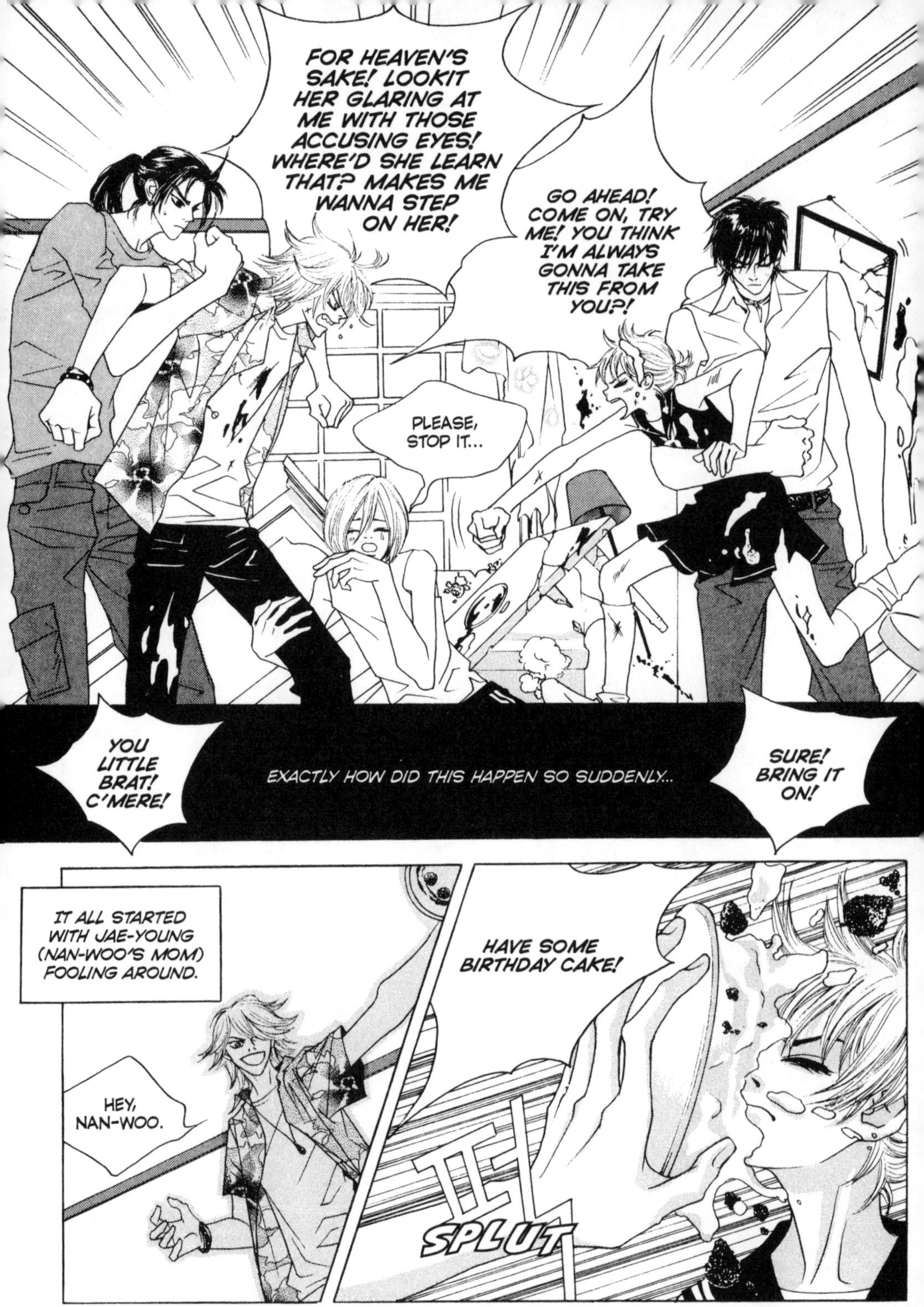
FOR HEAVEN'S SAKE! LOOKIT HER GLARING AT ME WITH THOSE ACCUSING EYES! WHERE'D SHE LEARN THAT? MAKES ME WANNA STEP ON HER!
GO AHEAD! COME ON, TRY ME! YOU THINK I'M ALWAYS GONNA TAKE THIS FROM YOU?!
PLEASE, STOP IT...
YOU LITTLE BRAT! C'MERE!
EXACTLY HOW DID THIS HAPPEN SO SUDDENLY...
SURE! BRING IT ON!
IT ALL STARTED WITH JAE-YOUNG (NAN-WOO'S MOM) FOOLING AROUND.
HEY, NAN-WOO.
HAVE SOME BIRTHDAY CAKE!
SPLUT

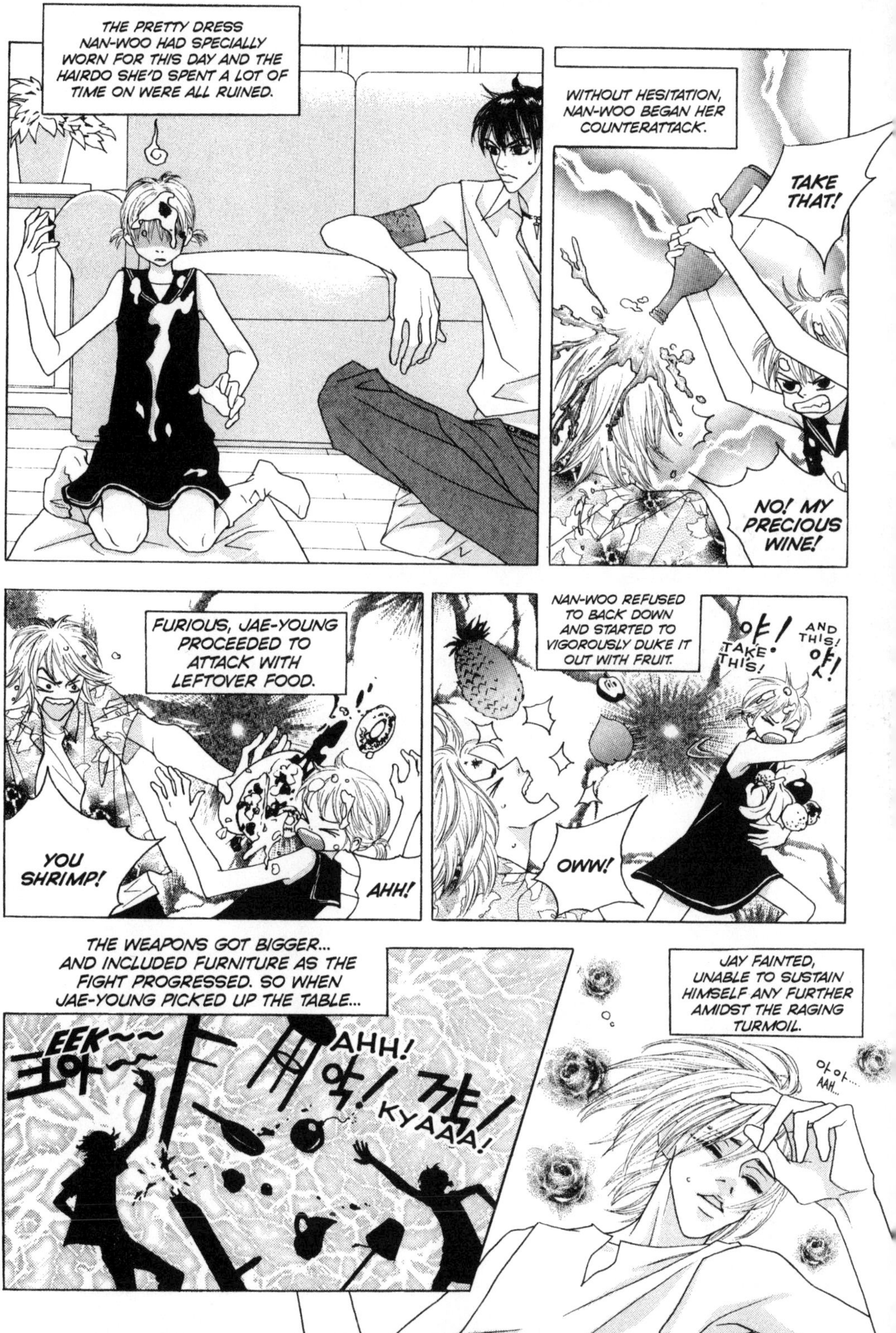

THE PRETTY DRESS NAN-WOO HAD SPECIALLY WORN FOR THIS DAY AND THE HAIRDO SHE'D SPENT A LOT OF TIME ON WERE ALL RUINED.
WITHOUT HESITATION, NAN-WOO BEGAN HER COUNTERATTACK.
TAKE THAT!
NO! MY PRECIOUS WINE!
FURIOUS, JAE-YOUNG PROCEEDED TO ATTACK WITH LEFTOVER FOOD.
YOU SHRIMP!
AHH!
NAN-WOO REFUSED TO BACK DOWN AND STARTED TO VIGOROUSLY DUKE IT OUT WITH FRUIT.
야!
TAKE THIS!
AND THIS!
야!
OWW!
THE WEAPONS GOT BIGGER... AND INCLUDED FURNITURE AS THE FIGHT PROGRESSED. SO WHEN JAE-YOUNG PICKED UP THE TABLE...
EEK~~
AHH!
KYAAAA!
JAY FAINTED, UNABLE TO SUSTAIN HIMSELF ANY FURTHER AMIDST THE RAGING TURMOIL.
아아...
AAH...

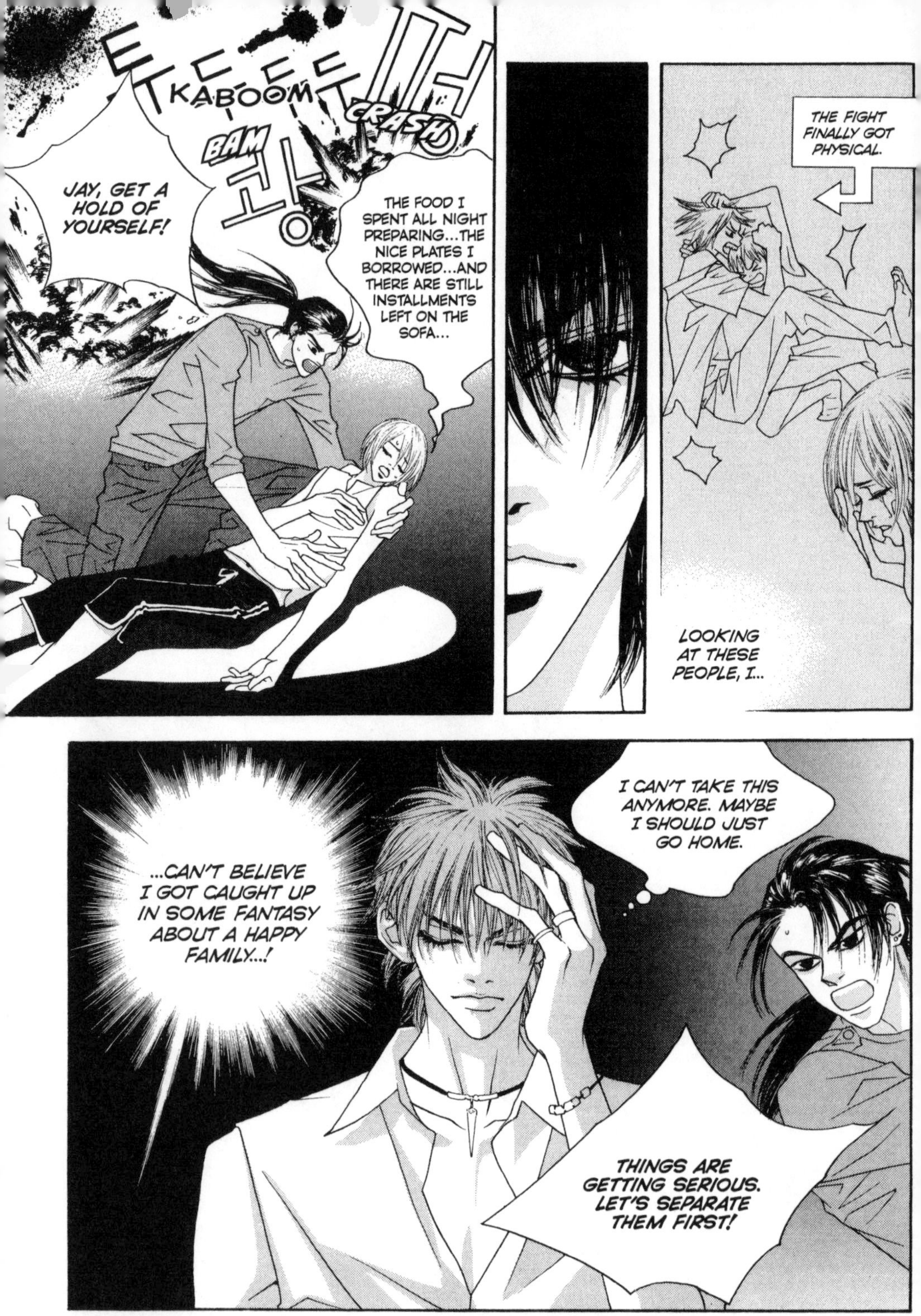
KABOOM
BAM
CRASH
JAY, GET A HOLD OF YOURSELF!
THE FOOD I SPENT ALL NIGHT PREPARING...THE NICE PLATES I BORROWED...AND THERE ARE STILL INSTALLMENTS LEFT ON THE SOFA...
THE FIGHT FINALLY GOT PHYSICAL.
LOOKING AT THESE PEOPLE, I...
...CAN'T BELIEVE I GOT CAUGHT UP IN SOME FANTASY ABOUT A HAPPY FAMILY...!
I CAN'T TAKE THIS ANYMORE. MAYBE I SHOULD JUST GO HOME.
THINGS ARE GETTING SERIOUS. LET'S SEPARATE THEM FIRST!

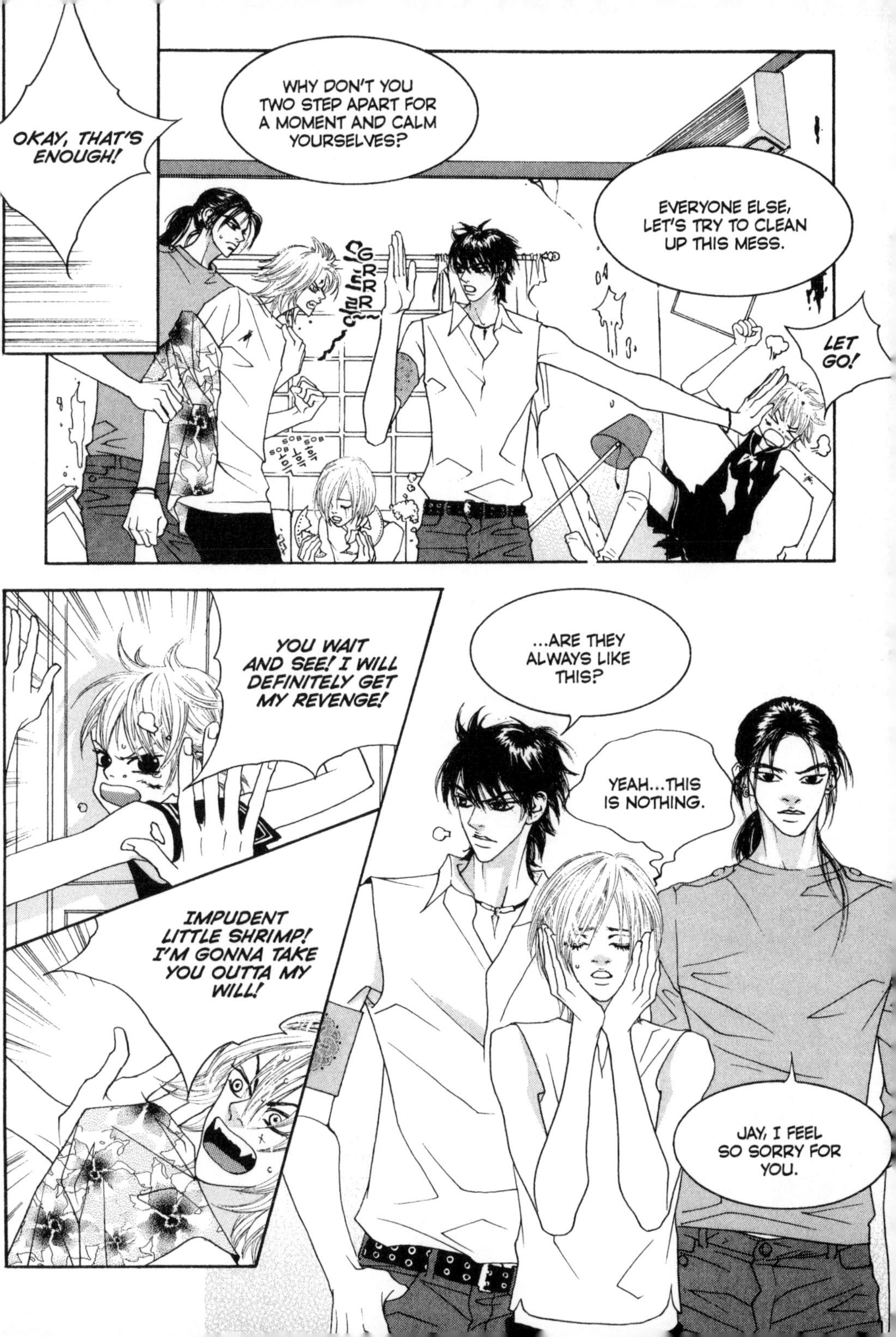

OKAY, THAT'S ENOUGH!
WHY DON'T YOU TWO STEP APART FOR A MOMENT AND CALM YOURSELVES?
GRRR
EVERYONE ELSE, LET'S TRY TO CLEAN UP THIS MESS.
SOB SOB
LET GO!
YOU WAIT AND SEE! I WILL DEFINITELY GET MY REVENGE!
IMPUDENT LITTLE SHRIMP! I'M GONNA TAKE YOU OUTTA MY WILL!
...ARE THEY ALWAYS LIKE THIS?
YEAH...THIS IS NOTHING.
JAY, I FEEL SO SORRY FOR YOU.

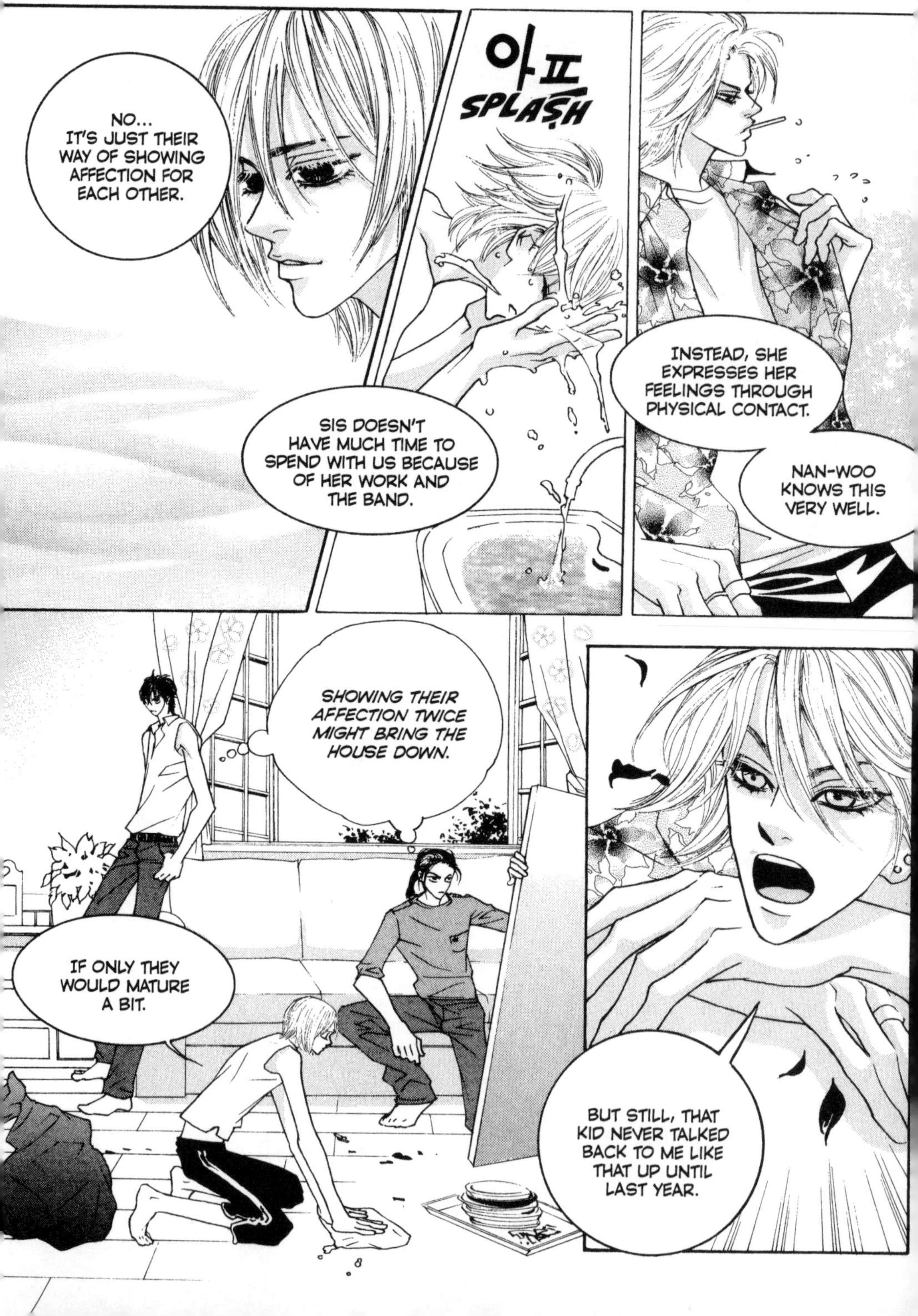
NO... IT'S JUST THEIR WAY OF SHOWING AFFECTION FOR EACH OTHER.
아ㅍ
SPLASH
SIS DOESN'T HAVE MUCH TIME TO SPEND WITH US BECAUSE OF HER WORK AND THE BAND.
INSTEAD, SHE EXPRESSES HER FEELINGS THROUGH PHYSICAL CONTACT.
NAN-WOO KNOWS THIS VERY WELL.
SHOWING THEIR AFFECTION TWICE MIGHT BRING THE HOUSE DOWN.
IF ONLY THEY WOULD MATURE A BIT.
BUT STILL, THAT KID NEVER TALKED BACK TO ME LIKE THAT UP UNTIL LAST YEAR.

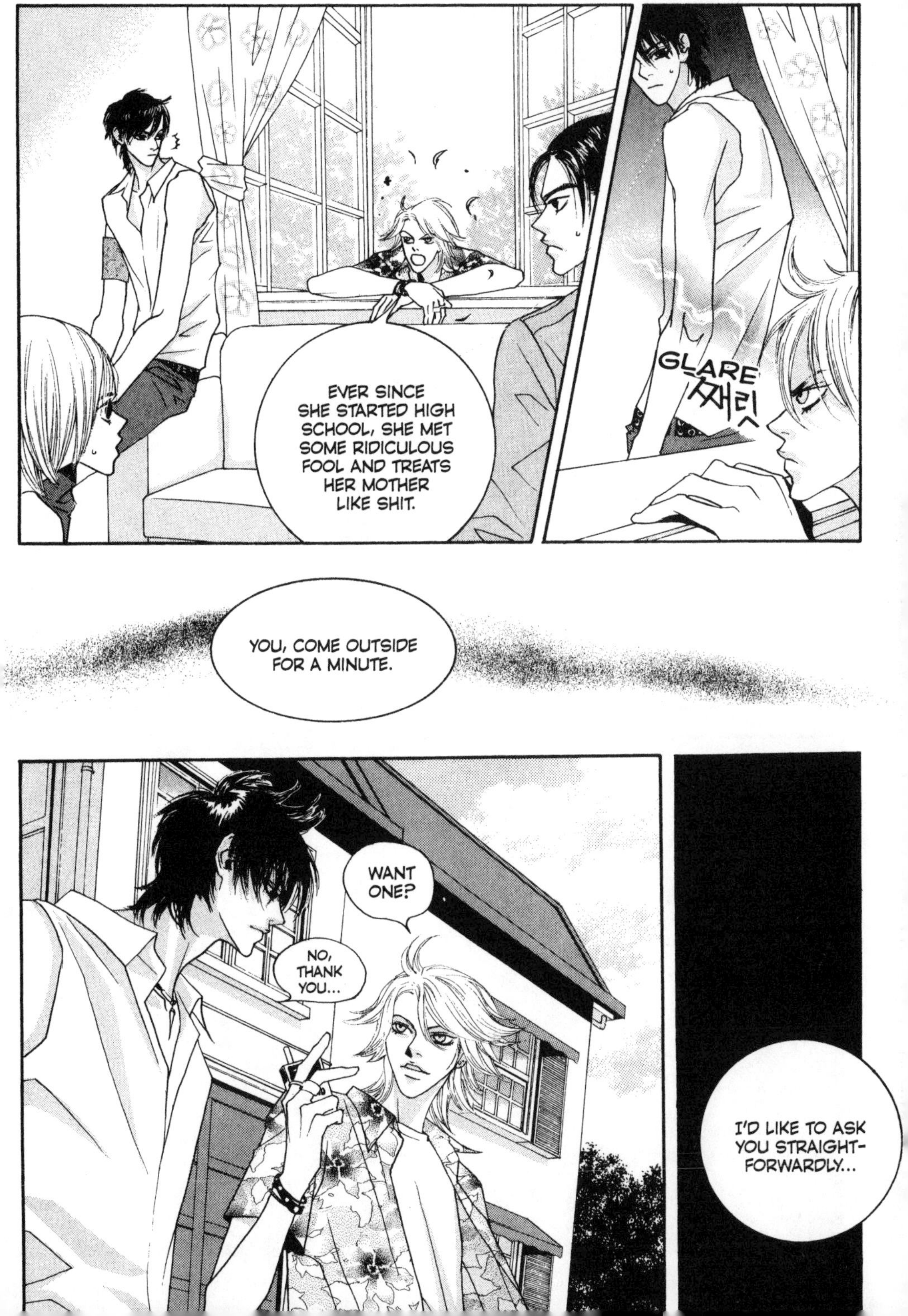
EVER SINCE SHE STARTED HIGH SCHOOL, SHE MET SOME RIDICULOUS FOOL AND TREATS HER MOTHER LIKE SHIT.
GLARE
째릿
YOU, COME OUTSIDE FOR A MINUTE.
WANT ONE?
NO, THANK YOU...
I'D LIKE TO ASK YOU STRAIGHT-FORWARDLY...

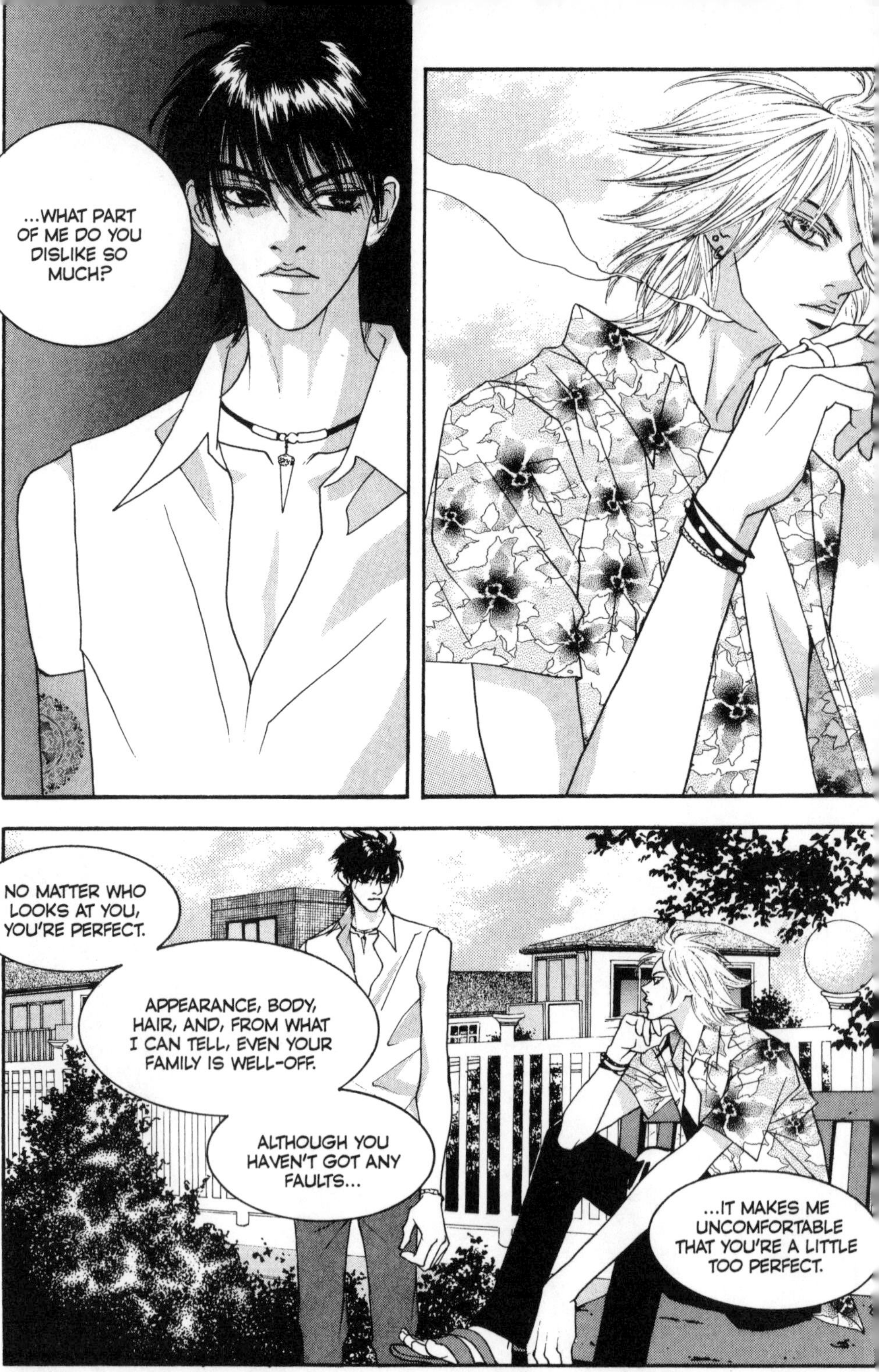
...WHAT PART OF ME DO YOU DISLIKE SO MUCH?
NO MATTER WHO LOOKS AT YOU, YOU'RE PERFECT.
APPEARANCE, BODY, HAIR, AND, FROM WHAT I CAN TELL, EVEN YOUR FAMILY IS WELL-OFF.
ALTHOUGH YOU HAVEN'T GOT ANY FAULTS...
...IT MAKES ME UNCOMFORTABLE THAT YOU'RE A LITTLE TOO PERFECT.

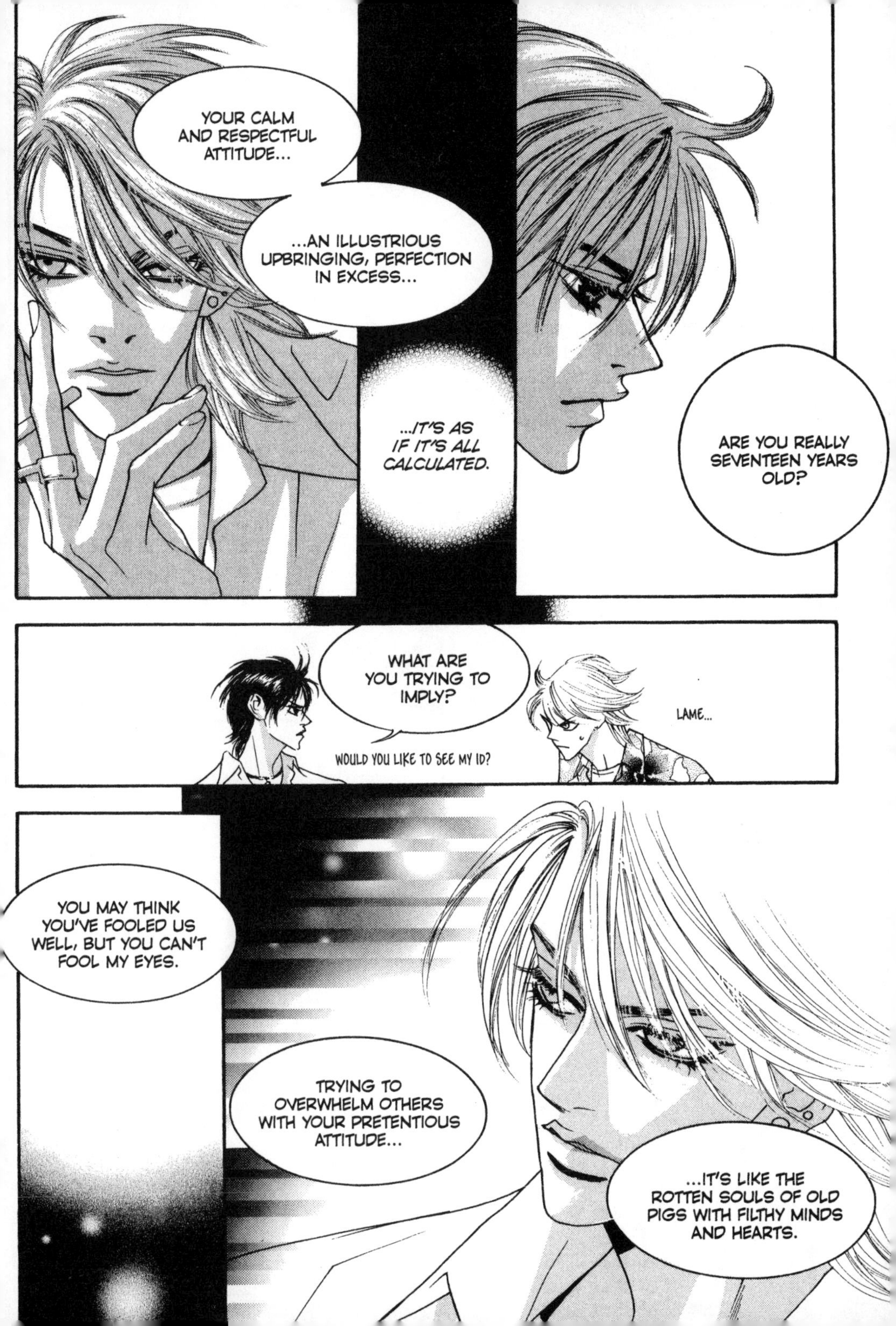
YOUR CALM AND RESPECTFUL ATTITUDE...
...AN ILLUSTRIOUS UPBRINGING, PERFECTION IN EXCESS...
...IT'S AS IF IT'S ALL CALCULATED.
ARE YOU REALLY SEVENTEEN YEARS OLD?
WHAT ARE YOU TRYING TO IMPLY?
WOULD YOU LIKE TO SEE MY ID?
LAME...
YOU MAY THINK YOU'VE FOOLED US WELL, BUT YOU CAN'T FOOL MY EYES.
TRYING TO OVERWHELM OTHERS WITH YOUR PRETENTIOUS ATTITUDE...
...IT'S LIKE THE ROTTEN SOULS OF OLD PIGS WITH FILTHY MINDS AND HEARTS.

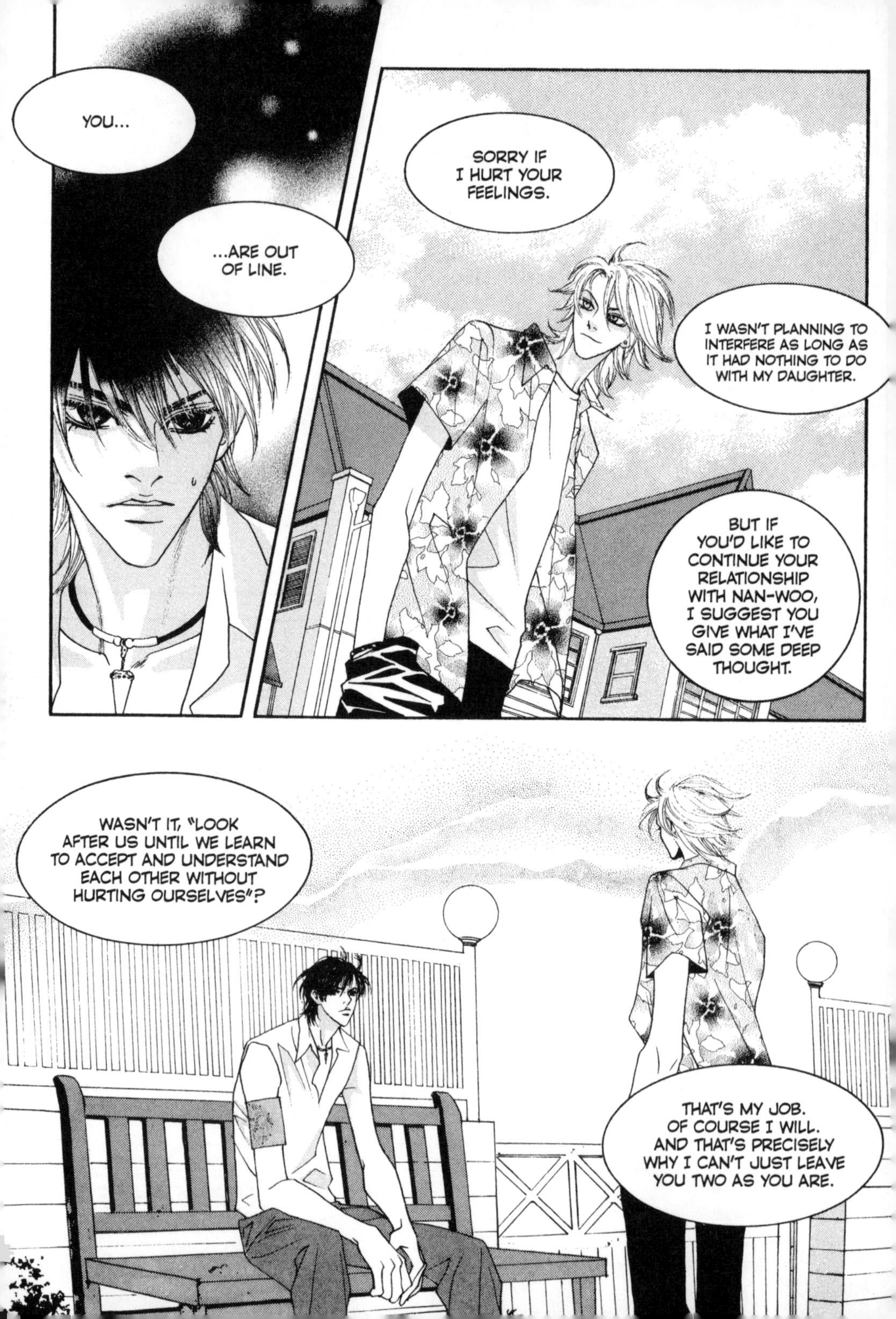
YOU...
...ARE OUT OF LINE.
SORRY IF I HURT YOUR FEELINGS.
I WASN'T PLANNING TO INTERFERE AS LONG AS IT HAD NOTHING TO DO WITH MY DAUGHTER.
BUT IF YOU'D LIKE TO CONTINUE YOUR RELATIONSHIP WITH NAN-WOO, I SUGGEST YOU GIVE WHAT I'VE SAID SOME DEEP THOUGHT.
WASN'T IT, "LOOK AFTER US UNTIL WE LEARN TO ACCEPT AND UNDERSTAND EACH OTHER WITHOUT HURTING OURSELVES"?
THAT'S MY JOB. OF COURSE I WILL. AND THAT'S PRECISELY WHY I CAN'T JUST LEAVE YOU TWO AS YOU ARE.

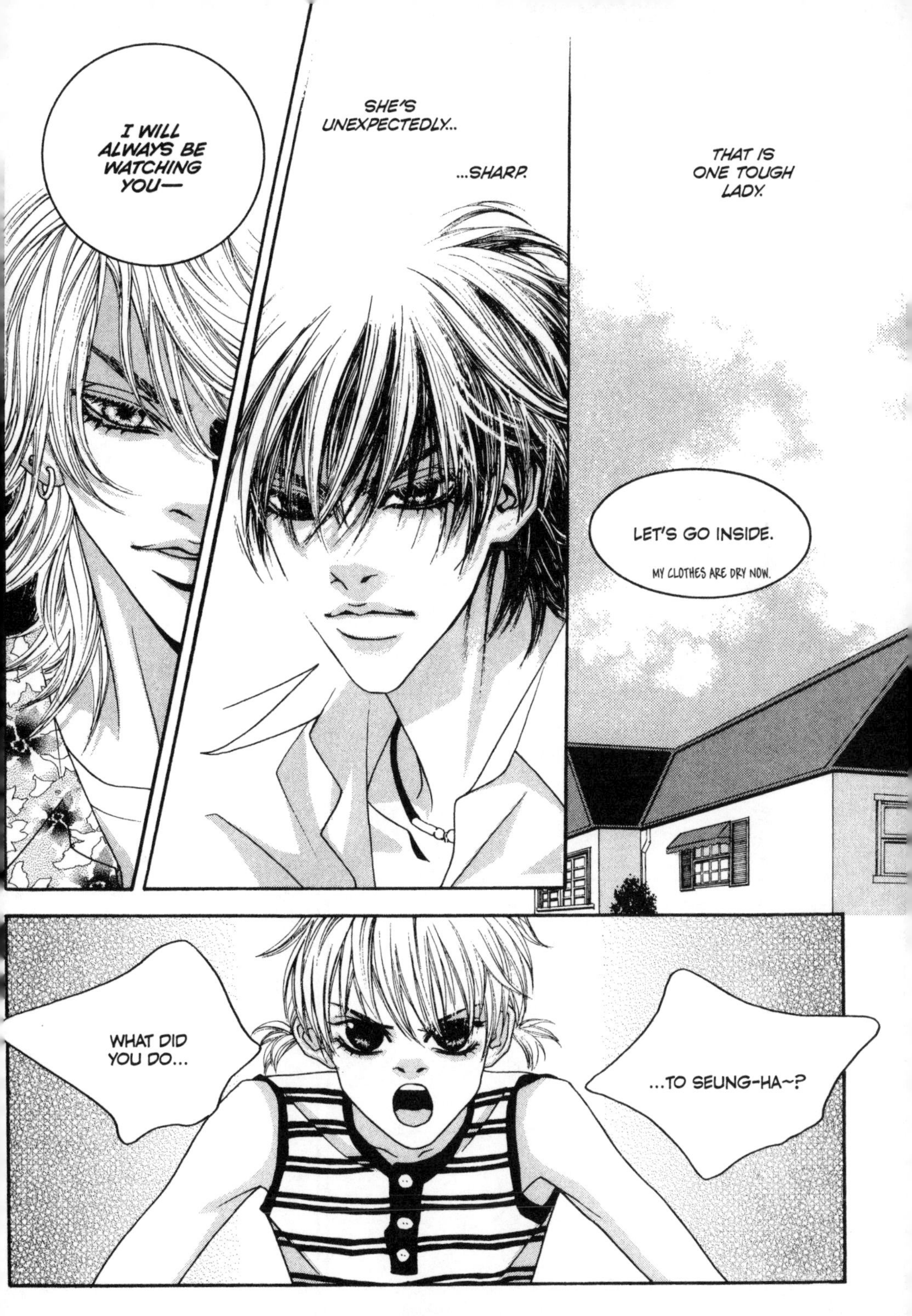
I WILL ALWAYS BE WATCHING YOU—
SHE'S UNEXPECTEDLY...
...SHARP.
THAT IS ONE TOUGH LADY.
LET'S GO INSIDE.
MY CLOTHES ARE DRY NOW.
WHAT DID YOU DO...
...TO SEUNG-HA~?

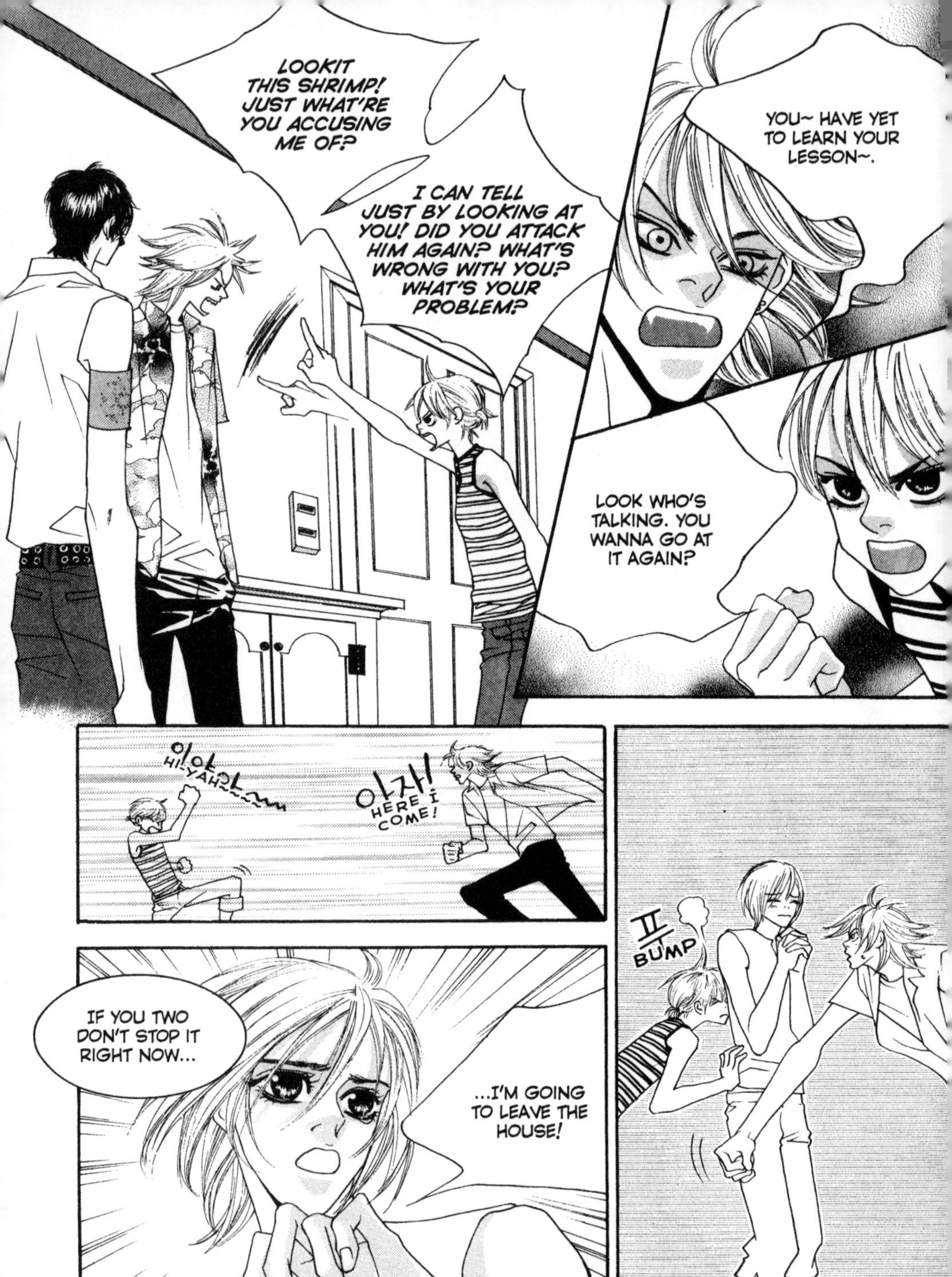
LOOKIT THIS SHRIMP! JUST WHAT'RE YOU ACCUSING ME OF?
I CAN TELL JUST BY LOOKING AT YOU! DID YOU ATTACK HIM AGAIN? WHAT'S WRONG WITH YOU? WHAT'S YOUR PROBLEM?
YOU~ HAVE YET TO LEARN YOUR LESSON~.
LOOK WHO'S TALKING. YOU WANNA GO AT IT AGAIN?
이야
HI-YAH!~~
아자!
HERE I COME!
IF YOU TWO DON'T STOP IT RIGHT NOW...
...I'M GOING TO LEAVE THE HOUSE!
BUMP

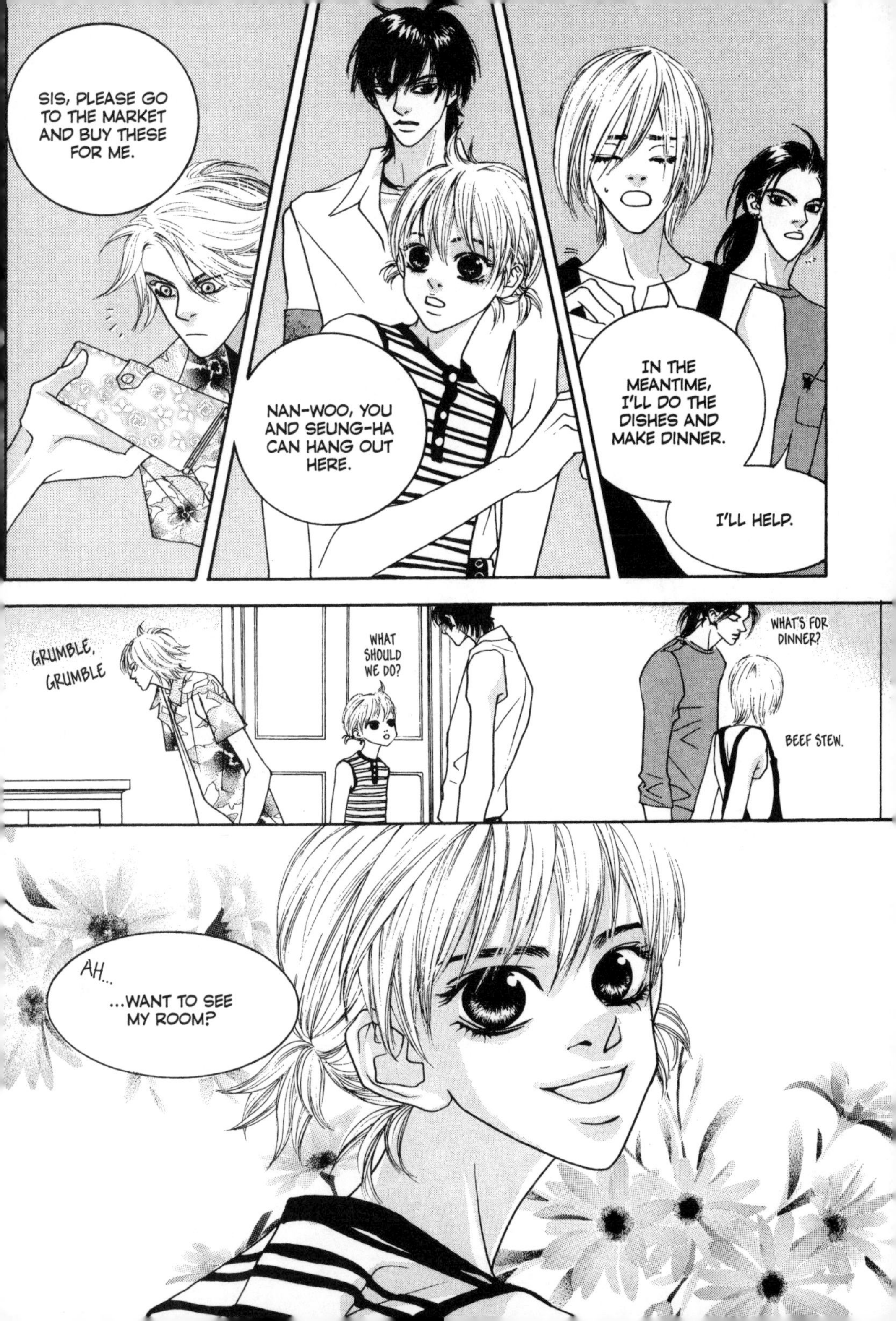
SIS, PLEASE GO TO THE MARKET AND BUY THESE FOR ME.
NAN-WOO, YOU AND SEUNG-HA CAN HANG OUT HERE.
IN THE MEANTIME, I'LL DO THE DISHES AND MAKE DINNER.
I'LL HELP.
GRUMBLE, GRUMBLE
WHAT SHOULD WE DO?
WHAT'S FOR DINNER?
BEEF STEW.
AH... ...WANT TO SEE MY ROOM?

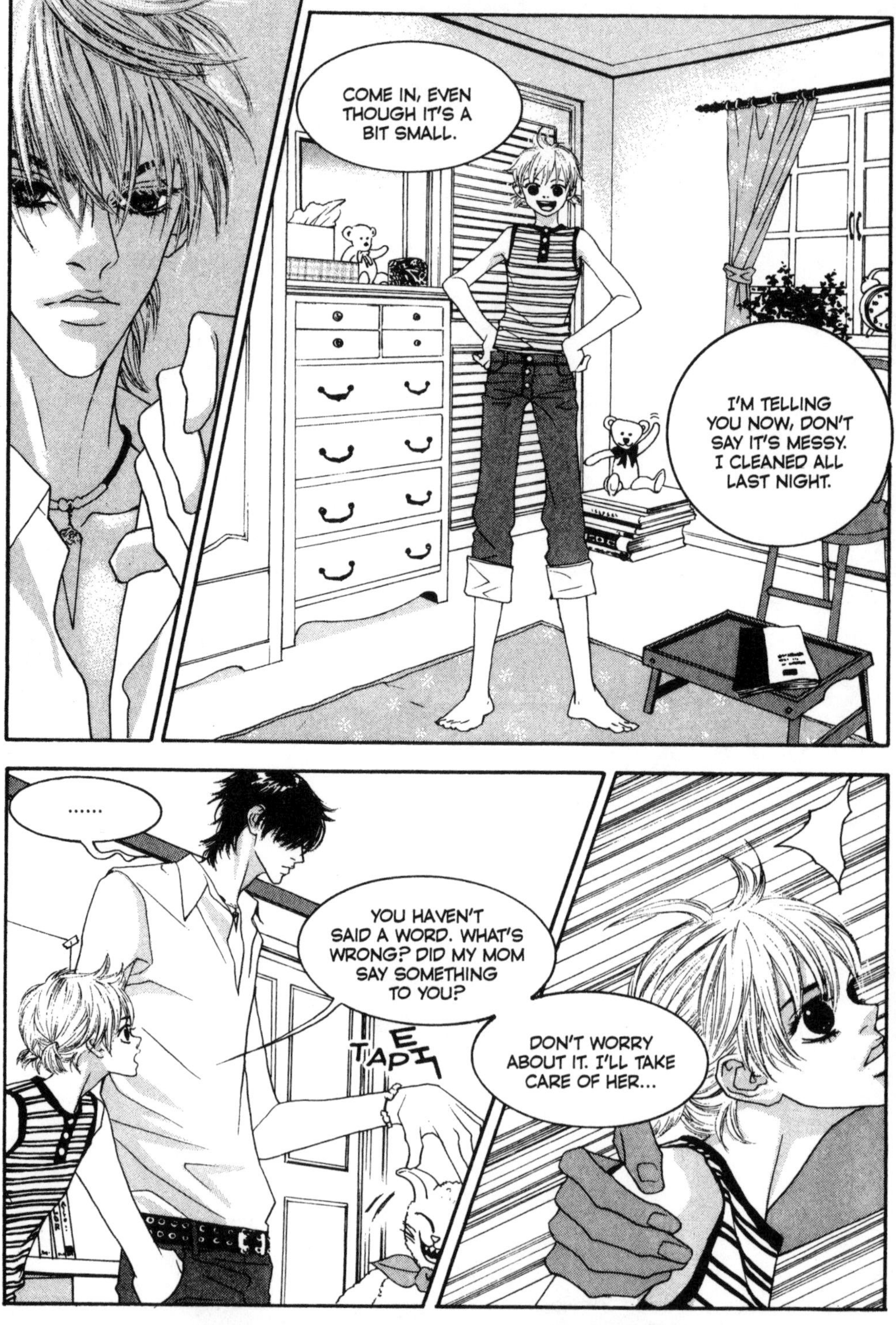
COME IN, EVEN THOUGH IT'S A BIT SMALL.
I'M TELLING YOU NOW, DON'T SAY IT'S MESSY. I CLEANED ALL LAST NIGHT.
......
YOU HAVEN'T SAID A WORD. WHAT'S WRONG? DID MY MOM SAY SOMETHING TO YOU?
TAP
DON'T WORRY ABOUT IT. I'LL TAKE CARE OF HER...

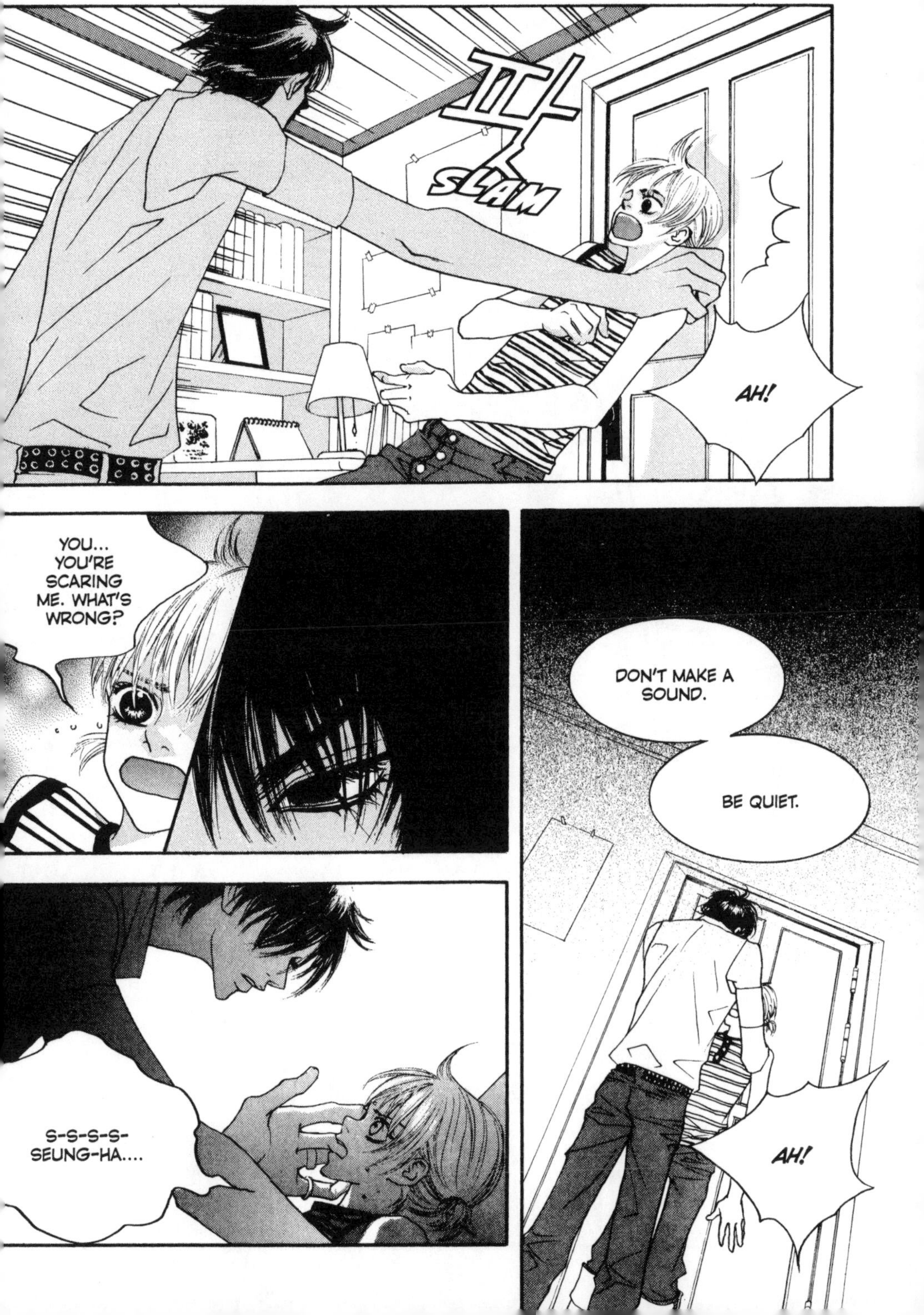
SLAM
AH!
YOU... YOU'RE SCARING ME. WHAT'S WRONG?
S-S-S-S-SEUNG-HA....
DON'T MAKE A SOUND.
BE QUIET.
AH!

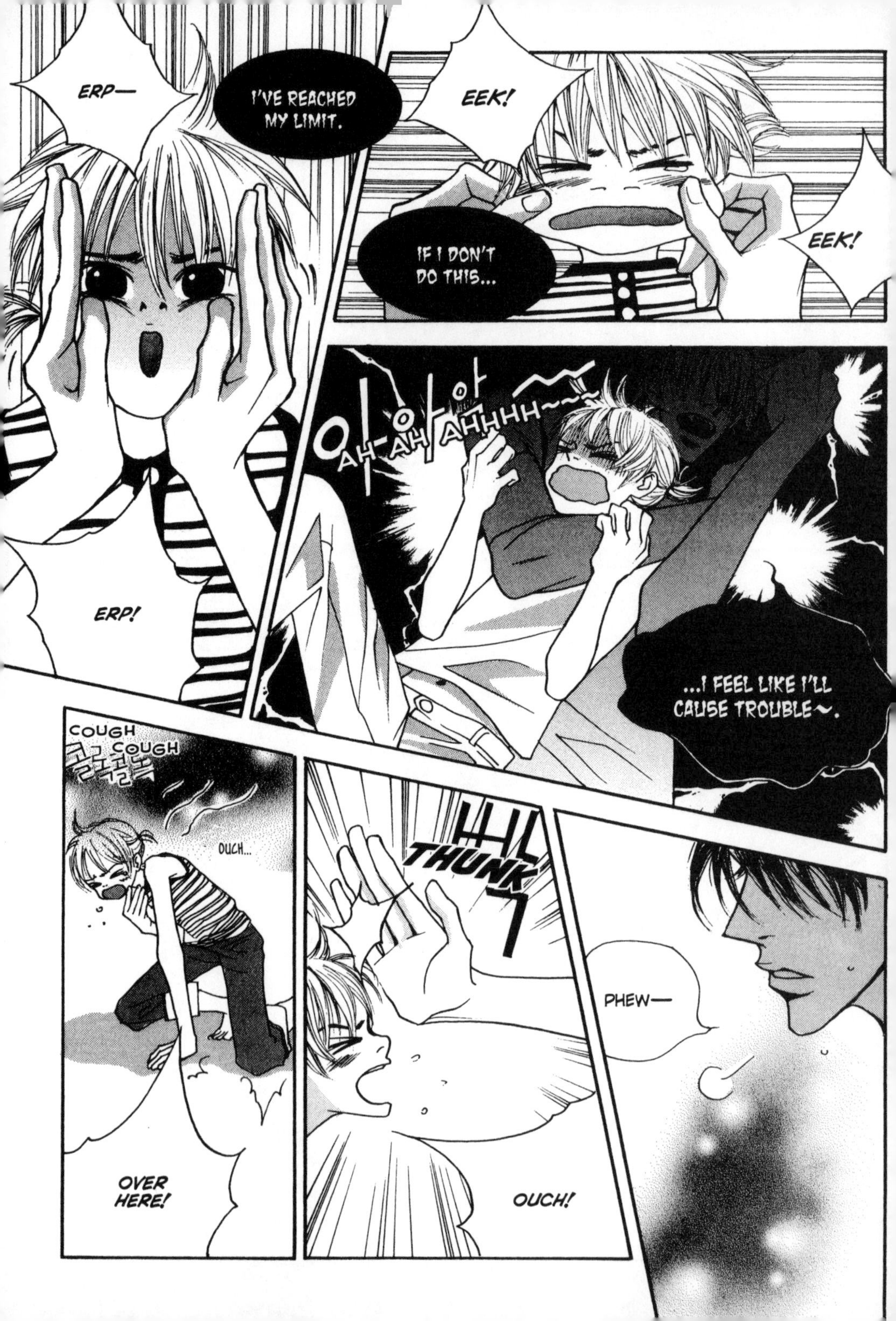
ERP—
I'VE REACHED MY LIMIT.
ERP!
EEK!
IF I DON'T DO THIS...
EEK!
AH-AH AHHHH~~~
...I FEEL LIKE I'LL CAUSE TROUBLE~.
COUGH COUGH
OUCH...
OVER HERE!
THUNK
OUCH!
PHEW—

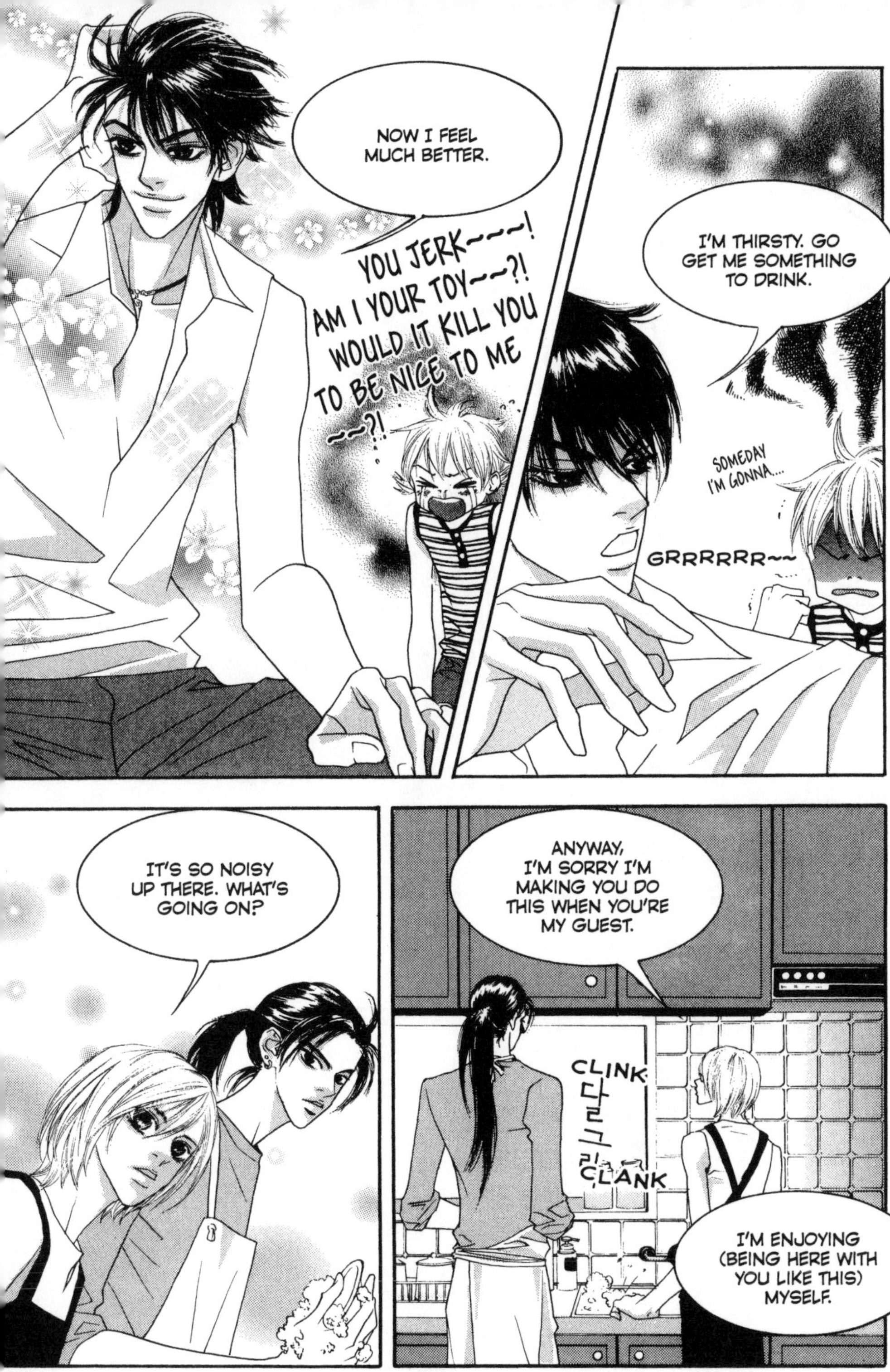
NOW I FEEL MUCH BETTER.
YOU JERK~~~! AM I YOUR TOY~~?! WOULD IT KILL YOU TO BE NICE TO ME ~~?!
I'M THIRSTY. GO GET ME SOMETHING TO DRINK.
SOMEDAY I'M GONNA....
GRRRRRR~~
IT'S SO NOISY UP THERE. WHAT'S GOING ON?
ANYWAY, I'M SORRY I'M MAKING YOU DO THIS WHEN YOU'RE MY GUEST.
CLINK
달그락
CLANK
I'M ENJOYING (BEING HERE WITH YOU LIKE THIS) MYSELF.

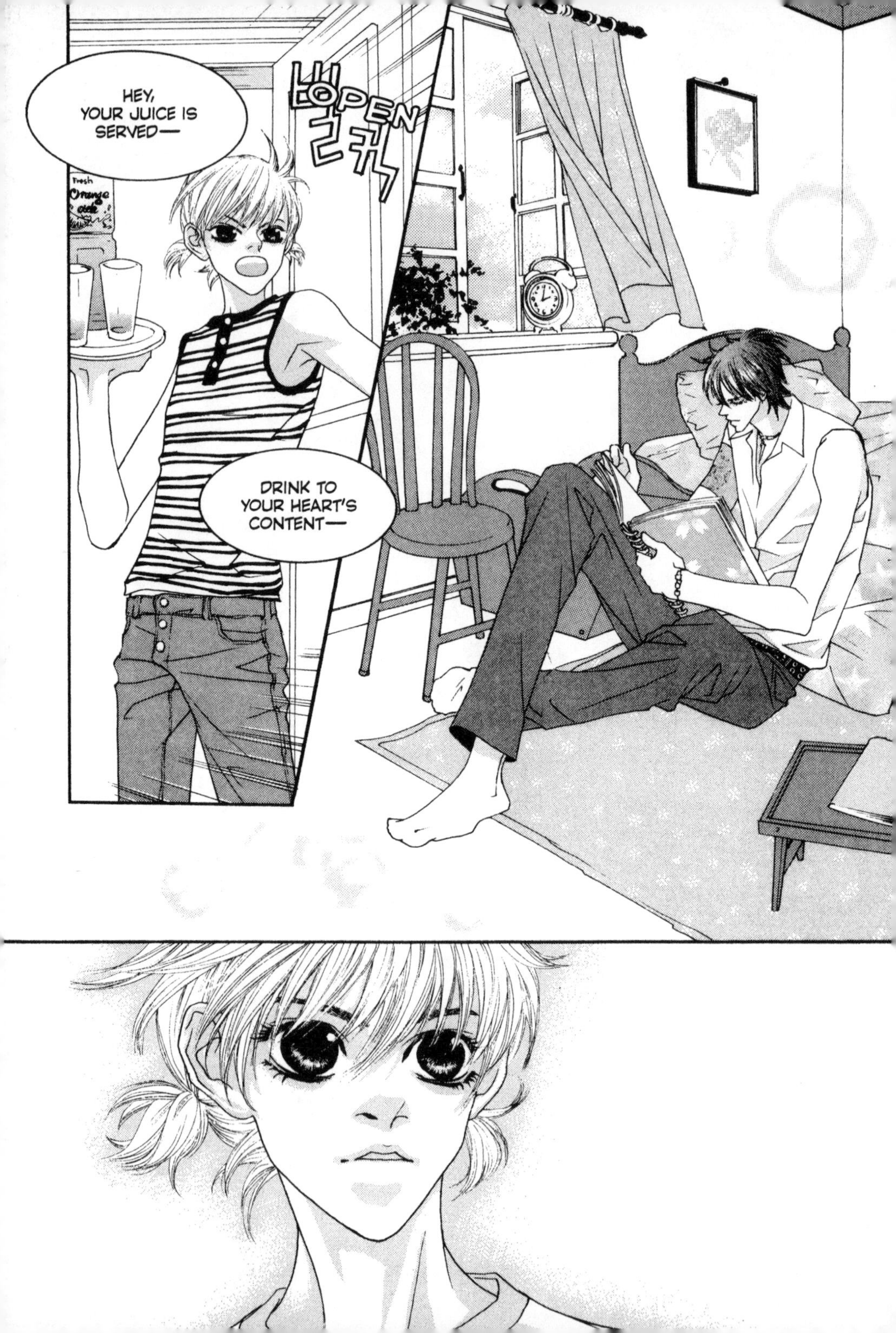
HEY, YOUR JUICE IS SERVED—
OPEN
DRINK TO YOUR HEART'S CONTENT—

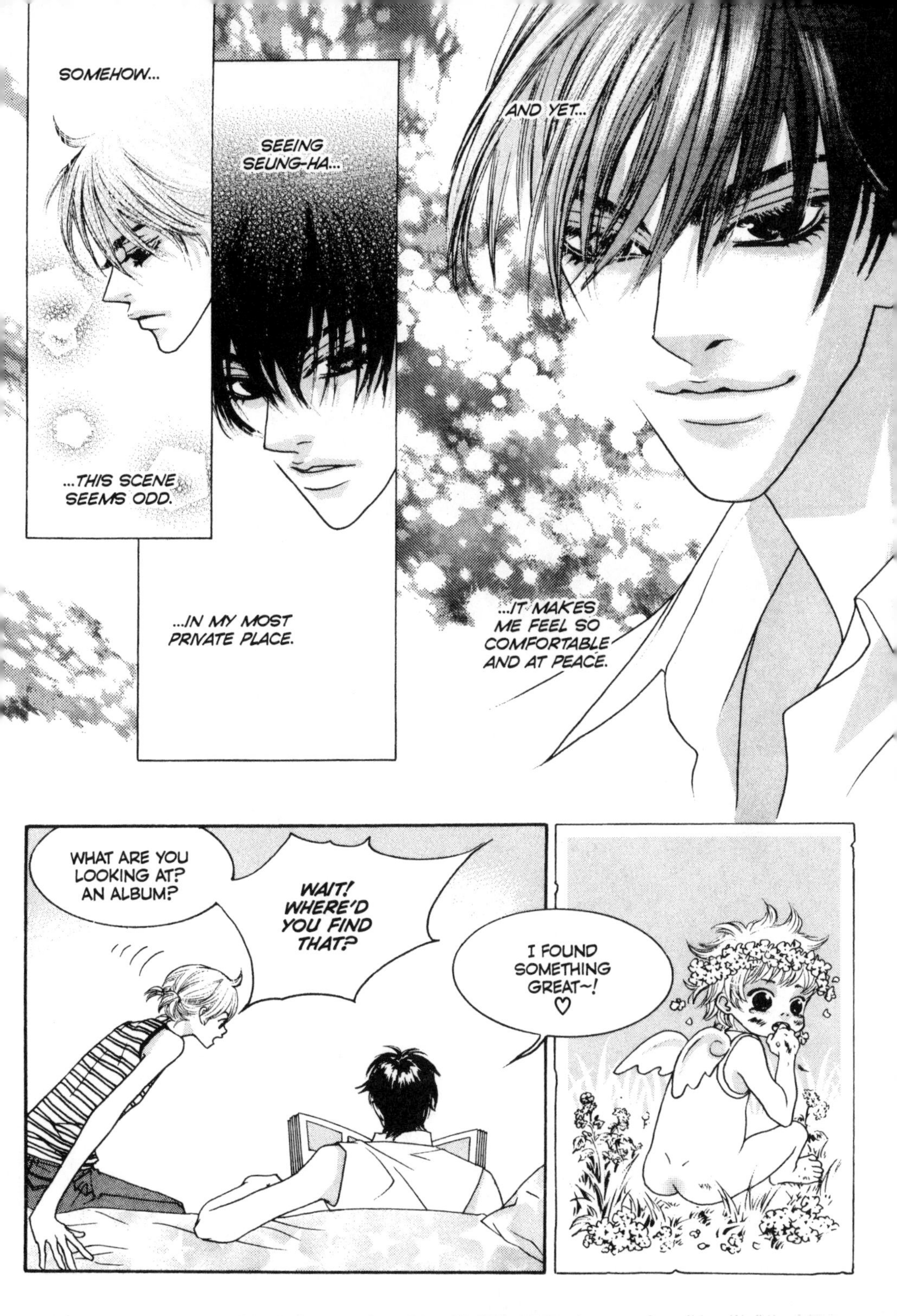
SOMEHOW...
...THIS SCENE SEEMS ODD.
SEEING SEUNG-HA...
...IN MY MOST PRIVATE PLACE.
AND YET...
...IT MAKES ME FEEL SO COMFORTABLE AND AT PEACE.
WHAT ARE YOU LOOKING AT? AN ALBUM?
WAIT! WHERE'D YOU FIND THAT?
I FOUND SOMETHING GREAT~! ♡

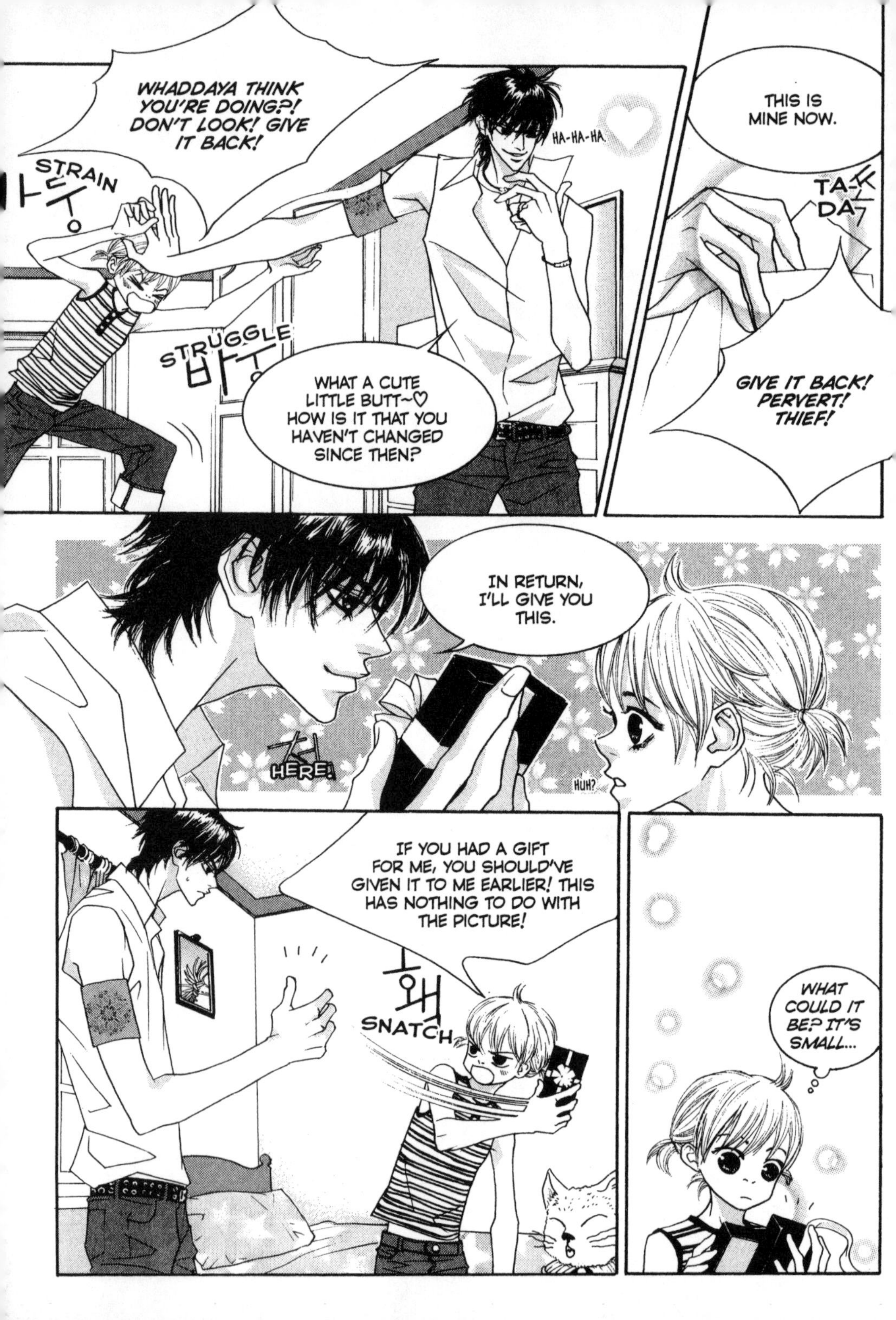
WHADDAYA THINK YOU'RE DOING?! DON'T LOOK! GIVE IT BACK!
STRAIN
HA-HA-HA.
STRUGGLE
WHAT A CUTE LITTLE BUTT~♡ HOW IS IT THAT YOU HAVEN'T CHANGED SINCE THEN?
THIS IS MINE NOW.
TA-DA
GIVE IT BACK! PERVERT! THIEF!
IN RETURN, I'LL GIVE YOU THIS.
HERE!
HUH?
IF YOU HAD A GIFT FOR ME, YOU SHOULD'VE GIVEN IT TO ME EARLIER! THIS HAS NOTHING TO DO WITH THE PICTURE!
SNATCH
WHAT COULD IT BE? IT'S SMALL...

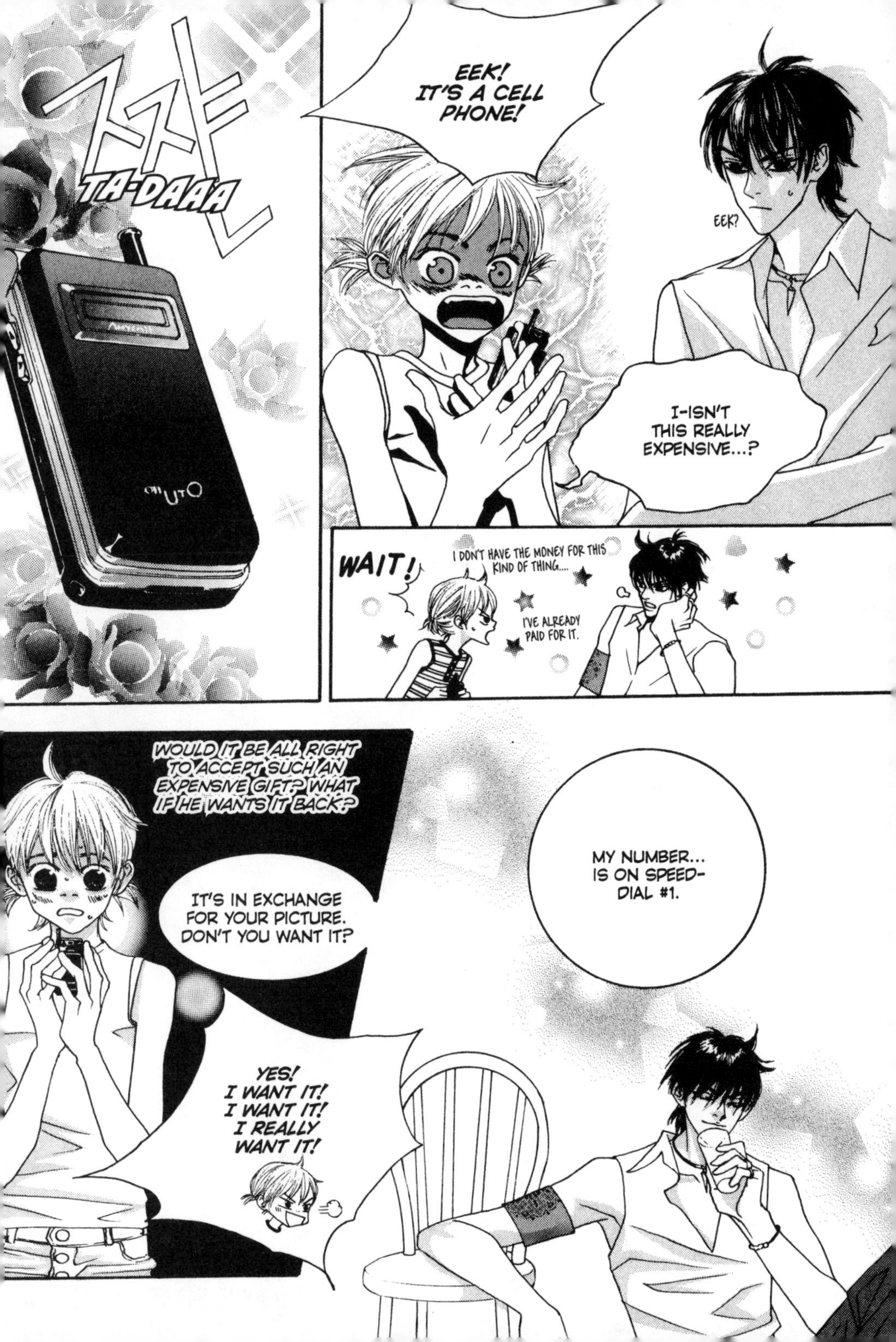
TA-DAAA
EEK! IT'S A CELL PHONE!
EEK?
I-ISN'T THIS REALLY EXPENSIVE...?
WAIT!
I DON'T HAVE THE MONEY FOR THIS KIND OF THING....
I'VE ALREADY PAID FOR IT.
WOULD IT BE ALL RIGHT TO ACCEPT SUCH AN EXPENSIVE GIFT? WHAT IF HE WANTS IT BACK?
IT'S IN EXCHANGE FOR YOUR PICTURE. DON'T YOU WANT IT?
YES! I WANT IT! I WANT IT! I REALLY WANT IT!
MY NUMBER... IS ON SPEED-DIAL #1.

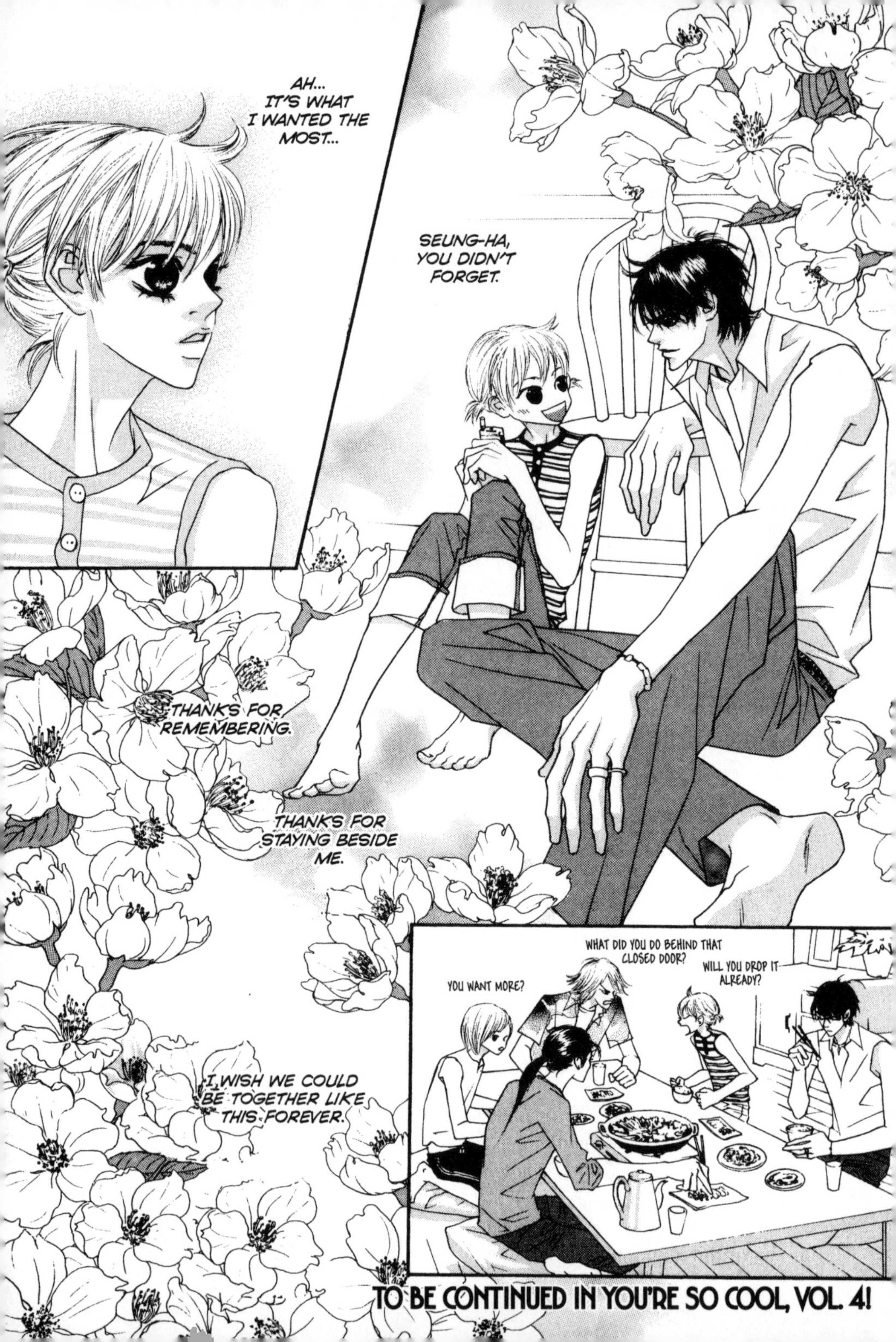
AH... IT'S WHAT I WANTED THE MOST...
SEUNG-HA, YOU DIDN'T FORGET.
THANKS FOR REMEMBERING.
THANKS FOR STAYING BESIDE ME.
I WISH WE COULD BE TOGETHER LIKE THIS FOREVER.
YOU WANT MORE?
WHAT DID YOU DO BEHIND THAT CLOSED DOOR?
WILL YOU DROP IT ALREADY?
TO BE CONTINUED IN YOU'RE SO COOL, VOL. 4!

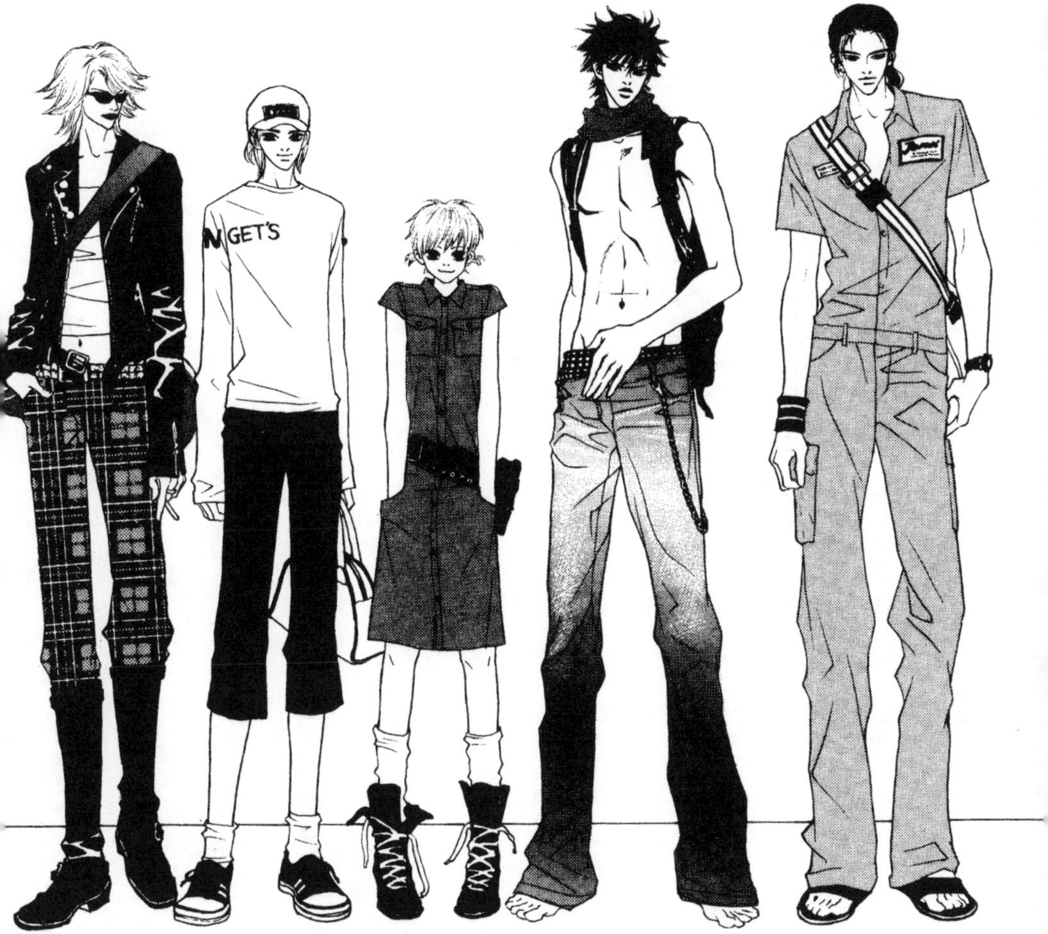
GET'S

◆ TA-DA! CHARACTER PROFILE + SHORT INTERVIEW ⟩⟩⟩

THIS INTERVIEW IS BROUGHT TO YOU BY ***YOU'RE SO COOL'S*** *YOUNG-HEE LEE AND THE QUESTIONS BY THE MEMBERS OF THE FAN CAFÉ— "HWA" CAFÉ (HTTP://CAFE.DAUM.NET/LEEYOUNGHEE).*

NAN-WOO JUNG <PROFILE>
AGE: 17 > BIRTHDAY: JUNE 15 > SIGN: GEMINI
BLOOD TYPE: O > HEIGHT: 158 CM > WEIGHT: 44 KG

>> INNOCENT? OR JUST OBLIVIOUS? NAN-WOO'S HEART AND PERSONALITY ARE VERY SIMPLE. THOUGH HER MIND AND BODY MAY SEEM LIKE SHE STILL HAS A WAYS TO GO UNTIL ADULTHOOD, SOMETIMES SHE'S MORE MATURE THAN SEUNG-HA IN DIFFERENT WAYS.

*NAN-WOO, WHY ARE YOU SO DENSE? (GAWUL, KANI)
---------------------HUH? WHAT? I'M NOT DENSE!

*WHAT'S YOUR BRA SIZE?! (OSOO)
-ASK THAT AFTER YOU TAKE CARE OF YOUR OWN.

*WHAT DO YOU THINK OF YOUR MOM...? (GAWUL)
-STUPID, PERVERTED, EVIL, DEMON OVERLORD, STOP TOUCHING ME!

*HOW DO YOU FEEL AS SEUNG-HA'S GIRLFRIEND? (GAWUL)
-HOW DO I MAKE HIM MORE HUMAN? I WISH HE'D STOP GLARING!

*EVER THOUGHT OF GROWING YOUR HAIR...? (GAWUL)
-I DON'T THINK IT LOOKS GOOD ON ME...LONG HAIR...

*IS THERE ANY PARTICULAR PLACE WHERE YOU WISH TO GO ON A DATE WITH SEUNG-HA? (HUMPHREY DUMPHREY)
-WELL...ANYWHERE IS FINE BY ME...REALLY...
SEUNG-HA'S KIND OF A PICKY GUY AND ALL...

*JAY'S NEW LOVE(?) HYUN-HO...WHAT DO YOU THINK OF HIM...? (GAWUL)
-WHO THE HELL ARE YOU CALLING JAY'S NEW LOVE?
PUKE~ NO WAY~ ...WAIT, IS IT TRUE?!

*BE STRONG, NAN-WOO! (SSAEGUH)
-...YEAH, OKAY...BUT WHAT'S UP WITH THAT?
YOU THINK I'M IN SOME SORT OF TROUBLE?

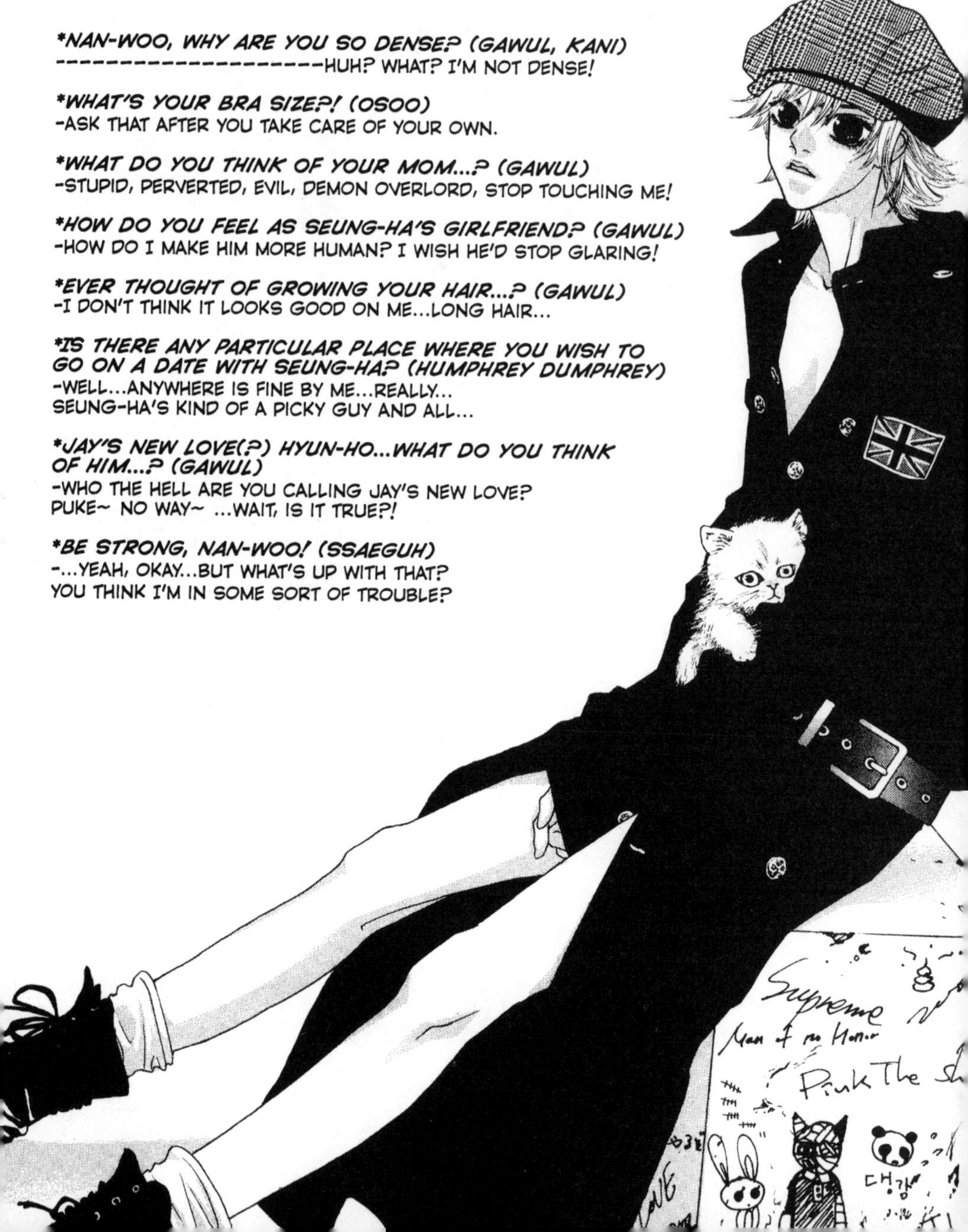
Supreme

SEUNG-HA RYU <PROFILE>
AGE: 17 > BIRTHDAY: NOVEMBER 2 > SIGN: SCORPIO
BLOOD TYPE: AB > HEIGHT: 181 CM > WEIGHT: 72 KG

>> IN SCHOOL, HE'S A MODEL STUDENT! BUT OUTSIDE, HE'S A GANGSTER! THE EPITOME OF MR. POPULAR, HE'S SHOWERED WITH LOVE FROM GIRLS ALL AROUND!! IN SCHOOL, HE SEEMS SO TRUSTWORTHY...BUT SOMETIMES (ESPECIALLY IN FRONT OF NAN-WOO), HE SHOWS OFF HIS REBELLIOUS AND CYNICAL STREAK, WHICH ONLY MAKES HIS APPEARANCE SHINE MORE. IT LOOKS LIKE HE'S GOT HIS REASONS, BUT WHEN WILL HIS DOUBLE LIFE END...?

WHAT DO YOU THINK ABOUT NAN-WOO'S CURRENT FEELINGS TOWARD YOU? SINCE WHEN HAVE YOU BEEN WEARING THAT MASK AND HIDING YOURSELF FROM EVERYONE? WHO WAS YOUR FIRST LOVE? (DID YOU HAVE ONE? +O+) WHY DID YOU CHOOSE NAN-WOO? WAS IT BECAUSE SHE'S FUN? HOW MANY STICKS OF TOBACCO DO YOU SMOKE PER DAY? -.- IT SEEMS YOU ENJOY RATHER TIGHT OUTFITS. EVER THOUGHT OF WEARING HIP-HOP GEAR?... (PANT PANT) (GAWUL)
-WHAT THE HELL? WHAT'S UP WITH SO MANY QUESTIONS?

SEUNG-HA, IN VOL. 2, WHEN CHAN-GYU SAW YOUR GANGSTER SIDE...WERE ASSISTANT LEE AND MS. 202 IN THE SCENE? (YUI)
-I DON'T KNOW THEM.

SEUNG-HA~ SO WHO PAYS FOR NAN-WOO'S CELL PHONE? (GENDER1004)
-OF COURSE, THE PERSON WHO USES THE PHONE.
WHAT KINDA QUESTION IS THIS?

I SEE SEUNG-HA AND NAN-WOO WALKING TOGETHER, HOLDING HANDS...SO TELL ME THAT STORY~. (SSAEGUH)
-THINK OF IT AS A LEASH.
THE KID KEEPS WANDERING OFF.

SO HOW DO YOU MAINTAIN THAT HOT BOD OF YOURS? DO YOU WORK OUT IN THE MIDDLE OF THE NIGHT UNDER THE MOON? OR DO 200 PUSH-UPS A DAY? OR DO YOU WORK OUT WITH "DO YOU WANT A HOT BOD" WORKOUT TAPES? I WANT TO KNOW YOUR SECRET. (OSOO)
-HEH.

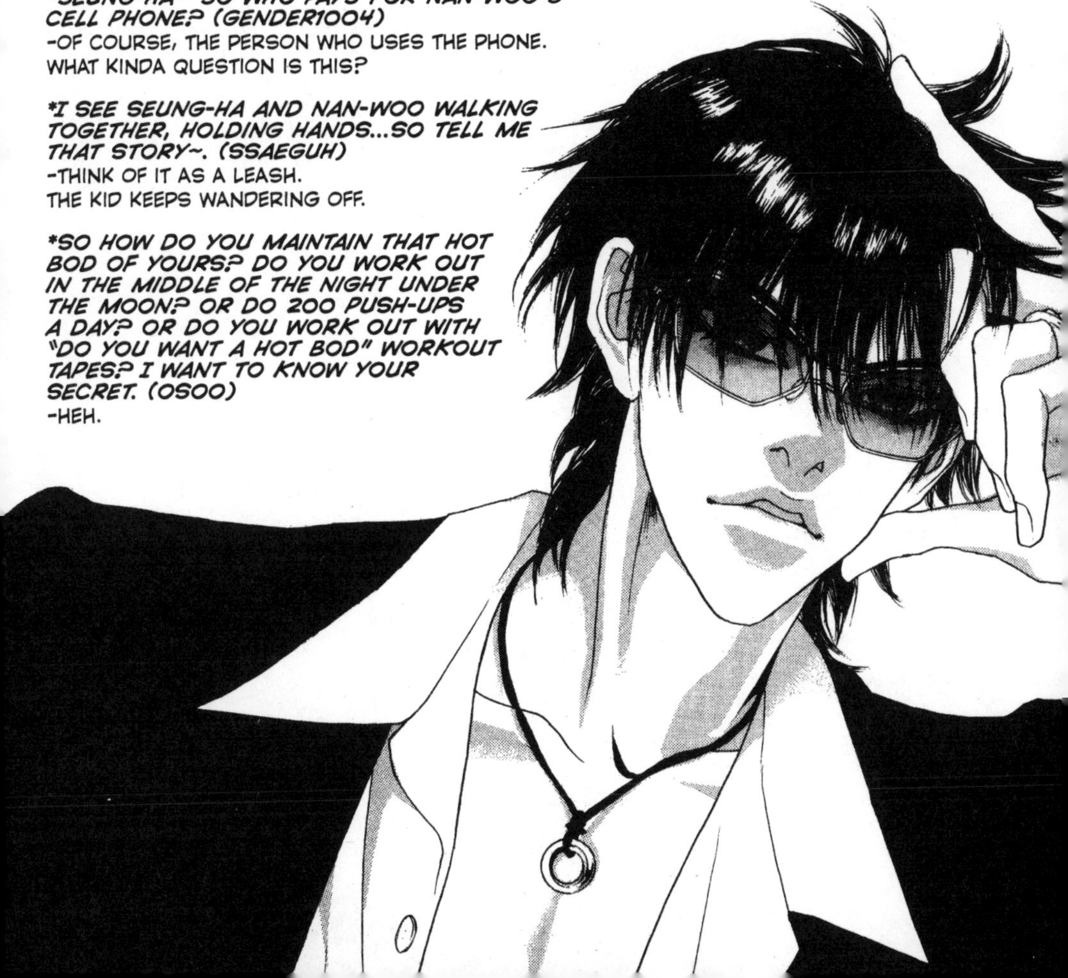

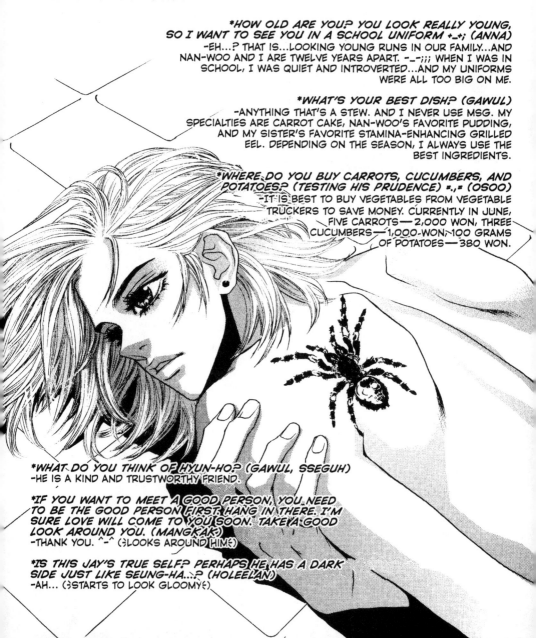

JAY JUNG <PROFILE>
AGE: 29 > SIGN: PISCES
BLOOD TYPE: A > HEIGHT: 172 CM > WEIGHT: 55 KG

>> NAN-WOO'S UNCLE AND JAE-YOUNG'S YOUNGER BROTHER. CURRENTLY, HE LIVES WITH
NAN-WOO AND JAE-YOUNG. HE COOKS, CLEANS, AND DOES ALL THE HOUSEHOLD CHORES...
ALMOST AT THE LEVEL OF A FULL-TIME HOUSEWIFE. HIS COOKING SKILLS ARE TOP-NOTCH.
HE HAS FEMININE FEATURES AND MANNERISMS; HE'S THE TYPE WHO LOOKS LIKE HE'LL
FAINT EASILY AND MAKES OTHERS WANT TO PROTECT HIM. WE'LL WATCH HOW HIS STORY
WITH HYUN-HO WILL UNFOLD IN THE FUTURE. A SECRET: HE'S BEEN KEEPING A DIARY SINCE
HIS ELEMENTARY SCHOOL DAYS.

*HOW OLD ARE YOU? YOU LOOK REALLY YOUNG,
SO I WANT TO SEE YOU IN A SCHOOL UNIFORM +_+; (ANNA)
-EH...? THAT IS...LOOKING YOUNG RUNS IN OUR FAMILY...AND
NAN-WOO AND I ARE TWELVE YEARS APART. -_-;;; WHEN I WAS IN
SCHOOL, I WAS QUIET AND INTROVERTED...AND MY UNIFORMS
WERE ALL TOO BIG ON ME.

*WHAT'S YOUR BEST DISH? (GAWUL)
-ANYTHING THAT'S A STEW. AND I NEVER USE MSG. MY
SPECIALTIES ARE CARROT CAKE, NAN-WOO'S FAVORITE PUDDING,
AND MY SISTER'S FAVORITE STAMINA-ENHANCING GRILLED
EEL. DEPENDING ON THE SEASON, I ALWAYS USE THE
BEST INGREDIENTS.

*WHERE DO YOU BUY CARROTS, CUCUMBERS, AND
POTATOES? (TESTING HIS PRUDENCE) =.,= (OSOO)
-IT IS BEST TO BUY VEGETABLES FROM VEGETABLE
TRUCKERS TO SAVE MONEY. CURRENTLY IN JUNE,
FIVE CARROTS—2,000 WON, THREE
CUCUMBERS—1,000 WON, 100 GRAMS
OF POTATOES—380 WON.

*WHAT DO YOU THINK OF HYUN-HO? (GAWUL, SSEGUH)
-HE IS A KIND AND TRUSTWORTHY FRIEND.

*IF YOU WANT TO MEET A GOOD PERSON, YOU NEED
TO BE THE GOOD PERSON FIRST. HANG IN THERE. I'M
SURE LOVE WILL COME TO YOU SOON. TAKE A GOOD
LOOK AROUND YOU. (MANGKAK)
-THANK YOU. ^-^ (:LOOKS AROUND HIM:)

*IS THIS JAY'S TRUE SELF? PERHAPS HE HAS A DARK
SIDE JUST LIKE SEUNG-HA...? (HOLEELAN)
-AH... (:STARTS TO LOOK GLOOMY:)

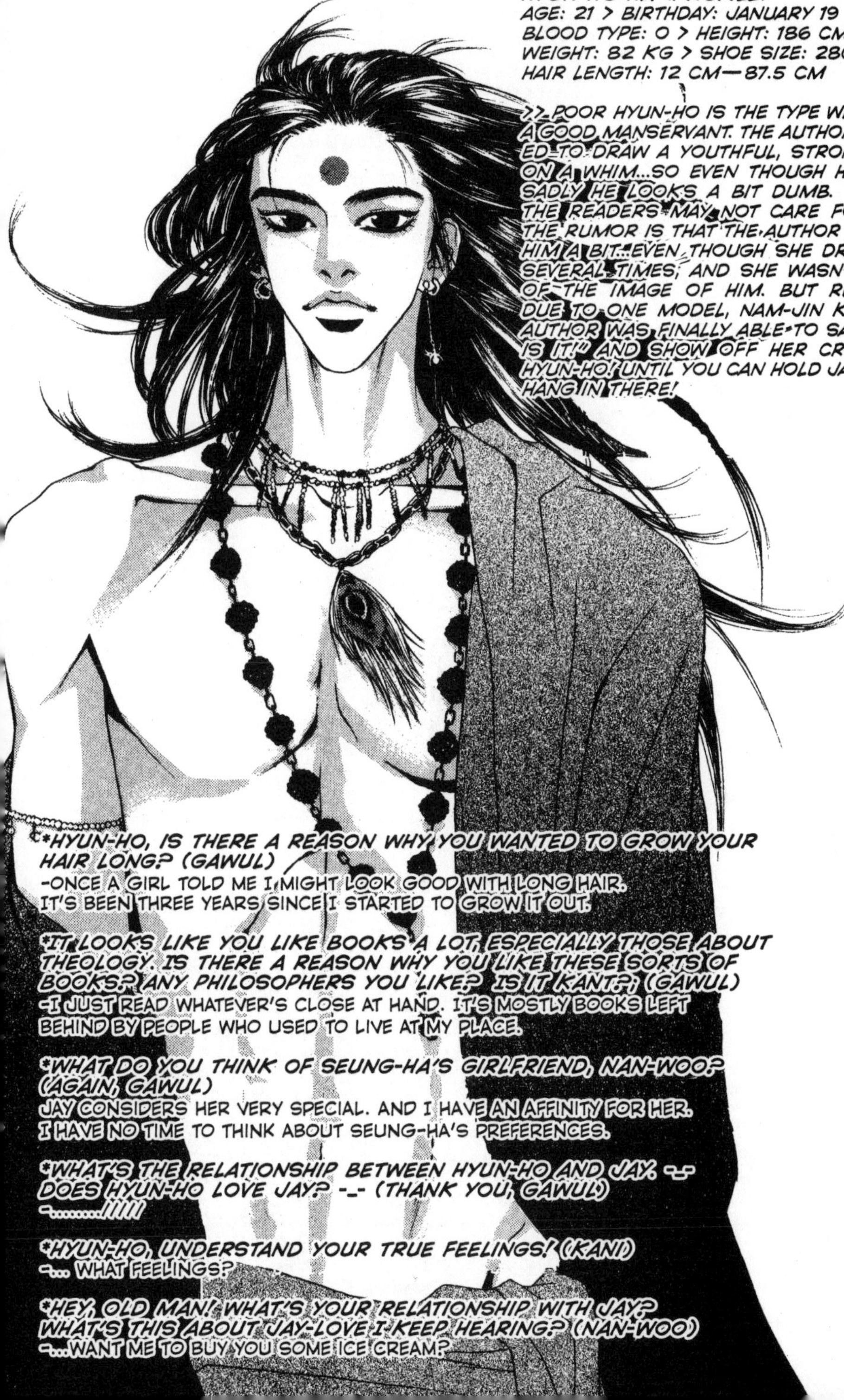

HYUN-HO HA <PROFILE>
AGE: 21 > BIRTHDAY: JANUARY 19 >
BLOOD TYPE: O > HEIGHT: 186 CM >
WEIGHT: 82 KG > SHOE SIZE: 280 MM >
HAIR LENGTH: 12 CM—87.5 CM

>> POOR HYUN-HO IS THE TYPE WHO'D BE A GOOD MANSERVANT. THE AUTHOR WANTED TO DRAW A YOUTHFUL, STRONG MAN ON A WHIM...SO EVEN THOUGH HE ISN'T, SADLY HE LOOKS A BIT DUMB. THOUGH THE READERS MAY NOT CARE FOR HIM, THE RUMOR IS THAT THE AUTHOR FAVORS HIM A BIT...EVEN THOUGH SHE DREW HIM SEVERAL TIMES, AND SHE WASN'T SURE OF THE IMAGE OF HIM. BUT RECENTLY DUE TO ONE MODEL, NAM-JIN KIM, THE AUTHOR WAS FINALLY ABLE TO SAY, "THIS IS IT!" AND SHOW OFF HER CREATIVITY. HYUN-HO! UNTIL YOU CAN HOLD JAY TIGHT, HANG IN THERE!

*HYUN-HO, IS THERE A REASON WHY YOU WANTED TO GROW YOUR HAIR LONG? (GAWUL)
-ONCE A GIRL TOLD ME I MIGHT LOOK GOOD WITH LONG HAIR. IT'S BEEN THREE YEARS SINCE I STARTED TO GROW IT OUT.

*IT LOOKS LIKE YOU LIKE BOOKS A LOT, ESPECIALLY THOSE ABOUT THEOLOGY. IS THERE A REASON WHY YOU LIKE THESE SORTS OF BOOKS? ANY PHILOSOPHERS YOU LIKE? IS IT KANT?; (GAWUL)
-I JUST READ WHATEVER'S CLOSE AT HAND. IT'S MOSTLY BOOKS LEFT BEHIND BY PEOPLE WHO USED TO LIVE AT MY PLACE.

*WHAT DO YOU THINK OF SEUNG-HA'S GIRLFRIEND, NAN-WOO? (AGAIN, GAWUL)
JAY CONSIDERS HER VERY SPECIAL. AND I HAVE AN AFFINITY FOR HER. I HAVE NO TIME TO THINK ABOUT SEUNG-HA'S PREFERENCES.

*WHAT'S THE RELATIONSHIP BETWEEN HYUN-HO AND JAY. -_- DOES HYUN-HO LOVE JAY? -_- (THANK YOU, GAWUL)
-........./////

*HYUN-HO, UNDERSTAND YOUR TRUE FEELINGS! (KANI)
-... WHAT FEELINGS?

*HEY, OLD MAN! WHAT'S YOUR RELATIONSHIP WITH JAY? WHAT'S THIS ABOUT JAY-LOVE I KEEP HEARING? (NAN-WOO)
-...WANT ME TO BUY YOU SOME ICE CREAM?

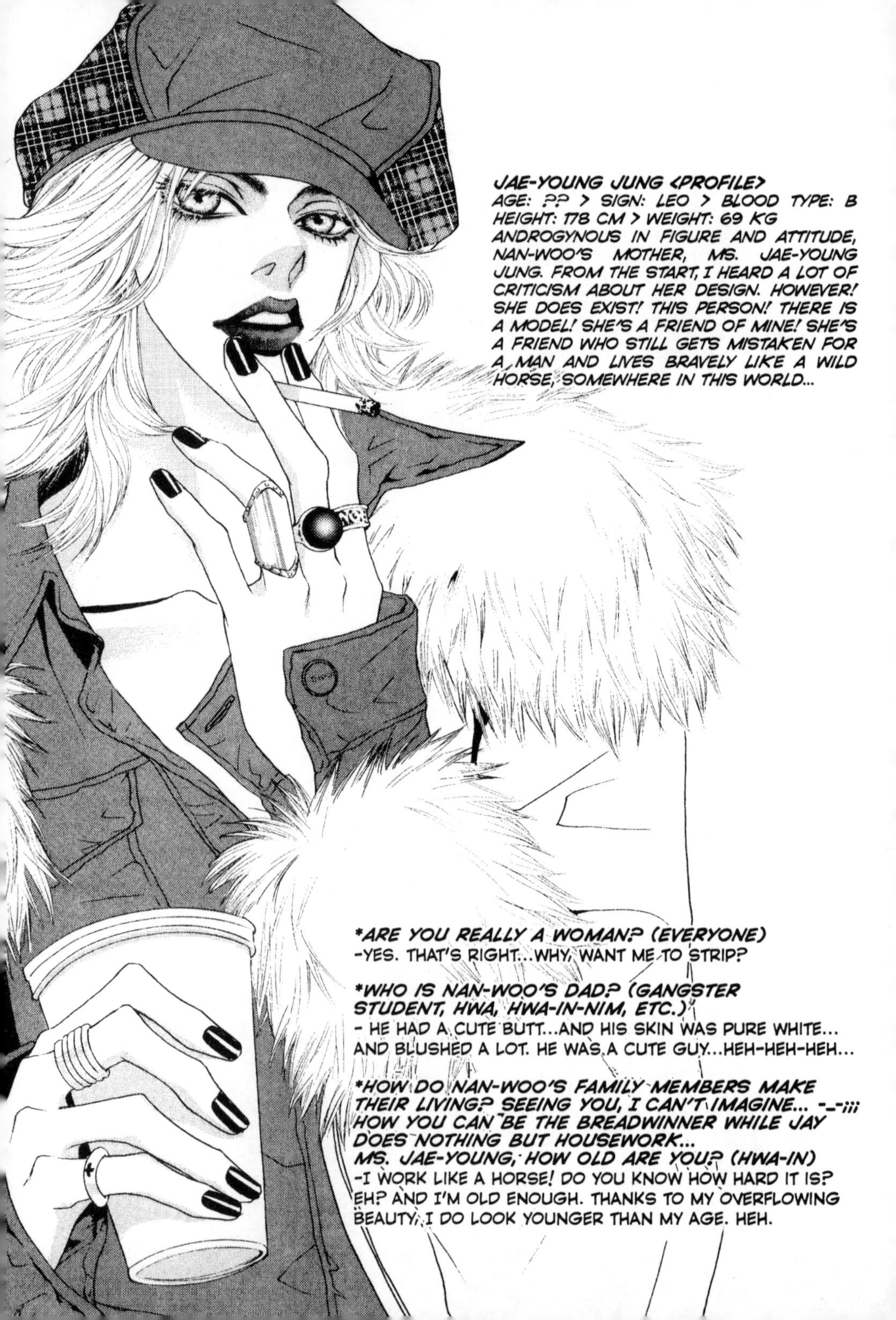

JAE-YOUNG JUNG <PROFILE>
AGE: ?? > SIGN: LEO > BLOOD TYPE: B
HEIGHT: 178 CM > WEIGHT: 69 KG
ANDROGYNOUS IN FIGURE AND ATTITUDE, NAN-WOO'S MOTHER, MS. JAE-YOUNG JUNG. FROM THE START, I HEARD A LOT OF CRITICISM ABOUT HER DESIGN. HOWEVER! SHE DOES EXIST! THIS PERSON! THERE IS A MODEL! SHE'S A FRIEND OF MINE! SHE'S A FRIEND WHO STILL GETS MISTAKEN FOR A MAN AND LIVES BRAVELY LIKE A WILD HORSE, SOMEWHERE IN THIS WORLD...

*ARE YOU REALLY A WOMAN? (EVERYONE)
-YES. THAT'S RIGHT...WHY, WANT ME TO STRIP?

*WHO IS NAN-WOO'S DAD? (GANGSTER STUDENT, HWA, HWA-IN-NIM, ETC.)
- HE HAD A CUTE BUTT...AND HIS SKIN WAS PURE WHITE... AND BLUSHED A LOT. HE WAS A CUTE GUY...HEH-HEH-HEH...

*HOW DO NAN-WOO'S FAMILY MEMBERS MAKE THEIR LIVING? SEEING YOU, I CAN'T IMAGINE... -_-;;; HOW YOU CAN BE THE BREADWINNER WHILE JAY DOES NOTHING BUT HOUSEWORK...
MS. JAE-YOUNG, HOW OLD ARE YOU? (HWA-IN)
-I WORK LIKE A HORSE! DO YOU KNOW HOW HARD IT IS? EH? AND I'M OLD ENOUGH. THANKS TO MY OVERFLOWING BEAUTY, I DO LOOK YOUNGER THAN MY AGE. HEH.

THOUGH NO ONE WANTED IT OR TOLD HER TO DO IT AND WITH JUST THE THOUGHT OF "THIS LOOK'S LIKE FUN" IN MIND, CRAZY AUTHOR 202 STARTED THIS PROJECT. IN THE FUTURE, SHE'LL DO HER BEST TO WORK HARD ON HER SCRIPTS.

AUTHOR OF "FLOWERS," 202-NIM!(?) WHAT IS YOUR FAVORITE TREE AND FLOWER?! PLEASE BE SPECIFIC~ +_+ (OSOO)
—I LIKE EVERYTHING THAT'S PRETTY! IN THE SUMMER, I LIKE HYDRANGEAS AND WILLOW TREES. DO YOU KNOW THE MYRTLE TREE (ALSO CALLED INDIAN LILAC)? IT'S A COMMON TREE, BUT I LOVE IT. CHARACTERS FROM *YOU'RE SO COOL* ALL HAVE A FLOWER IMAGE FOR EACH OF THEM; SEUNG-HA IS LIKE THE CONSTANCE SPRY (AN ENGLISH ROSE), NAN-WOO IS LIKE LILY BELL, JAY IS LIKE THE LITTLE PURPLE VIOLET, HYUN-HO IS LIKE BAMBOO, AND JAE-YOUNG IS A LILY.

202-NIM, WHERE DO YOU USUALLY READ YAOI? (SEUNGHANYANGHEE)
—HMM...BATHROOM? (WHAT A WEIRD QUESTION.)

IS NAN-WOO PERHAPS BASED ON YOUNG-HEE LEE-NIM? (HWA)
—HOW COULD YOU POSSIBLY COMPARE ME WITH THAT DENSE IDIOT? I'M A VERY SENSITIVE PERSON.

WHILE WORKING ON YOUR MANHWA, WHAT TYPE OF MUSIC DO YOU ENJOY LISTENING TO...? (ANNA)
—WHILE DRAWING, I PREFER TO LISTEN TO SOMETHING SOOTHING AND COMFORTABLE, LIKE ORIGINAL SOUND-TRACKS OR COMPILATION CDS. RECENTLY, I'VE BEEN LISTENING TO EVANESCENCE, THE CALLING, LOVEHOLIC, T.A.T.U., AND JOE HISAISHI.

WHAT TYPE OF CLOTHES DO YOU WEAR DAILY...? PERHAPS SOMETHING LOOSE...? (YONG-NAM)
—H...HOW DID YOU KNOW? DID YOU SEE ME? DID YOU? I NORMALLY WEAR SPORTS PANTS WITH VERY WORN-OUT T-SHIRTS. I'D LIKE TO HAVE FLOWER-PATTERNED PAJAMAS TO WEAR DURING WORK.

WHAT'S THE DIFFERENCE BETWEEN DRAWING AND WRITING THE STORY?!! (STRAWBERRY CAKE)
—WHEN I'M WRITING THE STORY, I (SORTA) TRY TO NATURALLY MIX THE ACTION AND THE FLOW OF EMOTION. WHEN I'M TRANSFERRING THE STORY TO MY DRAWING, I THINK OF IT IN MY HEAD LIKE FRAMES FROM A MOVIE. THEY'RE BOTH HARD TO DO, AND SOMETIMES I FEEL LIKE I'M DROWNING IN A SWAMP.

WHAT KIND OF STORY DO YOU WANT TO DRAW? (TAE-SUP SONG)
—IT'S A BIT OF AN ABSTRACT ANSWER, BUT I WANT TO DRAW A STORY THAT'S LIKE GOING INTO AN UNDERGROUND TUNNEL. I DON'T THINK EVEN I UNDERSTAND IT EXACTLY...IT'S LIKE A STORY THAT DOESN'T END WITH THE BOOK BUT CONTINUES ON IN THE IMAGINATION. IN THE END, I GUESS I WANT TO DO A COMIC THAT I CAN READ AND ENJOY TOO.

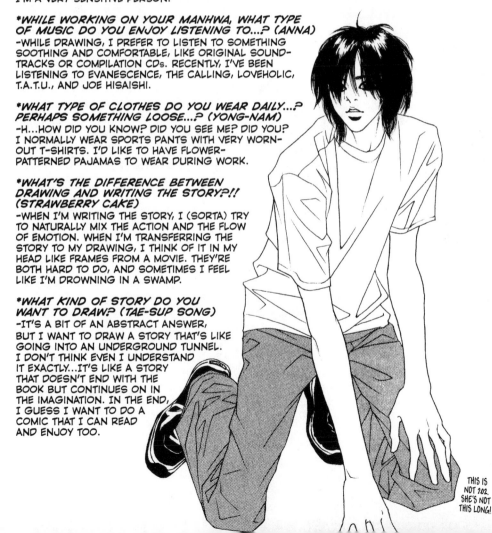

THIS IS NOT 202. SHE'S NOT THIS LONG!

MESSAGE...
From 202

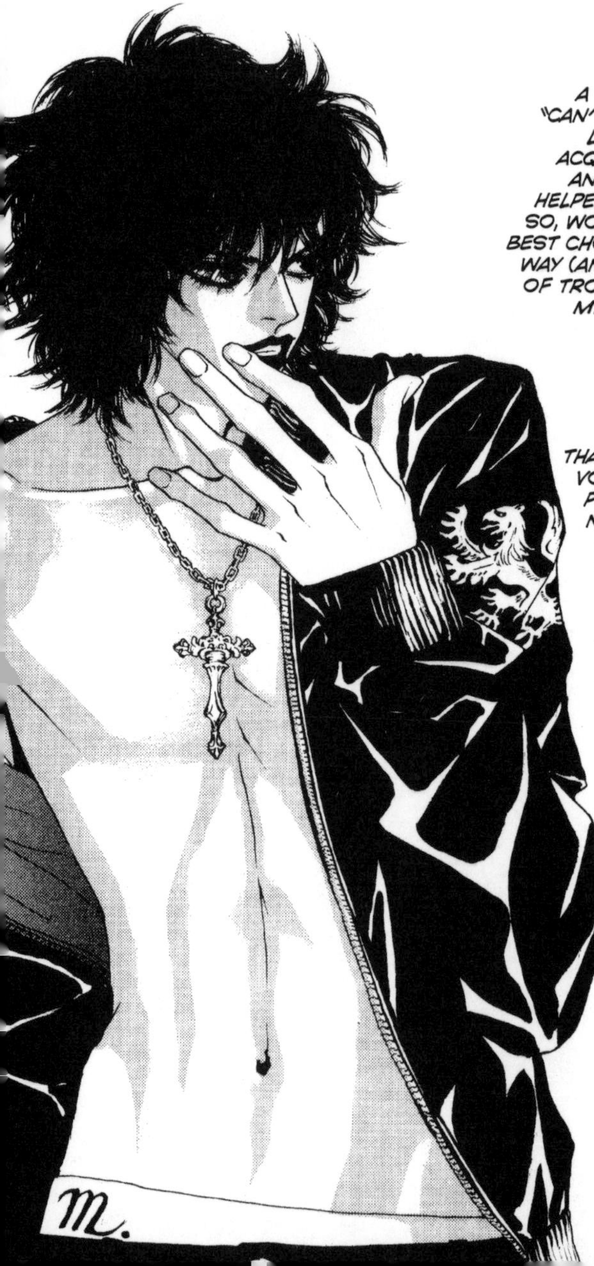

THERE'S A PHRASE I HATE A LOT—"IT CAN'T BE HELPED." BUT RECENTLY, A LOT OF SITUATIONS HAVE POPPED UP THAT "CAN'T BE HELPED." THOUGH I'VE LIVED A FAIRLY LONG LIFE AND IN THAT TIME SHOULD HAVE ACQUIRED SOME LIFE SKILLS (PAST, PRESENT, AND FUTURE), THERE ARE STILL "IT CAN'T BE HELPED" THINGS HAPPENING ALL THE TIME. EVEN SO, WORKING HARD IS THE BASIC IDEAL AND THE BEST CHOICE. SINCE I DON'T KNOW OF ANY OTHER WAY (AND THOUGH I'M SO LAZY AND CAUSE A LOT OF TROUBLE FOR OTHERS), I'M BASICALLY DOING MY BEST TO LIVE...SO IT'S NOT A BAD THING. LET HE WHO HAS NOT SINNED CAST THE FIRST STONE! (⊰SMACK!⊱) IT DOESN'T EVEN TICKLE ANYMORE!

... I'M SO SORRY FOR THE LONG RANT.

THANKS TO EVERYONE'S LOVE AND SUPPORT, VOLUME THREE (UNBELIEVABLY) MADE IT TO PUBLICATION. AS FOR MY NEW EDITOR AND NEW ASSISTANT, M, I'M STILL LEARNING TO GET TO KNOW THEM, BUT WE SHOULD BE ABLE TO STAND SIDE BY SIDE BY VOLUME FOUR. THEY HAD SO MUCH TROUBLE TO DEAL WITH FROM THE START (BECAUSE OF ME) THAT I...CAN'T...LOOK THEM... STRAIGHT IN THE FACE...E-EVEN SO, WE'LL STAND TOGETHER IN TRUST AND FRIENDSHIP, RIGHT? RIGHT?!

AND K! K! K! WITHOUT K, I COULDN'T EVEN THINK OF FINISHING IN TIME FOR MY DEADLINES! AND MY FIRST ASSISTANT, LEE, HAS SOME SHOCKING NEWS. IF YOU'RE CURIOUS, CHECK OUT THE NEXT BOOK! TO THE MEMBERS OF HWA CAFÉ WHO HELPED ME OUT SO MUCH WITH THE CHARACTER INTERVIEWS, I SEND YOU MY SPECIAL THANK-YOU: I LOVE YOU FOREVER~! MMM...

AM I DOING THIS RIGHT? I DON'T EVEN KNOW WHERE I'M GOING WITH THIS. ANYWAY, ONWARD TO THE NEXT VOLUME.

SEE YOU IN VOLUME FOUR!

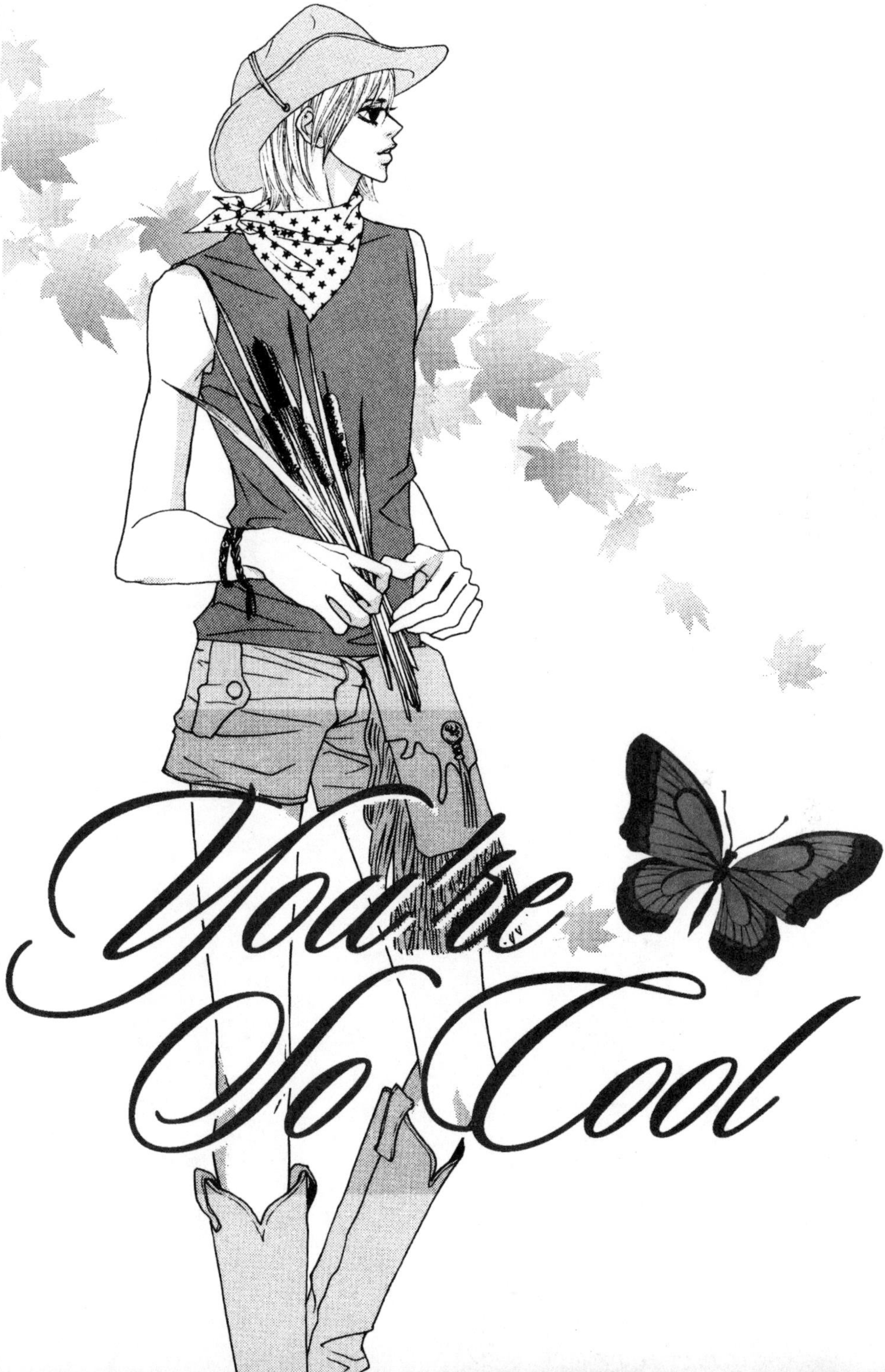
You're So Cool

Yen
Press
www.yenpress.com

Sometimes, just being a teenager is hard enough.

D a-Eh, an aspiring manhwa artist who lives with her father and her little brother, comes across Sun-Nam, a softie whose ultimate goal is simply to become a "Tough guy." Whenever these two meet, trouble follows. Meanwhile, Ta-Jun, the hottest guy in town, finds himself drawn to the one girl that his killer smile does not work on—Da-Eh. With their complicated family history hanging on their shoulders, watch how these three teenagers find their way out into the world!

Available at bookstores near you!

HISSING

1~4

Kang EunYoung

Yen
Press

www.yenpress.com

THE MOST BEAUTIFUL FACE, THE PERFECT BODY,
AND A SINCERE PERSONALITY...THAT'S WHAT HYE-MIN HWANG HAS.
NATURALLY, SHE'S THE CENTER OF EVERYONE'S ATTENTION.
EVERY BOY IN SCHOOL LOVES HER, WHILE EVERY GIRL HATES HER OUT OF JEALOUSY.
EVERY SINGLE DAY, SHE HAS TO ENDURE TORTURES AND HARDSHIPS FROM THE GIRLS.

A PRETTY FACE COMES WITH A PRICE.

THERE IS NOTHING MORE SATISFYING THAN GETTING THEM BACK.
WELL, EXCEPT FOR ONE PROBLEM...HER SECRET CRUSH, JUNG-YUN.
BECAUSE OF HIM, SHE HAS TO HIDE HER CYNICAL AND DARK SIDE
AND DAILY PUT ON AN INNOCENT FACE. THEN ONE DAY, SHE FINDS OUT
THAT HE DISLIKES HER ANYWAY!! WHAT?! THAT'S IT! NO MORE NICE GIRL!
AND THE FIRST VICTIM OF HER RAGE IS A PLAYBOY SHE JUST MET, MA-HA.

vol.1~4

CynicalOrange

Yun JiUn

Available at bookstores near you!

CHOCOLAT

1~6

Shin JiSang · Geo

Kum-ji was a little late getting under the spell
of the chart-topping band, DDL. Unable to
join the DDL fan club, she almost gives up
on meeting her idols, until she develops a
cunning plan–to become a member of a
rival fan club for the brand-new boy band
Yo-I. This way she can act as Yo-I's fan
club member and also be near Yo-I,

How far would you
go to meet your
favorite boy band?

who always seem to be in the
same shows as DDL. Perfect
plan...except being a fanatic is a lot
more complicated than she
expects. Especially when you're
actually a fan of someone else. This
full-blown love comedy about a fan
club will make you laugh, cry, and
laugh some more.

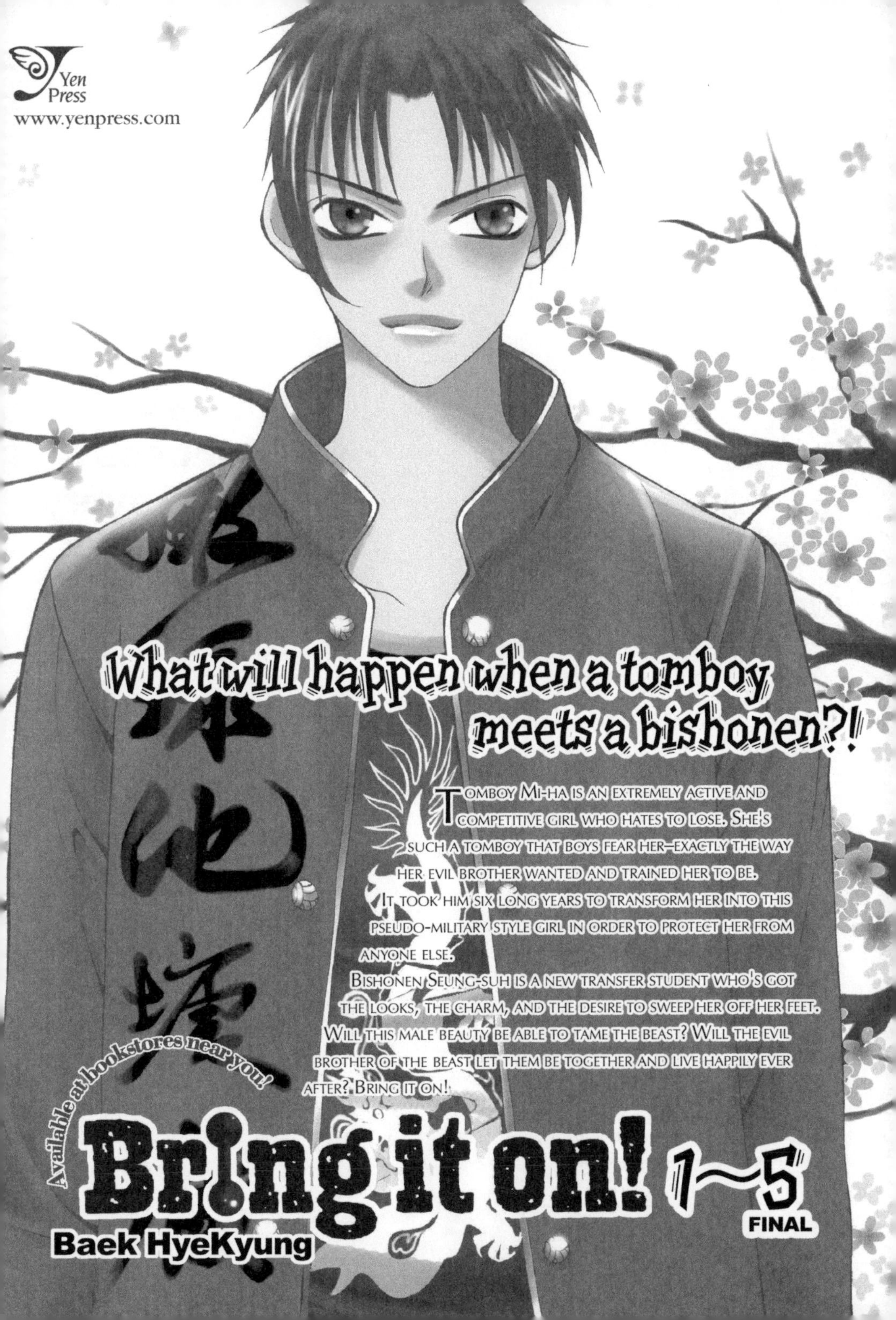

Yen Press
www.yenpress.com
What will happen when a tomboy meets a bishonen?!
Tomboy Mi-ha is an extremely active and competitive girl who hates to lose. She's such a tomboy that boys fear her—exactly the way her evil brother wanted and trained her to be. It took him six long years to transform her into this pseudo-military style girl in order to protect her from anyone else.
Bishonen Seung-suh is a new transfer student who's got the looks, the charm, and the desire to sweep her off her feet. Will this male beauty be able to tame the beast? Will the evil brother of the beast let them be together and live happily ever after? Bring it on!
Available at bookstores near you!
Bring it on! 1~5 FINAL
Baek HyeKyung

Yen Press

www.yenpress.com

Becoming the princess... Isn't that every girl's dream?!

Monarchy rule ended long ago in Korea, but there are still other countries with kings, queens, princes and princesses. What if Korea had continued monarchism? What if all the beautiful palaces, which are now only historical relics, were actually filled with people? What if the glamorous royal family still maintained the palace customs? Welcome to a world where Korea still has the royal family living in their everyday lives! Only for this one high school girl, Chae-Kyung, is this a tragedy, since she has to marry the prince — who apparently is a total bastard!

THE ROYAL PALACE
Goong
vol.1~2

Park SoHee

The Antique Gift Shop 1~5

Lee Eun

Available at bookstores near you!

CAN YOU FEEL THE SOULS OF THE ANTIQUES?
DO YOU BELIEVE?

Did you know that an antique possesses a soul of its own?
The Antique Gift Shop specializes in such items that charm and captivate the buyers they are destined to belong to. Guided by a mysterious and charismatic shopkeeper, the enchanted relics lead their new owners on a journey into an alternate cosmic universe to their true destinies.
Eerily bittersweet and dolefully melancholy, The Antique Gift Shop opens up a portal to a world where torn lovers unite, broken friendships are mended, and regrets are resolved. Can you feel the power of the antiques?

Wonderfully illustrated
modern day crossover
fantasy, available at
your local bookstore
or comic shop!

Apart from the fact her
eyes turn red when the moon
rises, Myung-Ee is your average,
albeit boy-crazy, 5th grader. After
picking a fight with her classmate
Yu-Da Lee, she discovers a startling
secret: the two of them are "earth
rabbits" being hunted by the "fox
tribe" of the moon!
Five years pass and Myung-Ee
transfers to a new school in search of
pretty boys. There, she unexpectedly
reunites with Yu-Da. The problem is
he doesn't remember a thing about
her or their shared past!

Moon Boy 월요일 소년 1~3

Lee YoungYou

Yen Press

www.yenpress.com

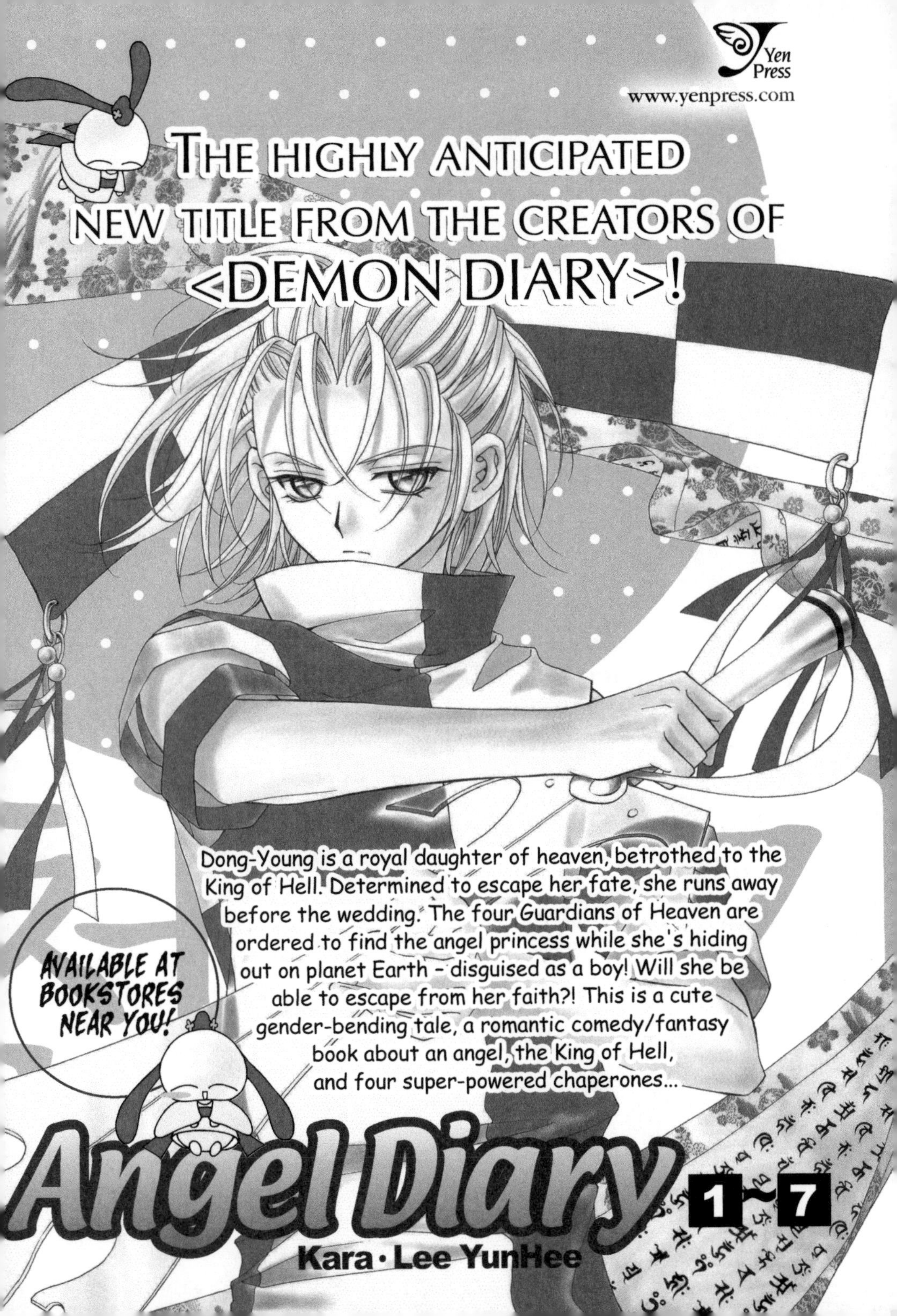
Yen Press
www.yenpress.com
THE HIGHLY ANTICIPATED
NEW TITLE FROM THE CREATORS OF
<DEMON DIARY>!
Dong-Young is a royal daughter of heaven, betrothed to the King of Hell. Determined to escape her fate, she runs away before the wedding. The four Guardians of Heaven are ordered to find the angel princess while she's hiding out on planet Earth - disguised as a boy! Will she be able to escape from her faith?! This is a cute gender-bending tale, a romantic comedy/fantasy book about an angel, the King of Hell, and four super-powered chaperones...
AVAILABLE AT BOOKSTORES NEAR YOU!
Angel Diary 1~7
Kara · Lee YunHee

The newest title from the creators of <Demon Diary> and <Angel Diary>!

Once upon a time, a selfish king summoned the monstrous Bulkirin into the real world. The monster killed half of all human beings, leaving the rest helpless as to what to do. That is, until one day when a hero appeared and defeated the Bulkirin with the legendary "Seven Blade Sword." But…what does all this have to do with 8th grader Eun-Gyo Sung?! First, she gets suspended from school for fighting. Then, she runs away from home. The last thing she needed was to be kidnapped—and whisked into the past by a mysterious stranger named No-Ah!

Available at bookstores near you!

Legend 1-3

K a r a · W o o S o o J u n g

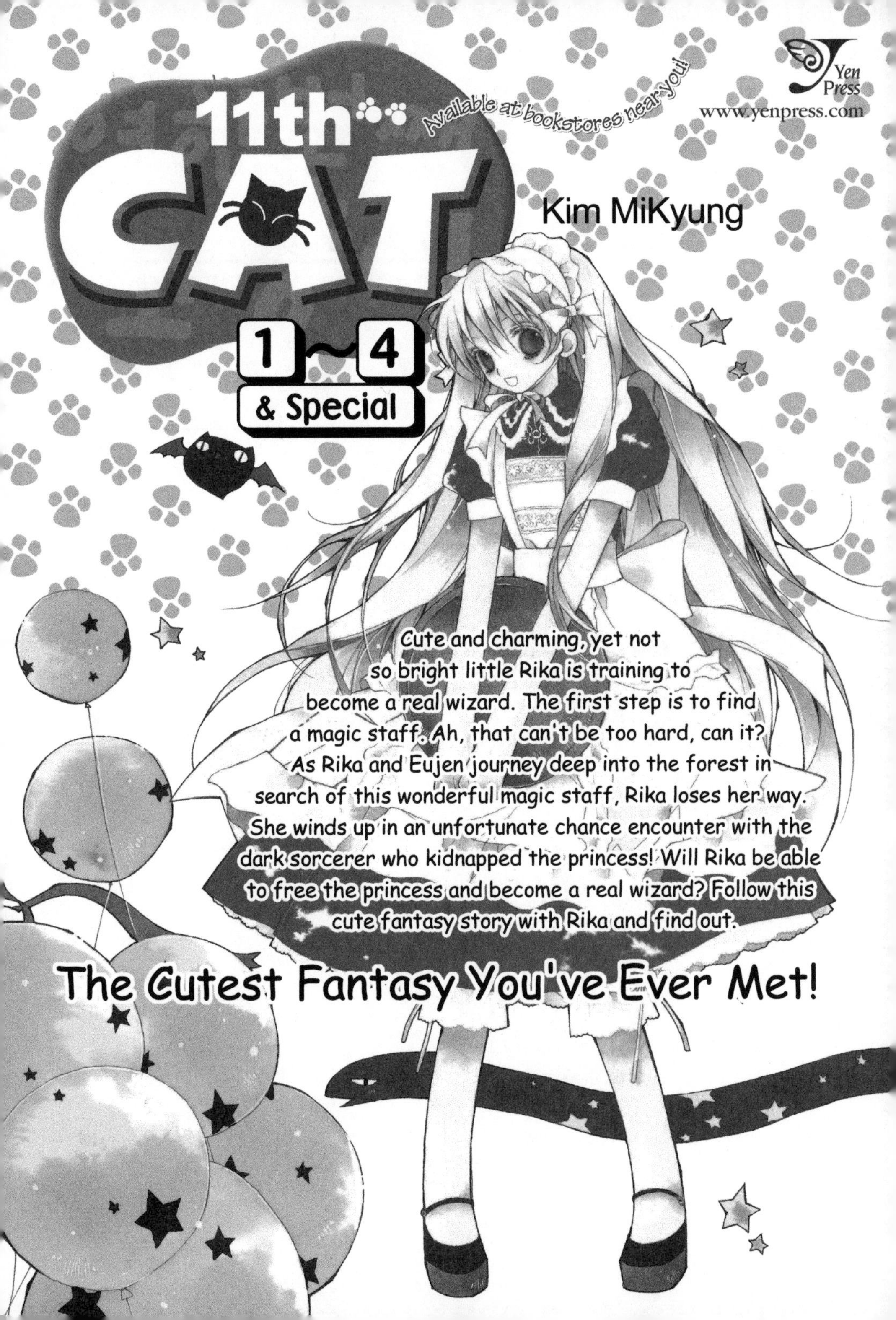
Yen Press
www.yenpress.com
11th CAT
Available at bookstores near you!
Kim MiKyung
1~4
& Special
Cute and charming, yet not so bright little Rika is training to become a real wizard. The first step is to find a magic staff. Ah, that can't be too hard, can it? As Rika and Eujen journey deep into the forest in search of this wonderful magic staff, Rika loses her way. She winds up in an unfortunate chance encounter with the dark sorcerer who kidnapped the princess! Will Rika be able to free the princess and become a real wizard? Follow this cute fantasy story with Rika and find out.
The Cutest Fantasy You've Ever Met!

YOU'RE SO COOL ③

YOUNGHEE LEE

Translation: Jackie Oh

Lettering: Terri Delgado

Yen Press
Hachette Book Group
237 Park Avenue, New York, NY 10017

Visit our Web sites at www.HachetteBookGroup.com and www.YenPress.com.

Yen Press is an imprint of Hachette Book Group, Inc. The Yen Press name and logo are trademarks of Hachette Book Group, Inc.

First Yen Press Edition: January 2009

ISBN: 978-0-7595-2864-2

10 9 8 7 6 5 4 3 2 1

BVG

Printed in the United States of America